FAITHFUL
FRIENDS

FAITHFUL FRIENDS

DOGS IN LIFE AND LITERATURE

Edited by
Frank Jackson

Foreword by
HRH Prince Michael of Kent

Carroll & Graf Publishers, Inc.
NEW YORK

Carroll & Graf Publishers, Inc.
19 West 21st Street
Suite 601
New York
NY 10010–6805

First published in the UK by Robinson
Publishing Ltd 1997

First Carroll & Graf edition 1997

Selection and editorial material copyright
© Frank Jackson 1997

ISBN 1–7867–0458–6

Printed and bound in the United Kingdom

Contents

Foreword by HRH Prince Michael of Kent   vii
Preface   ix

1 Character & Variety   1
2 A Great Friendship   41
3 Endlessly Useful   81
4 Dog Control   105
5 Rural Pursuits   119
6 Coarse Pastimes   171
7 Dogs as Pets   199
8 Love Me, Love My Dog   227
9 Curs & Mongrels   279
10 Extra Senses   315
11 Breeding   353
12 In Competition   359
13 A Dog's Worth   411
14 The Proper Remedy   449
15 A Too Short Life   477

   Acknowledgements   513
   Index of Authors   515
   Index of Subjects   525

Foreword
by HRH Prince Michael of Kent

No animal species has such a strong influence on man and civilization as the dog. It is therefore right that someone should explore the whole gamut of life and literature to highlight this association.

I have a close connection with my dogs, and have greatly enjoyed reading *Faithful Friends*. I commend this concatenation of canine culture to all who share the rapport. It reflects the debt mankind owes to the dog which in today's stressed society is often under-valued.

Michael

Kensington Palace, London

Preface

All the world's civilizations, past and present, share six interests in common: music, visual art, storytelling, alcohol consumption, religion, and – without exception – an interest in dogs. This extraordinary interest is and has been enjoyed by all ranks and ages in society.

Theories as to how the relationship between man and dog evolved are a source of contention, but almost certainly "the training of the dog seems to have been the first art invented by man, and the fruit of that art was the conquest and peaceable possession of the earth," as the great naturalist Buffon wrote.

Man's developing mastery over his canine companions led to their being used to control and guard flocks, to warn of intruders in the home, to guard if need be, to provide warmth, to hunt and retrieve game, to fight, chase and kill for man's pleasure, to be an ingredient in a stew, or material for warm clothing, or to pull heavy loads. There were times in the past when they were treated as gods, and times when they were objects of religious and political contempt and degradation.

Today they provide companionship for millions of people and are a source of pride to their owners. Primitive man's uses for them have been extended and refined. Dogs continue to herd and protect, to hunt and entertain and be used for competitions. But they also help in the search for catastrophe survivors, for drugs and explosives; they guide the blind, alert the deaf. They even give early warning of epileptic seizures. It has been scientifically proven that their mere presence can help people who are withdrawn and autistic to communicate, can lower the pulse rate, reduce anxiety and lift depression. A wide range of pastimes involving dogs provide enjoyment for both participants and spectators.

All this indicates a relationship which is far closer and far more important than even many dog lovers may suspect.

This anthology explores the wonderfully diverse, prolific agglomeration of material about dogs that has been written down in the English language through the ages. Previous anthologies have tended to be restricted to a particular theme – love of dogs, their fidelity, or expressions of sadness at the end of their all too short life. Others have looked at sport, or explored the work of a particular author. Some have confined themselves to mainstream literature. Such limitations fail to reflect the tremendous range of interest in dogs and written material about them.

This anthology's sources are as varied as the subjects they explore, and hopefully will contain something to please everyone. There are wonderfully funny pieces about them, as well as the more serious and informative, though there are occasions when the material may disturb, for sadly that too is an integral part of canine history.

Frank Jackson
Ashworth Moor, 1997

CHAPTER I

Character & Variety

Most dog owners and, for certain, all dog lovers will agree that dogs "possess a special and distinguishing excellence" that is uniquely their own, while, over the centuries, their characters and forms have developed into an amazing range. In fact, the domestic dog is probably the most varied species in the world.

Take first of all its character. Compare the willing propensity for instant obedience and the ability to accomplish complex tasks found among herding breeds with the sturdy self-reliance and independence of terriers, the haughty attitude of sight hounds, the wilfulness of some toy breeds, and others' fawning servility.

As for its size, it ranges from a 70 kg (154 lb) St Bernard to a 2.5 kg (5½ lb) Chihuahua, and in form from a slender, fragile-looking Italian Greyhound to a huge Dogue de Bordeaux. It can have luxuriant dreadlocks like a Komondor or, like a Xoloizcuintle, be entirely naked. The short, massive head of a Bulldog is very different from the aristocratic elegance of a Borzoi's. The Irish Wolfhound has very long legs, the Basset short ones. No other species, wild or domestic is so varied.

During the last 1,000 years and, particularly perhaps, during the last hundred, some breeds' physical appearance has changed in ways not always for the better. Occasionally physical form itself may have been altered through the efforts of breeders and veterinary surgeons. More often an apparent change is merely the result of a different style of hairdressing. Politicians and even some veterinarians who should know better have been given to generalized and indiscriminate criticism, yet many breeds, especially those which still enjoy the dignity of working for a living, are bigger, stronger, faster and more easily trained than their predecessors.

Nor are modern dogs just better at accomplishing traditional tasks, they offer services, of which earlier owners could not even have dreamt.

The following extracts explore dogs' character, formation and infinite variety of forms.

Theodorus Gaza

The gift which I am sending you is called a dog, and is in fact the most precious and valuable possession of mankind. For while other animals are each of them of use to us in virtue of one particular quality, and possess a special and distinguishing excellence, this one animal is responsible for greatest and highest points of excellence. A lion excels in courage, an ox in reliability and adaptability to agriculture, the horse in intelligence and speed, the ass and mule, as is stated by the poets, in patience and hard work; and other animals have other good points: this one animal combines the excellence of all others without one exception. He is naturally, suitable for war work and the pursuits of peace, and equally fitted to be of use and to be a pleasant companion. It would not be easy, as you will believe, to enumerate all the excellences and all the services to ourselves of this animal.

from *Laudatio Canis: an address to Mohammed II*, fifteenth century

Edward, 2nd Duke of York

An hounde is trewe to his lord or his maystere, and of good love or vrey. An hounde is of greet undirstondyng and of greet knowynge, a hound is of greet strength and greet bounte, an hounde is a wise beest and a kynde, an hound hath greet mynde and greet smellyng, an hounde hath grete bisynesse and greet mygt, an hounde is of greet wuthynes and of greet sotilte, a hound is of greet ligtnesse and of greet pursueaunce, an hounde is of good obeysaunce for he wil lerne as a man al that a man wil teche hym, a hounde is ful of good sport; houndes ben so good yat vunethes ther nys no man comonly yat ne wold have of hem some for oon craft and some for a nothr. Houndes ben hardy for oon hounde dar wel kepe his maister's hous and his beests and also he wil kepe al his maister's goodes and rathe he wil be dede yan eny thing be lost in his kepyng.

from *Mayster of the Game,* 1406–13

Oliver Goldsmith

Of all this tribe, the preference, being the most intelligent of all known quadrupeds, and the acknowledged friend of mankind. The dog, independent of the beauty of his form, his vivacity, force and swiftness, is possessed of all those internal qualifications that can conciliate the affections of man, and make the tyrant a protector. A natural share of courage, and angry and ferocious disposition, renders the dog, in its savage state, a formidable enemy to all other animals: but these readily give way to very different qualities in the domestic dog, whose only ambition seems the desire to please; he is seen to come crouching along, to lay his force, his courage, and all his useful talents, at the feet of his master; he waits his orders, to which he pays implicit obedience; he consults his looks, and a single glance is sufficient to put him in motion; he is more faithful even than the most boasted among men; he is constant in his affection, friendly without interest, and grateful for the slightest favours; much more mindful of benefits received, than injuries offered; he is not driven off by unkindness; he still continues humble, submissive, and imploring; his only hope to be serviceable; his only terror to displease; he licks the hand that has just lifted to strike him, and at last disarms resentment, by submissive perseverance.

More docile than man, more obedient than any other animal, he is not only instructed in a short time, but he also conforms to the dispositions and the manners of those who command him. He takes his tone from the house he inhabits. When at night the guard of the house is committed to his care, he seems proud of the charge, he continues a watchful sentinel, he goes his rounds, scents strangers at a distance, and gives warning of his being upon duty. If they attempt to break in upon his territories, he becomes more fierce, flies at them, threatens, fights, and either conquers alone, or alarms those

3

who have most interest in coming to his assistance; however, when he has conquered, he quietly reposes upon his spoils, and abstains from what he has deterred others from abusing; giving thus at once a lesson of courage, temperance, and fidelity.

The dog, thus trusted, exerts a degree of superiority over all animals that require human protection. The flock and the herd obey his voice more readily even than that of the shepherd or the herdsman; he conducts them, guards them, keeps them from capriciously seeking danger, and their enemies he considers his own. Nor is he less useful in the pursuits; when the sound of the horn, or the voice of the huntsman calls him to the field, he testifies his pleasure by every little art, and pursues with perseverance, those animals, which, when taken, he must not expect to divide.

Few quadrupeds are less delicate in their food; and yet there are many kinds of birds which the dog will not venture to touch. It should seem that water is more necessary to the dog than food; he drinks often, though not abundantly; and it is commonly believed, that when abridged in water, he runs mad. This dreadful malady, the consequences of which are so well known, is the greatest inconvenience that results from the keeping this faithful domestic.

from *An History of the Earth and Animated Nature,* 1774

Gace de la Vigne

A dog hath true love,
A dog hath right good understanding,
A wise dog knoweth all things,
A dog hath force and kindliness,
A dog hath mettle and is comely,
A dog is in all things seemly.
A knowing dog thinketh no evil,
A dog hath a memory that forgeteth not,
I say unto you again a dog forsaketh not his duty,
Hath might and cunning therewith and a great brave heart.

Poème sur la Chasse, 1359

Sir John Davies

Thou dogged Cineas, hated like a dogge,
For still thou grumblest like a Mastie dogge,
Comparst thy selfe to nothing but a dogge:
Thou saiest thou art as weary as a dogge,
As angry, sick, and hungry as a dogge,
As dull and melancholy as a dogge,
As lazie, sleepie, idle as a dogge.
But why dost thou compare thee to a dogge?
In that for which all men despise a dogge,
I will compare thee better to a dogge.

Thou art as faire and comely as a dogge,
Thou art as true and honest as a dogge,
Thou art as kind and liberall as a dogge,
Thou art as wise and valiant as a dogge.
But Cineas, I have often heard thee tell,
Thou art as like father as may be,
Tis like inough, and faith I like it well,
But I am glad thou art not like me.

"In Cineam", 1622

Plato

SOCRATES: The dog is a watcher, I said, and the guardian is also a watcher; and in this point of view, is not the noble youth very like a well-bred dog?

GLAUCON: How do you mean?

SOCRATES: I mean that both of them ought to be quick to see and swift to overtake the enemy; and strong too if, when they have caught him, they have to fight with him.

GLAUCON: All these qualities will certainly be required.

SOCRATES: Well, and your guardian must be brave if he is to fight well?

GLAUCON: Certainly.

SOCRATES: And is he likely to be brave who has no spirit, whether horse or dog or any other animal? Have you never observed how the presence of spirit makes the soul of any creature absolutely fearless and invincible?

GLAUCON: I have.

SOCRATES: Then now we have a clear idea of the bodily qualities which are required in the guardian.

GLAUCON: True.

SOCRATES: And also of the mental ones; his soul is to be full of spirit?

GLAUCON: Yes.

SOCRATES: But then, Glaucon, those spirited natures are apt to be furious with one another and with everybody else.

GLAUCON: There is the difficulty.

SOCRATES: Whereas they ought to be gentle to their friends, and dangerous to their enemies; or instead of the enemies destroying them, they will destroy themselves.

GLAUCON: True.

SOCRATES: What is to be done then; how shall we find a gentle nature which has also a great spirit, for they seem to be inconsistent with one another?

GLAUCON: True.

SOCRATES: And yet he will not be a good guardian who is wanting either of these two qualities; and as the combination of them appears to be impossible, this is equivalent to saying that to be a good guardian is also impossible.

GLAUCON: I am afraid that what you say is true.

SOCRATES: (*perplexed*) My friend, we deserve to be in a puzzle; for we have lost sight of the simile with which we started.

GLAUCON: What do you mean?

SOCRATES: I mean to say that there do exist natures gifted with those opposite qualities.

GLAUCON: And where do you find them?

SOCRATES: Many animals furnish examples of them; our friend the dog is a very good one; you know that well-bred dogs are perfectly gentle to their familiars and acquaintances and the reverse to strangers?

GLAUCON: Yes, I know.

SOCRATES: Then there is nothing impossible or out of the order of nature in our finding a guardian who has a similar combination of qualities?

GLAUCON: Certainly not.

SOCRATES: Would you say that he should combine with the spirited nature the qualities of a philosopher?

GLAUCON: I do not apprehend your meaning.

SOCRATES: The trait of which I am speaking may be also seen in the dog and is remarkable in an animal.

GLAUCON: What trait?

SOCRATES: Why, a dog, when he sees a stranger, is angry; when an acquaintance he welcomes him, although the one has never done him any harm, nor the other any good. Did this never strike you as curious?

GLAUCON: I never thought of it before.

SOCRATES: And surely this instinct of the dog is very charming; your dog is a true philosopher.

GLAUCON: Why?

SOCRATES: Why, because he distinguishes the face of a friend and of an enemy only by the criterion of knowing and not knowing. And must not the creature be fond of learning who determines what is friendly and what is unfriendly by the test of knowledge and ignorance?

> from *The Republic*, Book II, *c.* 350 BC,
> translated by Benjamin Jowett, 1817–93.

Jean-Jacques Rousseau

You will find them both charming,
You will find them both biting,
That is their point of resemblance.
One bites only your enemies,
The other bites all your friends . . .
That's the difference!

> from *Confessions*, 1782–9.

7

Ezra Pound

When I carefully consider the curious habits of dogs
I am compelled to conclude
That man is the superior animal.

When I consider the curious habits of man
I confess, my friend, I am puzzled.

from "Meditatio", 1916

Samuel Butler

The great pleasure of a dog is that you may make a fool of yourself with him and not only will he not scold you, but he will make a fool of himself too.

from *Notebooks*, 1912

Thomas Bewick

I have often amused myself in considering the character of the Canine Species, and of comparing it and its varieties, with those of the untutored part of mankind & it is curious & amusing to see the similarity between them – To his master the Dog is an uncommonly submissive, obedient & faithfull servant, & seems to look upon him as if he were an angel – his sagacity & courage are equally conspicuous, and in the defence of his master he will suffer death. But to his own Species he is ill behaved, selfish, cruel & unjust, he only associates with his fellows for the purpose of packing together to destroy other Animals, which cannot be effected otherwise. They will sometimes indeed let a supplicating Dog into which they have inspired terror, sneak off, & I have often watched to see the wary circumspect plan that a strange Dog adopts, on his being obliged to pass through a village, or through among those of their equally ill behaved brethren, the Butchers Dogs, in a town – it is curious to see the stranger upon these occasions view his danger and then to affect lameness and go hirpling through among them unmolested. I knew their instinct was surprizing, but to know some of their reasoning powers I had not tried, and for this purpose, when a Boy, I cut two thin slices of meat and plastered the insides with mustard, and then threw it to one of my fathers dogs. This, he being very apt at kepping, caught in his mouth, and as quickly as he could, got quit of it again, but from time to time, he would rather run the risk of losing it, than keep any more. And to prove how far selfness and malignity would operate upon him, – I have placed two Basons filled with very hot fat broth, at a distance from each other – he ran from one to the other, to prevent a beautiful spaniel bitch, from partaking of either of them – his attention was taken up with thus watching & preventing her, 'till at length his patience was exhausted by going so often from one Bason to the other, and then, with the utmost vengeance he seized her & tore away his mouthful of skin from her side.

from *A Memoir*, nineteenth century

Diogenes the Cynic

I am called a dog because I fawn on those who give me anything, I yelp at those who refuse, and I set my teeth in rascals.

from *Diogenes*, fourth century BC

Charles Darwin

Many carnivorous animals, as they crawl towards their prey and prepare to rush or spring on it, lower their heads and crouch, partly, as it would appear, to hide themselves, and partly to get ready for their rush; and this habit in an exaggerated form has become hereditary in our pointers and setters. Now I have noticed scores of times that when two strange dogs meet on an open road, the one which first sees the other, though at the distance of one or two hundred yards, after the first glance always lowers its head, generally crouches a little, and even lies down; that is he takes the proper attitude for concealing himself and for making a rush or a spring, although the road is quite open and the distance great. Again, dogs of all kinds when intently watching and slowly approaching their prey, frequently keep one of their fore-legs doubled up for a long time, ready for the next cautious step; and this is eminently characteristic of the pointer. But from habit they behave in exactly the same manner whenever their attention is aroused.

From *The Expression of the Emotions in Man and Animals,* 1873

Isaac Watts

Let dogs delight to bark and bite,
For God hath made them so;
Let bears and lions growl and fight,
For 'tis their nature too.

"Against quarrelling",
Divine Songs for the Use of Children, 1715

Sir Walter Scott

The females are testy, petulant, and very apt to indulge their impatient dislike of each other's presence, of the spirit of rivalry which it produces, in a sudden bark and snap, which last is generally made as much at advantage as possible. But these ebullitions of peevishness lead to no very serious or prosecuted conflict; the affair begins and ends in a moment. But not so the ire of the male dogs, which, once produced and excited by growls of mutual offence and defiance, leads generally to a fierce and obstinate contest, in which, if the parties be dogs of game and well matched, they grapple, throttle, tear, roll each other in the kennel, and can only be separated by choking them with their own collars till they lose wind and hold at the same time, or by surprising them out of their wrath by sousing them with cold water.

from *St Ronan's Well,* 1823

Lieutenant Commander George Washington DeLong

When they fight, how they fight, and whom they fight, seem to be purely abstract questions with them, so long as it is a fight. For instance dogs one and two will see dog three in a good position, perhaps enjoying a meat can that has been empty for months and has, of course, no nutriment. As if by concerted plan one and two will spring on three, roll him over, and seemingly tear him to pieces. Fortunately the wool is so long and thick that an attacking dog gets a mouth full of hair before his front teeth reach the flesh, so no great damage is generally done. The vulnerable places are the ears, and the belly.

I have seen an attacked dog run, and, lying on his stomach, shove his head into a snow bank with impunity, while his foes are choking over the hair they tore from his back. However, this is a long digression. Suddenly dog three will turn on dog two and be promptly aided by dog one, his previous foe. By this time the whole pack has gathered as if by magic, and a free and indiscriminate fight occurs, until the advent of the quartermaster, and a merciless application of the whip breaks up the row.

From *Diary of the Jeanette expedition to the North Pole,* 1879

William Henry Hudson

If a dog could be taught to turn a spit, find truffles, save a man from drowning or from perishing in a snow-drift, point out a partridge, retrieve a wounded duck, kill twenty rats in as many seconds, and herd a flock of sheep, then it would indeed be an animal to marvel at. These are special instincts or incipient instincts, and to bestow such epithets as "generous" and "noble" on a dog for pulling a drowning man out of the water, or scratching him out of a snow-drift, is fully as irrational as it would be to call the swallow and cuckoo intrepid explorers of the Dark Continent, or to praise the hive-bees of the working caste for their chastity, loyalty, and patriotism, and for their profound knowledge of chemistry and the higher mathematics, as shown in their works. Cross dogs and these various propensities, which being useful to man and not to the animals themselves are preserved artificially, fade away and disappear, and from moving artificially apart in twenty different grooves the animals revert to the old simple groove in which they were first found by man.

. . . It ought to be a great comfort to those who devote themselves to canine pets, and to canophilists generally, to know that the philosophers are at one with them. To some others it will perhaps add a new terror to existence if students of dog-psychology generally should feel themselves tempted to imitate a recent illustrious example, and go about the country lecturing on the marvellous development of mind in their respective pets. Leibniz once gave an account of a dog that talked; and quite recently a writer in a London journal related how, in a sheltered spot among the rocks on a lonely Scotch moor, he stumbled on an old shepherd playing whist with his collie. Nothing approaching to these cases in dramatic interest can be looked for in the apprehended discourses. The animal to be described will as a rule be of a quiet, thoughtful character proper in a philosopher's dog; not fond of display or much given to wild flights of imagination. He will only show that he possesses that faculty when asleep or barking at the heels of a dream-hare. He will show deep affection for his master . . . also a strong sense of proprietorship, . . . – a display of intellect which strangely simulates an instinct common to all creatures. And he will also show an intelligent curiosity, and examine things to find out what they are, and prove himself a very agreeable companion; as much so as Mr Benjamin Kidd's pet humble-bee. Moreover he will be accomplished enough to sit up and beg, retrieve a walking-stick from the Serpentine, close an open door, etc.; and besides these ordinary things he will do things extraordinary, such as picking up numbered or lettered cards, red, blue, and yellow, at his master's bidding; in fact such tricks as a pig will perform without being very learned, not a Porson of its kind, but only possessing the ordinary porcine abilities. In conclusion the lecturer will bring up the savage, not in person, but a savage evolved from his inner consciousness, and compare its understanding with that of the dog, or of his dog, and the poor savage will have very much the worst of it.

Dr Romanes, in his work on *Mental Evolution in Animals*, speaks of what he calls unpleasant survivals in the dog, such as burying food until it becomes offensive before eating it, turning round and round on the hearth-rug before lying down, rolling in filth, etc. etc., and he says that they have remained unaffected by contact with man because these instincts being neither useful nor harmful have never been either cultivated or repressed. From which it may be inferred that in his opinion these disagreeable habits may be got rid of in time. But why does he call them survivals? If the action, so frequently observed in the dog, of turning round several times before lying down, is correctly ascribed to an ancient habit in the wild animal of treading down the grass to make a bed to sleep on, it is rightly called a survival, and is a habit neither useful nor harmful in the domesticated state, which has never been either cultivated or repressed, and will in time disappear. Thus far it is easy to agree with Dr Romanes. The other offensive instinct of the dog, of which burying meat to make it putrid, rolling in filth, etc., etc., are different manifestations, is not a survival, in the sense in which zoologists use that word, any more than the desire of the well-fed cat for the canary, and of the hen-hatched ducklings for the pond, are survivals.

from "The Great Dog-superstition', *The Book of a Naturalist,* 1919

Charles Dickens

"Dogs, sir?"

"Not just now," said Mr Winkle.

"Ah! you should keep dogs – fine animals – sagacious creatures – dog of my own once – pointer – surprising instinct – out shooting one day – entering enclosure – whistled – dog stopped – whistled again – Ponto – no go; stock still – called him – Ponto, Ponto – wouldn't move – dog transfixed – staring at a board – looked up, saw an inscription – 'Gamekeeper has orders to shoot all dogs found in this enclosure.' – wouldn't pass it – wonderful dog – valuable dog that – very."

"Singular circumstance that," said Mr Pickwick. "Will you allow me to make a note of it?"

"Certainly, sir, certainly – hundred more anecdotes of the same animal."

from *Pickwick Papers,* 1837

Judith Anne Lytton, Baroness Wentworth

Like the dogs of Constantinople, he has a great idea of the laws of boundaries. For instance, he is most polite to James, the house boy, so long as he is in the pantry, but let him cross the threshold of the swing door which opens on to the stairs, and there is a fearful uproar as James is chivvied away. This is all a game to which James very good-naturedly lends himself. In the same way Fizzy is always respectful to my nursery maids in the nursery, but he won't have them on the stairs nor in the pantry. I have had several and he always treats them in the same way. Out of doors he is always amiable to everybody, evidently considering it neutral ground. He has also no objection to the housekeeper going anywhere in the house so long as she does not touch anything he thinks I am using.

from *Toy Dogs and their Ancestors*, 1911

Virginia Woolf

He nosed his way from smell to smell; the rough, the smooth, the dark, the golden. He went in and out, up and down, where they beat brass, where they bake bread, where women sit combing their hair, where the birdcages are piled high on the causeway, where the wine spills itself in dark red stains on the pavement, where leather smells and harness and garlic, where cloth is beaten, where vine leaves tremble, where men sit and drink and spit and dice – he ran in and out, always with his nose to the ground, drinking in the essence; or with his nose in the air vibrating with the aroma. He slept in this hot patch of sun – how sun made the stone reek! he sought the tunnel of shade – how acid shade made the stone smell! He devoured whole bunches of grapes largely because of their smell; he chewed and spat out whatever tough relic of goat or macaroni the Italian housewife had thrown from the balcony – goat and macaroni were raucous smells, crimson smells. He followed the swooning sweetness of incense into the violet intricacies of dark cathedrals; and, sniffing, tried to lap the gold on the window-stained seat.

from *Flush*, 1933

James Joyce

Their dog ambled about a bank of dwindling sand, trotting, sniffing on all sides. Looking for something lost in past life. Suddenly he made off like a bounding hare, ears flung back, chasing the shadow of a lowskimming seagull. The man's shrieked whistle struck his limp ears. He turned, bounded back, came nearer, trotted on twinkling shanks. On a field tenney a buck, trippant, proper, unattired. At the lacefringe of the tide he halted with stiff forehoofs seawardpointed ears. His snout lifted barked at the wavenoise, herds of seamorse. They serpented towards his feet, curling, unfurling many crests, every ninth, breaking, plashing, from far, from farther out, waves and waves.

Cocklepickers. They waded a little way in the water and, stooping, soused their bags, and, lifting them again, waded out. The dog yelped running to them, reared up and pawed them, dropping on all fours, again reared up at them with mute bearish fawning. Unheeded he kept by them as they came towards the drier sand, a rag of wolf's tongue redpanting from his jaws. His speckled body ambled ahead of them and then loped off at a calf's gallop. The carcass lay in his path. He stopped, sniffed, stalked round it, brother, nosing closer, went round it, sniffing rapidly like a dog all over the dead dog's bedraggled fell. Dogskull, dogsniff, eyes on the ground, moves to one great goal. Ah, poor dogsbody. Here lies dogsbody's body.

– Tatters! Out of that, you mongrel.

The cry brought him skulking back to his master and a blunt bootless kick sent him unscathed across a spit of sand, crouched in flight. He slunk back in a curve. Doesn't see me. Along by the edge of the mole he lolloped, dawdled, smelt a rock and from under a cocked hindleg pissed against it. He trotted forward and, lifting his hindleg, pissed quick short at an unsmelt rock. The simple pleasures of the poor. His hindpaws then scattered sand: then his forepaws dabbled and delved. Something he buried there, his grandmother. He rooted in the sand, dabbling, delving and stopped to listen to the air, scraped up the sand again with a fury of his claws, soon ceasing, a pard, a panther, got on spousebreach, vulturing the dead.

from *Ulysses*, 1922

William Hamilton

Calm though not mean, courageous without rage,
Serious not dull, and without thinking sage;
Pleas'd at the lot that Nature has assign'd,
Snarl as I list, and freely bark my mind;
As churchman wrangle not with jarring spite,
Nor statesman-like caressing whom I bite;
View all the canine kind with equal eyes,
I dread no mastiff, and no cur despise:
True from the first, and faithful to the end.
My days and nights one equal tenour keep,
Fast but to eat, and only wake to sleep:
Thus stealing along life I live incog,
A very plain and downright honest dog.

"On a Dog", eighteenth century

* * *

Professor Thomas Bell

Now we find that there are several different instances of the existence in dogs of such a state of wildness as to have lost even that common character of domestication, variety of colour and marking. Of these, two very remarkable ones are the dhole of India and the dingo of Australia. There is, besides, a half-reclaimed race amongst the Indians of North America, and another also partially tamed in South America, which deserve attention. And it is found that these races in different degrees, and in a greater degree as they are more wild, exhibit the lank and gaunt form, the lengthened limbs, the long and slender muzzle, and the great comparative strength which characterise the wolf; and that the tail of the Australian dog, which may be considered as the most remote from the state of domestication, assumes the slightly bushy form of that animal.

We have here a remarkable approximation to a well-known wild animal of the same genus, in races which, though doubtless descended from domesticated ancestors, have gradually assumed the wild condition; and it is worthy of especial remark that the anatomy of the wolf, and its osteology in particular, does not differ from that of the dog in general, more than the different kinds of dogs do from each other. The cranium is absolutely similar, and so are all, or nearly all, the other essential parts; and, to strengthen still further the probability of their identity, the dog and wolf will readily breed together, and their progeny is fertile. The obliquity of the position of the eyes in the wolf is one of the characteristics in which it differs from the dogs; and, although it is very desirable not to rest too much upon the effects of habit on structure, it is not perhaps straining the point to attribute the forward direction of the eyes in the dog to the constant habit, for many successive generations, of looking forward to his master, and obeying his voice.

from *British Quadrupeds, c.* 1860

Will H. Ogilvie

Pepper or Mustard — what's the odds?
Valiant, varmint, lithe and low,
These were the hounds that the wise old gods
Took to their hunting an aeon ago,
These when the wild boar stamped and stood
These when the gaunt wolf snapped at bay,
Grim and relentless, rash and rude,
Went for the throat in the Dandie way.

Deep in the slope of that dome-like head,
Under that topknot crimped and curled,
Surely the fighting fire was fed
Before the fires were cool in the world!
Surely 'twas these that the cave-man kept,
Comrades in hunting, sport and war,
Sharing the shelves where their masters slept,
Tearing the bones that their masters tore!

No? – Well, have it the way you please;
But I'll wager it wasn't a show-ring Fox,
Poodle or Pom or Pekingese,
That bayed the mammoth among the rocks;
But something tousled and tough and blue,
Lined like a weasel – arch and dip,
Coming up late, as the Dandies do,
And going right in with the Border grip.

"Dandie Dinmonts", *The Collected Sporting
Verse of Will H. Ogilvie,* 1932

Marcus Terentius Varro

There are two kinds [of dog], one for hunting connected with the wild beasts of the woods, the other trained for purposes of defence, and used by shepherds.

In the first place you must obtain dogs of the proper age; puppies and old dogs are no good to themselves or to the sheep either and sometimes become the prey of wild beasts. They should possess a handsome shape, and be of great size, their eyes black or yellowish, with nostrils to match; the lips should be blackish or red, the upper lips neither turned up too much nor hanging down too low. The lower jaw should be short and the two teeth that spring from it on the right and left side should project a little, while the upper teeth should be rather straight. The incisors should be covered by the lip; the head and ears large, and the latter broad and hanging; the neck and throat thick, the parts between the joints long, the legs straight and turned out rather than in; the feet big and broad, spreading out as they walk; the toes being well separated, and the claws hard and curved. The soles be neither horny nor over hard, but rather sponge-like and soft; the body tucked in near the top of the thighs, the spine neither prominent nor curved, and the tail thick. The bark should be deep, the stretch of the jaw extensive, the colour preferably white, because they are then more easily recognized in the dark, and the appearance should be lion-like. Breeders also prefer that the bitches should have breasts with teats of equal size.

from *De Re Rustica, c.* 40 BC

Edward, 2nd Duke of York

A rennyng hounde is a kynde of houndis ther be fewe men yat ne have seie some of hem, natheless I shall devyse how a tennyng hounde shal be holed for good and faire, and also I shal devyse of her maners, of alle hewes of rennyng houndes, which be good and whiche be bad or evyl, as of greihoundes; but ye beest hewe of rennyng houndes and moost comon for to be good, is i cleped broun tawne; also, ye goodnesse of rennyng houndes and of al other maner kynde of good houndes, cometh of verray corage, and of ye good nature of here good fadir and hir good modir; and also as towchyng greyhoundes men may helpe to make hem good techyng as to lede hem to wode and to feelres and to be ay nye hem in makyng of many good quyrreis whan hei han wel I don, and astyng and biteng hem whan the done amys, for thei byn beestis and therefore thei have nede to be lernyd to yat men wil yat thei shuld do.

After a rennyng hounde shuld be wel bore and wel grove of bodie, and shulde have greet nosethrelles and open and longe snowte, but not smale, and greet lippis and hangyng adoun, grete jeu and rede or blak, greet forhede and grete hede, and large erys wel longe and wel hangyng adoun and brood and nye ye hede; a grete neke, and a greet brest, grete shuldres, and grete leggis, and stronge and not to longe, grete feet and rounde, and grete clees and ye foot a litel availede; smale bi the flanks, and longe sydes a litel pintel, and long smale hangyng balloks, and wel trussyd to gideris; a good chyne bone, a grete bak, good thies and greet hynder legges and ye heghes streight and not bowed: ye taile grete and hie and not crompyng upon ye bak, but streight with a litel crompyng upward . . .

from *Mayster of the Game* (1406–13)

Dame Julyans Barnes

A greyhounde should be headed lyke a snake,
An neckyd lyke a drake,
Fotyd lyke a cat,
Tayled lyke a rat,

Syded lyke a teme,
And chyned lyke a bream,
The fyrste year he most lerne to fede,
The secund yere to felde hym lede,
The .iii. yere he is felow-lyke,
The .iiii. yere ther is noon syke,
The .v. yere he is good ynough,
The .vi. yere he shall holde the plough,
The .vii. yere he will avayle,
Grete bikkys for to assayle.
The .viii. yere likladill;
The .ix. yere cartsadyll.
And when he is commyn to that yere,
Have hym to the Tanner,
For the best hownde that ever bikke hade,
At .ix. yere he is full badde.

from *Boke of St Albans*, 1479

Julian Grenfell

Shining black in the shining light,
    Inky black in the golden sun,
Graceful as the swallow's flight,
    Light as a swallow's winged one,
Swift as driven hurricane,
    Double-sinewed stretch and spring,
Muffled thud of flying feet –
    See the black dog galloping,
    Hear his wild foot-beat.

See him lie when the day is dead,
    Black curves curled on the boarded floor.
Sleepy eyes, my sleepy-head –
    Eyes that were aflame before.
Gentle now, they burn no more:
    Gentle now and softly warm,
With the fire that made them bright

Hidden — as when after storm
Softly falls the night.

God of speed, who makes the fire —
  God of Peace, who lulls the same —
God who gives the fierce desire,
  Lust for blood as fierce as flame —
God who stands in Pity's name —
  Many may ye be or less,
Ye who rule the earth and sun:
  Gods of strength and gentleness,
  Ye are ever one.

"To a Black Greyhound", *c.* 1912

Randle Cotgrave

Allan: a kinde of big, strong, thicke-headed, and short-snowted dog;
the brood whereof came first out of Albania.

Allan de boucherie: is like our mastive, and serves butchers, to
bring in fierce oxen, and to keepe their stalls.

Allan gentil: is like a grayhound in all properties and parts, his
thicke and short head excepted.

Allan vautre: a great and ougly curre of that kind (having a big
head, hanging lips, and slowching eares), kept onely to bait the Beare
and wild Boare.

A French and English Dictionaire, 1611

Gervase Markham

I will heere describe as neere as I can the best proportion of a perfect
Water dogge.

First, for the colour of the best watr Dogge, all be it some which
are curious in all things will ascribe more excellency to one colour
than to another as the Blacks to be the best and hardest; the
lyverhued swiftest in swimming, and the Pied or Spotted Dogge,

quickest of scent; yet in thruth it is nothing so, for all colurs are alike and so a Dogge of any of the former colours, may be excellent good Dogge, and of any may bee most notable curres, according to their first ordering and trayning; for Instruction is the liquor where-with they are seasoned, and if they be well handled at the first, they will ever smell of that discresion, and if they bee ill handled they will ever stink of that folloey: for nature is a true mistress and bestowes her guifts freely, and it is onely nature which abuseth them.

To proceede then, your Dogge may be of any colour and yet excellent, and his hairs in generall would be long and curled, not loose and shagged; for the first showes hardnesse and ability to endure the water, the other much tendernesse, making his sport grievous; his head would be round and curled, his ears broad and hanging, his Eye full, lively and quicke, his nose very short; his lippe, Hound-like, side and rough bearded, his Chappes with a full set of strong Teeth, and the genral features of his whole countenance being united together would be as Lyon-like as might be, for that shewes fierceness and goodnesse: his Necke would bee thicke and short, his Brest like the brest of a Shippe, sharpe and compact, his Shoulders broad, his fore Legs straight, his Chine square, his Buttockes rounde, his ribbes compassed, his belly gaunt, his Thyes brawny, his Cambrels crooked, his Pasterns strong and dewe clawde, and his foure feet spatious, full and round, and closed together to the cley, like a watr Ducke, for they bring his oars to rowe him in the water, having that shape, will carry his body away faster. And thus you have the trye description of a perfect Water Doggee.

from *Hunger's Prevention; or the whole Arte of Fowling by Water and Land*, 1615

John Gay

How falsely is the spaniel drawn!
Did man from him first learn to fawn?
A dog proficient in the trade!
He, the chief flatt'rer nature made!
Go, man, the ways of courts discern,
You'll find a spaniel still might learn.

How can the foxe's theft and plunder
Provoke his censure, or his wonder?

from "Fable IX: The Elephant
and the Bookseller," 1727

John Taylor

In shapes and forms of dogges; of which there are but two sorts that
are usefull for man's profit, which are the mastiffe and the little
whippet, or house dogge; all the rest are for pleasure and recreation.

from *All the Workes of John Taylor, the Water Poet*, 1630

Barnabe Googe

But now will I onely speake of Dogges for the husbands, and keepers
both of the house and the Cattell, and first of the Mastie that keepeth
the house; for this purpose you must provide you such a one as hath
a large and a mightie body, a great and a shrill voyce, that both his
barking he may discover, and with his sight dismay the theefe, yea,
being not seene, with the horror of his voice put him to flight. His
stature must be neither long nor short, but well set; his head, great;
his eyes, sharp and fiery, either browne or grey; his lippes, blackish,
neither turning up nor hanging too much down; his mouth black
and wide; his neather jaw, fat, and coming out of it on either side a
fang appearing more outward than his other teeth; his upper teeth
even with his neather, not hanging too much over, sharpe, and
hidden with his lippes; his countenance, like a lion; his brest, great
and shag hayrd; his shoulders, broad; his legges, bigge; his tayle,
short; his feet, very great. His disposition must neither be too gentle
nor too curst, that he neither faune upon a theefe nor flee upon his
friends; very waking; no gadder abroad, nor lavish of his mouth,
barking without cause; neither maketh it any matter though he be
not swifte, for he is but to fight at home, and to give warning of the
enemie.

The Dogge that is for the folde must neyther be so gaunt nor

23

swyft as the Greyhound, nor so fatte nor heavy as the Masty of the house, but very strong, and able to fight and followe the chase, that he may be able to beate away the Woolfe or other beastes and to follow the theefe and recover the praye and therefore his body would rather be long than short and thicke: in all other poyntes he must agree with the Bandogge.

. . . For his colour . . . The white they commend, because he may be discerned from the Woolfe in the night, whereby they shall not strike the Dogge insteede of the Woolfe. The blacke agayne for the house is best commended, because of his Terrour to the Theefe in the day and for the hurt that he may doo by night, by reason of his not being seene . . . To arme them agaynst the Woolf, or other wyld beastes, you may put brode collars about theyr neckes full of nayles, and iron studdes, lyning it with soft leather within.

from *Foure Bookes of Husbandry*, 1631

Gratius Faliscus

Besides our Mastiffe which seems to be an Indigena or Native of England; we train up most excellent Grey-hounds (which seem to have been brought hither by the Galls) in our open Champaines. Then for hounds, the West Country, Cheshire and Lancashire, with other Wood-land and Mountainous Countries, breed our Slow-Hound; which is a large, great dog, tall and heavy. Then Worcestershire, Bedfordshire and many well mixt soiles, where the Campaigne and covert are of equall largenesse, produce a middle-siz'd dog of a more nimble composure than the former. Lastly the North-parts, as Yorkshire, Cumberland, Northumberland, and many other plain champaign Countries bred the light, nimble, swift, slender, Fleet-hound (which Mr Markham with his wonted curiosity doth observe). After all these the little Beagle is attributed to our Country; this is by Ulitius shown to be the Canis Agassoeus of Oppian against Caius. All these Dogs have deserved to be famous in adjacent and remote countries whither they are sent for great rarities, and ambitiously sought for by their Lords and Princes, although only the fighting Dogs seem to have been known to the antient Authors:

and perhaps in that Age hunting was not much cultivated by our own Countrymen.

Dogs have innumerable countries from which they spring and the disposition of each corresponds with his origin. The Mede dog shows great fight, though untaught, and the far distant Celt is celebrated with high renown.

Some prefer to breed Chinese dogs, a race of implacable anger, with which contrast those of Arcadia, that are traceable yet combative. The Hyrcanian (this near the Caspian) race of dogs have all the ferocity and more, for they interbreed with the savage monsters of the forests.

But the Umbrian dog runs away even from the enemies whom he has himself discovered. Would that he had as much courage and pluck in fight as he has loyalty and sagacity in scent! What if you were to go to the English Channel, surging with treacherous sea, and reach as far as the Britons themselves! How small the charge and expense if you do and are not attracted merely by deceptive look and form (this is the only danger about British dogs): nay, when a great work is to be done and courage to be displayed and the hazard of approaching war gives the final summons, then you would not admire even the well-known Molossian hounds so much as these.

from *Cynegeticon*, c. 20 BC

Gervase Markham

Now there are divers kinds [of hounds] as the slow hound, which is a large, great dog, tall and heavy, and are bred for the most parts in the West Counties of this Land, as also in "Cheshire" and "Lancashire", and most woodland and mountainous Countries; then the middle siz'd dog, which is fit for the Chase, being of a more nimble composure, and are bred in "Worcestershire", "Bedfordshire", and many other well mixt soyls, where the Chapain and Covert are of equal largeness; then the light, nimble, swift, slender Dog, which is bred in the North parts of this land as "Yorkshire", "Cumberland", "Northumberland", and many other plain Champion Countries: and lastly, the little "Beagle", which may be carried in a mans glove, and are bred in many Countries for delight only, Being of curious scents and passing cunning in their hunting; for the most part tyring, (but seldome killing) the prey, except at some strange advantage.

These Hounds are of divers colours, and according to their colours, so we elect them for the chase: as thus for example: The White Hound, or the white with black spots, or the white with some few liver spots, are the most principal, both to compose your Kennel of, and will indeed hunt any chase exceeding well, especially the Hare, Stag, Buck, Roe or Otter; for they will well endure both woods and waters: yet if you demand which is the best and most beautiful of all colours, for the general Kennel, then I answer, the white with the black ears, and a black spot at the setting on of the tayl, and are ever found both of good scent, and good condition. The black hound, the black tann'ed, or he that is all liver hew'd, or the milk white, which is the true Talbots, are best for the string or line, for they do delight most in blood, and of these the largest is ever best, and most comely. The grissel'd which are ever most commonly shag-hair'd or any other colour, whether it be mixt or unmixt, so it be shag-hair'd are the best verminers, and therefore are chosen to hunt the Fox, Badger, or any other hot scents: they are exceeding good and cunning finders: and therefore have Huntsmen thought not amiss to have one, or a couple in every Kennel.

For the shape of your Hound, it must be according to the Climate where he is bred, and according to the natural composition of his body, as thus: If you would chuse a large, heavy, slow, true, Talbot-like Hound, you must chuse him which hath a round, big, thick head, with a short nose uprising, and large open nostrils, which shews that he is of a good and quick scent, his ears exceeding large, thin, and down-hanging, much lower than his chaps, and the flews of his upper-lips almost two inches lower than his nether chaps, which shews a merry deep mouth, and a loud ringer, his back strong, and streight, yet rather rising, than inwardly yielding, which shews much toughness and indurance; his fillets will be thick and great, which approves a quick gathering up of his legs without pain, his huckle-bones round and hidden, which shews he will not tire, his Thighs round, and his Hams streight, which shews swiftness; his Tail long, and rush grown, that is big at the setting on, and small downward, which shews a perfect strong chine, and a good wind; the hair under his belly hard and stiff, which shews willingness and ability to endure labour in all weathers, and in all places; his Legs large and lean, which shews nimbleness in leaping or climbing; his Foot round, high knuckled and well claw'd, and a general composure of his Body so just and even, that no level may distinguish whether his hinder or fore-part be the higher: all which shew him of much ability, and that in his labour he will seldom find any annoyance.

But if you will chuse a swift light Hound, then must his head be more slender, and his nose more long, his ears and flews more shallow, his back broad, his belly gaunt, his tail small, his joynts long, his foot round, and his general composure much more slender, and Gray-hound-like: and thus in the generality for the most part, are all your "Yorkshire" Hounds, whose vertues I can praise no farther than for scent and swiftness: for to speak of their mouths they have only a little sharp sweetness like Gig, but no depth or ground like more solemn musick.

When you intend to set up a Kennel of Hounds, examine your fancie what be the best pleasures you take in Hounds, whether it be cunning in hunting, sweetness, loudness, or deepness of cry; whether it be for the training of your Horse, or else but meerly for the exercise of your own body, being otherwise subject to grossness and infirmity: If it be for cunning hunting, you shall breed your dogs from the slowest and largest of the Northern Hounds, and the swiftest and slendrest of the West-country Hounds, being both Male and Female, approved to be staunch, fair, and even-running, of perfect fine scent, and not given to lie off, or look for advantages.

These Hounds will neither be so exceeding slow, that you will waste many days without some Fruit of your labor, or so unnimble, that you shall need men to help them over every hedge, as I have many times seen to my much wonder; but having both strength and nimbleness, will hold you in continual delight and exercise; for these middle siz'd dogs are neither so swift that they will far out-run the scent, and let it grow cold by their own laziness, but being ever and anon upon it, bring Chase to such a narrow exigent, that the poor Beast shall be forc'd to try all the skill, nature and strength hath lent it, to preserve life: and the Hounds on the other side, all their pains and the Huntsman's cunning, to undo intricate doubles, Skips, Squats and windings with which they shall be perplexed: and in this mediocrity of hunting, shall your eye (if the covert be not to extream thick) take a perfect view of all the art and cunning in every passage; so that I conclude the middle sized Hound, of good strength, sound mouth, and reasonable speed, which will make a Horse gallop fast, and not run, is the best for the true Art and use of hunting.

> from *Countrey Contentments, or, the Husbandman's Recreations, containing the Wholesome Experience, in which any ought to Recreate himself, after the toyl of more Serious Business, As namely Hunting, Hawking, Coursing with Grey-Hounds, and the Laws of Leash, Shooting in the Long-Bow or Cross-Bow, Bowling, Tennis, Baloon; the whole Art of Angling; And the use of the Fighting Cock, 1631*

Peter Beckford

There are necessary points in the shape of a hound, which ought always to be attended to by a sportsman; for, if he be not of a perfect symmetry, he will neither run fast, nor bear much work: he has much to undergo, and should have strength proportioned to it. Let his legs be straight as arrows; his feet round, and not too large; his shoulders back; his breast rather wide than narrow; his chest deep; his back broad; his head small, his neck thin; his tail thick and brushy: if he carry it well, so much the better.

> From *Thoughts upon Hunting, in a series of Familiar Letters*, 1733

William Somervile

See there with count'nance blithe,
And with a courtly grin, the fawning hound
Salutes thee cow'ring, his wide op'ning nose
Upwards he curls, and his large sloe-black eyes
Melt in soft blandishments and humble joy:
His glossy skin, or yellow pied, or blue,
In lights or shades, by Nature's pencil drawn,
Reflects the various tints: his ears and legs

Fleckt here and there in gay enamel'd pride,
Rival the speckled pard; his rush-grown tail
O'er his broad back, bends in an ample arch,
On shoulders clean upright and firm he stands:
His round cat feet, straight hams, and widespread thighs
And his low drooping chest, confess his speed,
His strength, his wind, or on the steepy hill
Or far extended plain; on every part
So well proportioned, that the nicer skill
Of Phidias himself can't blame thy choice.
Of such compose thy pack.

The Chace, 1735

Edith Somerville

I have visited several kennels of foxhounds in America, and there I
have been introduced to packs of pure-bred English foxhounds, and
pure-bred American hounds, and hounds that were a cross between
the two breeds. The American hounds have a tall, light elegance,
with the rather light bone and "hare's feet" that again bring the
Kerry Beagles to mind. I hope I may be pardoned for quoting what I
have said elsewhere of a very beautiful pack of this breed.

"The hounds . . . were pure American. . . . They were of the
orthodox three colours, black, white and tan, with the long hanging
ears (that irresistibly suggest the portraits of Mrs Barrett Browning)
and beautiful romantic eyes, and pointed tan toes, that again suggest
the poetess, and would look charming in black satin sandals."

Little as they conformed to Peterboro' standards they were
singularly attractive in their own way. I am reminded of a tale of
an intelligent little girl who was, for the first time, taken to a meet. She
regarded the pack gravely and remarked, "What a lot of dogs!" She
was corrected. "Those are hounds, darling!" She again studied the
pack, and then said, controversially, "Well, they're very like dogs."

Thus with this pack. They were very like hounds.

The supreme merit of the pure-bred American hounds is their
fitness for their business. They can take a line unfalteringly through
sandy wood-lands, and speak to it on hot and dusty roads. They have

perseverance while the mere fact that they are the breed that is favoured by Colonel John Weatherford is enough to sanction their appearance in the most select foxhound circles. I once had the good luck to see a pack of them in full cry after a fox, and tongue more tunable one could not wish to hear, though, for all their likeness, in build, though not in colour, to the Black and Tans, their cry had not the lonesome, wailing, contralto lament that one may listen to in the Kerry mountains, when the dark hounds are away in the high places, merged in the darkness of the heather.

from *An Appreciation, The Silver Horn,* 1934

J. Wentworth Day

The odd thing about the Chesapeake is that you always think of him, quite instinctively, as "a grand old dog." That is precisely what I felt about my friend Mr Nigel Holder's seven-months-old Chesapeake, when I found him plugging through the water on his own on my fen in Cambridgeshire. He struck me as being slightly rude in his stand-offish way, but obviously a person to know, to admire, and, later on, to like. That applies to all Chesapeakes.

Their impression of power is remarkable. They give one the feeling of immense reserves of energy, of great reservoirs of knowledge, of tolerance of disposition, obstinacy of purpose, and tenacity of principle. They are responsive, and they have a lot of quiet good sense. It will take many generations of stupid women in Bayswater and suede-footed young men in Kensington to ruin the character of this eminently sensible working dog. He has all the dignity, the native aristocracy, the quiet good sense, and the instinctive judgement of human nature of the British working man. Foreigners can never understand that it is because of those qualities that revolutions happen in this country with, to them, such depressing infrequency.

It is just the same with the Chesapeake. If you have two or three Chesapeakes in the kennel there will never be any disturbances in your shooting routine – none of that hoity-toity flightiness of the Gordon setter, the kiss-me-quick slobberings of the spaniel or the mental whimperings of the golden retriever. Do not imagine for a moment that I dislike any of these three excellent breeds of sporting dogs. But I mourn for individuals among them. The show-bench and the drawing-room have made fools of them, undermined their character, ruined their stamina, set their nerves on edge, reduced them from working dogs to park paddlers, tea-table sycophants, and drawing-room druggets. I doubt if you could ever do that with a Chesapeake. He will probably bite someone finally, just as a protest, and then walk out of the house, a dog in search of a man for a master.

from *The Dog in Sport,* 1938

Oliver Goldsmith

The want of that degree of discernment which is found in so many of the canine varieties, added to the ferocity of the bulldog, make it extremely dangerous when its courage and strength are employed to protect the person and property of its owner, or for any domestic purpose; since, unlike many of the more sagacious, though less powerful dogs, which seem rather more anxious to give alarm when danger threatens by their barking, than to proceed immediately to action, the bulldog, in general, makes a silent but furious attack, and the persisting powers of its teeth and jaws enable it to keep its hold against any but the greatest efforts, so that the utmost mischief is likely to ensue, as well to the innocent visitor of its domicile as to the felonious intruder.

from *An History of the Earth and Animated Nature,* 1774

Jerome K. Jerome

I remember being in the lobby of the Haymarket Stores one day, and all round about me were dogs, waiting for the return of their owners, who were shopping inside. There were a mastiff, and one or two collies, and a St Bernard, a few retrievers and Newfoundlands, a boar-hound, a French poodle, with plenty of hair round its head, but mangy about the middle, a bulldog, a few Lowther Arcade sort of animals, about the size of rats, and a couple of Yorkshire tykes.

There they sat, patient, good, and thoughtful. A solemn peacefulness seemed to reign in that lobby. An air of calmness and resignation – of gentle sadness pervaded the room.

Then a sweet young lady entered, leading a meek-looking little fox-terrier, and left him, chained up there, between the bulldog and the poodle. He sat and looked about him for a minute. Then he cast up his eyes to the ceiling, and seemed, judging from his expression, to be thinking of his mother. Then he yawned. Then he looked round at the other dogs, all silent, grave, and dignified.

He looked at the bulldog, sleeping dreamlessly on his right. He looked at the poodle, erect and haughty, on his left. Then, without a word of warning, without the shadow of a provocation, he bit that poodle's near fore-leg, and a yelp of agony rang through the quiet shades of that lobby.

The result of his first experiment seemed highly satisfactory to him, and he determined to go on and make things lively all round. He sprang over the poodle and vigorously attacked a collie, and the collie woke up, and immediately commenced a fierce and noisy contest with the poodle. Then Foxey came back to his own place, and caught the bulldog by the ear, and tried to throw him away; and the bulldog, a curiously impartial animal, went for everything he could reach, including the hall-porter, which gave that dear little terrier the opportunity to enjoy an uninterrupted fight of his own with an equally willing Yorkshire tyke.

Anyone who knows canine nature need hardly be told that, by this time, all the other dogs in the place were fighting as if their hearths and homes depended on the fray. The big dogs fought each other indiscriminately; and the little dogs fought among themselves, and filled up their spare time by biting the legs of the big dogs.

The whole lobby was a perfect pandemonium, and the din was terrific. A crowd assembled outside in the Haymarket, and asked if it was a vestry meeting; or, if not, who was being murdered, and why? . . .

And in the midst of the riot that sweet young lady returned, and snatched up that sweet little dog of hers (he had laid the tyke up for a month, and had on the expression, now, of a newborn lamb) into her arms, and kissed him, and asked him if he was killed, and what those great nasty brutes of dogs had been doing to him; and he nestled up against her, and gazed up into her face with a look that seemed to say: "Oh, I'm so glad you've come to take me away from this disgraceful scene!" . . .

Such is the nature of fox-terriers.

*

To look at Montmorency you would imagine that he was an angel sent upon earth, for some reason withheld from mankind, in the shape of a small fox-terrier. There is a sort of Oh-what-a-wicked-world-this-is-and-how-I-wish-could-do-something-to-make-it-better-and-nobler expression about Montmorency that has been known to bring tears into the eyes of pious ladies and gentlemen.

When first he came to live at my expense, I never thought I should be able to get him to stop long. I used to sit down and look at him, as he sat on the rug and looked up at me, and think: "Oh, that dog will never live. He will be snatched up to the bright skies in a chariot, that is what will happen to him."

But when I had paid for about a dozen chickens that he had killed; and had dragged him, growling and kicking, by the scruff of his neck, out of a hundred and fourteen street fights; and had had a dead cat brought round for my inspection by an irate female, who called me a murderer; and had been summoned by the man next door but one for having a ferocious dog at large, that had kept him pinned up in his own tool-shed, afraid to venture his nose outside the door for over two hours on a cold night; and had learned that the gardener, unknown to myself, had won thirty shillings by backing him to kill rats against time, then I began to think that maybe they'd let him remain on earth for a bit longer, after all.

To hang about a stable, and collect a gang of the most disreputable dogs to be found in the room, and lead them out to march round the shims to fight other disreputable dogs, is Montmorency's idea of "life": and so, as I before observed, he gave to the suggestion of inns, and pubs, and hotels his most emphatic approbation.

from *Three Men in a Boat*, 1889

Revd Gilbert White

My near neighbour, a young gentleman in the service of the *East-India* Company, has brought home a dog and a bitch of the

Chinese breed from *Canton*; such as are fattened in that country for the purpose of being eaten; they are about the size of a moderate spaniel; of a pale yellow colour, with coarse bristling hair on their backs; sharp upright ears and peaked heads which give them a very fox-like appearance. Their hind legs are unusually straight without any bend at the hock or ham to such a degree as to give them an awkward gait when they trot. When they are in motion their tails are curved high over their backs like those of some hounds, and have a bare place each on the outside from the tip midway, that does not seem to be matter of accident, but somewhat singular. Their eyes are jet black, small and piercing; the insides of their lips and mouths of the same colour and their tongues blue. The bitch has a dew claw on each hind leg; the dog has none. When taken out into a field the bitch showed some disposition for hunting, and dwelt on the scent of a covey of partridges till she sprung them, giving tongue all the time.

The dogs in *South America* are dumb; but these bark much in a short thick manner, like foxes; and have a surly, savage demeanour like their ancestors, which are not domesticated, but bred up in sties, where they are fed for the table with rice-meal and other farinaceous food. These dogs, having been taken on board as soon as weaned, could not learn much from their dam; yet they did not relish flesh when they came to *England*. In the islands of the *Pacific* ocean the dogs are bred up on vegetables, and would not eat flesh when offered them by our circumnavigators.

We believe that all dogs, in a state of nature, have sharp, upright fox-like ears; and that hanging ears, which are esteemed so graceful, are the effect of choice breeding and cultivation. Thus, in the Travels of *Ysbrandt Ides* from *Muscovy* to *China*, the dogs which draw the *Tartars* on snow-sledges near the river *Oby* are engraved with prick-ears, like those from *Canton*. The *Kamschatdales* also train the same sort of sharp-eared peaked-nosed dogs to draw their sledges; as may be seen in an elegant print engraved for Captain *Cook's* last voyage round the world.

from *Natural History and Antiquities of Selborne*, 1788

William Taplin

The dog so called [Pomeranian] in this country is but little more than 18 in or 20 in in height, and is distinguished by his long, thick, and rather upright coat, forming a most tremendous ruff about the neck, but short and smooth on the head and ears. They are mostly of a pale yellow or cream colour, and lighter on the lower parts. Some are white, some few are black, and others, but rarely, spotted; the head broad towards the neck, and narrowing to the muzzle; ears short, pointed, and erect; nose and eyes mostly black; the tail large and bushy, and invariably curled in a ring upon the back. Instances of smooth or short coated ones are very rarely seen. In England he is much more familiarly known by the name of fox dog, and this may originally have proceeded from his having much affinity to that animal about the head; but by those who in their writings describe him as a native of Pomerania, he passes under the appellation of the Pomeranian dog.

In general opinion as a house dog he is held in but slender estimation, being by nature frivolous, artful, noisy, quarrelsome, cowardly, petulant, deceitful, snappish and dangerous with children, without one prominent property of perfection to recommend him. The breed is common in Holland, and has occasionally been introduced as a hieroglyphic by the caricatured partisans of the House of Orange (in opposition to the pug) to ridicule in their political disputes.

> from *The Sportsman's Cabinet, or a Correct Delineation of the Various Dogs used in the Sports of the Field; including the Canine Race in general,* 1803

Harriet Beecher Stowe

Every animal has its own character, as marked and distinct as a human being. Many people who have not studied much into the habits of animals don't know this. To them a dog is a dog . . . and no more, — that is the end of it.

But domestic animals that associate with human beings develop a very different character from what they would possess in a wild state.

Dogs, for example, in those countries where there is a prejudice against receiving them into man's association, herd together, and become wild and fierce like wolves. This is the case in many Oriental countries, where there are superstitious ideas about dogs; as, for instance, that they are unclean and impure. But in other countries, the dog, for the most part, forsakes all other dogs to become the associate of man. A dog without a master is a forlorn creature; no society of other dogs seems to console him; he wanders about disconsolate, till he finds some human being to whom to attach himself, and then he is a made dog, – he pads about with an air of dignity, like a dog that is settled in life.

There are among dogs certain races or large divisions, and those belonging purely to any of those races are called blood-dogs. As examples of what we mean by these races, we will mention the spaniel, the mastiff, the bull-dog, the hound, and the terrier; and each of these divisions contains many species, and each has a strongly-marked character. The spaniel tribes are gentle, docile, easily attached to man; from them many hunting dogs are trained. The bull-dog is irritable, a terrible fighter, and – fiercely faithful to his master. A mastiff is strong, large, not so fierce as the bull-dog, but watchful and courageous, with a peculiar sense of responsibility in guarding anything which is placed under his charge. The hounds are slender, lean, wiry, with a long, pointed muzzle, and a peculiar sensibility in the sense of smell, and their instincts lead them to hunting and tracking. As a general thing, they are cowardly and indisposed to combat; there are, however, remarkable exceptions, as you will see if you read the account of the good black hound which Sir Walter Scott tells about in "The Talisman", – a story which I advise you to read at your next leisure. The terriers are, for the most part, small dogs, smart, bright, and active, very intelligent, and capable of being taught many tricks. Of these there are several varieties, – as the English black and tan, which is the neatest and prettiest pet a family of children can have, as his hair is so short and close that he can harbour no fleas, and he is always good-tempered, lively, and affectionate. The Skye terrier, with his mouse-coloured mop of hair, his great bright eyes, is very loving and very sagacious; but, alas! unless one can afford a great deal of time for soap, water, and fine tooth-comb exercises, he will bring more company than you will like. The Scotch terriers are rough, scraggy, affectionate;

but so nervous, frisky, and mischievous that they are only to be recommended as out-door pets in barn and stable. They are capital rat-catchers, very amicable with horses, and will sit up by the driver or a coach-boy with an air of great sagacity.

There is something very curious about the habits and instincts of certain dogs which have been trained by man for his own purposes. In the mountains of Scotland, there is a tribe of dogs called shepherd dogs, which for generations and ages have helped the shepherds to take care of their sheep, and which look for all the world like long-nosed, high-cheekboned, careful old Scotchmen. You will see them in the morning, trotting out their flock of sheep, walking about with a grave, care-taking air, and at evening, all bustle and importance – scurrying and scurrying hither and thither, getting their charge all together for the night. An old Scotchman tells us that his dog, Hector, by long sharing his toils and cares, got to looking so much like him, that once, when he felt too sleepy to go to meeting, he sent Hector to take his seat in the pew, and the minister never knew the difference, but complemented him the next day for his good attention to the sermon.

There is a kind of dog employed by the monks of St Bernard, in the Alps, to go out and seek in the snow for travellers who may have lost their way; and this habit becomes such a strong instinct in them, that I once knew a puppy of this species which was brought by a ship-master to Maine, and grew up in a steady New England town, which used to alarm his kind friends by rushing off into the pine forest in snow-storms, and running anxiously up and down burrowing in the snow as if in quest of something.

I have seen one of a remarkable breed of dogs that are brought from the island of Manilla. They resemble mastiffs in their form, but are immensely large and strong. They are trained to detect thieves, and are kept by merchants on board of vessels where the natives are very sly and much given to stealing. They are called holders, and their way is, when a strange man, whose purposes they do not understand, comes on board the ship, to take a very gentle but decisive hold of him by the heel, and keep him fast until somebody comes to look after him. The dog I knew of this species stood about as high as an ordinary dining-table, and I have seen him stroke off the dinner-cloth with one wag of his tail in his pleasure when I patted his head. He was very intelligent and affectionate.

There is another dog, which may often be seen in Paris, called the Spitz dog, He is a white, smooth-haired, small creature, with a great muff of stiff hair round his neck, and generally comes into Paris riding on the back of the cart-horses which draw the carts of the washerwomen. He races nimbly up and down on the back of the great heavy horses, barking from right to left with great animation, and is said to be a most faithful little creature in guarding the property of his owner. What is peculiar about these little dogs is the entireness of their devotion to their master. They have not a look, not a wag of the tail, for any one else; it is vain for a stranger to try to make friends with them, – they have eyes and ears for one alone.

All dogs which do not belong to some of the great varieties, on the one side of their parentage or the other, are classed together as curs, and are very much undervalued and decried; and yet among these mongrel curs we have seen individuals quite as sagacious, intelligent, and affectionate as the best blood-dogs.

And now I want to say some things to those young people who desire to adopt as domestic pets either a dog or a cat. Don't do it without making up your mind to be really and thoroughly kind to them, and feeding them as carefully as you feed yourself, and giving them appropriate shelter from the inclemency of the weather.

Some people seem to have a general idea that throwing a scrap, or bone, or bit of refuse meat, at odd intervals, to a dog, is taking abundant care of him. "What's the matter with him? he can't be hungry, – I gave him that great bone yesterday." Ah, Master Hopeful, how would you like to be fed on the same principle? When you show your hungry face at the dinner-table, suppose papa should say, "What's that boy here for? He was fed this morning." You would think this hard measure; yet a dog's or cat's stomach digests as rapidly as yours. In like manner, dogs are often shut out of the house in cold winter weather without the least protection being furnished them. A lady and I looked out once, in a freezing, icy day, and saw a great Newfoundland cowering, in a corner of a fence to keep from the driving wind; and I said, "Do tell me if you have no kennel for that poor creature." "No," said the lady. "I didn't know that dogs needed shelter. Now I think of it, I remember last spring, he seemed quite poorly, and his hair seemed to come out; do you suppose it was being exposed so much in the winter?" This lady had taken into her family a living creature, without ever having reflected on what that creature needed, or that it was her duty to provide for its wants.

Dogs can bear more cold than human beings, but they do not like cold any better than we do; and when a dog has his choice, he will very gladly stretch himself on a rug before the fire for his afternoon nap, and show that he enjoys the blaze and warmth as much as anybody.

from *Our Dogs and Other Stories,* 1862

Charles Stuart Calverley

The piper he piped on the hill-top high,
  (Butter and eggs and a pound of cheese)
Till the cow said "I die", and the goose asked why?
  And the dog said nothing, but search'd for fleas.

from *Verses and Translations,* 1862

CHAPTER 2

A Great Friendship

From the outset of their relationship with man, dogs have provided services. While possibly no more than scavengers to begin with, they later became hunting companions, herders, guards and much more. Dogs have also acquired a – largely deserved – reputation for fidelity, but neither the services they provide nor their constancy have always protected them from man's often perverse attitudes.

When in 1307 Sir Aymer de Valance led a party of Englishmen, guided by Scottish collaborators, to search for the fugitive king, Robert the Bruce, not only did they have local assistance, but they also had one of Bruce's own dogs – a sleuth-hound.

Once the king's party had been located it split into three groups to confuse its pursuers. However, the hound was able to identify the route taken by the group which included the king. Thereupon Bruce and his foster-brother abandoned their friends to make their own way across country. Once this new strategy had been perceived, John of Lorn who had joined the English contingent, selected five of his most hardy and fleetfooted men to continue the pursuit.

The stratagem failed because when the party came up with the fugitive pair all were killed, four by Bruce, one by his foster brother. The main party had travelled more slowly but, led by Bruce's own hound, were inexorably closing in on him; whereupon Bruce took to the water.

Bishop Barbour recorded the scene in suitably heroic verse:

> But the sleuth-hound made stinting there
> And wavered long time to and fro

> That he no certain gait could go,
> Till at last that John of Lorn
> Perceived the hound the scent had 'lorn,
> And said, "We have lost this travail;
> To pass further may not avail,
> For the wood is both broad and wide,
> And he is well far by this tide."

Blind Harry, a Border minstrel, provided a less heroic record of the event:

> In Gelderland, there was that bratchet bred,
> Siker of scent to follow them that fled:
> So was she used in Eske and Liddesdail,
> While she gar blood no fleeing might avail.

Sir Peers Legh of Lyme Hall in Cheshire was wounded at Agincourt but was protected from further injury by his Mastiff dog. The dog stayed at his side throughout the night and only relinquished its vigil when Sir Peers was found by his colleagues on the following day.

Unfortunately Sir Peers died of his wounds before reaching his Cheshire home but his faithful Mastiff followed his coffin to the grave. A distinctive strain of Mastiffs continued to be kept at Lyme Hall until well into the twentieth century.

A. Sloan and A. Farquar

This is the tale of a very great friendship which began many, many years ago, when Time was yet at its dawn. It is the tale of an enduring friendship which has braved the change of climates, times, and customs, and is very much alive even to this day.

In this tale there are two central characters: first Dog, because, according to tradition, he was created amongst the creatures early on the sixth day of God's creation; then Man, for he was created, but later in that same day, to be a ruler over all the beasts of the earth.

Now, Dog is a word which comprises all varieties of the Dog-kind, from those feathery-tailed, proud-spirited morsels of Chinese

Royalty, the Pekingese, to the large, broad-headed, kindly-hearted St Bernard of the snowy heights of Helvetia.

Man is a term no less broad, for it includes the black and brown and yellow men of the East, and the white and red men of the West; and even as there are bad men and good men, kind and friendly men, as well as others cold and evil-hearted, so, besides our many loving and faithful friends, there are Dogs that delight to "bark and bite." But when you consider the example that some of us set them, can you blame them?

It is difficult to say exactly when Man and Dog became partners in the game of life – as difficult as it is to trace any great friendship to its root. Can you say when first you ceased to eye your friend with the cold, critical stare of acquaintance, and do you remember when first you saw him through the warm, kind eye of the heart? Probably on the day the seeds of love were planted, and since then the warmth of the sun of friendship has ripened that seed to maturity.

And so it came about between Man and Dog. But please do not forget that this all happened some little while ago – say 10,000 years or so – when Man was in the Neolithic stage of development, and not the stiff-shirted, top-hatted creature he is to-day. He and Dog met on a far more level footing, and, liking each other, struck a bargain and formed a very limited company of two. It probably happened somewhat after this fashion.

Man, having laboriously caught his food by digging a deep hole and covering it over with branches or brush and then waiting hungrily till some unwary beast fell into his trap, would eat it raw, pulling bone from bone, and would suck and pick, smacking his lips, happily unconscious of bad manners or present-day restrictions and conventions. Then, as each bone was picked clean, Man threw it out of his cave on to his midden or rubbish-heap, and, feeling brutishly happy, he would curl up with a grunt and go to sleep.

Outside in the dense darkness a pair of glowing yellow eyes had watched Man's doings, and those eyes had flashed a brighter gold when he saw those delicious bones thrown out on to the heap.

Seeing and hearing that Man slept, Dog (for it was none other than he) crept out of the undergrowth to negotiate the bone-pile, where he saw a meal worthy (to him) of the Ritz Restaurant. Of course, the bones had been pretty well picked by Man; still, they looked delicious; and so Dog gathered together his courage, which at first had oozed out of the very ends of his bristling coat, and stealthily advanced to the bone-heap. Nearer and nearer he crept; and then, with one sudden movement, he seized a nice, medium-sized bone and carried it back to his hiding-place beneath the forest trees.

Finding that Man slept on, Dog became more and more bold; and, as time went on, increasingly less cautious. At last he did not wait for the snoring evidence of Man's slumber, but prowled round the bone-heap all the time. It was probably in this way that Dog came into the habitation of Man. Gradually their bowing acquaintance ripened into something better, something close, for the seed of friendship and love to be sown.

So began the great partnership in the business of life, Dog brought to Man's use his scent, teeth, and so helped him to stalk, catch and kill his food. Man shared the food thus caught with his new friend, and invited him to sit beside him within the narrow circle of firelight, to give a feeling of companionship in that great unbroken silence of the early world. This feeling of warmth and friendliness towards Dog in Man was perhaps the first stirring of human kindness, friendship, and love in his wild, brutish heart; and it was surely then that the appealing, longing look first crept into Dog's hunted, wild gaze.

So they would sit, darkly silhouetted against the firelight, whilst all around them and over the sleeping world was purple night; and the only moving things that were seen were the shining stars which leapt and twinkled to the tune played by the dancing flames of Man's fire.

from *Dog and Man, The Story of a Friendship*, 1925

Woods Hutchinson

There is increasing body of evidence that, instead of man adopting the dog into his family, the dog adopted man into his pack! This sounds at first distinctly improbable . . . yet those who have watched the ways of wild men and wild animals together most closely are the most inclined to regard it as not merely possible, but probable.

The mechanism of the process would appear to have been that a certain number of the more intelligent of the wolves or wild dogs of the region found that it was more profitable to follow man in his hunting expeditions and let him do the killing, for their share of the entrails and waste parts of the animal, than it was to kill for themselves. From following him on his hunting expeditions, they gradually came to following him home; and finding that bones and offal, and occasionally human bodies, were to be picked up around these encampments, they became a sort of permanent hanger-on of the tribe. In a little time, doubtless, man took the hint, and after he had wounded an animal found it was more profitable to sit down (savages always have plenty of time) and let his canine followers run in upon the quarry and chase it down, endeavouring to get in at the death himself, than to track it on his own account.

from *The Contemporary Review* (date unknown)

Rudyard Kipling

When Wild Dog reached the mouth of the Cave he lifted up the dried horse-skin with his nose and sniffed the beautiful smell of the roast mutton, and the Woman, looking at the blade bone, heard him, and laughed, and said, "Here comes the first. Wild Thing out of the Wild Woods, what do you want?"

Wild Dog said, "O my Enemy and Wife of my Enemy, what is this that smells so good in the Wild Woods?"

Then the Woman picked up a roasted mutton-bone and threw it to Wild Dog, and said, "Wild Thing out of the Wild Woods, taste and try." Wild Dog gnawed the bone, and it was more delicious than anything he had ever tasted, and he said, "O my enemy and Wife of my Enemy, give me another."

The Woman said, "Wild Thing out of the Wild Woods, help my Man hunt through the day and guard this Cave at night, and I will give you as many roast bones as you need."

"Ah!" said the cat, listening. "This is a very wise Woman, but she is not so wise as I am."

Wild Dog crawled into the Cave and laid his head on the Woman's lap, and said, "O my Friend and Wife of my Friend, I will help your Man to hunt through the day, and at night I will guard your Cave."

"Ah!" said the Cat, listening. "That is a very foolish Dog." And he went back through the Wet Wild Woods waving his wild tail, and walking by his wild lone. But he never told anybody.

. . . When the Man waked up he said, "What is Wild Dog doing here?" And the Woman said, "His name is not Wild Dog any more, but the First Friend, because he will be our friend for always and always and always. Take him with you when you go hunting."

from "The Cat that Walked by Himself", *Just So Stories*, 1902

★ ★ ★

William Youatt

[The fact that from] the very earliest periods of history, the [dog] seemed to be as sagacious, as faithful, and as valuable as at the present day, strongly favour the opinion that he is descended from no inferior and comparatively worthless animal, – that he was not the progeny of the wolf, the jackal, or the fox, but he was originally created, somewhat as we now find him, the associate and the friend of man.

If, within the first thousand years after the Deluge, we observe that divine honours were paid him, we can scarcely be brought to believe his wolfish genealogy. The most savage animals are capable of affection for those to whom they have been accustomed, and by whom they have been well treated, and therefore we give full credit to several accounts of this sort related to the wolf, the lion, and even the cat and the reptile: but in no other animal – in no other, even in the Genus Canis – do we find the qualities of the domestic dog, or the slightest approach to them. "To his master he flies with alacrity," says the eloquent Buffon, "and submissively lays at his feet all his courage, strength, and talent. A glance of the eye is sufficient; for he understands the smallest indications of the will. He has all the ardour of friendship, and fidelity and constancy in his affections, which man can have. Neither interest nor desire of revenge can corrupt him, and he has no fear but that of displeasing. He is all zeal and obedience. He speedily forgets ill-usage, or only recollects it to make returning attachment the stronger. He licks the hand which causes him pain, and subdues his anger by submission. The training of the dog seems to have been the first art invented by man, and the fruit of that art was the conquest and peaceable possession of the earth." "Man," says Burns, "is the God of the dog; he knows no other; and see how he worships him. With what reverence he crouches at his feet – with what delight he fawns upon him, and with what cheerful alacrity he obeys him!"

If any of the lower animals bear about them the impress of the Divine hand, it is found in the dog: many others are plainly and decidedly more or less connected with the welfare of the human being; but this connexion and its effects are limited to a few points, or often to one alone. The dog, different, yet the same, in every region, seems to be formed expressly to administer to our comforts and to our pleasure. He displays a versatility, and yet a perfect unity of power and character, which mark him as our destined servant, and, still more, as our companion and friend. Other animals may be brought to a certain degree of familiarity, and may display much affection and gratitude. There is scarcely an animal in the menagerie of the Zoological Society that did not acknowledge the super-intendent as his friend; but it was only a casual intercourse.

Cuvier eloquently states that the dog exhibits the most complete and the most useful conquest that man has made. Each individual is entirely devoted to his master, adopts his manners, distinguishes and defends his property, and remains attached to him even unto death; and all this springing not from mere necessity, or from constraint, but simply from gratitude and true friendship. The swiftness, the strength, and the highly developed power of smelling of the dog, have made him a powerful ally of man against the other animals; and, perhaps, these qualities in the dog were necessary to the establish-ment of society. It is the only animal that has followed the human being all over the earth.

In process of time man began to surround himself with many servants from among the lower animals, but among them all he had only one friend – the dog; one animal only whose service was voluntary, and who was susceptible of disinterested affection and gratitude. In every country, and at every time, there has existed between man and the dog a connexion different from that which is observed between him and any other animal. The ox and the sheep submit to our control, but their affections are principally, if not solely, confined to themselves. They submit to us, but they can rarely be said to love, or even to recognise us, except as connected with the supply of their wants. . . .

The dog is the only animal that is capable of disinterested affection. He is the only creature that regards the human being in his compassion, and follows him as his friend; the only one that seems to possess a natural desire to be useful to him, or from a spontaneous impulse attaches himself to man. We take the bridle from the mouth of the horse, and turn him free into the pasture, and he testifies his joy in his partially recovered liberty. We exact from the dog the service that is required of him, and still he follows us. He solicits to be continued as our companion and our friend. Many an expressive action tells us how much he is pleased and thankful. He shares in our abundance, and he is content with the scantiest and most humble fare. He loves us while living, and has been known to pine away on the grave of his master.

from *The Dog,* 1845

Homer

Thus, near the gates conferring as they drew,
Argus, the dog, his ancient master knew;
He, not unconscious of the voice and tread,
Lifts to the sound his ear, and rears his head;
Bred by Ulysses, nourish'd at his board,
But, ah! not fated long to please his lord!
To him, his swiftness and his strength were vain;
The voice of glory call'd him o'er the main.
Till then in every sylvan chase renown'd,
With Argus, Argus, rung the woods around:
With him the youth pursued the goat or fawn,
Or traced the mazy leveret o'er the lawn.
Now left to man's ingratitude he lay,
Unhous'd, neglected, in the public way;
And where on heaps the rich manure was spread,
Obscene with reptiles, too his sordid bed.

from *The Iliad, c.* 800 BC, translated by Alexander Pope

Plutarch

As Pyrrhus was journeying through the country he came across a dog guarding the body of his master who had been murdered; and according to the testimony of neighbours, the dog had been there already for three days without moving, or eating, or drinking. Pyrrhus ordered that the man should be buried and he took the dog with him commanding that he should be well treated. A few days afterwards there was a muster and a review of all the soldiers who paraded before the king seated on his throne with the dog near him. The dog lay still until he perceived the murderers of his master when he rushed upon them incontinently with loud barks, and raging fury, turning often towards Pyrrhus in such a way that not only the king but all his attendants conceived a strong suspicion that these must be the men who had killed his master. They were made prisoners, and at their subsequent trial further evidence, both direct and circumstantial, was produced against them, so that in the end they confessed the murder and were put to death. The dog belonging to the sage Hesiod did the same, having convinced the children of "Garyctor" of "Naupactus" of the murder committed on the person of his master.

from *Symposiaca*, AD c.100

Cicero

Dogs watch for us faithfully: they love and worship their masters: they hate strangers: their power of tracking scent is extraordinary: great is their keenness in the chase: – what can all this mean but that they were made for man's advantage?

from *De Officiis*, c.50 BC

Claudius Aelianus

When Darius, the last of the Persian kings, was killed by Bessus in his battle with Alexander, and lay dead, all the men left the corpse

49

behind but the dog alone he had bred remained faithful. The dog belonging to King Lysimachus chose to die by the same fate as his master, although he could, had he so wished, have saved himself. Again, when there was civil war in Rome, a Roman citizen called Calvus was killed. Many of his enemies strove in rivalry to accomplish the glorious deed of cutting off his head, but none could do so until they had killed the dog who stood by his side.

De Natura Animalum, AD 200

Theodorus Gaza

I would ask, who does not know how gentle and affectionate he is by nature also? For when his master is at home, he remains at home; and when he goes out, the dog goes out with him, and neither the length of the journey, nor rough country, nor thirst, nor storm, nor heat will deter him from following his master everywhere. And while he follows, he sometimes runs forward, and sometimes runs back to his master, and at other times plays about and wags his tail and does everything he can to sport pleasantly with him. If his master calls him, he approaches; and if he threatens him, cowers to the ground; and if he strikes him, shows no resentment.

from *Laudatio Canis, an address to Mohammed II,* fifteenth century

Thomas Chestre

The good grehounde for wele ne wo
Wolde not fro the knyght go
But laye and lycked his wounde
He wente to haue heled hym agayne
And therto he dyde his payne
Lo suche love is in a hounde
This knight laye tylle he dyde stynke
The grehounde than began to thynke
And scraped a pytte anone
Therein he drewe the deed corse

So he covered with erth and mose
And from hym he wolde not gone
The grehounde laye styll there
This quene gan forthe fare
For drede of her sone.

Sir Launfal, late fourteenth century

Abraham Fleming

In Latine *Canes defensores* defending dogges in our mother tongue.

If it chaunce that the master bee oppressed, either by a multitude, or by the greater violence & so be beaten downe that he lye grovelling on the grounde, (it is proved true by experience) that this Dogge forsaketh not his master, no not when he is starcke deade: But induring the force of famishment and the outrageous tempestes of the weather, most vigilantly watcheth and carefully keepeth the deade carkasse many dayes, endevouring, furthermore, to kil the mutherer of his master, if he may get any advantage. Or else by barcking, by howling, by furious iarring, snarring, and such like meanes betrayeth the malefactor as desirous to have the death of his aforesayde Master rigorouslye revenged. And example hereof fortuned within the compass of my memory.

The Dogge of a certaine wayefaring man travailing from the Citie of London directly to the Towne of Kingstone . . . passing over a good portion of his journey was assaulted and set upon by certaine confederate theefes laying in waight for the spoyle in *Comeparcke*, a perilous bottom, compassed about wyth woddes to well knowne for the manyfolde murders & mischiefeous robberies theyr committed. Into whose handes this passinger chaunced to fall, so that his ill luck cost him the price of his lyfe. And that Dogge whose syer was Englishe . . . manifestly perceavyng that his Master was murthered (this chaunced not farre from *Parsi*, by the handes of one which was a suiter to the same woman, whom he was a wooer unto), dyd both bewraye the bloudy butcher, and attempted to teare out the villons throate if he had not sought meanes to avoyde the revenging rage of the Dogge.

In fyers also which fortune in the silence and dead time of the night, or in stormy weather of the sayde season, the older dogges barcke, ball, howle, and yell (yea notwithstandyng they bee roughly rated) neyther will they stay their tounges till the householde servantes awake, ryse, search, and see the burning of the fyre, which beyng perceaved they use voluntary silence, and cease from yolping. This hath bene, and is founde true by tryall, in sundry partes of England.

There was no faynting faith in that Dogge, which when his Master by a mischaunce in hunting stumbled and fell toppling downe a deepe dytche beyng unable to recover of himselfe, the Dogge signifying his masters mishappe, reskue came, and he was hayled up by a rope, whom the Dogge seeying almost drawne up to the edge of the dytche, cheerefully saluted, leaping and skipping upon his master as though he woulde have imbraced hym, beyng glad of his presence, whose longer absence he was lothe to lacke.

Some Dogges there be, which will not suffer fyery coales to lye skattered about the hearthe, but with their pawes wil rake up the burnyng coales, musying and studying fyrst with themselves how it might be conveniently be done. And if so bee that the coales caste to great a heate then will they buyry them in ashes and so remove them forwarde to a fyt place wyth theyr noses.

Other Dogges bee there which exequute the office of Farmer in the nyghte tyme. For when his master goeth to bedde to take his naturall sleepe. And when,

A hundred barres of brasse and yron boltes,
Make all things safe from startes and from revoltes.
When Ianus keepes the gate with Argos eye,
That daungers none approch, ne mischiefes nye.

As Virgill vautheth in his verses. Then if his master byddeth him go abroade, he lingereth not, but raungeth over all his lands lying there about, more diligently, I wys, then any farmer himselfe. And if he finde anything their that is straunge and pertaining to other persons besides his master, whether it be man, woman, or beest, he driveth them out of the ground, not meddling with any thing which doth belong to the possession and use of his master. But how much faythulnes, so much diversite there is in their natures.

from *Of Englishe Dogges,* 1576

Joachim Camerarius

Of any beast, none is more faithful found
  Nor yeelds more pastime in house, plaine, or woods,
  Nor keepes his master's person, nor his goods,
With greater care, than doth the dog or hound.

Command; he thee obeys most readily.
  Strike him; he whines and falls down at thy feet.
Call him: he leaves his game and comes to thee
  With wagging taile, offring his service meeke.

In summer's heat he follows by thy pace:
  In winter's cold he never leaveth thee:
In mountains wild he by thee close doth trace;
  In all thy feares and dangers true is he.

Thy friends he loves; and in thy presence lives
  By day: by night he watcheth faithfully
That thou in peace mayst sleepe; he never gives
  Good entertainment to thine enemie.

Course, hunt, in hills, in vallyes, or in plaines;
  He joyes to run and stretch out every lim:
To please but thee, he spareth for no paines:
  His hurt (for thee) is greatest good to him.

Sometimes he doth present thee with a Hare,
  Sometimes he hunts the Stag, the Fox, the Boare,
Another time he baits the Bull or Beare,
  And all to make thee sport, and for no more.

If so thou wilt, a Collar he will weare;
  And when thou list to take it off againe
Unto thy feet he coucheth downe most faire,
  As if thy will were all his good and gaine.

In fields abroade he lookes unto thy flockes,
  Keeping them safe from Wolves, and other beasts:
And oftentimes he beares away the knocks
  Of some odd theife, that many a fold infests.

And as he is the faithful bodies guard,
  So is he good within a fort or hold,
Against a quicke surprise to watch and ward;
  And all his hire is bread mustie and old.

Canst thou then such a creature hate and spurne?
  Or barre him from such poore and simple food?
Being so fit and faithfull for thy turne,
  And no beast else can do thee halfe such good!

from *Living Librarie*, 1583, translated by J. Mole.

William Cecil, Lord Burghley

Then one of the executioners, pulling off her garters, espied her little dogg, which was crept under her clothes, which could not be gotten forth but by force, yet afterwards would not depart from the corpse, but came and lay betweene her head and her shoulders, which being imbrued with her bloode was caryed away and washed, as all things ells were that had any bloode was either burned or clean washed.

Account of Mary Queen of Scots' execution, c. 1589

Michael Drayton

He called his dog (that sometimes had the praise)
Whitefoot, well known to all that keep the plain,
That many a wolf had worried in his days,
A better cur there never followed swain;
Which, though as he his master's sorrows knew,
Wagged his cut tail, his wretched plight to rue.

"Farewell to Whitefoot", *c.* 1600.

Matthew Prior

His prudence and his wit were seen
In that, from Mary's grace and mien,
He own'd the power, and lov'd the queen.
By long obedience he confess'd
That serving her was to be bless'd.
Ye murderers, let True evince
That men are beasts, and dogs have sense.
   His faith and truth all Whitehall knows,
He ne'er could fawn or flatter those
Whom he believed were Mary's foes;
Ne'er skulk'd against the hand that fed him —
Read this, ye statesmen now in favour,
And mend your own, by True's behaviour.

"True's Epitaph", 1700

Again: the lonely fox roams far abroad,
On secret rapine bent, and midnight fraud;
Now haunts the cliff, now traverses the lawn,
And flies the hated neighbourhood of man:
While the kind spaniel, or the faithful hound,
Likest that fox in shape and species found,
Refuses through these cliffs and lawns to roam,
Pursues the noted path, and covets home;
Does with kind joy domestic faces meet,
Takes what the glutted child denies to eat,

And, dying, licks his long lov'd master's feet.

from "Solomon on the
Vanity of the World", 1718

William Cowper

Forth goes the woodman, leaving unconcern'd
The cheerful haunts of man to wield the axe
And drive the wedge in yonder forest drear,
From morn to eve his solitary task.
Shaggy and lean and shrewd, with pointed ears
And tail cropp'd short, half lurcher and half cur –
His dog attends him. Close behind his heel
Now creeps he slow; and now with many a frisk
Wide-scamp'ring, snatches up the drifted snow
With iv'ry teeth or ploughs it with his snout;
Then shakes his powder'd coat, and barks for joy.

The Task, 1785

William Wordsworth

A barking sound the shepherd hears,
A cry as of a dog or fox;
He halts – and searches with his eyes
Among the scattered rocks:
And now at distance can discern
A stirring in a brake of fern,
And instantly a dog is seen,
Glancing through that covert green.

The dog is no mountain breed;
Its motions, too, are wild and shy;
With something, as the shepherd thinks,
Unusual in its cry:
Nor is there anyone in sight
All round, in hollow or on height;
Nor shout, nor whistle strikes his ear;
What is the creature doing here?

It was a cove, a huge recess,
That keeps, till June, December's snow;
A lofty precipice in front,
A silent tarn below!
Far in the bosom of Helvellyn,
Remote from public road or dwelling,
Pathway, or cultivated land,
From trace of human foot or hand.

There sometimes doth a leaping fish
Send through the tarn a lonely cheer;
The crags repeat the raven's croak,
In symphony austere;
Thither the rainbow comes – the cloud –
And mists that spread the flying shroud;
And sunbeams, and the sounding blast,
That, if it could, would hurry past;
But that enormous barrier holds it fast.

Not free from boding thoughts, a while
The shepherd stood; then makes his way
O'er rocks and stones, following the dog
As quickly as he may;
Nor far had gone before he found
A human skeleton on the ground;
The appalled discoverer with a sigh
Looks round, to learn the history.

From those abrupt and perilous rocks
The man had fallen, that place of fear!
At length upon the shepherd's mind
It breaks, and all is clear:
He instantly recall'd the name,
And who he was, and whence he came;
Remembered, too, the very day
On which the traveller passed this way.

But hear a wonder, for whose sake
This lamentable tale I tell!

A lasting monument of words
This wonder merits well.
The dog, which still was hovering nigh,
Repeating the same timid cry,
This dog had been, through three months' space,
A dweller in that savage place.

Yes, proof was plain that, since the day
When this ill-fated traveller died,
The dog had watched about the spot,
Or by his master's side:
How nourished there through such long time
He knows, who gave that love sublime;
And gave that strength of feeling, great
Above all human estimate!

"Fidelity", 1805

Thomas Hodgkins

But if this be I,
    As I do hope it be,
I have a little dog at home
    And he knows me;
If it be I,
    He'll wag his little tail,
And if it be not I
    He'll loudly bark and wail!

Home went the little woman
    All in the dark,
Up starts the little dog,
    And he began to bark;
He began to bark,
    And she began to cry,
Lawk a mercy on me,
    This is none of I!

"Little woman and her dog", 1806

George Crabbe

There watch'd a cur before the Miser's gate —
A very cur, whom all men seem'd to hate;
Gaunt, savage, shaggy, with an eye that shone
Like a live coal, and he possess'd but one;
His bark was wild and eager, and became
That meagre body and that eye of flame;
His master prized him much, and Fang his name.
His master fed him largely; but not that,
Nor aught of kindness, made the snarler fat.
Flesh he devour'd, but not a bit would stay;
He bark'd, and snarl'd, and growl'd it all away.
His ribs were seen extended like a rack,
And coarse red hair hung roughly o'er his back.
Lamed in one leg, and bruised in wars of yore,
Now his sore body made his temper sore.
Such was the friend of him who could not find
Nor make him one 'mong creatures of his kind.
Brave deeds of Fang his master often told,
The son of Fury, famed in deeds of old;
From Scratch and Rabid sprung; and noted they
In earlier times — each dog will have his day.

from "The Dealer and Clerk", c 1807

Attr. "Vincent"

Curled on their warm and strawy beds, repose
My dogs, save two, whose coats sable and white,
And speckled legs, and tail well fringed and ears
Of glossy silken black, declare their kind
By land or water, equally prepared
To work their busy way. My steps alone
These follow in the depth of Winter's reign.

from *Fowling*, 1808

Samuel Pratt

Stand forth thou champion of a ruffian band,
At mercy's bar uplift thy savage hand;
Brought to thine eye, what thou, perforce must see,
The dread account betwixt thy slave and thee.
First, answer to thy Dog, as first in place,
Friend at thy board, companion of thy chase;
His no foul crime of "friend remembered not,"
Each kindness cherish'd, and each wrong forgot;
And though full oft he feels thy stripes unjust
He bears them all, and humbles to the dust;
Unmurmuring bears them, and one slight caress,
Tho' smitten to the bone, again can bless.
Thy day of labour he is proud to share,
And guards thy slumbers with a lover's care;
The presence hails, thy absence fondly mourns,
While bounding raptures mark thy wish'd returns;
To rage, to anguish, e'en to death, resigned, –
What nobler feelings boast thy nobler kind?

. . . through the pressing throng,
See how yon terrier gently leads along
The feeble beggar, to his custom'd stand,
With piteous tale to woo the bounteous hand;
In willing bonds, but master of the way,
Ne'er leads that trusted friend his charge astray:
With slow, soft step, as conscious of his care,
As if his own deep sorrows form'd the prayer –

Should yielding charity the scrip supply,
Tho' hunger press'd, untouch'd the boon would lie;
Eyes to the blind, he notes the passing thief,
And guards the good Samaritan's relief;
A faithful steward, amidst unbounded power,
Patient he waits the home-returning hour;
Then reconducts his master to his shed,
And grateful banquets on the coarsest bread.

And were that cheerless shed, by fortune plac'd
In the chill cavern, or the naked waste,
The sport of every storm, unroof'd and bare,
This faithful slave would find a palace there;
Would feel the labours of his love o'erpaid
Near to his monarch master's pillow laid;
Unchang'd by change or circumstance or place:
A sacred lesson to a prouder race!

But, reasoner, say, are these thy gifts of art,
Or, native graces of the canine heart?
Say, does he owe this social change of state
To imitation of the fair and great?
Copied from thee, and do his virtues rise
From man's example of the good and wise?
If thou hast thus reclaimed from savage strife,
And made him thus a link of social life,
Ask thy own soul — that every harshness knows —
How oft his joys are follow'd by his woes;
And if like thee, this slave could count his gains,
Say, would his pleasures balance to his pains?

"The Lower World", 1810

George Crabbe

With eye uprais'd, his master's looks to scan,
The joy, the solace, and the aid of man;
The rich man's guardian, and the poor man's friend,
The only being faithful to the end.

from *The Borough*, 1810

Washington Irving

Dame Van Winkle regarded them as companions in idleness, and
even looked upon Wolf with an evil eye, as the cause of his master's

going so often astray. True it is, in all points of spirit fitting an honourable dog, he was as courageous an animal as ever scoured the woods – but what courage can withstand the ever-during and all-besetting terrors of a woman's tongue? Like a sensible man, to escape from the clamours of his wife, Rip would stroll in the woods. Here he would sometimes seat himself at the foot of a tree, and share the contents of his wallet with Wolf, with whom he seemed as a fellow-sufferer in persecution. "Poor Wolf," he would say, "thy mistress leads thee a dog's life of it, but never mind, my lad, whilst I live thou shalt never want a friend to stand by thee." Wolf would wag his tail, looking wistfully in his master's face, and if dogs can feel pity, I verily believe he reciprocated the sentiment with all his heart.

from "Rip van Winkle", *The Sketch Book,* 1819

James Hogg

There's nae sic perfeck happiness, I suspeck, sir, as that o' the brutes. No that I wuss I had been born a brute – yet aften hae I been tempted to envy a dowg. What gladness in the cretur's een, gin ye but a single word to him, when you and him's sittin thegither by your two sels on the hill. Pat him on the head and say "Hector, ma man!" and he whines wi' joy – snap your thooms, and he gangs dancin round you like a whirlwind – gie a whusslin hiss, and he loups frantic ower your heid – cry halloo, and he's aff like a shot, chasing naething, as if he were made.

from "Noctes Ambrosianae",
Blackwood's Edinburgh Review, 1822–1835

Henry Hallam

But looking towards the grassy mound
Where calm the Douglas chieftains lie,
Who, living, quiet never found,
I straightway learnt a lesson high;
For there an old man sat serene,

And well I knew that thoughtful mien
Of him whose early lyre had thrown
O'er mouldering walls the magic of its tone.

It was a comfort, too, to see
Those dogs that from him ne'er would rove,
And always eyed him reverently,
With glances of depending love.
They know not of the eminence
Which marks him to my reasoning sense;
They know but that he is a man,
And still to them is kind, and glads them all he can.

And hence their quiet looks confiding;
Hence grateful instincts, seated deep,
By whose strong bond, were ill betiding,
They'd lose their own, his life to keep.
What joy to watch in lower creature
Such dawning of a moral nature,
And how (the rule all things obey)
They look to a higher mind to be their law and stay.

from "On Sir Walter Scott", *c.* 1832

Charles Dickens

At his feet, sat a white-coated, red-eyed dog; who occupied himself, alternately, in winking at his master with both eyes at the same time, and in licking a large, fresh cut on the side of his mouth, which appeared to be the result of some recent conflict. "Keep quiet, you warmint! keep quiet!" said Mr Sikes, suddenly breaking silence. Whether his meditations were so intense as to be disturbed by the dog's winking, or whether his feelings were so wrought upon by his reflections that they required all the relief derivable from kicking an unoffending animal to allay them, is a matter for argument and consideration. Whatsoever was the cause, the effect was a kick and a curse bestowed upon the dog simultaneously.

63

Dogs are not generally apt to revenge injuries inflicted upon them by their masters; but Mr Sikes's dog, having faults of temper in common with his owner: was labouring, perhaps at this moment, under a powerful sense of injury, made no more ado but at once fixed his teeth in one of the half-boots. Having given it a hearty shake, he retired, growling, under a form; thereby just escaping the pewter measure which Mr Sikes levelled at his head.

"You would, would you?" said Sikes, seizing the poker in one hand, and deliberately opening with the other a large clasp-knife, which he drew from his pocket. "Come here, you born devil! Come here! D'ye hear?"

The dog no doubt heard; because Mr Sikes spoke in the very harshest key of a very harsh voice; but, appearing to entertain some unaccountable objection to having his throat cut, he remained where he was, and growled more fiercely than before: at the same time grasping the end of the poker between his teeth, and biting at it like a wild beast.

This resistance only infuriated Mr Sikes the more; who, dropping on his knees, began to assail the animal most furiously. The dog jumped from right to left, and from left to right: snapping, growling, and barking; the man thrust and swore, and struck and blasphemed; and the struggle was reaching a most critical point for one or other, when, the door suddenly opening, the dog darted out, leaving Bill Sikes with the poker and clasp-knife in his hands.

from *Oliver Twist*, 1837–9

Thomas Carlyle

Poor little Nero, the dog, must have come this winter, or "Fall" (1839)?. Railway guard (from Dilberoglue, Manchester) brought him in one evening late. A little Cuban (Maltese? and otherwise mongrel) shock, mostly white – a most affectionate, lively little dog, otherwise of small merit, and little or no training. Much innocent sport there arose out of him; much quizzical ingenuous preparation of me for admitting of him: "My dear, it's borne in upon my mind that I'm to have a dog, etc., etc.," and with such a look and style!

We had many walks together, he and I, for the next ten years; a great deal of small traffic, poor little animal, so loyal, so loving, so naïve and true with what of dim intellect he had!

Letter, December 1849

Elizabeth Barrett Browning

You see this dog. It was but yesterday
I mused forgetful of his presence here
Till thought on thought drew downward tear on tear,
When from my pillow, where wet-cheeked I lay,
A head as hairy as Faunus, thrust its way
Right sudden against my face, — two golden-clear
Great eyes astonished mine, — a drooping ear
Did flap me on either cheek to dry the spray!
I started first, as some Arcadian,
Amazed by goatly god in twilight grove;
But, as the bearded vision closlier ran
My tears off, I knew Flush, and rose above
Surprise and sadness — thanking the true PAN,
Who, by low creatures, leads to heights of love.

"Flush, or Faunus," *c.* 1855

Darkly brown thy body is,
Till the sunshine striking this,
    Alchemise its dulness, —
When the sleek curls manifold
Flash all over into gold,
    With a burnished fulness.

Underneath my stroking hand,
Startled eyes of hazel bland
    Kindling, growing larger, —

Up thou leapest with a spring,
Full of prank and curvetting,
   Leaping like a charger.

Leap! thy broad tail waves a light;
Leap! thy slender feet are bright,
   Canopied in fringes.
Leap — those tasselled ears of thine
Flicker strangely, fair and fine,
   Down their golden inches.

Yet, my pretty sportive friend,
Little is't to such an end
   That I praise thy rareness!
Other dogs may be thy peers
Haply in these drooping ears
   And this glossy fairness.

But of thee it shall be said,
This dog watched beside a bed
   Day and night unweary, —
Watched within a curtained room,
Where no sunbeam brake the gloom
   Round the sick and dreary.

Roses, gathered for a vase,
In that chamber died apace,
   Beam and breeze resigning —
This dog only, waited on,
Knowing that when light is gone,
   Love remains for shining.

Other dogs in thymy dew
Tracked the hares and followed through
   Sunny moor or meadow —
This dog only, crept and crept
Next a languid cheek that slept,
   Sharing in the shadow.

Other dogs of loyal cheer
Bounded at the whistle clear,
   Up the woodside hieing —
This dog only, watched in reach
Of faintly uttered speech,
   Or a louder sighing.

And if one or two quick tears
Dropped upon his glossy ears,
   Or a sigh came double, —
Up he sprang in eager haste,
Fawning, fondling, breathing fast,
   In a tender trouble.

And this dog was satisfied,
If a pale thin hand would glide,
   Down his dewlaps sloping, —
Which he pushed his nose within,
After, — platforming his chin
   On the palm left open.

This dog, if a friendly voice
Call him now to blyther choice
   Than such chamber-keeping,
"Come out!" praying from the door,
Presseth backward as before,
   Up against me leaping.

Therefore to this dog will I,
Tenderly not scornfully,
   Render praise and favour!
With my hand upon his head,
Is my benediction said
   Therefore, and for ever.

        "To Flush, my dog," *c.* 1855

Mrs Gaskell

The feeling, which in Charlotte partook of something of the nature of an affection, was, with Emily, more of a passion. Some one speaking of her to me, in a careless kind of strength of expression, said, "she never showed regard to any human creature; all her love was reserved for animals." The helplessness of an animal was its passport to Charlotte's heart; the fierce, wild, intractability of its nature was what often recommended it to Emily. Speaking of her dead sister, the former told me that from her many traits in Shirley's character were taken; her way of sitting on the rug reading, with her arm round her rough bull-dog's neck; her calling to a strange dog, running past, with hanging head and lolling tongue, to give it a merciful draught of water, its maddened snap at her, her nobly merciful presence of mind, going straight into the kitchen, and taking up one of Tabby's red-hot Italian irons to sear the bitten place, and telling no one, till the danger was well-nigh over, for fear of the terrors that might beset their weaker minds. All this, looked upon as a well-invented fiction in "Shirley", was written down by Charlotte with streaming eyes; it was the literal true account of what Emily had done. The same tawny bull-dog (with his "strangled whistle", called "Tartar" in "Shirley", was "Keeper" in Haworth parsonage, a gift to Emily. With the gift came a warning. Keeper was faithful to the depths of his nature as long as he was with friends; but he who struck him with a stick or whip, roused the relentless nature of the brute, who flew at his throat forthwith, and held him there till one or the other was at the point of death. Now Keeper's household fault was this. He loved to steal up-stairs, and stretch his square, tawny limbs, on the comfortable beds, covered over with delicate white counterpanes. But the cleanliness of the parsonage arrangements was perfect; and this habit of Keeper's was so objectionable, that Emily, in reply to Tabby's remonstrances, declared that, if he was found again transgressing, she herself, in defiance of warning and his well-known ferocity of nature, would beat him so severely that he would never offend again. In the gathering dusk of an autumn evening, Tabby came, half triumphant, half trembling, but in great wrath, to tell Emily that Keeper was lying on the best bed, in drowsy voluptuousness. Charlotte saw Emily's whitening face, and set mouth, but dared not speak to interfere; no one dared when Emily's eyes glowed in that manner out of the paleness of her face, and when her lips were so compressed into stone. She went upstairs, and Tabby and Charlotte stood in the gloomy passage below, full of the dark shadows of the coming night. Down-stairs came Emily, dragging after her the unwilling Keeper, his hind legs set in a heavy attitude of resistance, held by the "scruff of his neck," but growling low and savagely all the time. The watchers would fain have spoken, but durst not, for fear of taking off Emily's attention, and causing her to avert her head for a moment from the enraged brute. She let him go, planted in a dark corner at the bottom of the stairs; no time was there to fetch stick or rod, for fear of the strangling clutch at her throat – her bare clenched fist struck against his red fierce eyes, before he had time to make his spring, and, in the language of the turf, she "punished him" till his eyes were swelled up, and the half-blind, stupefied beast was led to his customary lair, to have his swelled head fomented and cared for by the very Emily herself. The generous dog owed her no grudge; he loved her dearly ever after; he walked first among the mourners to her funeral, and never, so to speak, rejoiced, dog fashion, after her death. Let us somehow hope, in half Red Indian creed, that he follows Emily now; and, when he rests, sleeps on some soft white bed of dreams, unpunished when he awakens to the life of the land of shadows.

from *The Life of Charlotte Brontë*, 1857

Charles Dickens

At a small butcher's in a shy neighbourhood (there is no reason for suppressing the name, it is by Notting-hill, and gives upon the district called the Potteries), I know a shaggy black and white dog who keeps a drover. He is a dog of an easy disposition, and too frequently allows this drover to get drunk. On these occasions it is the dog's custom to sit outside the public-house, keeping an eye on a few sheep and thinking. I have seen him with six sheep, plainly casting up in his mind how many he began with when he left the market, and at what places he has left the rest. I have seen him perplexed by not being above to account to himself for any particular sheep. A light has gradually broken on him, he has remembered at what butcher's shop he left them, and in a burst of grave satisfaction has caught a fly off his nose, and shown himself much relieved. If I could at any time have doubted the fact that it was he who kept the drover, and not the drover who kept him, it would have been abundantly proved by his way of taking undivided charge of the six sheep when the drover came out, besmeared with red ochre and beer, and gave him wrong directions, which he calmly disregarded.

He has taken the sheep entirely into his own hands, has merely remarked, with respectful firmness, "That instruction would place them under an omnibus; you had better confine your attention to yourself, you will want it all;" and has driven his charge away, with an intelligence of ears and tail, and a knowledge of business, that has left his lout of a man very, very far behind.

from *All the Year Round*, 1859–1870

Sir Sidney Colvin

With Pomero, Landor would prattle in English and Italian as affectionately as a mother to a child. Pomero was his darling, the wisest and most beautiful of his race; Pomero had the brightest eyes and the most wonderful yaller tail ever seen. Sometimes it was Landor's humour to quote Pomero in speech and writing as a kind of sagacious elder brother whose opinion had to be consulted on all subjects before he would deliver his own. This creature accompanied his master wherever he went, barking "not fiercely but familiarly" at friend and stranger, and when they came in would either station himself upon his master's head to watch the people passing in the street, or else lie curled up in his basket until Landor, in talk with some visitor, began to laugh, and his laugh to grow and grow, when Pomero would spring up and leap upon and fume about him, barking and screaming for sympathy until the whole street resounded. The two together, master and dog, were for years to be encountered daily on their walks about Bath and the vicinity, and there are many who perfectly well remember them; the majestic old man, looking not a whit the less impressive for his rusty and dusty brown suit, his bulging boots, his rumpled linen, or his battered hat; and his noisy, soft-haired, quick-glancing, inseparable companion.

from *The Life of W. S. Landor,* 1881

W. H. Davies

My dog went mad and bit my hand,
   I was bitten to the bone:
My wife went walking out with him,
   And then came back alone.

I smoked my pipe, I nursed my wound,
   I saw them both depart:
But when my wife came back alone,
   I was bitten to the heart.

"D is for Dog", *c.* 1930

Jack London

A rest comes very good after one has travelled three thousand miles, and it must be confessed that Buck waxed lazy as his wounds healed, his muscles swelled out, and the flesh came back to cover his bones. For that matter, they were all loafing – Buck, John Thornton, and Skeet and Nig – waiting for the raft to come that was to carry them down to Dawson. Skeet was a little Irish setter who early made friends with Buck, who, in a dying condition, was unable to resist her first advances. She had the doctor trait which some dogs possess; and as a mother cat washes her kittens so she washed and cleansed Buck's wounds. Regularly, each morning after he had finished his breakfast, she performed her self-appointed task, till he came to look for her ministrations as much as he did for Thornton's. Nig, equally friendly, though less demonstrative, was a huge black dog, half bloodhound and half deerhound, with eyes that laughed and a boundless good nature.

To Buck's surprise these dogs manifested no jealousy toward him.

They seemed to share the kindliness and largeness of John Thornton. As Buck grew stronger they enticed him into all sorts of ridiculous games, in which Thornton himself could not forbear to join; and in this fashion Buck romped through his convalescence and into a new existence. Love, genuine passionate love, was his for the first time. This he had never experienced at Judge Miller's down in the sun-kissed Santa Clara Valley. With the Judge's sons, hunting and tramping, it had been a working partnership; with the Judge's grandsons a sort of pompous guardianship; and with the Judge himself, a stately and dignified friendship. But love that was feverish and burning, that was adoration, that was madness, it had taken John Thornton to arouse.

This man had saved his life, which was something; but, further, he was the ideal master. Other men saw to the welfare of their dogs from a sense of duty and business expediency; he saw to the welfare of his as if they were his own children, because he could not help it. And he saw further. He never forgot a kindly greeting or a cheering word, and to sit down for a long talk with them (gas, he called it) was as much his delight as theirs. He had a way of taking Buck's head roughly between his hands, and resting his own head upon Buck's, of shaking him back and forth, the while calling him ill names that to Buck were love names. Buck knew no greater joy than that rough embrace and the sound of murmured oaths, and at each jerk back and forth it seemed that his heart would be shaken out of his body so great was his ecstasy. And when, released, he sprang to his feet, his mouth laughing, his eyes eloquent, his throat vibrant with unuttered sound, and in that fashion remained without movement, John Thornton would reverently exclaim, "God! you can all but speak!"

Buck had a trick of love expression that was akin to hurt. He would often seize Thornton's hand in his mouth and close so fiercely that the flesh bore the impress of his teeth for some time afterward. And as Buck understood the oaths to be love words, so the man understood this feigned bite for a caress.

For the most part, however, Buck's love was expressed in adoration. While he went wild with happiness when Thornton touched him or spoke to him, he did not seek these tokens. Unlike Skeet, who was wont to shove her nose under Thornton's hand and nudge and nudge till petted, or Nig, who would stalk up and rest his great head on Thornton's knee, Buck was content to adore at a distance. He would lie by the hour, eager, alert, at Thornton's feet, looking up into his face, dwelling upon it, studying it, following with keenest interest each fleeting expression, every movement or change of feature. Or, as chance might have it, he would lie farther away, to the side or rear, watching the outlines of the man and the occasional movements of his body. And often, such was the state in which they lived, the strength of Buck's gaze would draw John Thornton's head around, and he would return the gaze, without speech, his heart shining out of his eyes as Buck's heart shone out.

For a long time after his rescue, Buck did not like Thornton to get out of his sight. From the moment he left the tent to when he entered it again, Buck would follow at his heels. His transient masters since he had come into the Northland had bred in him a fear that no master could be permanent. He was afraid that Thornton would pass out of his life as Perrault and François and the Scotch half-breed had passed out. Even in the night, in his dreams, he was haunted by this fear. At such times he would shake off sleep and creep through the chill to the flap of the tent, where he would stand and listen to the sounds of his master's breathing.

from *The Call of the Wild,* 1903

J. M. P.

Rover, mi dog, kind, true, an' brave,
To thee aw'll warble eawt a stave
   Ov hearty song.
An' iv it doesna seawnd so weel,
Aw'll sing chusheaw just what aw feel,
   Reet or wrong.

When theau looks up wi' moistened e'e,
What admiration do aw see
   Depicted theer.
Aw'm king o' men to thee, aw know,
Whether aw'm heigh i' th' world or low
   Theau'rt sincere.

Theau'rt th' staunchest dog aw've seen fur grit,
As theau con prove aboon a bit
   When danger's nigh.
An' iv sum villain threatened me,
He'd ha' to square his books wi' thee –
   Theau'd stond by.

To some theau'rt fierce as ony gale;
But, oh, a've seen the wag thi tail
   Wi' whinin' glee.
When th' little childer stroke thi yure
Theau'rt gradely gentle then, for shure,
   Pleeosed as con be.

An' mony a time theau's guarded, too,
Ti master's dwelling aw t' neet through,
   Still and dark;
Ready on th' slightest seawnd to spring
Straight to attention, threatening
   Wi' warnin' bark.

Com' Rover, then, fond, faithful mate,
Theau'll understond, at any rate,
   So aw suppose;
An' neaw, as th' rain eawtside's gan o'er,
We'll have a ramble reawnd once mooar,
   E'er twileet fo's.

     "To My Dog", *Our Dogs, 19 February* 1909

Alfred Ollivant

There below him, in a scoop of the ground, crouched a hump-backed boulder in hideous deformity; huge, grey, uncouth, like the back of some stranded Leviathan, flinging a deathly shade far across the green. And as he looked he was aware of a black form fluttering about it – the creak of wings, and the muffled grunt and cackle of a raven in excess of agitation.

All around the boulder fluttered the ominous bird, dabbing, darting, retreating, croaking, like a witch flirting. M'Adam could see the shut-shears beak, the little lusty eye, the low head screwing round to gaze at him, and hunching shoulders; and he wondered.

Then something arose, flapped, and fell again. It was the lappet of a man's coat. Staring intently, he now discerned a long, prone, ragged figure beneath the grey-glooming boulder.

Such a resemblance to the dead had the sleeper, that for a moment a sudden dread fell on him. And as the evil bird stooped lower and fluttered furiously, eager to strike and yet afraid, he yelled, –

"Houts, awa' wi' ye, blasphemin' corbie!" and advanced to wake the sleeper.

There was no need. The beggar had his guard.

As the bird stooped, a tiny yellow bomb burst from the sleeper's rags, and the bird wheeled away in hideous bustle.

The guardian dragged back to his position with drooping tadpole head, tongue out, and the heavy legs of puppyhood; and a bloody gash upon his neck revealed that the unequal combat had been long sustained.

The little man advanced with alluring thumb and finger to coax the puppy to him. But the fire-eyed defender, cornering back among the rags, would have none of him; and, as his antagonist drew nearer, he bared his little teeth, raised his little bristles, and growled a hideous menace – type of brute baby at bay.

Finally, as this fresh assailant still drew on, he dashed out, but fell, pitifully spent; and lay watching, his head along his paws, too weak to move, but resolute while he had life to fulfil his charge.

M'Adam bent and raised him tenderly. The puppy gurgled and slobbered in desperate fury, and then hung limp. A few weeks' baby, yet like his master an outcast, more wolf than dog; large, wicked head, cropped ears, and for tail a yet raw red button – no more; while the stark ribs and jagged spine were wearing through their owner's yellow coat.

"Why, wee one," cried M'Adam with wrathful pity, "ye're nigh to starvit!" And turning on the shred-robed sleeper at his feet, –

"Man!" he called angrily, "hoo daur ye starve yer dog? Ha' ye no peety? Wak', man!" and he kicked him in the ribs.

The man's arm fell away and discovered his face. And then

M'Adam knew there was no more waking for the gaunt starveling at his feet; knew by the evidence of a nibbled crust that this drawn-faced dead had given his last to his puppy, and died for want of the wherewithal to feed himself.

In the ground beside him was a cleft stick, and in the cleft a paper. On it, in the hand of one whose grim humour forsakes him not in death, –

"Beware the dog!"

And that, as any man in the Dale-land could tell you, is the story of the coming of the Tailless Tyke.

Owd Bob, The Grey Dog of Kenmuir, ?c. 1925

Stephen Vincent Benét

There was a man I knew near Pigeon Creek,
Who kept a kennel full of hunting-dogs,
Young dogs and old, smart hounds and silly hounds,
He'd sell the young ones every now and then,
Smart as they were and slick as they could run.
But the one dog he'd never sell or lend
Was an old half-deaf foolish-looking hound
You wouldn't think had sense to scratch a flea,
Unless the flea were old and sickly too.
Most days he used to lie beside the stove,
Or sleeping in a piece of sun outside.
Folks used to plague the man about that dog,
And he'd agree to everything they said:
"No – he ain't much on looks – or much on speed –
A young dog can outrun him any time,
Outlook him and outeat him and outleap him;
But, Mister, that dog's hell on a cold scent,
And, once he gets his teeth in what he's after,
He won't let go until he knows it's dead.

from *John Brown's Body,* 1928

William Henry Davies

The dog was there, outside her door,
She gave it food and drink,
She gave it shelter from the cold:
It was the night young Molly robbed
An old fool of his gold.

"Molly," I said, "you'll go to hell –"
And yet I half believed
That ugly, famished, tottering cur,
Would bark outside the gates of Heaven,
To open them for her.

"The Dog", 1925

E. Darbyshire

Seven-and-sixpence a year, dus ta 'ear?
    Fur a good-for-nowt dog like thee;
Thah kno's very well thah't not worth it.
    Er why dus ta blink so at me?
Come, lift up them ears o' thine, wil'ta
    And 'eer what thi gaffer's to say,
Thah's been a good useful servant,
    But, for aw that, thi time's up to-day;
Thah's fowt for thi friends like a tiger,
    Thah's play'd wi' these bairns like a lamb –
But we can't find brass for thi licence,
    Thah'll a' to be thrown in t' dam.
Why, thah's whinin! Thi tail's stop'd waggin –
    Thah must understand what ah say;
Very well, then, thah shan't go i't watter,
    We'll tak' thee and gi' thee away;
Else loise thee – but thah's owt but a beauty:
    Foaks al' say thah wur best lost ner fun:
But we, that have reared thee and kno' thee,

Al' loise a good friend when thah't gone.
When we come dahnstairs in a mornin'
  When s'll miss thi owd friendly wag:
And at neet, when we come fro't factory,
  Thah'll not meet us, so fussy and glad.
And these childer, how they'll miss thee,
  When they haven't thi long ears to pull:
Here, come and lay dahn upo' t' arston –
  Can't ta see that me heart is full?
But thah't not gone yet, and thah kno's it,
  Er, why ar' ta' waggin' thi tail?
Can't ta see what ah've just been thinkin',
  To do wi' less bacca and ale?
Ay, thah't an owd un! Where's me hat
  Thah's helped me to get ah't o' t' fix.
Stop here; tak' care o' these childer,
  Ah'll go and get Seven-and-six.

"Ahr Pincher", *c.* 1930

John Galsworthy

Man, no doubt, first bound or bred the dog to his service and companionship for purely utilitarian reasons; but we of to-day, by immemorial tradition and a sentiment that has become almost as inherent in us as the sentiment towards children, give him a place in our lives utterly different from that which we accord to any other animal (not even excepting cats); a place that he has won for himself throughout the ages, and that he ever increasingly deserves. He is by far the nearest thing thing to man on the face of the earth; the one link that we have spiritually with the animal creation; the dumb creature into whose eyes we can look and tell pretty well for certain what emotion, even what thought, is at work within; the dumb creature which – not as a rare exception, but almost always – steadily feels the sentiments of love and trust. This special nature of the dog is our own handiwork, a thing instilled into him through thousands of years of intimacy, care, and mutual service, deliberately and ever more carefully fostered; extraordinarily precious even to those of us who profess to be without sentiment. It is one of the prime factors of our daily lives in all classes of society – this mute partnership with dogs.

from *A. Sheaf, c.* 1934

Siegfried Sassoon

Who's this – alone with stone and sky?
It's only my old dog and I –
It's only him; it's only me;
Alone with stone and grass and tree.

What share we most – we two together?
Smells, and awareness of the weather.
What is it makes us more than dust?
My trust in him; in me his trust.

Here's anyhow one decent thing
That life to man and dog can bring;
One decent thing, remultiplied
Till earth's last dog and man have died.

"Man and Dog", *c.* 1960

Maurice Maeterlinck

Pelléas had a great, bulging, powerful forehead, like that of Socrates or Verlaine; and, under a little black nose, blunt as a churlish assent, a pair of large, hanging and symmetrical chops, which made his head a sort of massive, obstinate, pensive, and three-cornered menace. He was beautiful after the manner of a beautiful natural monster that has complied strictly with the laws of his species. And what a smile of attentive obligingness, of incorruptible innocence, of affectionate submission, of boundless gratitude, and total self-abandonment, lit up, at the least caress, that adorable mask of ugliness.

from "Pelléas et Mélisande", 1892

Anonymous

Sometimes dogs are restrained portraits, sometimes the fiercest of satires [of their owners]. A sheep dog has exactly a shepherd's air of having to work hard and anxiously for his living; he has his master's shyness in company, his deep concentration in repose, his resource and unflagging energy in action. If two mastiffs are employed, one to guard valuable possessions from thieves, the other as a companion for children, the first bears in its poise and gait the fierce, possessive pride of ownership, and the second becomes as mild and gentle as an old nurse behind a perambulator.

The public parks are delightful, full of people who go about with four-legged replicas of themselves upon a leash. The likeness is often remarkable enough to win a smile, even in the case of men who obscure it sometimes by their uniform habits of dress; but all the world may instantly know a woman by her dog. If she is by nature of tweed and heather, she will own a canine trifle of silk and scent. If she is selfish and pampered, her dog will yap at every disturbance of its leisured comfort, will fume and fret as she scolds and complains, and will be saved, as she is, from the outward troubles of life, not because it is wise, but because it seldom ventures far from shelter of its comfortable basket.

Dogs not only absorb the characters of their individual masters, but exhibit the idiosyncrasies of their natures. Among sheep dogs alone, England, Scotland, and Wales are divided with true racial distinctness, and a glance into the faces of the dogs we have imported from China proves them to be decorative aliens in this land of setters and terriers.

The observant traveller would discover, in every kennel through-out the world, more and more data for the problems of human psychology – so many, indeed, that he might at last return with relief to the imperturbable and international cat, "who walks by himself, and to who all places are alike."

"The Tell-Tale Dog", *The Times,* 1924

CHAPTER 3

Endlessly Useful

G iven the incredible diversity of size and form exhibited by domestic dogs it is perhaps not surprising that the uses to which they have been and are put by man should be just as varied. Yet in spite of diversity of size and form domestic dogs are all of the same species and are the product of the same lupine ancestors. The inherently natural behaviour of all breeds of domestic dog, the way in which they care for their young, the way in which they express emotions and communicate remain the same across all breeds. Tiny Chihuahuas from Mexico speak the same language as huge Neapolitan Mastiffs. Monastery dogs from Tibet have no difficulty in communicating with dogs reared in British hunt kennels. Diversity of form contrasts sharply with uniformity of basic behaviour and expression.

The behaviour of wild ancestors contains all the ingredients which have, over thousands of years, allowed man to breed dogs which are not just capable but positively eager to undertake a huge variety of tasks. No other species, except perhaps our own, exhibits such a wide range of talents.

Adaptation of basic hunting routines has produced dogs which will herd and protect livestock. Adaptation of territorial instincts has produced dogs which will guard home and property; dogs even guard the entrance to Hades just as the ancient Egyptians used dogs to guard the graves of their ancestors. It was a dog which pioneered space travel. The calming effect of the presence of a dog on emotionally and physically disturbed people has long been recognized and is being increasingly taken up by the medical profession. Dogs are also beginning to be used to predict the onset of epileptic seizures, a use which, even a very few years ago, could never have been imagined.

Dogs have long been used to guide the blind and are now also being used to assist deaf and physically handicapped people. Dogs are used to search for illicit substances and for people lost in hostile conditions. Even after thousands of years in the service of man, their talents are being put to use in exciting new ways.

Hector Boece

There are among the Scotch, besides the common domestic dogs, three kinds of dogs, which you will not (I think) find anywhere else in the world: one kind is used for hunting (ane grew hownd) which is both very fast and very bold: nor (is it used) only against wild beasts, but against enemies and thieves: especially if it see its master or leader attacked, or if it be incited against them. The second (ane rache) is used for discovering *by scent* horses, wild beasts, birds, nay, even fishes lurking among stones. The third kind (ane sluth hownd) is not larger than the scent-following dogs: but is usually reddish with black spots, or black with reddish spots. So great is their power of smell that they follow up thieves and stolen objects, and attack them when found. Nay even if a thief, to throw them off, cross a river, they fling themselves in, where he entered the water, and crossing to the other side do not cease to search all round until they have picked up the scent again. . . .

The third kind is mair than ony rache; reid hewitt, or ellis blak, with small sprainges or spottis; and ar callit be the peple, Sleuthoundis. This doggis hes sae mervellus with, that serche thevir and followis on thaim allanerlie be sent of the guddis that are tane away; and nocht allanerlie findis the theif, but invadis him with watter, quhair they pass, to caus the hound to tine the sent of thaim and the guddis, yet he serchis heir and thair with sic diligence that, be his fut, he findis baith the trace of the theif and the guddis. The mervellous nature of thir houns will have na faith with uncouth people; howbeit, the samin ar richt frequent and rife on the bordouris of Ingland and Scotland; attour it ih statue, be the lawis of the Bordouris, he that denyis entres to the sleuthound, in time of chace and serching of guddis, sal be haldin participant with the crime and thift committis.

from *History of Scotland*, translated by Raphael Holinshed, and included in his *Chronicles*, 1577

Abraham Fleming

Of the Dogge called a Bloudehounde in Latine *Sanguinarius*.

The greater sort which serve to hunt, having lippes of a large syze & eares of no small lengtht, doo, not onely chase the beast whiles it liveth . . . but beyng dead also by any maner of casualtie, make recourse to the place where it lyeth, having in this poynt an assured and infallible guyde, namely, the sent and savour of the bloud sprinckled heere and there upon the ground. For whether the beast beyng wounded, doth notwithstanding enjoye life, and escapeth the handes of the huntesman, or whether the said beast beyng slayne is convayed clenly out of the parcke (so that there be some signification of bloud shed) these Dogges with no lesse facilitie and easiness, then aviditie and greedinesse, can disclose and bewray the same by smelling, applying to their pursuit, agilitie and nimblenesse, without tediousnesse, for which consideration, of a singuler specialitie they deserved to bee called *Sanguinarij* bloudhounds. And albeit peradventure it may chaunce . . . that a peece of fleshe be subtily stolen and conningly convayed away with such provisos and precaveats as thereby all apparaunce of bloud is eyther prevented, excluded, or concealed, yet these kinde of dogges by a certaine direcion of an inwarde asured notyce and privy marcke, pursue the deede dooers, through long lanes, crooked reaches, and weary wayes, without wandring awry out of the limites of the land whereon those desperate purloyners prepared their speedy passage. Yea, the natures of these Dogges is such, and such, and so effectuall is their foresight, that they can bewray, seperate, and pycke them out from among an infinite multitude and an innumerable company, creepe they never so farre into the thickest thronge, they will finde him out notwith standyng he lye hidden in wylde woods, inclose and overgrown groves, and lurcke in hollow holes apte to harbour such ungracious guestes.

Moreover, although they should passe over the water, thinking thereby to avoyde the pursute of the houndes, yet will not these dogges give over their attempt, but presuming to swym through the streame, persver in their pursute, and when they be arrived and gotten the further bancke, they hunt up and downe, to and fro runne they, from place to place shift they, until they have attained to that plot of grounde where they passed over. And this is their practise, if perdie they canot at ye first time smelling, finde out the way which the deede dooers tooke to escape. So at length get they that by arte, cunning, and dilligent indevour, which by fortune and lucke they cannot otherwyse overcome. . . . For they wyll not pause or breath from their pursute untill such tyme as they bee apprehended and taken that committed the facte.

The owners of such houndes use to keepe them in close and darke channells in the day time, and let them lose at liberty in the night season, to th'intent that they myght with more courage and boldnesse practise to follow the fellon in the evening and solitarie houres of darkenesse, when such yll disposed varlots are principally purposed to play theyr impudent pageante, and imprudent pranckes. These houndes when they are to follow such fellowes as we have before rehearsed, use not that liberty to raunge at wil, which they have otherwise when they are in game (except upon necesary occasion, whereon dependeth an urgent an effectuall perswasion), when such purloyners make spedy way in flight, but beyng restrained and drawne backe from running at random with the lease, the ende whereof the owner holding in his hand is led, guyed and directed with such swiftnesse and slownesse (whether he go on foote or whether he ryde on horsebacke), as he himselfe in harte would wishe for the more easie apprehension of those venturous varlots.

In the borders of England and Scotland (the often and accustomed stealing of cattell so procuring) these kinde of Dogges are very much used and they are taught and trayned up first of all to hunt cattell as well of the smaller as of the greater grouth, and afterwardes (that qualitie relinquished and lefte) they are learned to pursue such pestilent persons as plant theyr pleasure in such practises of purpoyning as we have already declared. Of this kinde there is nene that taketh the water naturally, except it please you so to suppose of them whych follow the Otter, whych sometimes haunte the lande, and sometime useth the water. And yet neverthelesse all the kind of them boyling and boyling with greedy desire of the pray which by swymming passeth through river and flood, plung amyds the water, and passe the streame with their pawes. But this propertie proceedeth from an earnest desire wherwith they be inflamed, rather then from any inclination issuyng from the ordinance and appoyntment of nature.

The shepherds hounds is very necessarye and profitable for the avoyding of harmes and inconveniences which may come to men by the means of beastes. The second sort sere to succour against the snares and attemptes of mischiefous men. Our shepherdes dogge is not huge, vaste, and bigge, but of an indifferent stature and growth, because it hath not to deal with the bloudthyrsty wolf, sythence there be none in England, which happy and fortunate benefite is to be ascribed to the puisant Prince *Edgar*, who to thintent ye the whole counterey myght be evacuated and quite clered from wolfes, charged & commanded the welsheme (who were pestered with these butcherly beastes above measure) to paye him yearely tribute which was (note the wisdomes of the King) three hundred Wolfes. Some there be which write that *Ludwall* Prince of Wales paide yeerly to King *Edgar* three hundred wolves in the name of an exaction (as we have sayd before.) And that by the meanes hereof, within the compasse and tearme of foure yeares none of those noysome, and pestilent Beastes were left in the coastes of England and Wales.

But to returne to our shepherds dogge. This dogge either at the hearing of his masters voyce, or at the wagging and whisteling in his fist, or at the shrill and horse hissing bringeth the wandring weathers and straying sheepe, into the selfe same place where his master will and wishe, is to have them, whereby the shepherd reapeth this benefite, namely, that with litle labour and no toyle or moving of his feete he may rule and guide his flocke, according to his owne desire, either to have them go forward, or to stand still, or to drawe backward, or to turne this way, or to take that way. For it is not in Englande, as it is in *Fraunce*, as it is in *Flaunders*, as it is in *Syria*, as it is in *Tartaria*, where the sheepe follow the shepherd, for heere in our country the sheepherd followeth the sheepe. And sometimes the straying sheepe, when no dogge runneth before them, nor goeth about & beside them, gather themselves together in a flocke, when they heere the sheepherd whistle in his fist, for feare of the Dogge (as I imagine) remembering this (if unreasonable creatures may be reported to have memory) that the Dogge commonly runneth out

85

at his masters warrant which is his whistle. This have we oftentimes diligently marcked in taking our journey from towne to towne, when wee have hard a sheepherd whistle we have rayned in our horse and stoode styll a space, to see the proofe and triall of this matter.

Furthermore with this dogge doth the sheepherd take sheepe for ye slaughter, and to be healed if they be sicke, no hurt or harme in the world done to the simple creature.

from *Of Englishe Dogges,* 1576

Edmund Spenser

Thilk same Shepheard mought I well marke;
He has a dogge to byte or to barke;
Never had shepheard so kene a kurre,
That waketh and if but a leafe sturre.
Whilome there wonned a wicked wolfe,
That with many a lambe had glutted his gulfe.
And ever at night wont to repaye
Unto the flocke, when the welkin shone faire,
Ycladde in clothing of seely sheepe,
When the good old man used to sleepe.
Tho at midnight he would barke and ball,
(For he had eft learned a curres call,)
As if a woolfe were emong the sheepe.
With that the shepheard would breake his sleepe,
And send out Lowder (for so his dog hote)
To raunge the fields with wide open throte.
Tho, whenas Lowder was farre awaye,
This wolvish sheepe would catchen his pray . . .
At end, the shepheard his practise spyed,
(For Roffey is wise, and as Argus eyed)
And when at even he came to the flocke,
Fast in theyr folds he did them locke . . .
For it was a perilous beast above all,
And eke had he cond the shepherds call,
And oft in the night came to the shepecote,
And called Lowder, with a hollow throte,

As if it the old man selfe had bene.
The dog his maisters voice did it weene,
Yet halfe in doubt he opened the dore,
And ranne out, as he wont of yore.
No sooner was out but swifter than thought,
Fast be the hyde the wolfe Lowder caught;
And had not Roffy renne to the steven,
Lowder had be slaine thilke same even.

from *The Shepheards Calendar*: "September," 1579

Thomas Nashe

Yea, there be of them, as there be of men,
Of every occupation more or less:
Some carriers and they fetch; some watermen,
And they dive and swim when you do bid them;
Some butchers, and they worry sheep by night;
Some cooks, and they do nothing but turn spits,
Cynics they are, for they will snarl and bite;
Right courtiers to flatter and to fawn;
Valiant to set upon their enemies;
Most faithful and most constant to their friends.

from *Summer's Last Will and Testament*, 1600

Samuel Pepys

With Mr Pierce, the surgeon, to see an experiment of killing a dog, by letting opium into his hind leg. He and Dr Clerke did fail mightily in hitting the vein, and in effect did not do the business after many trials; but, with the little they got in, the dog did presently fall asleep; and a little dog, also, which they put it down his throat; he also staggered first, and then fell asleep, and so continued. Whether he recovered or not, after I was gone, I know not.

Diary, 16 May 1664

A gentleman arrived here this day, Mr Brown, of St Maloes, among other things, tells me the meaning of the setting out of dogs every night out of the town walls, which are said to secure the city; but it is not so, but only to secure the anchors, cables, and ships that lie in the dry, which might otherwise in the night be liable to be robbed. And these dogs are set out every night, and called together in every morning by a man with a horse and they go in very orderly.

Diary, 25 May 1666

Dr Croome told me that, at the meeting at Gresham College to-night, which, it seems, they have now every Wednesday again, there was a pretty experiment of the blood of one dog let out, till he died, into the body of another on one side, while all his own ran out on the other side. The first died upon the place, and the other very well, and likely to do well. This did give occasion to many pretty wishes, as of the blood of a Quaker to be let into an Archbishop, and such like; but, as Dr Croome says, may, if it takes, be of mighty use to man's health, for the mending of bad blood by borrowing from a better body.

Diary, 14 November 1666

This noon I met with Mr Hooke, and he tells me the dog which he filled with another dog's blood at the College the other day is very well, and likely to be so as ever, and doubts not its being found of great use to men; and so do Dr Whistler, who dined with us at the tavern.

Diary, 16 November 1666

John Gay

The dinner must be dished at once,
Where's this vexatious turnspit gone?
Unless the skulking cur is caught,
The sirloin's spoilt, and I'm at fault.

Thus said (for sure you'll think it fit
That I the cook maid's oaths omit)
With all the fury of a cook,
Her cooler kitchen Nan forsook:
The broom-stick o'er her head she waves,
She sweats, she stamps, she puffs, she raves —
The sneaking cur before her flies;
She whistles, calls, fair speech she tries;
These nought avail. Her choler burns;
The fist and cudgel threat by turns.
With hasty stride she presses near:
He slinks aloof, and howls with fear.

from *Rural Sports,* 1713

William Somervile

A diff'rent hound for ev'ry diff'rent chace
Select with judgement; nor the tim'rous hare
O'er-match'd destroy, but leave that vile offence
To the mean, murd'rous coursing crew, intent
On blood and spoil.

from *The Chace,* 1735

William Cowper

The noon was shady, and soft airs
  Swept Ouse's silent tide,
When, 'scaped from literary cares,
  I wander'd on his side.

My spaniel prettiest of his race,
  And high in pedigree, —
(Two nymphs adorn'd with every grace
  That spaniel found for me,)

Now wanton'd lost in flags and reeds,
  Now starting into sight,
Pursued the swallow o'er the meads
  With scarce a slower flight.

It was the time when Ouse display'd
  His lilies newly blown;
Their beauties I intent survey'd,
  And one I wish'd my own.

With cane extended far I sought
  To steer it close to land;
But still the prize, though nearly caught,
  Escaped my eager hand.

Beau mark'd my unsuccessful pains
  With fix'd considerate face,
And puzzling set his puppy brains
  To comprehend the case.

But with a cherup clear and strong
  Dispersing all his dream,
I thence withdrew, and follow'd long
  The windings of the stream.

My ramble ended, I return'd;
  Beau, trotting far before,
The floating wreath again discern'd,
  And plunging left the shore.

I saw him with the lily cropp'd
  Impatient swim to meet
My quick approach, and soon he dropp'd
  The treasure at my feet.

Charm'd with the sight, "The world," I cried,
  "Shall hear of this thy deed;
My dog shall mortify the pride
  Of man's superior breed;

"But chief myself I will enjoin,
   Awake at duty's call,
To show a love as prompt as thine
   To Him who gives me all."

"The dog and the water-lily"

John Clare

The barking dogs by lane and wood
Drive sheep afield from foddering ground
And eccho in her summer mood
Briskly mocks the cheery sound
The flocks as from a prison broke
Shake their wet fleeces in the sun
While following fast a misty smoke
Recks from the moist grass as they run
No more behind their masters heels
The dog creeps o'er his winter pace
But cocks his tail and o'er the fields
Runs many a wild and random chase.

from *The Shepherd's Calendar,*
"February: A Thaw", 1827

Anonymous

On Monday a strange looking animal having been seen in the fields near Wheathamstead, Hert, a small party went in search, supposing it was a deer, out of Brocket Hall Park. Great was their surprise at finding in the hedge a large leopard, which stole away, followed at a respectful distance by the sportsmen, who were only loaded with swan shot. As it was endeavouring to escape, it met with a labourer in the field whom it attacked and dangerously wounded, but his life was saved by a mastiff fastening on the leopard, and enabling Mr Norman Thrale to approach within a few yards, and disable it with a charge of swan shot. It was shortly afterwards destroyed, and was found to weigh 14 stone. It had breakfasted off a dog, whose head was found. It is not known where the beast had escaped from.

Hampshire Chronicle, 6 June 1836

Henry Mayhew

THE DANCING DOGS

I received the following narrative from the old man who has been so long known about the streets of London with a troop of performing dogs. He was especially picturesque in his appearance. His hair, which was grizzled rather than grey, was parted down the middle, and hung long and straight over his shoulders. He was dressed in a coachman's blue greatcoat with many capes. His left hand was in a sling made out of a dirty pocket-handkerchief and in his other he held a stick, by means of which he could just manage to hobble along. He was very ill, and very poor, not having been out with his dogs for nearly two months. He appeared to speak in great pain. The civility, if not politeness of his manner, threw an air of refinement about him, that struck me more forcibly from its contrast with the manners of the English belonging to the same class. He began –

"I have de dancing dogs for de street – now I have nothing else. I have tree dogs – One is called Finette, anoder von Favorite, that is her nomme, an de oder von Ozor. Ah I," he said, with a shrug of the shoulders, in answer to my inquiry as to what the dogs did, "un danse, un valse, un jomp a de stick and troo do hoop-non, noting else. Sometimes I had de four dogs – I did lose de von. Ah! she had beacoup d'esprit – plenty of vit, you say – she did jomp a de hoop better dan all. Her nomme was Taborine! – she is dead dare is long time. All ma dogs have des habillements – the dress and de leetle hat. Dey have a leetle jackette in divers colours en étoffe – some de red, and some de green, and some de bleu. Deir hats is de rouge et noir – red and black, with a leetle plume-fedder, you say. Dere is some 10 or 11 year I have been in dis country. I come from Italie – Italie – Oui, Monsieur, oui. I did live in a leetle vile, trento miglia, dirty mile, de Parma. Je travaille dans la campagne, I vork out in de countrie – je ne sais comment vous appellez la campagne. There is no commerce in de montagne. I am come in dis country here. I have leetle business to come. I thought to gagner ma vie – to gain my life wid my leetel dogs in dis countrie. I have dem déjà when I have come here from Parma – j'en avait dix. I did have de ten dogs – je les apporte. I have carried all de ten from Italie. I did learn – yes – yes – de dogs to dance in ma own countrie. It did make de cold in de montagne in winter, and I had not no vork dere, and I must look for to gain my life some oder place. Après ça, I have instruct my dogs to danse. Yes, ils learn to danse; I play de music, and dey do jomp. Non, non – pas du tout! I did not never beat ma dogs; dare is a way to learn de dogs without no vip. Premièrement, ven I am come here I have gained a leetel monnaie – plus que now – beaucoup d'avantage plenty more. I am left ma logement – my lodging, you say, at 9 hours in de morning, and am stay away vid ma dogs till 7 or 8 hours in de evening. Oh! I cannot count how many times de leetel dogs have danse in de day – twenty – dirty – forty peut-être – all depends: sometimes I would gain de tree shilling – sometime de couple – sometime not nothing – all depend."

from *London Labour and London Poor,* 1851

Florence Nightingale

A small pet is often an excellent companion for the sick, for long chronic cases especially.

from *Notes on Nursing,* 1859

Charles Dickens

There is a dog residing in the borough of Southwark, who keeps a blind man. He may be seen most days in Oxford-street, hauling the blind man away on expeditions wholly uncontemplated by, and unintelligible to the man; wholly of the dog's conception and execution. Contrariwise, when the man has projects, the dog will sit down in a crowded thoroughfare and meditate. I saw him yesterday wearing the money-tray, like an easy-collar, instead of offering it to the public, taking the man against his will, on the invitation of a disreputable cur, apparently, to visit a dog at Harrow – he was so intent on that direction. The north wall of Burlington House-gardens, between the Arcade and the Albany, offers a shy spot for appointments among blind men at about two or three o'clock in the afternoon. They sit, very uncomfortably, on a sloping board there, and compare notes. Their dogs may always be observed at the same time, openly disparaging the men they keep to one another, and settling where they shall respectively take their men when they begin to move again.

from *All the Year Round,* 1859–1870

Robert Browning

Sing me a hero! Quench my thirst
Of soul, ye bards!
   Quoth Bard the first
"Sir Olaf, the good knight, did don
His helm and eke his habergeon . . ."
Sir Olaf and his bard –!

"That sin-scather brow" (quoth Bard the second)
"That eye wide ope as though Fate beckoned
My hero to some steep beneath
Which prejudice smiled tempting death . . ."
You too without your host have reckoned!

"A beggar-child" (let's hear this third!)
"Sat on a quay's edge: like a bird
Sang to herself at careless play,
And fell into the stream. Dismay!
Help, you the standers-by!" None stirred.

"Bystanders reason, think of wives
And children ere they risk their lives.
Over the balustrade has bounced

A mere instinctive dog, and pounced
Plumb on the prize. "How well he dives!

"Up he comes with the child, see, tight
In mouth, alive too, clutched from quite
A depth of ten feet – twelve, I bet!
Good dog! What, off again? There's yet
Another child to save? All right!

"Here he comes, holds in mouth this time – What may
the thing be? Well, that's fine!
Now, did you ever? Reason reigns
In man alone, since all Tray's pains
Have fished – the child's doll from the slime!"

And so amid the laughter gay,
Trotted my hero off, – old Tray –
Till somebody, prerogatived
With reason, reasoned: "Why he dived,
His brain would show us, I should say.

"John, go and catch, or if needs be,
Purchase – that animal for me!
By vivisection, at expense
Of half-an-hour and eighteen pence,
How brain secretes dog's soul we'll see!"

"Tray", 1870

Josh Billings (pseud.)

Newfoundland dogs are good to save children from drowning, but
you must have a pond of water handy and a child, or else there will
be no profit in boarding a Newfoundland.

from *Essays*, c. 1880

George R. Krehl

Sir,

As I see from this morning's papers that official information has been supplied to the press upon the subject of the bloodhounds that have been brought to London to track the Whitechapel murderer, I shall presume I shall not be making any indiscreet disclosure by giving an account of the trial run that was made this morning in Hyde Park in the presence of the Commissioner of the Police. I will preface the description by a few remarks showing how bloodhounds were introduced in this matter.

It has long been the opinion among breeders and exhibitors of dogs that the keen scenting power of the bloodhound should be more generally employed in the detection of crime.

The chief objection to the proposal has been the one of a sentimental nature. An important number of the public abhor the idea of employing a means which calls up having thoughts of the days when escaped slaves were trapped by bloodthirsty dogs and the very name bloodhound possesses a terror for many minds.

These objectives may be dismissed in a couple of words as far as they affect the hounds Sir Charles Warren has summoned to London. In the first place, the dogs used for hunting slaves in America were not bloodhounds at all but a variety of crossbreds – Mastiff type predominantly. Secondly, the title "Bloodhound" is an unfortunate misnomer as applied to the animals we recognise nowadays by this name. For our bloodhound is a descendant from the French St Hubert hound as anybody can recognise who's seen the same breed in France, where it is still used for its natural purpose hunting in packs, deer and other quarry.

Last Thursday an eminent veterinary surgeon of the South West district was summoned by telegraph to attend Sir Charles Warren to advise upon the question of employing bloodhounds for the discovery of the Whitechapel murderer.

His views being favourable to the plan, he was instructed to procure hounds. He immediately communicated with two well known breeders who were known to have trained their hounds to hunt man. Mr Hood Wright offered his famous Hector II who so distinguished himself at the Warwick dog show trials that on condition that should any harm come to it he should be compensated to the extent of £1200. Mr Edwin Brough replied that he would bring to town two thoroughly trained hounds, Barnaby and Burgho, if expenses were paid. The second offer was accepted. They arrived last Saturday in time for what was expected by police would take place on Sunday night. They were kennelled by Mr W. K. Taunton. Yesterday, Monday 7 a.m. they were tried in Regents Park by the owner and the veterinary surgeon. They were out again last night and hunted on the leash in the dark.

. . .

At a quarter to the hour [7 a.m] I was the first on the ground. A few minutes later a gentleman, one of the chief surgeons to the police arrived. At 7, Mr Brough, Mr Taunton and a friend came in a trap with the two hounds. Six minutes later, Sir Charles Warren rode up on a stout cob directly after the veterinary surgeon arrived attended by his assistant.

No time was lost in making a start; the morning was fine, but misty and a slight wind blew from the east. It felt like a fine hunting morning, but it turned out to be the contrary again proving how difficult it is until the hounds are on, to say if scent will lie.

Sir Charles immediately offered to act as a hunted man. No scent of any shape was used. The hounds were to hunt nothing but the plain boot of a man they had no previous knowledge of.

The Chief Constable set off at a trot in the direction of Bayswater. After he had been given ample time and had passed out of sight, Mr Brough with a wave of his hat and an encouraging cheer slipped the intelligent couple of hounds who galloped off carrying their heads low with their long pendulous ears sweeping the morning dew from the grass. They did not bay but hunted perfectly mute.

Sir Charles made a circle round and the hounds went at a fair pace, not fast – when he traversed about half the circle he called to a constable to cross his track which the man did. This point the hounds checked – they made a careful slow cast, Barnaby hitting it off, Burgho followed then they ran closely until they winded their man some twenty yards from the track and then were at fault and we came up to them. Sir Charles having plenty of wind left, decided to give us another run. Again the hounds were laid on but did not work so well and it became apparent to us that it was a very bad morning for scent.

The Chief Commissioner agreed that another member of our party, Mr H. E. Shepard, who is well up in drag and showhound work should give us a run. Mr Shepard set off in a northerly direction. After he had gone some seven hundred yards, a baker's boy crossed and directly after, a man walked over the track. We then lost sight of our man in the mist. When we viewed him again emerging from Kensington way, we laid on. The hounds swept along pausing a moment where the track had been foiled by the footsteps of the boy and the man. About half the distance they were at fault and Burgho ran back, but Barnaby casting forward found and finished well. By this time the park was filling so we called up the hounds. In spite of the event not allowing, Sir Charles Warren was able to see sufficient to recognise the value of the hounds for the purpose. They hunted perfect strangers and stuck to them when others crossed the scent. They had no scent but the odour of man and leather.

These hounds will be kept where they can be summoned instantly and within reach of Whitehall in less than half an hour. Should another murder take place, the man who discovers the body must without a word to passers-by repair to the nearest police station whence the hounds will be wired for.

If this be done as I've described, the complications of track by many feet will be avoided and I have no doubt whatever that the murderer will be run down.

Hounds that can hunt a boot with a bad injury scent, will never check after a man who in addition to his natural body odour animated by excitement will most probably get splashed by a little blood and then in addition to these advantages the man after having his hands in the abdomen will bear fresh and strong that sickly smell which surgeons know clings to the hands for days and after repeated washing with carbolic soap, and, further this murderer by removing and retaining one of the organs when he takes the uterus or kidney will be actually carrying the drag for the hounds. With such an accumulation of scent particles these bloodhounds will track hours after the man has got away . . . I gather that it is believed by those best able to form an opinion that the man is a slaughterer and that he is still within the neighbourhood where the crimes have been committed. If he is a maniac, all his cunning, should he kill another poor creature, will not avail him against the sure hounds that will be laid in his track. Then when London rings the news of his capture, humanity will be under another obligation to the service of man's best friend, the most intelligent of the brute creation, our dogs.

I am Sir, your obedient servant,
George R. Krehl
Kennel Editor to the *Stockkeeper and Fancier's Chronicle*

Letter to the *Evening News*, 9 October 1888

Anonymous

Our attention has been called by the Exhibitions branch of the Board of Trade to a series of interesting demonstrations to be given at the International Exhibitions to be held at Ghent for a period of six months from the 26th of April in the present year – in which His Majesty's Government are officially participating – of the "chien Policier," as the trained police dog is called in the Continent.

The history of the development of this system is interesting. Dogs, as every one knows, have been frequently called in to the assistance of police in all countries ever since the force existed, but their use as a regular organized adjunct arose out of the necessity which occurred in Ghent of strengthening the police in the most economical method to be found. This was in 1899, and the then Chief of the force, Van Wesomael introduced three sheep dogs as an experiment. So successful was this found to be that to-day there are forty-three dogs in the police kennels, and to the visitor they certainly present the most interesting and instructive lesson.

The breed is the Malines sheep dog, something after the type of the smooth haired Scottish collie – a tawny light brown, hardy, fierce and full of vital force. Broad of chest, alert in appearance, he gives the impression of a truly formidable antagonist. And formidable he would be were he not so perfectly trained as to be completely under the control of the policeman whom he accompanies on his rounds.

This fact is evident at once to any one visiting the kennels, for the fierce barking which the entrance of a stranger naturally evokes is instantly checked at the command of the trainer. This trait of implicit obedience is even carried so far that at a word from the trainer any of the dogs will at once attack the kennelman who feeds them, and to whom they are obviously devoted, even though a moment before they have been licking his hand which caressed them.

And the manner in which the training is carried out is perfectly simple. "I have never struck one of them. A dog beaten is a dog spoiled," the trainer declares; and it is easy to believe, for there is no sign of fear to be observed – no cringing at the word of command. Every dog is anxious to obtain the caress of the trainer and evinces the most perfect happiness thereat. The test of obedience is then the first lesson in the training. If the dog shows his capability of understanding this readily, he is worthy of the trouble to be taken with his education; if not, his training as a police dog goes no further.

"Police Dogs at the Ghent International Exhibition", *The Foxhound*,
April 1913

Anonymous

Dedicated to the indomitable spirits of the sled dogs that relayed antitoxin six hundred miles over rough ice across treacherous waters through arctic blizzards from Nenana to the relief of stricken Nome in the Winter of 1925.

Endurance   Fidelity   Intelligence

Inscription on the statue of Balto in Central Park, New York, 1925

Dorothy Eustis

It was as though a complete transformation had taken place before my eyes. One moment it was an uncertain, shuffling blind man, tapping with a cane, the next it was an assured person, with his dog firmly in hand and his head up, who walked towards us quickly and firmly, giving his orders in a low confident voice. That one quick glimpse of the crying need for guidance and companionship in the lonely, all-enveloping darkness stood out clearly before my swimming eyes. To think that one small dog could stand for so much in the life of a human being, not only in his usual role of companion but as his eyes, sword, shield and buckler! How many humans could fill those roles with the same uncomplaining devotion and untiring fidelity? Darned few, I think.

"The Seeing Eye", *Saturday Evening Post*, 5 November 1927

Shannon Garst

The young Chasseurs, or "Blue Devils" seemed much amused at the sight of these dogs who had come half-way around the world to accomplish what men, horses and mules had failed to do: the task of hauling supplies over the steep and snowy Vosges Mountains looming like a natural and formidable barricade between France and Germany.

Now Scotty had the job of training the Blue Devils to handle dogs. First, he got some white paint and a brush and numbered from one to sixty the posts of the high fence that enclosed the kennels. There were sixty teams and twenty extra dogs.

Lieutenant Haas explained in French about the tags and what each position meant: leader, left and right swing, left pointer, right pointer, left wheel and right wheel, and Scotty showed them how to harness the dogs.

"Tell them not to be afeerd," he cautioned Lieutenant Haas. "Tell them that a dog smells the fear scent on a mon and reacts to it ferociously."

"These men afraid!" Lieutenant Haas scoffed. "They are Frenchmen. They fear not dog, the Boche or the devil."

"A' right," Scotty said. "I forgot Frenchmen are never afeerd."

It was not difficult to teach the Chasseurs the few English words they must know in order to command the dogs. "Gee," "Haw," "whoa," and "mush" were sufficient.

"Mush on was originally a French term," Haas told him. "It is a corruption of the *marchons*, march on, first used by French traders in the North."

Twice a day the dogs, half at a time, were let off the chains. Scotty had the Chasseurs unsnap the buckles so that the dogs would get used to their new masters.

During these first manoeuvres Scotty kept himself well in sight, ready instantly to stop any trouble that might start. Any dog that came out growling, snarling, or showing any signs of ill-nature was instantly sent back to be tied up. The dogs were very sensitive to this sort of humiliation and the punishment was usually effective.

One day before entraining for the Front, Scotty went to Le Havre to get some new chains and snaps. While he was gone, the dogs got into a terrific fight. The Chasseurs were at a complete loss to know what to do and the dogs realized that no one was in real authority over them. When Scotty returned he found the biggest dog fight he had ever seen in progress.

He got busy with blacksnake and voice and in a short time he had the animals quelled, giving a good demonstration of how one small man could handle four hundred fighting dogs.

The following day they entrained for the Front in the Vosges Mountains. Scotty was given officers' quarters and was treated like one, although the French general in command was at first very sceptical as to the amount of services the dogs would be able to perform.

Scotty got busy amid exploding shells, showing what the dogs could do in snowy country. Before long the general was congratulating him on the amazing performance of the K9 Blue Devils, as they were now called.

There first feat was to carry ninety tons of ammunition to a battery that was cut off and out of shells and bullets. For two weeks horses and mules had been trying to get to the soldiers' rescue, without success. The dogs reached the isolated French battery within four days.

Another section of dogs strung more than twenty miles of telephone wire in a single night and so established communication with another detachment that had been cut off by the Germans.

On several occasions the dogs got ammunition and supplies to various detachments in the nick of time. By no other means could they have been reached.

There were also times when the speedy teams brought wounded men in on sledges to receive medical attention to save their lives.

When Scotty made his departure, the general told him that he did not see how his Chasseurs could possibly carry out their mountain operations successfully without his dogs . . .

Later Scotty was thrilled by the news that three of Baldy's descendants were decorated for valour in battle, and René Haas was made a captain because of his work with the K9 Corps.

After the war the wonderful dogs were given to the men who worked with them and learned to love them.

Little did anyone realise that these Alaskan dogs, many of them descendants of Baldy, would be used in another world-wide struggle. When the Japanese gained their first foot hold on the Aleutians, the huskies and the malemutes were ready again to lend their valuable services to soldiers.

from *Scotty Allan, King of the Dog-team Drivers*, 1948

Desmond Morris

Those disturbed individuals who pour out hatred for dogs are missing a great deal. And those who are merely interested are also losing out on an amazingly rewarding man/animal relationship. Since such people will almost certainly ignore this book, they will be unaware of an intriguing fact: people who keep dogs (and cats, for that matter) live longer on average than those who do not. This is not some kind of procanine campaigning fantasy. It is a simple medical fact that the calming influence of the company of a friendly pet animal reduces blood pressure and therefore the risk of heart attack. To stroke a cat, pat a dog or cuddle any sort of furry pet has a de-stressing influence that goes directly to the root of many of today's ailments. Most of us suffer from too much tension and stress in the hustle of modern urban living, where minute-by-minute considerations are frequently complex and demand a whole range of conflicting compromises. By contrast, the friendly contact of a pet dog or cat serves to remind us of the survival of simple, direct innocence even inside the dizzy whirlpool we refer to as advanced civilization.

from *Dogwatching,* 1986

CHAPTER 4

Dog Control

From Canute's Forest Laws (1016) to the 1991 Dangerous Dogs Act the means used to exert official control over dogs and constrain ownership have largely been repressive, inhumane, unjust and ineffective. At times they have even been politically cynical.

King Canute set aside "certaine territorie of woody grounds and fruitful pastures, privileged for wilde beasts and foules, chase and warren, to rest and abide in, in the safe protection of the King for his princely delight and pleasure". Anyone, not a freeman, who kept greyhounds within ten miles of the first could under his law have their dogs mutilated, a practice known as "hambling".

Additionally, all mastiffs kept in the proscribed area were required to be "expedited" – made lame.

A forefoot was placed "on a piece of wood eight inches thick and a foot square, and then setting a chisel of two inches broad upon the three claws, he struck them off with one blow of a mallet". The operation was carried out on both forefeet. "If any Mastiff was found on any wild animal and he was mutilated, he whose dog he was was quit of the deed; but if he was not mutilated, the owner of the mastiff was guilty as if he had given it with his own hand."

Small dogs – "because it stands to reason there is no danger in them" – could be kept without mutilation. A small dog was defined as one which could be passed through a metal hoop of about seven inches in diameter.

Surgical mutilation in various forms has continued to be a legal constraint, even reappearing, in the 1980s, when potentially dangerous breeds of dogs were required to be neutered, a campaign supported by welfare organizations and the veterinary profession.

The first Scottish Forest Laws of 1130 required that "both inhabitants of the wood and others are forbidden to enter any enclosure of the woods with their animals in time of pannage. . . . After this time and month eight cows shall be forfeit only if the beasts be found by the forester scattered with a keeper who has a fire or a horn or a dog which is called 'warset'."

Should a dog run after a beast into the king's forest a free man or hunter could follow his running dog, after first removing his bow and arrows.

If a greyhound was found running and causing damage within a forest, it was retained and presented to the forester or verderer, who in turn sent it to the king. A mastiff, however, was not guilty of any such offence if it were still chained to its owner!

The term "warset" was derived from "wardefet", meaning a watchdog used to prevent animals from straying. The law appears to differentiate between animals which had strayed into the forest and those which had legally been taken into it but had subsequently strayed.

Throughout successive reigns, especially those of Elizabeth I and James I, it became increasingly apparent that mutilation and even the threat of heavy fines were proving ineffective in controlling dog ownership. The problems were further increased as numerous exemptions to the law were sought and granted. Slowly mutilation fell from favour, not because of the cruelty involved or its effect on the dogs themselves, but simply because of its ineffectiveness.

In 1584 a statute of the University of Oxford allowed students to keep only a "spannell" and then only with the prior permission of the Vice-Chancellor. The same statute also discouraged students, on pain of a fine, from "encouraging an inordinate growth of hair".

In 1738 Edinburgh Magistrates ordered "that all dogs of the mastiff kind be forthwith put to death under penalty of £5 Sterling and imprisonment of the owner for twelve calendar months. Also all citizens and inhabitants to remove their dogs from the City and Liberties, empowering the City Guard and Town Officers to kill all dogs that are seen after 12 noon the next day. The Town Treasurer to pay 1/- Sterling reward for each dog killed."

The proclamation was a reaction to a bull bitch which belonged to James Grieg, a local butcher, which had indiscriminately attacked every dog it saw. Magistrates were convinced that the dog was mad and that it might well have infected a great many others.

Wholesale slaughter, such as the British Government considered prior to introducing the Dangerous Dogs Act, was also regarded as a legitimate method of control. During the 1665 outbreak of bubonic plague 40,000 dogs were destroyed in London in an effort to control the spread of infection. The plague spread through fleas which not only infested rats, but also, presumably, the dogs which might have killed the rats and thus reduce the spread of the epidemic.

Cynicism surfaced in 1791 when Mr George Clark addressed Parliament on the subject of a Tax upon Dogs as a means to raise funds for "effectually suppressing the oppressive practice of impressing seamen and more expeditions by manning the Royal Navy". Clark believed that more dogs were kept "for fancy or for pleasure, than from necessity" and that since they could be regarded as luxuries they should be taxed. Since he suggested that the tax should be collected by the collectors of the window tax we might also conclude that he also regarded windows as luxuries. However Clark was more honest than some of his successors and accepted that the tax "would no doubt cause a devastation among those creatures" and even considered the possibility that "laying the tax upon dogs will cause so many to be destroyed that the tax will be unproductive". He, therefore, set out to "enumerate some of the dangers and evils which arise from dogs" and so justify his proposal other than as a means to raise revenue. Foremost among these were the fear of rabies, the unnecessary consumption of food by dogs, the prevalence of poaching and harassment to farm livestock. Clark's proposals enjoyed the support of a small but vociferous minority but it was perhaps largely the prospect of raising an estimated £150,000 through such a dog tax which most attracted Parliament and led to several debates during the next five years. The anticipated annual income assumed that half a million households in Britain owned a dog, yielding £125,000, and taxation on the estimated 5,000 gentlemen who kept packs of dogs for hunting would yield another £25,000.

Press gangs continued for another forty years, until the 1830s, when they were were replaced by a form of taxation, which eventually became a dog licensing system which remained in force until 1986.

In 1983 the Dog Order (Northern Ireland) led to a new system of dog licensing with a £5 annual fee. In the first year 86,000 licences were issued, against 59,000 in the previous year. Unlicensed dogs were to be summarily destroyed. During the year 8,297 dogs were impounded and 2,167 handed in by owners who no longer wanted them. Of these 7,850 were destroyed.

In 1986 the British Government took a very different and far more realistic attitude towards dog control when it announced that it intended to abolish dog licensing which was costing £3.5 million to collect £750,000 in fees and was having no discernible effect as a means to control dog related problems.

Canute the Great

No meane person may keepe any Greyhounds: but freemen may keep Greyhounds, so that their knees be cut before the Verderors of the Forest and without cutting of their knees also, if they doe abide ten miles from the bounds of the Forest. But if they doe come any nearer to the Forest, they shall pay twelve pence for every mile: but if the Greyhounds bee found within the Forest, the master or owner of the Dog shall forfeit the Dog, and ten shillings to the King.

Para. 31, Carta de Foresta, of King Canutus a Dane, and a King of this realme, graunted at a Parliament holden at Winchester, in the yeare of our Lord 1016

Anonymous

Item the Mundaye afore Mychaelmes Daye cam in a dogge of Iohnsons of Denygtone, the shoemaker, and kyllyd .ii. dooes, and there the dogge was take up, and I sende to hym to wete wether he wold have the dogge agayne and he sende word nayer, and then I hynge hym upon a tre.

from *The Framlington Game Roll*, 1515

John Manwood

This verbe Expeditor, to make lame, or to make one halt, or unable to run, is a made Latine word, used in stead of Mutilo, to make one lame: and in the Assizes and Customes of the Forest, that were made in the time of Edward the First, there this word Mutilatus is used for Expeditatus, as a word of better Latine bee used for that purpose. Canutus, in his one and thirtieth Canon, doth call the lawing of dogges Genuiscissio; but that was a kind of cutting or laming of dogges in the hammes, and that sort of laming of dogs the old foresters were wont to call Hambling, or Hoxing, and of some Hocksynew-ing. King Henry the Second was the first that began to cut off the claws of the forefeet of mastives: And therefore he called that maner of torment of lawing dogs, Expeditatio Mastiuorum, the expeditating of mastives, taking that name (Expeditating) of making them lame and unable to run, Expede, of the hurt or mayhem that they have of the foot, by the cutting off of the three clawes of the forefoot.

from *A Treatise and Discourse of the Laws of the Forest*, 1598

George R. Jesse

The cutting of the knees of greyhounds, enforced by the laws of Canute, was one method of maiming dogs kept in or near forests, and incapacitating them for killing or chasing game. In the laws of Henry the First it is called "the wretched expedition of dogs," and Odericus Vitalis said of that king, "Reserving for his own sport the beasts of chace in the forests of England, he even caused all dogs kept on the verge of woods to be mutilated by having one of their claws chopped off, and reluctantly licensed some few of the greater nobles and his particular friends to have the privilege of hunting in their own forests." In the 14 Henry II. [*sic*] men of Northumberland were amerced 22s. 10d. for not cutting the feet of their dogs – "non truncaverant pedes canum suorum;" and in the 18th of the same reign, Roger Mantell and William Fitz Ralf rendered account to the Exchequer of the paunage of the king's forests throughout England for that and the previous year, paying £7 12s. for that year for the New Forest; £6 for Windsor, &c.; and among the smaller perquisites as bark, honey, wax, &c., 5s for each dog unexpedited – "et de 10s. pro 2 canibus non expedatis." John enforced the game laws rigorously, indeed, exceeded them, for, besides creating more forests, he, according to Henry de Knyghton, the canon of Leicester, ordered all dogs and mastiffs in every forest in the kingdom to be slaughtered. "Canes et mastivi per omnes forestas Angliae occiduntur." But it is probable the good canon's statement must be received with the usual reserve necessary when monks write of that king. King and clergy hated each other heartily.

Researches into the History of the British Dog from Ancient Laws, Charters, and Historical Records, with Original Anecdotes, and Illustrations of the Nature and Attributes of the Dog, from the Poets and Prose Writers of Ancient, Mediaeval, and Modern Times, 1866

Magnus VI Haakonsson, the Law-Reformer

Whoso shall set savage dog or tame bear on his neighbour shall suffer exile, provided always that no injuries arise from the assault. But if there shall be bruises, or bites arising therefrom so that the skin becomes blue or red, or if blood well up or drop upon the ground, then he who set the animal on shall be judged an outlaw, the people from roundabout the place where the attack occurred having been summoned to be witness to the assault.

The law holds it as firm-founded that no trust is to be put in a dog. He who possesses a savage dog shall fasten it to a stake in such a way that it shall not be able to reach men going and coming out of the house. And when a dog is tied up by the door of a shop, or of a tavern, or of a chamber in an upper story, he who fastens it shall see to it that the length of the tie between the dog's collar and the stake is not longer than two cubits [i.e. the length of two forearms]. If the dog is fastened in a bath-house, it shall not be fastened to the leg of the bench where it could reach and bite men walking about the floor. If a dog is tied up in a privy it must not be allowed to reach men going therein, or sitting on the seat, or stretching out for the wiping-cloth. If anyone shall tie a dog without due care, or in any other way than that which has been set out above, or if it shall bite any freeman so that his skin turn red or blue, or blood gushes out, the owner of the dog shall be fined three marcs.

Gragasse, c. 1270

William of Wykeham, Bishop of Winchester

Whereas we have convinced ourselves by clear proofs that some of the nuns of your house bring with them to church birds, rabbits, hounds and such like frivolous creatures, to which they give more heed than to the offices of the church, with frequent hindrance to their own psalmody and to that of their fellow nuns, and to the grievous peril of their souls, therefore we strictly forbid you, jointly and singly, in virtue of the obedience due to us, that from henceforth you do not presume to bring to church and birds, hounds, rabbits or other frivolous creatures that are harmful to good discipline. . . . What is more, because through hunting hounds, and other dogs living within the confines of your nunnery, the alms which should be given to the poor are devoured.

Letter to the nuns of Romsey Abbey, Hampshire, c. 1390

Revd Robert Poole

Remember the Sabbath day to keep it holy, and carefully attend the Worship of God. But bring no Dogs with you to church, and carefully attend the Worship. Consider where they are going when they bring Dogs with them to the Assembly of Divine Worship; disturbing the Congregation by their Noise and Clamour. Be thou careful, I say, of this Scandalous Thing, which all ought to be advised against as indecent.

from *A Choice of Seraphic Love,* 1724

Anonymous

The king's heighnes alsoe straightlie forbiddeth and inhibiteth that no person, whatsoever they be, presume to keep any greyhounds, mastiffs, hounds, or other doggs in the Court, then some small spanyells for ladies or for others: nor bring any unto the same except it be by the King's or Queen's commandment. But the said greyhounds and doggs to be kept in kennell and other meete places out of court as is convenient soe as the premisses duelie observed, and the houses abroade, may be swete, wholesome, cleane and well furnished as to a prince's house and state apperteyne.

Regulation of the Royal Household of Henry VIII, c. 1515

Jean de la Fontaine

But as they went, he spied his friend's bald scruff.
"What's that?" he questioned him. "'Tis naught,"
"How naught?" "Well, nothing much," "But what?"
"The collar of my chain, 'tis like enough,
Has caused the trifling mark you see."
"Your chain?" exclaimed the Wolf, "then you're not free
To come and go?" "Not always – but no matter."
"Indeed? It wouldn't do for me,"
Replied the starveling. "You may be fatter,
But I prefer my own sweet will
To all the riches of your platter."
Therewith he ran. I guess he's running still.

from "The Wolf and the Dog", 1668

William Byrd

The Captain's bitch killed a lamb yesterday, for which we put her into a house with a ram that beat her violently to break her of that bad custom.

from *Secret Diary for the Years* 1709–12

Horace Walpole

In London there is a more cruel campaign than that waged by the Russians: the streets are a very picture of the murder of the innocents

– one drives over nothing but poor dead dogs! The dear, good-natured, honest, sensible creatures! Christ! how can anybody hurt them? Nobody could but those Cherokees the English, who desire no better than to be halloo'd to blood: – one day Admiral Bynge, the next Lord George Sachville, and to-day the poor dogs!

Letter to Lord Stafford, c. 1780

Sir John Sinclair

The most unaccountable part of the conduct of the lower classes of people in many parishes and which can be least easily reconciled to the hardships of their situation, is their fondness for dogs. Almost every family has one, and some two or three. Even paupers were threatened to be struck off the poor's roll to make them part with them. There are 400 in the parish of Kilculmonel and Kilberry. The food devoured by them would fed 400 pigs, which at a year old, would sell for 400£. Deduct 40£ for prime cost, and 360£ would be the prime savings to this parish alone by such a substitution, besides preventing canine madness, worrying sheep, of which 140 were destroyed by dogs in eight miles in a few weeks.

Statistical Account of Scotland, 1791

Lt Col. Peter Hawker

If you have occasion to punish a dog, which I should recommend having recourse to as little as possible, never kick him, for by such means you may do him an injury. I know a sportsman in Hampshire who had the misfortune to lose a dog by giving him an unlucky kick! Always, therefore, flog your dog with a whip or switch. To do this, and, at the same time, avoid the risk of his getting loose, or biting you, hold his head between your knees, by which means you properly secure him, and have a full commend of his back, without being liable to strike in a tender part.

Instructions to Young Sportsmen, 1833

Anonymous

An Act to consolidate and amend the several laws relating to the cruel and improper treatment of animals and the mischiefs arising from the driving of cattle, and to make other provisions in regard there-to, laid down "that any person wantonly and cruelly beating, ill-treating, abusing, or torturing any Horse, Mare, Gelding, Bull, Ox, Cow, Heifer, Steer, Calf, Mule, Ass, Sheep, Lamb, Dog, or any other cattle, or domestic animal, or improperly driving the same whereby any mischief shall be done, shall upon conviction be fined or imprisoned."

"That any person keeping, or using, any House, Room, Pit, Ground, or other place, for running, baiting, or fighting any Bull, Bear, Badger, Dog, or other Animal (whether of a domestic or wild nature or kind), or for Cock-fighting, shall be liable to a penalty of £5 for every day he shall so keep and use the same."

The Humane Act, 1835, promoted by Mr Pease of the Society of Friends, J. G. Merriott of the SPCA and by W. A. Makinnon MP

Anonymous

The Chief Commissioner of the Metropolitan Police, in his monthly report to the Home Secretary with regard to the seizure of stray and ferocious dogs during the last month reports that no fewer than 1,530 dogs, for whom no owners could be found, were found and sent to the Dogs' Home at Battersea; 55 dogs were killed in the streets (36 by the police and 19 by private persons). An examination of these by veterinary surgeons showed that 18 suffered from rabies, 13 from epilepsy, 3 from convulsions, 1 not examined, 3 ferocious or mad, whilst 1 dog died from rabies at the Dogs' Home. No fewer than 144 persons were bitten by dogs during the month.

Kennel Gazette, July 1889

Thomas Huxley

One of the unpardonable sins, in the eyes of most people, is for a man to go about unlabelled. The world regards such a person as the police do an unmuzzled dog, not under proper control.

from *Evolution and Ethics*, 1893

Theophilus Marples

From the 17th February, when the latest metropolitan muzzling edict was put in force, up to the end of June, London has been depopulated of its itinerant canine population to the tune of something like 22,000 head of its inhabitants. Surely, such a wholesale onslaught must have cleared the city of most of the mongrel dogs which prowled about its streets to the peril of the public, and which propagate rabies more than any other section of the canine community. The receptacle for this colossal collection of canines has been the Battersea Dogs' Home, and which, plus the more respectable moiety claimed by their owners, have found their way to the lethal chamber and from thence to the crematorium, no more to act as a menace to humanity or a trouble to the tax collector. One London daily, in commenting on the case, points to the fact that England, as a manufacturing country, makes some use of almost all waste products in her manufactures, and asks is it to the credit of London that this huge mass of dog flesh should not be utilised in some way; but our contemporary suggests no uses for the carcases, or any part of them, beyond the idea that a 'Dogs' Home Residual Products Utilisation Company (Limited)' should be brought out at once. We quite agree with our contemporary that we do seem wanting in our scientific enterprise to allow so much, maybe very valuable, "material" to be destroyed. The hides of dogs free from disease certainly ought to be valuable; whilst the "oil" from dogs is, we believe, without equal for the cure of many human afflictions. Then again, as dogs are impervious to that dreadful human disease, consumption, it seems within the range of possibility that the lungs of these thousands of dogs might in some way be utilised for the alleviation, if not complete cure, of the disease in man, a disease from which so many are brought to an untimely end in this country. These are, of course, purely commercial and scientific questions, and as such do not come within the scope of subjects upon which this journal treats. In the same way, the subject of rabies is a purely medical and scientific question; yet as both relate to dogs, we are bound to touch upon them at times. It occurred to us that as the "poor dog" is the innocent cause of much agony and many deaths from hydrophobia, that he might be made the medium of alleviating human suffering, and possibly saving human life, by a utilisation of his carcase in some way or other. This would in a measure expiate his crimes in connection with rabies, of which, however, the dog has a good set off in his splendid life-saving deeds, which are written on the pages of history.

Our Dogs, 18 July 1896

Lt Col. Peter Hawker

Among the many lamentable cases of persons and animals getting bitten by mad dogs, we may safely say that nineteen in twenty of them originate from people keeping useless curs, which they turn loose to forage on the town, and for which there is paid no tax. (I always invoke the tax-gatherers, when I want to get rid of a nuisance; but, Lord knows, for no other purpose!) Let me suggest, therefore, that every one should have on his dog a collar, with name and address, by which the owners of dogs may be found, and be made to answer for any depredations committed by, or default in payment of duty for them. A muzzle may be added; or a penalty for not having one. Let all dogs that are found loose without collars be taken by the police, and advertised in their district; and if, within a certain time, no one comes forward to take charge of a dog and pay the tax (which, if an animal of any apparent value, plenty of people would be glad to do, on speculation, or for the chance of reward from the owner), let the magistrate have the full power of passing sentence of death. This may appear cruel; but the riddance of useless curs is a minor evil when compared to the distressing events that have so lately occurred in the metropolis. It may be asked, how are the dogs to be caught? But it would be a bad policy to publish the many ways which there are of doing this, at the risk of giving finishing lessons to dog-stealers.

from *Instructions to Young Sportsmen,* 1824

CHAPTER 5

Rural Pursuits

There are cogent arguments to advance for and against using dogs to pursue, kill or assist in the killing of other animals. It is not part of the purpose of this book to examine those arguments, still less to support one or other viewpoint. Whatever one thinks about the sports in which dogs were engaged for many hundreds of years – and still are – the simple and unavoidable fact is that sporting activities have produced the majority of the breeds now recognized by kennel clubs throughout the world. These breeds cannot be fully appreciated unless one is aware of the demands which shaped their temperament and appearance.

The conduct of field sports has over the years reflected changing definitions of sportsmanship and fair play. What was once acceptable behaviour is now regarded by many as abominable.

"Queen Elizabeth in her progress, in the fifteenth year of her reign, came to Berkeley Castle, where at this time Henry Lord Berkeley had a stately herd of red deer in a park near the castle called 'The Worthy', of which Henry Ligon was the keeper. During the time she stayed there she made such slaughter that twenty-seven stags were killed in the nets in one day and many others on that day and the next day stolen and havocked. When his lord, who was then at Callowden, heard about what had happened, he suddenly and impulsively ordered that 'The Worthy' should be disparked, because he had greatly delighted in his herd of game."

On this occasion the herd of red deer were slaughtered by the Queen and her attendants after they had been driven into nets by dogs.

"On Monday, August 17th [1591], at eight of the clock in the morning, her Highness took horse, with all her train, and rode into the park, where there was a delicate bower prepared, under which were placed her Highness' own musicians. After a sweet song, a girl dressed as a nymph gave the Queen a crossbow so that she could shoot at the deer. There were about thirty of them, in a paddock, and of this number she killed three or four and the Countess of Kildare one. Then her Majesty rode to Cowdray for dinner, and about six o'clock in the evening from a turret in the house, she saw sixteen bucks, all having a fair start, pulled down by greyhounds on the lawn."

Nor does the behaviour of human participants provide the only cause for comment. In America the behaviour of native foes showed that they had little semblance of understanding as to how immigrant British foxhunters and their imported packs of hounds expected them to behave. John Lawson writing in his *A New Voyage to Carolina* (1709) wrote that "the fox of Carolina is gray but smells not as the foxes in Great Britain and elsewhere. They have reddish hair about their ears and are generally very fat; yet I never saw anyone eat them. When hunted they make a sorry chace because they run up trees when pursued."

Xenophon

[Your hounds] ought to be big; and should have light, flat, well-knit heads. The lower part of the face should be sinewy and the eyes black, bright and prominent: face, large and broad, with a deep space between the eyes: ears long, thin and bare on the outside: neck long, soft and flexible: breast broad and fleshy: shoulder-blade not at much distance from the shoulders: the forelegs small, straight, round and firm: the bend in the legs square, sides not altogether deep but coming together in oblique fashion; loins fleshy and in size medium, neither too soft nor too hard, sides neither large nor small: rounded hips, fleshy at the back and not close together in the upper parts but contracted inwardly, the lower flanks themselves loose; tail long, straight, and pointed: thighs hard, lower thighs long, mobile and compact: legs much more highly developed before than behind, and somewhat slender: agile feet.

If your hounds are as I have described in appearance they will be strong, light, well proportioned, swift runners, bright eyed and clean mouthed.

In hunting they ought soon to learn to quit the beaten tracks, slanting their heads towards the ground, smelling at the tracks but dropping their ears downwards, and while they dart quick glances this way and that, and wag their tails, they should go forward in a body towards the lairs, making many deviations. When they are near the hare, then they should give the sign to the huntsman, by running about much more quickly than before, signifying by their eagerness, and with the head, their eye and their entire change of carriage, by their looking towards or at the hare's hiding-place, and moving their bodies forwards, backwards and sideways, by their obvious joy and delight, that they are near the hare.

They should pursue that animal unremittingly and steadily, with great noise and barking, penetrating everywhere where the hare does, and run quickly and vigorously after him, twisting with him this way and that, barking loudly withal. And let them not leave the track and return to the huntsman.

Apart from having such appearance and being fitted for such duties, they should be of the superior kind in spirit, in speed, in scent and in hair. In the first place they will show spirit if they do not leave scenting when the stifling heat comes on: and good at scent if they apprehend the hare in bare, dry and sunny localities at the advent of the dog-star; sound of foot if during the same season of the year their feet are not blistered when they run over mountainous grounds. As to the coating of the hair, it should be fine and thick and soft. As to colour, a dog ought not to be red or black or white altogether: a uniform colour is not a sign of breeding but rather of a common animal.

from *Cynegeticus,* fourth century BC

Horace (trans. Alexander Pope)

Up, up! cries Gluttony, 'tis break of-day,
Go drive the deer, and drag the finny-prey;
With hounds and horns go hunt an appetite —
So Russel did, but could not eat at night,
Call'd, happy dog! the beggar at his door,
And envied thirst and hunger to the poor.

from *The Sixth Epistle of the First Book*

Ovid

As when th' impatient greyhound, slipped from far,
Bounds o'er the glade to course the fearful hare,
She in her speed does all her safety lay,
And he with double speed pursues the prey;
O'erruns her at the sitting turn, but licks
His chaps in vain, yet blows upon the flix;
She seeks the shelter, which the neighbouring covert gives
And, gaining it, she doubts if yet she lives.

from *Metamorphoses,* Book IV

Edward the Confessor

To Randolph Peperking, and to his Kynlyng,
With Hart and Hynde, Doe and Bucke,
Hare and Foxe, Cat and Brocke,
Wyldfowle with his flocke,
Partridge, Fezant Hen, and Fezant Cocke,
With greene and wilde stub and stocke
To keepen, and two yoemen by all their might,
Both by day and eke by night,
And hounds for to hould,
Good, swift and bould,
Foure Greyhounds, and sixe Ratches,
For Hare and Foxe, and wyld Cattes.

Letter, c. 1050

Marco Polo

The Emperor hath two Barons who are own brothers, one called
Baian and the other Mingan; and these two are styled Chinuchi,
which is as much as to say, "The Keepers of the Mastiff Dogs".
Each of these brothers hath 10,000 men under his orders, each

body of 10,000 being dressed alike, the one in red and the other in blue, and whenever they accompany the Lord to the chase, they wear livery, in order to be recognised. Out of each body of 10,000 there are 2,000 men who are each in charge of one or more mastiffs, so that the whole number of these is very great. And when the Prince goes a-hunting, one of these Barons, with his 10,000 men and something like 5,000 dogs, goes towards the right, whilst the other goes towards the left with his party in like manner. The move along, all abreast of one another, so that the whole line extends over a full day's journey, and no animal can escape them. Truly it is a glorious sight to see the working of the dogs and the huntsmen on such an occasion. And as the Lord rides a-fowling across the plains, you will see these big hounds come tearing up, one pack after a bear, another pack after a stag, or some other beast, as it may hap, and running the game down now on this side and now on that, so that it is really a most delightful sport and spectacle.

from *Divisament dou Monde* 1298, translated by Sir Henry Yule

Anonymous

When he had heard Mass, and taken a hasty mouthful,
He hurried with his horn, hot for the hunting field.
Before the first beam of the sunshine brightened the earth
He and his knights were in the saddle, high on their horses.
Then the handy huntsmen coupled up their hounds,
Cast open the door of the kennel and called them out;
Blew loud on the bugles, three plain blasts;
Brachets bayed at the horns, and gave their brave cries;
Those which chased off were chivvied back and chastised;
A hundred hunters, as I have heard tell,
    Of the finest.
  Fewterers joined those at the trysts;
  Huntsmen uncoupled their hounds.
  The forest was woken and stirred
  By the echoing notes of the horn.

The wild beasts quivered at the cry of the questing hounds;
Deer ran through the dale, distracted by fear,
Hastened up the high slopes, but hotly were met
By the stout cries of the stable, staying their flight.
They let through the antlered harts, with their handsome heads,
For this fine lord had forbidden, in fermison time
That any man should molest the male of the deer.
The hinds were held in the valley with hey! and ware!,
The does driven with din to the depth of the dale.
Then the shimmering arrows slipped from the bowstring,
    and slanted,
Winging their way from every tree in the wood. Their broad
    heads pierced the bonny flanks of brown;
The deer brayed and bled, as on the banks they died.
The hurrying hunters still chased them, and harried them still;
Hunters came after with high hue of the horn,
Cleaving the cliffs with the clear noise of their cry.
The beasts which ran on and broke through the ranks of
    the bowmen
Died at the resayt, seized and dragged down by the dogs;
They were harried from the slopes and teased down to the streams,
So skilled were those who stood down at the sets,
And the greyhounds so great and so swift to grip them
And to fling them down, faster than one could follow
        With the flick of an eye.
    The lord, in high good humour,
    Now galloping, now on foot,
    Saw the merry day wear on
    Till the fall of night . . .

Hunters unhardled hounds beside the holt;
Rocks rang in the trees to the roar of horns.
Some hounds fell on the fewte left by the fox,
Using their craft to cross and cross again.
A kennet cries, the huntsman calls his name,
His fellow hounds, milling and snuffling, follow,
Romp on the track, racing on in a rabble.
The fox flees on before; they find him soon,
Settling to run as soon as he is in sight,

Crying his doom full clear with clamour and noise.
Many a thorny thicket he dodges through;
Loops back by many a bush, and lies to listen,
Leaping at last a hedge and a little ditch
To steal out secretly beside a spinney;
Thinks him away from the wood and the hounds with his wiles;
But now, unaware, finds himself faced by a fewterer,
With three grim greyhounds, eager to grasp him.
    He sees,
  And starts away again,
  And, still strong, flees,
Dismayed, but running yet
To his stronghold in the trees.
Then would your heart have been high with the cry of hounds,
When all the pack came on him, and pressed in pursuit.
They cried the view, and called such a curse on his head
That all the towering tops of the cliffs might have tumbles.
Here he met a halloo, when the hunters came on him;
There he was sworn at, and swerved at a snarling word.
Here he was threatened; there he was damned for a thief,
Unable to tarry, his trackers still at his tail.
Whenever he raked away to the fields, he was run at,
And as often went back to the wood, the wily Reynard.

from Sir Gawain and the Green Knight, fourteenth century

Edward, 2nd Duke of York

Rennyng hondis hunten i dveris maners, for sum folowying ye hert
fast at ye first, for thei good lightly and fast and whan thei han ronne
so a while thei han hyed hem so fast yat yei be reluixed and breethles,
and abiden stille and leven ye hert whan yei shuld enchace. This
manner of rennyng houndis men shulde fynde comonly in ye lande
of Basco and Spayne; yei be right good for ye weylde boor, but thei
ben not good for ye hert for thei ben not good to enchace at a longe
flight, but only for to a trest hym, for thei seche not wel, ne thei
rennen not wel, ne thei hunte not longe for yei be custumed to hunt
nye and at ye bigynnyng thei han shewed ye best.

Other maner of rennyng houndis ther byn ye which hunten somdele moor slowly and hevyli, but as thei begynne thei holde on all day. Thise houndis athresten not so sone an as ye othir, but thei bryng hym best bi maistrie and strengthe to his eende, for thei retreve and senteh ye fues better and ferther, for bicause yat yei byn somdele slow thei must hunt the hert from ferther and therfore thei sentyn better yan other yat goon hasteley with out abiding in to ye tyme that thei byn wery. A bold hounde shuld never pleyn, neither youle . . . A bold hound huntethe with ye wynde whan he seeth his tyme: and credeth his maistre and understondeth hym and doth as he biddeth hym. A bold hounde shuld not leve ye hert neither for wynde, neither for reyn, neither for hete ne for cold, ne for non evyl wedir; but in this tyme ther ben fewe soche: and also wel shuld he hunt ye hert by hym slef with out helpe of man as yif ye man were alway with hym . . . [They] shuld overcome ye hert wel and perfitly and maisterfully thorgh out al ye change. Thes houndes ben not so good and so pfite as ye bold houndes to aforesaid to move me by to seye some rennyng hondes with grete horrede taylles ye which were fulle good.

Rennynge houndes hunten in diveris maners, for sum folowyn ye hert fast at first for thei goon lightly and fast and whan thei han ronne so a while yei han hied hem so fast yat yei be reliuxed and breethles, and abiden stille, and leven ye herte whan yei shuld enchase.

This maner of rennyng houndes . . . be right good for ye weylde boor, but their ben not good for ye hert for thei ben not good to enchace at a longe flight.

Other maner of rennyng houndes ther byn ye which hunten somdele moor slowly and hevily, but as thei bigynne thei holde on alle day. Thise houndes athresten not so sone an hert as ye other, but thei bryng hym best by maistrie and strength to his eende, for thei retreve and senteth ye fues bettir and ferther, for bicause yat yei bene somdele slowe yei muste hunte the hert from ferther and therfore thei senten bettir than (the other). Thei ben wel wyse, for thei knowe wel that thei shuld not hunt ye chaunge; and thei ben not so wise for to dissevere ye hert fro ye chaunge for yei a bide stil and restif.

Thise houndes I hold full good, for ye hunter yat knoweth hem may wel helpe hem to sle ye hert. Noon of alle thies thre maneres of houndes, ne hunten not atte hert in Rutsomtyme, but if it be ye good bolde hounde ye whiche is best of akke other houndes.

The best sport yat men have is ye rennyng houndes; for yif ye hunte at hare, or at ye roo, or at buk, or at hert, or at any other beast with out greihound, it is a faire thinge and a pleasaunt to hym that loveth hem: ye sechyng and ye fyndyng is also a fair thing, and gret likyng to sle hym with strenght and for to se ye witt and ye knowleche yat god hath geven to good houndes, and for to se ye rekeveryng, and ye retreiving, and ye maistries, and sootiltees yat be in good houndews. For of greihoundes and othir nature of houndes, what ever thei be ne lesteth not ye disport; for a non a good greihounde, or a good Alaunt taketh, or failleth of ye beest; and so doon all maner of houndes save rennyng houndis, ye whiche moost hunt all ye day questyng and makyng gret melody in her langage, and seyng gret villeny and chydeng ye beest yat yei enchace, and therfore I hold me with hem bifore al othir nature of houndes for thei han moo virtues as me semeth yan every other beest.

from *Mayster of the Game*, 1406–13

Gace de la Vigne

Later you may hear hunters talk of their sport,
And for me there can be no finer pastime in the world.
I believe no ears ever heard such dazzling marvels;
Even the King has to smile a little at what he hears.
Still, I shall forbear to suggest that untruths are said
– However much the ill-natured may hint at falsehood –
For in hunting there are feats so frequent and so testing
That the layman would refuse them credence.

from *Poème sur la Chasse*, 1359

Dame Julyans Barnes

With the bowellis and with the bloode
Rewarde ye yowre howndis, my sonnys so goode;

And eche foote ye shall cutte in .iiii., I yow kenne.
Take the bowellis and the bloode and do all togedre then.
Yevyth hit then to yowre howndys so,
And moche the glaadder then thay will go.

from *Boke of St Albans*, 1479

Sir Thomas More

What greater pleasure is there to be felte, when a dogge followeth a
hare, than when a dogge followeth a dogge? For one thing is done in
bothe, that is to saye, runnynge, yf thou haste pleasure therein. Byt
yf the hope of slaughter and the expectation of tearynge in peces the
beaste doth please thee; thou shouldst rather be moved with pities to
see a selye innocente hare murdered by a dogge.

from *Utopia*, 1516

Martin Luther

I was lately two days sporting in the country; we killed a brace of
hares and took some partridges, a very pretty employment for an idle
man! However, I could not help theologizing amidst dogs, missile
weapons and nets; for I thought to myself, do not we, in hunting
innocent animals to death, very much resemble the devil who by
crafty wiles, and the instrument of wicked priests, is seeking
continually whom he may devour?

from *Letters and Sermons*, c. 1535

Abraham Fleming

That kinds of dogge whom nature hath indued with the vertue of
smelling, whose property it is to use a lustiness, a readiness, and a
courageousnes in hunting, and draweth into his nostrells the ayre or
sent of the beast pursued and followed, we called by this word *Sagax*,

the *Grecians* by thys word ετ of tracing or chasing by ye foote, or ατ of the nostrells, which be the instruments of smelling. Wee may knowe these kinde of Dogges by their long, large, and bagging lippes, by their hanging eares, reachyng downe both sydes of their chappes, and by the indifferent and measurable proportion of their making. This sort of Dogges we call *Levararios* Hariers, that I may comprise the whole number of them in certaine specialities, and apply to them their proper and peculier names, for so much as they cannot all be reduced and brought under one sorte, considering both the sundrye uses of them, and the difference of their service whereto they be appointed.

	the Hare	
	the Foxe	
	the Wolfe	
	the Harte	
	the Bucke	
Some for	the Badger	Some for one thing and
	The Otter	some for another.
	The Polcat	
	The Lobster	
	The Weasell	
	The Conny, &c. . . .	

Another sorte there is which hunteth the Foxe and the Badger or Greye onely, whom we call Terrars, because they (after the maner and custome of ferrets in searching for Connyes) creepe into the grounde, and by that means make afrayde, nyppe, and byte the Foxe and the Badger in such sort, that eyther they teare them in pieces with theyr teeth beyng in the bosome of the erth, or else hayle and pull them perforce out of their lurking angles, darke dongens, and close caves, or at the least through coceved feare, drive them out of their hollow harbours, in so much that they are compelled to prepare speedy flight, and being desirous of the next (albeit not the safest) refuge, are otherwise taken and intrapped with snares and nettes layde over holes to the same purpose. But these be the least in that kynde called *Sagax*.

Of the Dogge called the Gasehounde, in Latine *Agaseus*.

This kinde of Dogge which pursueth by the eye, prevayleth little, or never a whit, by any benefite of the nose that is by smelling, but excelleth in perspicuitie and sharpnesse of sight altogether, by the vertue whereof, being singuler and notable, it hunteth the Foxe and the Hare. . . . These Dogges are much and usually occupied in the Northern partes of England amore then in the Southern parts, and in fealdy landes rather then in bushy and woddy places, horsemen use them more then footmen to th'intent that they might provoke their horses to a swift galloppe (wherwith they are more delighted then with the pray it selfe), and that they might accustome theyr horse to leape over hedges and ditches. . . .

There is another kinde of dogge which for his incredible swiftenesse is called *Leporarius* a Grehounde because the principall service of them dependeth and consisteth in starting and hunting the hare, which Dogges likewyse are indued with no lesse strength then lightnes in maintenance of the game, in serving the chase, in taking the Bucke, the Harte, the Dowe, the Foxe, and other beastes of semblance kinde ordained for the game of hunting.

Another sort of dogges be there, in smelling singuler, and in swiftnesse incomparable. This is (as it were) a myddle kinde betwixt the Harrier and the Grehounde, as well for his kinde, as for the frame of his body. And it is called in latine *Levinarius, a Levitate*, of lyghtnesse, and therefore may well be called a lyght hounde, it is also called by this worde *Lorarius, a Loro*, wherewith it is led. This Dogge for the excellency of his conditions, namely smelling and swift running, doth followe the game with more eagernes, and taketh the pray with a jolly quicknes.

Of the Dogge called a Tumbler, in Latine *Vertagus*.

This sorte of Dogges, which compasseth all by craftes, fraudes, subtelties and deceiptes, we Englishe men call Tumblers, because in hunting they turne and tumble, winding their bodyes about in circle wise, and then fearcely and violently venturing upon the beast, doth soddenly gripe it, at the very entrance and mouth of their receptacles, or closets before they can recover meanes, to save and succour themselves. This dogge useth another craft and subteltie, namely, when he runneth into a warren, or setteth a course about a connyburrough, he huntes not after them, he fayes them not by barcking, he makes no countenance or show of hatred against them, but dissembling friendship, and pretending favour, passeth by with silence and quietness, marking and noting their holes diligently, wherin (I warrant you) he will not be overshot nor deceaved. When he commeth to the place where

Connyes be, of a certaintie, he cowcheth downe close with his belly to the ground, Provided alwayes by his skill and polisie, that ye the winde bee never with him but against him in such an enterprise. And that the Connyes spie him not where he lurcketh. By which meanes he obtaineth the sent and savour of the Connyes, carryed towardes him with the wind & the ayre, either going to their holes, or coming out, eyther passing this way, or running that way, and so provideth by his circumspection, that the selly simple Conny is debarred quite from his hole (which is the haven of their hope and the harbour of their health) and fraudiulently circumvented and taken, before they can get the advantage of their hole. Thus having caught his pray he carryeth it speedily to his Master, wayting his Dogges returne in some conveneient lurcking corner.

from *Of Englishe Dogges*, 1576

George Turbervile

Ther are sundrie sortes of Terriers, whereof wee hold opinion that one sorte came out of Flaunders or the low Countries, as Artoys and thereabouts, and they have crooked legges, and are shorte heared moste commonly. Another sorte there is which are shagged and streight legged: those with the crooked legges will take earth better than the other, and are better for the Badgerd, bycause they will lye longer at a vermine: but the others with streight legges do serve for twoo purposes, for they wyll Hunte above the grounde as well as other houndes, and enter the earthe with more furie than the others: but they will not abide so long, bycause they are too eagre in fight, and therefore are constreyned to come out to take the ayre: there are both good and badde of bothe sortes.

You shall beginne to enter them as soone as they be eyght or tenne moneths old: for if you enter not a Terrier before he be a yeare old, you shall hardly make him take the earth. And you must take goode heede that you encourage them, and rebuke them not at the firste: nor that the Foxe or Badgerd do hurt them within the earth, for then they will never love the earth agayne. And therefore never enter a yong Terryer in an earth where there is an olde Foxe or Badgerd: But first lette them be well entred, and be a yeare old full or more. You shall do well also to put an old Terryer before them which may abide and endure the furie of the Foxe or Badgerd. You may enter them and fleshe them sundrie wayes. First when Foxes and Badgerds have yong cubbes, take all your olde Terryers and put then into the grounde: and when they beginne to baye (which in the earth is called yearning), you muste holde your yong Terryers every one of them at a sundrie hole of some angle or mouth of the earth, that they may herken and heare theyr fellowes yearne. And when you have taken the old Foxes and Badgerdes, and that there is nothing left in the earth but the yong Cubbes, take out then all your old Terryers, and couple then, crying, To him, To him, To him; and if they take any yong Cubbe, lette them take theyr pleasure of him, and kill him within the grounde: and beware that the earth fall not downe upon them and smoother them. That done, take all the rest of the Cubbes and Badgerds pigges home with you, and frie theyr livers and theyr bloud with cheese, and some of theyr owne greace, and thereof make your Terryers a rewarde . . .

He that will be present at such pastimes, may do well to be booted: For I have lent a Foxe or a Badgerd ere nowe, a piece of my hose, and the skyn and fleshe for companie, which he never restored agayne.

from The Noble Arte of Venerie or Hunting, 1576

Sir John Harington

And as the hound that men the tumbler name,
When a hare or cunnie doth espie,
Seemeth another way to course to frame,
As though he meant not to approch more nie
But yet he meeteth at the last his game,
And shaketh it vntill he make it die.

from Orlando Furioso, 1591

Cervantes

"Mercy on me, what pleasure can you find, any of ye all, in killing a poor beast that never meant any harm!"

"You are mistaken, Sancho: hunting wild beasts is the most proper exercise for knights and princes; for in the chase of a stout noble beast, may be represented the whole art of war, stratagems, policy, and ambuscades, with all other devices usually practised to overcome an enemy with safety. Here we are exposed to the extremities of heat and cold: ease and laziness can have no room in this diversion. By this we are inured to toil and hardship; our limbs are strengthened, our joints made supple, and our whole body hale and active: in short, it is an exercise that may be beneficial to many, and can be prejudicial to none."

from *The Adventures of Don Quixote de la Mancha*, 1605

John Taylor

After we had stayed there three hours or thereabouts, we might perceive the deer appear on the hill round about us (there heads making a show like wood), which, being followed by Tinchel, are chased down into the valley, with a hundred couple of strong Irish grey-hounds. they are let loose as occasion serves upon the herd of deer.

from *The Pennylesse Pilgrimage, All the Workes of John Taylor, the Water Poet*, 1630

Lord William Pitt Lennox

In the year 1638 lived Mr Hastings, second son of an Earl of Huntingdon. He was, peradventure, an original in our age, or rather the copy of our ancient nobility in hunting, not in warlike times. He was very low, very strong, and very active, of a reddish flaxen hair. His clothes, always green cloth, and never worth (when new) five pounds; his house was perfectly of the old fashion, in the midst of a large park, well stocked with deer, and near the house rabbits to deserve his kitchen; many fish-ponds, great store of wood and timber, a bowling green in it (long and narrow), full of high ridges, it being never levelled since it was ploughed. They used round lead bowls, and it had a banqueting house, like a stand, built in a tree.

He kept all manner of sport-hounds, that ran buck, fox, hare, otter and badger; and hawks, long and short-winged. He had all sorts of nets for fish; he had a walk in the New Forest and the Manor of Christ Church.

This last kept him well supplied with red deer, sea and river fish; and, indeed, all his neighbours grounds and royalties were free to him, who bestowed all his time in these sports. He was popular with his neighbours; and was ever a welcome guest at their houses; he, too, kept open house, where beef, pudding and small beer were to be had in plenty; his great hall was full of marrow bones, and full of hawk's perches, hounds, spaniels and terriers, the upper side of which was hung with fox's brushes, here and there a polecat intermixed.

The parlour was a very large room, and properly furnished. On a great hearth, paved with brick, lay some terriers, and the choicest hounds and spaniels. Seldom but two of the great chairs had litters of young cats in them, which were not to be disturbed, he having always three or four attending him at dinner, and a little white round stick of fourteen inches lying by his trencher, that he might defend such meat as he had no mind to part with to them.

from *Recreations of a Sportsman,* 1862

Jean de la Fontaine

The argument was very sound,
And coming from a master's mouth
Would have been lauded for its truth.
But since the author was a hound,
Its merit went unrecognized.

"The Farmer, the Dog, and the Fox", 1668

John Aubrey

It was the Right hon. Philip Earle of Pembroke, that was the great Hunter. It was in his Lordship's time (cs. tempore Jacobi I and Caroli I) a serene calme of Peace, that Hunting was at its greatest Heigth that ever was in tis Nation. The Roman Governours had not (I thinke) the leisure; the Saxons were never at quiet; and the Baron's Warres, and these of Yorke and Lancaster, took up the greatest part of the time since the Conquest: So that the Glory of the English Hunting breath'd its last with this Earle: who deceased about 1644, and shortly after the Forests and Parkes were sold, and converted into Arable.

'Twas after his Lordship's Decease, that I was a Hunter: that is to say with the right Honble William, Lord Herbert of Cardiff, the aforesaid Philip's Grandson.

This present Earl of Pembroke (1680) has at Wilton, 52 Mastives and 30 Grey-hounds, some Bears, and a Lyon, and a matter of 60 fellowes more bestial than they.

from *Brief Lives*, 1693

Alexander Pope

To plains with well-breath'd beagles we repair,
And trace the mazes of the circling hare:
(Beasts, urged by us, their fellow beast pursue,
And learn of man each other to undo).

from "Windsor Forest: Winter," 1713

Thomas Tickell

Seest thou the gaze-hound! how, with glance severe,
From the close herd he marks the destin'd deer:
How ev'ry nerve the greyhound's stretch displays,
The hare preventing in her airy maze;

The luckless prey how treach'rous tumblers gain,
And dauntless wolf-dogs shake the lion's mane:
O'er all, the bloodhound boasts superior skill
To scent, to view, to turn, and boldly kill. –
His fellows' vain alarms rejects with scorn,
True to the master's voice and learned horn: –
His nostrils oft, if ancient fame sing true,
Traced the sly felon thro' the tainted dew;
Once snuff'd, he follows with unalter'd game:
Nor odours lure him from the chosen game;
Deep-mouth'd he thunders, and inflamed he views,
Springs on relentless, and to death pursues.

from *Hunting*, eighteenth century

Anonymous

Let Terriers small be bred, and taught to bay,
When Foxes find unstopt Badjers earthe,
To guide the Delvers, where to sink the Trench;
Peculiar in their breed, to some unknown,
Who choose a fighting biting Curr, who lyes
And is scarce heard, but often kills the Fox;
With such a one, bid him a Beagle join,
The smallest kind, my Nymphs for Hare do use,
That Cross gives Nose, and wisdom to come in
When Foxes earth, and hounds all bayeing stand.

quoted in the "Records of the Old Charlton Hunt
by the Earl of March", the poem is dated 1737

James Macpherson

"Call," said Fingal, "call to the chase,
Dogs slim and choice in travelling the moor:
Call Bran of the whitest chest;
Call Neart and Kiar and Lu-a;

Fillan, Ryno – he is in his grave,
My son is in the sleep of death!
Fillan and Fergus, blow the horn;
Let joy arise on hill and cairn,
Let deer start up in Cromala,
And by the lake of roes – their home.

The shrill sound rang throughout the wood;
Slowly started a herd in Chrome.
A thousand dogs sprang over the heath;
A deer fell down to every dog:
Fell three to Bran alone;
And towards Fionn he turned the three,
To give great joy to the king.

from *Fingal, an Ancient Epic Poem,* 1762

William Taplin

Previous to the present improved state of hunting, and polish of field sports, packs of beagles were frequently seen in the possession of gentlemen whose age and infirmities prevented their enjoyment of sport of a different description; but in proportion to the gradational improvements made in the different kinds of hounds (according to the different chases they were intended to pursue), the former attachment to beagles has been observed to decline. They are the smallest of the hound race used in this country, are exquisite in their scent of the hare, and indefatigably vigilant in the pursuit of her. Though wonderfully inferior in point of speed, yet equally energetic in persevering pursuit, they follow her through all her windings, unravel all her mazes, explore her labyrinths, and by the scent alone trace, and retrace her footsteps to a degree of admiration that must be seen to be properly understood; during all of which the soft and melodious tone of their emulous vociferation seems to be the most predominant inducement to the well-known ecstatic pleasures of the chase.

This slow kind of hunting was admirably adapted to age and the feminine gender; it could be enjoyed by ladies of the greatest timidity as well as gentlemen labouring under infirmity; to both of whom it was a consolation, that if they were occasionally a little way behind, there was barely a possibility of their being thrown out. A pack of this description was perfectly accommodating to the neighbouring rustics, the major part of those not being possessed of horses found it a matter of no great difficulty to be well up with them on foot. The spirit of emulation seemed formerly to be who should produce the greatest degree of merit in the smallest compass; and packs were to be seen in different parts of the most diminutive description.

from *The Sportsman's Cabinet,* 1803

Thomas Bewick

The Terrier has a most acute smell, is generally an attendant on every pack of Hounds, and is very expert in forcing Foxes or other game out of their coverts. It is the determined enemy of all the vermin kind; such as Weasels, Foumarts, Badgers, Rats, Mice, &c. It is fierce, keen, and hardy; and in its encounters with the Badger, sometimes meets with very severe treatment, which it sustains with great courage and fortitude. A well-trained Dog frequently proves more than a match for that hard-biting animal.

There are two kinds of Terriers, – the one rough, short-legged, long-backed, very strong, and most commonly of a black or yellowish colour, mixed with white; the other is smooth, sleek, and beautifully formed, having a shorter body, and more sprightly appearance: it is generally of a reddish brown colour, or black, with tanned legs; and is similar to the rough Terrier in disposition and faculties, but inferior in size, strength, and hardiness.

from *History of Quadrupeds,* 1790

Sir Walter Scott

The eager pack, from coules freed,
    Sash through the bush, the brier, the brake,

While, answering hound, and horn and steed,
   The mountain echoes starting wake.

from "The Wild Huntsman", *c.* 1810

Two dogs of black Saint Hubert's breed,
Unmatch'd for courage, breath, and speed,
Fast on his flying traces came,
And all but won that desperate game;
For, scarce a spear's length from his haunch,
Vindictive toil'd the blood hounds stanch;
Nor nearer might the dogs attain,
Nor farther might the quarry strain.

from "*The Lady of the Lake*," 1810

The Druid (pseud.)

During the summer he spent nearly all his time among "my lambs," and cared very little to wander afield. The Yarborough, Beaufort, and Belvoir kennels were what he principally used; but during his last two seasons he dipped deeply into Mr Selby Lowndes's Royal, an old-fashioned-looking dog, and rather wild in his work. "Ah! my lad, the dam is the secret," was his constant remark to young huntsmen. Like most reserved men, he was tough in his opinion, both in the field and the kennel, and no one but the boiler knew what the puppies were by, till they were ready to go out to quarters. He hung very much to the notion that in breeding two negatives would make a positive, both in style of work and make, and enforced it pretty generally in all his correspondence. It was delightful to hear him tell, almost under his breath, when you asked after the cream of entry, that they were "perhaps just the most beautiful I ever had," and believing himself most implicitly, summer after summer. "A thing of beauty" was most truly his "joy for ever." If he was showing one of his hounds, which he thought a little out of the common way, he would indicate his delight by thrusting his hands deep into his breeches pocket, and kicking out his little right leg. He would then draw his hand over the hound from head to stern, and remark, in his gentle tone, that "it couldn't be more beautiful if it had been spoke-shaved."

from *Scott and Sebright*, 1842

Angus Bethune Reach

I may as well state here that the country weavers of Saddleworth are, like Nimrod, mighty hunters. Every third or fourth man keeps his beagle or his brace of beagles, and the gentlemen who subscribe to the district hunt pay the taxes on the dogs. There are no foxes in Saddleworth – the country, indeed, is too bare for them to pick a living: but hares abound, and occasionally the people have "trail" hunts – the quarry being a herring or a bit of rag dipped in oil, dragged across the country by an active runner, with an hour's law. A few, but only a very few, pursue the sport on horseback; the weavers, who form the great majority of the hunt, trusting to their own sound lungs and well-strung sinews to keep within sight of the dogs. Even the discipline of the mills is as yet in many instances insufficient to check this inherent passion for the chase. My informant, himself a millowner, told me that he had recently arranged a hunt to try the mettle of some dogs from another part of Yorkshire against the native breed. He had tried to keep the matter as quiet as he could but it somehow leaked out, and that more than 500 carders, slubbers, spinners, and weavers formed the field. The masters, however, are often too keen sportsmen themselves to grudge their hands an occasional holiday of the sort. The Saddleworth weavers must be excellent fellows to run. A year or two ago, a gentleman, resident there, purchased a fox at Huddersfield, and turned him loose at Upper Mill, a spot almost in the centre of the hills. There started on the trail upwards of 300 sports, men on foot. Reynard led the chase nearly to Manchester, a distance of about twenty miles, and then doubled back almost to the place where he was unbagged, favouring his pursuers with an additional score of miles' amusement. Of the 300 starters, upwards of twenty-five were in at the death.

from "The Rural Cloth-Workers of Yorkshire", the *Morning Chronicle*, 1849

Scrutator (pseud.)

An old hound I had, called Pilgrim, showed most extraordinary sagacity one day which may be considered too romantic to be true, but I vouch for the fact. He was out with us in the early part of the season, when we brought a fox to our home coverts and ran him to ground there in a large rabbit pipe. As we tried on for another fox the earth was stopped up, but not finding again, I returned home and fed the hounds. Old Pilgrim was with us then, and the terriers, which after feeding were, as usual, let run about. This was about two o'clock in the day.

At four o'clock I went down to see the hounds again, and, not finding the terriers or old Pilgrim in their usual sleeping apartment, I made inquiries where they were. No one could tell; but the feeder had seen them about an hour previously in the yard together. We searched and looked everywhere for them, but in vain. It being a fine afternoon, and having nothing to do, I walked across to the covert where we had run the fox to ground in the morning, to see if he had scratched his way out again, as some loose stones only had been thrown into the earth. Great, indeed, was my surprise when I discovered old Pilgrim lying at the mouth of the pipe, having removed all the stones, and dug a hole nearly large enough to hold himself; greater still was my surprise, when upon listening at the earth, I heard the two terriers inside at the fox.

The old dog wagged his tail, and gave me a knowing look, as much as to say, "That will do, we shall soon have him out;" and I was so much pleased with his cunning, that I resolved he should not be disappointed. I accordingly hallooed to a man I saw at work, and sent him home for the whipper-in and a spade. We soon dug the fox out, and carried him home in a sack. Nothing could exceed the delight of the old hound when he saw the fox safely bagged – he danced and jumped about, and led the way in high glee, as much as to say, "Here he come! this is my doing." Having deposited the fox in a safe place, the old hound appeared quite satisfied; but when it became dark, we turned him loose again.

from Letters on the Management of Hounds, 1852

(Robert Smith) Surtees

And but for the fortunate friendship of Abraham Brown, the village blacksmith, who had given his young idea a sporting turn, entering him with ferrets and rabbits, and so training him on with terriers and rat-catching, badger-baiting, and otter-hunting, up to the noble sport of fox-hunting itself, in all probability his lordship would have been a regular miser. As it was, he did not spend a halfpenny upon anything but hunting.

from Mr Sponge's Sporting Tour, 1853

Sir J. Eardley-Wilmot

Nor was Mr Smith in any way sparing of expense in securing the very best blood for his pack. In addition to Sir R. Sutton's hounds, he bought those belonging to Sir Thomas Boughey, and, later, the pack of the Duke of Grafton. In particular he prized most highly the stock of Mr Warde, and, as a proof of this, on one occasion he deputed Mr F— to offer Mr Horlock, who had purchased Mr Warde's pack for £2000, 1000 guineas for twenty couples, which Mr Smith was to pick out from the kennel, without any other to guide him than his own well-practised eye, in making the selection.

One of the most surprising, and at the same time interesting, scenes to witness was the "fascination" he seemed to possess over hounds, and the strong attachment they always evinced towards their master. "I recollect," relates one of his friends, "his once having out five couples of drafts whom he had never seen before. Sharp, his kennel huntsman at that time, gave him their names written down; he then called each hound separately, and after giving him a piece of bread, returned the list to the huntsman, saying, "I know them now;" and so they did him. On other occasions when the fixture was "Dare Hill" and the hounds were awaiting his arrival, Dick Buton used to say, "Master is coming I perceive by the hounds;" and this, too, long before he made his appearance. When he came within three hundred yards, no huntsman or whip in the world could have stopped the pack from bounding to meet him. In the morning when let loose from the kennel, they would rush to his study window or to the hall door, and stand there till he came out. . . .

It may not be out of place here to describe the animated and interesting scene which invariably occurred when the squire joined his hounds at the meet. Directly he appeared, every hound rushed towards him, and if ever there was a hearty welcome given to man by "dumb animals", theirs was that welcome. It could not be said, however, to be given by "dumb animals", for each hound had a peculiar winning note of its own to express its joy, and no one could for a moment doubt the reciprocal delight both of master and hounds. This was the more singular as Mr Smith never fed his hounds in the kennel, but, directly the hunting was over for the day, he mounted his hack and galloped home, while the hounds returned quietly with the whippers-in.

from *The Reminiscences of a Fox-hunter*, 1860

Surtees

Wideawake was a yellow or light tan-coloured hound, with bright hazel eyes and a very Spanish-pointer-like head and expression of countenance. Indeed Jack Rogers, who was a bit of a utilitarian, used to say he wouldn't despair of making him point still. He – the hound, that is to say – stood twenty-five inches high, with a drooping kangaroo-like back, terminating in a very abruptly docked tail, looking, indeed, more like an Italian iron, as used in laundries, than a hound's stern. Nor were his personal defects his sole demerits. He ran mute, and being a queer, unaccountable-looking animal, was often taken for a stag as for a hound. "Yeas, ar seed him," the countrymen would reply to Jack's inquiry if they had seen the stag, "yeas, ar seed him: short tail and arl, a-goin as hard as ivir he could lick."

Wiseacre was a different description of animal, being of the bull-dog-like order, black and white in colour; very much the sort of animal one sees chained under a carrier's cart. He was short and thick, with a bald face, loaded shoulders, crooked legs, and flat feet. Unlike Wideawake, he was of the vociferous order; and though he did not throw his tongue prodigally, he yet did it in such a solemn sententious sort of way as always to carry conviction to the pack. He could hunt both the stag and Wideawake, and run under Wide-awake's belly when he came up with anything. Between the two, Jack reckoned he could catch almost anything; Wideawake making the running, and Wiseacre keeping the clamorous party on the line.

from *Mr Facey Romford's Hounds*, 1865

John Woodcock Graves

Did ye ken John Peel wie his cwote seay gray,
Did ye ken John Peel at the breck o'day;
Did ye ken John Peel gang far – far away,
Wid his hounds an' his horn in the mwornin'.

For the sound of his horn cawt me frae my bed,
An' the cry o' the hounds has me oft me led
John Peel's view-hollo wad 'waken the dead
Or a fox frae his lair in a mwornin'.

Did ye ken that bitch whaes tongue was death?
Did ye ken her sons of peerless faith?
Did ye ken that a fox wid his last breath
Curst them, O, as he died in the mwornin'.

Yes, I kenn'd John Peel, an aul Ruby, too,
Ranter and Royal and Bellman as true;
Fra the drag to the chase, an' the chase to the view,
An' the view to the deeth in a mwornin'.

An' I kenn'd John Peel beath oft an' far,
Ower many a "yett" an' toplin bar,

Fra Low Dentonhowm up to Scratchmere Scar,
When we struggled for the brush in the mwornin'.

Here's to John Peel fra the heart an' the soul;
Come fill, O fill to him another bowl;
An' swear that we'll follow thro' fair an' fouwl,
Wheyle weare waked by his horn in the mwornin'.
    'Twas the sound of his horn etc.,

"D'ye ken John Peel?",

from the original dialect manuscript, early nineteenth century

Somerville and Ross (pseud.)

Throughout these excursions I noticed, as far I was able to notice anything, the independent methods of the O'Reilly draft. They ignored the horn, eluded Michael, and laughed at Hickey and me; they hunted with bloodthirsty intentness and entirely after their own devices. Their first achievement was to run the earth-stopper's dog, and having killed him, to eat him. This horrid feat they accomplished, secure from interruption, in the briary depths of the ravine, and while the main body of the pack were industriously tow-rowing up and down the stream after their lawful fox, a couple of goats were only saved from the Whiteboys by miracles of agility and courage on the part of the countrymen. The best that could be said of them was that, "linking one virtue to a thousand crimes," whenever the hounds got fairly out of covert, the Whiteboys were together, and were in front.

It was about eight o'clock, and the fierce red and grey sunrise had been overridden by a regiment of stormy clouds, when one of the foxes met his fate, amid ear-piercing whoops, and ecstatic comments from the onlookers, who had descended from the hill-tops with the speed of ski-runners.

"Aha! that's the lad had many a fat duck under his rib!"

"He had, faith! I'll go bail 'twas him that picked me wife's fashionable cocks!"

from "The Man that came to Buy Apples",
Further Experiences of an Irish R. M., 1908

John Masefield

He halted at the Cock and Pye,
The hounds drew round him on the green,
Arrogant, Daffodil and Queen,
Closest, but all in little space.
Some lolled their tongues, some made grimace,
Yawning, or tilting nose in quest,
All stood and looked about with zest,
They were uneasy as they waited.
Their sires and dams had been well-mated,
They were a lovely pack for looks;
Their forelegs drumsticked without crooks,
Straight, without over-tread or bend,
Muscled to gallop to the end,
With neat feet round as any cat's,
Bright, clean, short-coupled, broad in shoulder,
With stag-like eyes that seemed to smoulder.
The heads well-cocked, the clean necks strong,
And all like racers in the thighs;
Their minds being memories of smells;
Their voices like a ring of bells;
Their colours like the English weather,
Magpie and hare, and badger-pye,
Like minglings in a double dye,
Some smutty-nosed, some tan, none bald;
Their manners were to come when called,
Their flesh was sinew knit to bone,
Their courage like a banner blown.
Their joy to push him out of cover,
And hunt him till they rolled him over.

from *Reynard the Fox, or
The Ghost Heath Run,* 1919

Richard Jefferies

There ain't no such chaps for poaching as they navigators in all England: I means where there be a railway a-making. I've knowed forty of 'em go out together on a Sunday, and every man had a dog, and some two; and good dogs too – lots of 'em as you wouldn't buy for ten quid. They used to spread out like, and sweep the field clean as the crown of your hat. Keepers weren't no good at all, and besides they never knowed which place us was going to make for. One of the chap gave I a puppy, and he growed into the finest greyhound as you'd find in a day's walk. The first time I was took up before the bench I had to go to gaol, because the contractor had broke and the works was stopped, so my mates hadn't no money to pay the fine.

The dog was took away home to granny by my butty [comrade], but one of the gentlemen as seed it in court sent his groom over and got it off the old woman for five pound. She thought if I hadn't the hound I should give it up, and she come and paid me out of gaol. It was a wonder I didn't break her neck; only her was a good woman, you see, to I. But I wouldn't have parted with that hound for a quart-full of sovereigns. Many's a time I've seed his name – they changed his name, of course – in the papers for winning coursing matches. But we let that gent as bought him have it warm; we harried his pheasants and killed most of 'em.

from *The Amateur Poacher*, 1879

John Watson

At night the poacher's dogs embody all his senses. An old black bitch is his favourite; for years she has served him faithfully – in the whole of that time never having once given mouth. Like all good lurchers, she is bred between the greyhound and the sheepdog. The produce of this cross have the speed of the one, and the "nose" and intelligence of the other. Such dogs never bark, and, being rough coated, are able to stand the exposure of cold nights. They take long to train, but when perfected are invaluable to the poacher. Upon them almost wholly depends success.

Every poacher knows that the difficulty lies not so much in obtaining the game as in transporting it safely home. Their dogs are always trained to run on a couple of hundred yards in advance, so as to give warning of anyone's approach. If a constable or keeper is met on the highway the dog immediately leaps the fence, and, under its cover, runs back to its master. Seeing this the game-bag is dropped in a dry ditch, and the dog and man make off in opposite directions. County constables loiter about unfrequented lanes and by-paths at daybreak. The poachers know this and are rarely met with with game upon them.

from *Poachers and Poaching*, 1891

Moorman (pseud.)

It is necessary to discriminate between those dogs which poach regularly and others which only do so occasionally, because the indiscriminate taking of dogs in traps is not altogether judicious, and may land one into serious trouble. There are, however, up and down the country hundreds of what may be called professional poaching dogs which exist solely upon what they can pick up in the preserves and elsewhere. The man who is engaged in trapping rabbits and vermin is sure to meet with them and suffer indirectly from their depredations. These brutes are for the most part of a mongrel sheepdog type, owned, if owned at all, by those who have no possible use for them, except as a reason for the employment of bad language and the administering of stray kicks. They are usually sleepy and listless by day, but develop symptoms of activity and intelligence towards night-time. As a rule it is difficult to identify the owners of regular poaching dogs, as the brutes work far afield from their homes. This is an advantage to anyone trapping them, as he is not likely to be bothered by inquiries.

The true poaching dog is a most unmitigated nuisance, and fearfully destructive. . . .

Their chief depredations will be the taking of rabbits from traps or snares, failing which they will mouth and maul and partly consume them, abjuring the head, as a rule – just the opposite to the methods of the poaching cat. Then they will frequent the keeper's rearing-fields, get amongst his young birds when first turned away in the coverts, and also at an earlier season champ up any nest of eggs or young birds they may come across, and chop up young rabbits and leverets.

from *How to Trap and Snare*, c. 1900

Patrick Chalmers

All along the moorland road a caravan there comes
Where the piping curlew whistles and the brown snipe drums;
   And a long lean dog
   At a sling jig-jog,
A poacher to his eyelids, as all the lurcher clan,
Follows silent as a shadow, and clever as a man.

His master on the splash-board, oh, of ancient race he is;
He came down out of Egypt, as did all the Romanys;
   With, the hard hawk face
   Of an old king race,
His hair is black and snaky, and his cheek is brown as tea,
And pyramids and poacher-dogs were made by such as he.

Now the dog he looks so solemn as the beak upon the bench,
But he'll pounce and pick a hare up, and he'll kill it with a wrench,
   Or he'll sneak around a rick
   And bring back a turkey chick;
And you'll wonder how they got him all his cock-a-leerie fakes.
Well, his master comes of people who turn walking sticks to snakes!

There was once a god in Egypt, when the gods they first began,
With the muzzle of a lurcher on the body of a man;
   But the Pharaoh of to-day
   He has changed the ancient way,
And has found him a familiar by his caravan to jog
With the head piece of a Solomon, the body of a dog!

"The New Anubis", twentieth century

Thomas Thompson

Rats! Eggs were missed and chicken killed. "We's ha' to do summat about it," said Billy at a Court meeting hurriedly assembled to discuss the situation. "Yo' could put pizen down," said Fred Jackson. "Oh, aye," said Billy. "Art tha not satisfied wi' ten cats or does tha want a cock chicken or two to flavour thi grapes." Fred looked sheepish. "Ah'd never thwot o' that," he said. "We'll get Billy Bowker to bring his dogs an' ferrets," said Billy. "That'll put paid to 'em."

Billy Bowker came down on Sunday morning. Billy Bowker always came on Sunday mornings. In a way his ratting was a form of escapism. Neither he nor his wife was a strict Sabbatarian. To her Sunday morning was one wild orgy of cooking and cleaning. When there was anything to cook cooking predominated. When rations were thin cleaning won. In either case Billy was in the way, so he took engagements for himself, three lurchers of cosmopolitan breed, and two evil-looking ferrets. The lurchers were perfectly disciplined and always to heel. They were sensible, for Billy's toes were encased in steel-capped clogs.

When Billy got down to the Court he let the dogs explore the ground. Soon they became excited and dashed about one particular hencote. "They're on th' scent," said Billy. Fred Jackson was holding his nose and asthmatically wheezing. "By gow!" he said. "They are th' scent. They niff a bit, don't they?"

"There's no rat con live long in that atmosphere," said Billy Feather, heaving slightly. "Well, ston' away," said Billy Bowker. "It'll be better for me if there's not too mony round."

Billy Feather had already moved behind another pen and Fred Jackson backed about twenty yards into the wind. Billy Bowker was examining a stone under the cote. "This is wheer they run," he said. "They allus leave their mark so wheer they goo." He ducked under the cote and found one hole. Then he went round the other side and discovered another. "Allus a road out an' a road in," he said.

He placed a net over one hole, untied a dirty bag and took out a snaky ferret, which he placed in the other hole, down which it promptly disappeared. Then Billy "kenched down" near the net and waited with his hands spread expectantly like a wicket-keeper. The dogs sat in a row with ears cocked. Suddenly there was a rush. Two rats bolted from the hole. Billy grabbed them as they came and swung them under his arm. The dogs jumped about and barked furiously. Billy put the live rats in another dirty bag and waited for the ferret. Its sinister face appeared and Billy put the animal away. "Them'll not trouble yo' any more," he said, "Ah've another job on. Good morning."

Fred Jackson lit a piece of tarred rope and let it smoulder. Billy Feather came out of hiding with a very white face. "He doesn't wesh them dogs wi'" rose-watter," said Fred. "That," said Billy, "is a hunderstatement."

On the Scent

Abraham Fleming

The Dogge called the Setter, in Latine *Index*.

Another sort of Dogges be there, serviceable for fowling, making no noise either with foote or with tounge, while they followe the game. These attend diligently upon theyr Master and frame their conditions to such beckes, motions, and gestures, as it shall please him to exhibite and make, either going forward, drawing backeward, inclining to the right hand, or yealding toward the left, (In making mencion of fowles my meaning is of Partridge and the Quaile) when he hath founde the byrde, he keepeth sure and fast silence, he stayeth his steppes and wil proceede no further, and with a close, covert, watching eye, layeth his belly to the grounde and so creepeth forward like a worme. When he approcheth neere to the place where the birde is, he layes him downe, and with a marcke of his pawes, betrayeth the place of the byrdes last abode. . . . The place being knowne by the meanes of the dogge, the fowler immediately openeth and spreedeth his net, intending to take them, which being done the dogge at the accustomed becke and usually signe of his Master ryseth up and by and by, and draweth neerer to the fowle that by his presence they might be the authors of their owne insnaring, and be ready intangled in the prepared net, which conning and artificiall indevour in a dogge (being a creature domesticall or householde servaunt brought up at home with offalls of the trencher and fragments of victualls) is not much to be marvailled at. . . .

Of the Dogge called the water Spaniell, or finder, in Latine *Aquaticus sevinquisitor*. That kinde of dogge whose service is required in fowling upon the water, partly through a naturall towardness, and partly by diligent teaching, is indued with that property. . . . He frequenteth and hath usual recourse to the water where all his game & exercise lyeth, namely, waterfowles, which are taken by the helpe & service of them, in their kind. And principaly duckes and drakes, whereupon he is lykewise named a dogge for the ducke, because in that qualitie he is excellent. With these dogges also we fetche out of the water such fowle as be stounge to death by any venemous worme, we use them also to bring us our boultes & arrows out of the water (missing our marcke) wherat we directed our levell, which otherwise we should hardly recover, and oftentimes the restore to us our shaftes which we thought never to see, touche or handle againe, after they were lost, for which circumstaunces they are called *Inquisitores*, searchers, and finders.

Although the ducke otherwhiles notably deceaveth both the dogge and the master, by dyving under the water, and also by naturall subtilty, for if any man shall approche to the place where they builde, brede, and syt, the hennes go out of their neastes, offering themselves voluntarily to the hands, as it were, of such as draw nie their neastes. And a certaine weakenesse of their wings pretended, and infirmite of their feete dissembled, they go so sloweley and so leasurely, that to a mans thinking it were no masteryes to take them. . . . [Or if] they have an ynkling that they are espied they hide themselves under turfes or sedges, wherewith they cover and shrowde themselves so closely and so craftly, that (notwithstanding the place where they lurke be found and perfectly perceaved) there they will harbour without harme, except the water spaniell by quicke smelling discover theyr deceiptes.

from *Of Englishe Dogges,* 1576

George Markland

Halloo-Halloo-See, see from yonder Furze
The Lurchers have alarm'd and started Puss!
Hold! What d'ye do? Sure you don't mean to Fire?
Constrain that base, ungenerous Desire,
And let the Courser and the Huntsman share
Their just and proper Title in the Hare.
Let the poor Creature pass, and have fair play,
And fight the Prize of Life out her own Way.
The tracing Hound by Nature was design'd
Both for the Use and Pleasure of Mankind;
In enmity each to each is bound:
Then he who dares by different means destroy
That Nature meant, offends 'gainst NATURE'S LAW.

from *Pteryplegia, or, The Art of Shooting Flying*, 1727

William Fawcett

The Haydon at this time were hunting fox solely, and consequently the expenses became larger, though they were still trencher-fed, as witness the following:

"Also proposed and carried unanimously:
That Robert Bruce be huntsman to the said Hunt, and that he is to hunt the hounds two days in each week, and gather the same for the same sum as the previous year, £31 10s."

It seems to have been Bruce's practice to dismiss his hounds one by one on the road home, only taking back to Haydon Bridge those whose "walks" were adjacent to the town. When at a convenient point fairly near any hound's residence, he would pull up and name the hound he wanted, which, upon the order "Gan away heam, lad," would trot off with his stern up across the fields or over the fell to his "walk" and his food. Probably Bruce had the great gift of obedience from his pack without roughness or severity. Old hunters record that his custom was, when a hound first spoke in West Dipton or some other large fastness, to caution him. If the hound spoke again he would cheer him to the echo with his fine high voice. On hearing challenge it would be: "Noo, Lovelace, mind what thou's deein, be canny," and on the second note, "Hark to, Lovelace. Ha-a-a-a-a-rk." If a hound had spoken riot the first time, the caution from the huntsman was enough to prevent a further mistake.

from *Hunting in Northumbria*, 1927

Will H. Ogilvie

The white hound runs at the head of the pack,
   And mute as a mouse is he,
And never a note he flings us back
   While the others voice their glee.
With nose to the ground he holds his line
   Be it over the plough or grass;
He sets a pace for the twenty-nine
   And won't let one of them pass.

The white hound comes from a home in Wales,
   Where they like them pale in hue
And can pick them up when the daylight fails
   And the first gold stars look through.
They can see them running on dark hill-sides
   If they speak to the scent or no,
And the snow-white hounds are welcome guides
   Where the wild Welsh foxes go.

The white hound runs with our dappled pack
   Far out behind him strung;
He shows the way to the tan-and-black
   But he never throws his tongue.
At times he leads by a hundred yards,
   But he's always sure and sound;
All packs, of course, have their picture cards,
   And ours is the old white hound. .

The Master says he is far too fast
  For our stout, determined strain,
And the huntsman curses him – "D-n and blast
  He's away by himself again!"
But the Field is glad when it sees him there,
  For we know when a fox is found
The pace will be hot and the riding rare
  In the track of the old white hound.

"The White Hound",
The Collected Sporting Verse of Will H. Ogilvie, 1932

Richard Clapham

Gray lay on a blaeberry-covered ledge nearly two thousand feet above the dale. Below him mile after mile of country was spread out, while in the distance a glint of silver marked the sea. Gray's shoulder had healed after his encounter with the hind, but a slight mark still showed amongst the fur. He was licking himself when he heard the first faint sounds. They came from the direction of the wood near the farm. He ceased licking, and lay with ears a-cock. Faintly a hound spoke, and then another. Soon there was a steady clamour that grew louder. Tiny white figures poured over the boundary wall, and spread themselves about the fell. The huntsman's voice mingled with the cry of as he cheered his favourites. Overnight showers had damped the ground and scent lay well. Hounds started to shove along. It was Gray's drag they had struck, and from where he lay Gray watched them working it out along the fellside. They were still a long way off. Following every twist and turn he had made, they veered towards the big earth. Beyond it the pace increased, and soon they were in the opposite cove. Then they began to sink the hill. They crossed the beck where it issued from his birthplace, and began to climb the scree-beds below Gray's crag. Still he did not move. From where he lay he could look right down on them. It was precipitous going, and Barmaid, the light coloured bitch who led the pack, spoke at intervals, for she needed all her breath. Strung out behind her came the rest of the pack in single file. At last they cleared the screes and began to scale the crag. Up and up from ledge to ledge they scrambled, and Gray thought it was time to make a move. Ten seconds later he was out of the crag and cantering smoothly across the fell top.

Behind him rang a screaming chorus. Hounds hit his line, and by the way they began to run there was evidently a breast-high scent. Across the top they flew, and Gray – not so far in front – lengthened his stride. It was good going on the top and hounds could race. Heading straight north, Gray suddenly turned in at the foot of the adjoining valley. Below him lay a crag seamed with heather-covered ledges and sheep trods. As he shot into it, two stags raised their heads, and hearing the cry of hounds climbed out towards the top. Through the crag Gray ran, and as hounds came in at the lower end he was out on the rough fellside again. He gained a lead, and as he headed south he picked the very roughest ground. It was rough, too. Under the rocky edge of the fell lay scree-beds and deep watercourses, where stones and gravel avalanched downhill at the slightest touch. Light as a feather, Gray cantered across the dangerous face, hardly disturbing a pebble in his passage. Behind him ran hounds throwing their tongues vociferously, while silhouetted on the sky-line the two stags watched the chase swing past below them.

Ahead of Gray lay the pass beyond which was his home dale. Above it stood the huntsman, a spot of scarlet on the sunlit fell. Gray slanted down the slope, and crossed the grassy bottom of the pass. Someone halloed as he went through. Turning right-handed he was on rough going again as he climbed to the foot of the Black Crag. Behind him relentless chorus still pursued.

Up and up he went to a wide cove beneath the fell top, and then he turned straight south towards the big earth. Between lay a sea of rocks and boulders. As he dodged his way amongst them, hounds swung through the pass. They were running hard. Gray reached a grassy flat clear of the rocks, and began the last descent to the great borran. As he did so a chorus of view-halloas rang out. A whip cracked, and two terriers voiced their excitement shrilly. There were five men on the terrace, and what with halloas, whip-cracking and hurtling stones, Gray deemed it best to turn aside. For once the place was too well guarded for him to risk a dash, so he turned uphill and headed for the ridge. Over a wall he went and slanted north again towards the felltop. It was good grass all the way. As he reached the sky-line he glanced back. Hounds were jumping the wall, the leaders already stretching out again.

Gray held a comfortable lead, but his tongue was out for the pace had been fast. He was in no way distressed, however. Across the open top he ran, then swerved sharply to the left and slipped over the edge. Beneath him lay a steep fell breast, strewn with scree-beds and here and there a clump of junipers. Lower still the road to the pass wound snake-like up the hill, the last steep gradient one in four. As he slanted down towards the road, hounds came screaming in above him. They were gaining now, and Gray put on a spurt. Several cars stood on the road. Their drivers had heard hounds and stopped to see the fun. As Gray jumped the wall and crossed the road in three long strides, he was greeted with a volley of noises. Some of the people tried to halloa, and succeeded in making raucous sounds, while others ran to get a better view.

Ahead of Gray lay a towering fell, its scree-beds red in the sunlight. He climbed some distance up the breast, then turned and headed south. Hounds were over the road and the cry was drawing nearer. Gray's objective was his old quarry. As he neared it, hounds were only three hundred yards behind. A solitary watcher stood on guard, and he halloed for very life. He might as well have saved his breath, for Gray ignored him, climbed the face of the rubbish heap and slipped inside. A minute later hounds arrived and marked their fox to ground. The whipper-in, with four coupled terriers trotting at his heels, was the first to reach the place, and soon after came the huntsman. "Let Turk off," said he, and into the rubbish heap darted the black terrier. It was almost dark inside. Gray, lying on a ledge, heard the terrier scrambling amongst the stones, and slipped through a narrow crevice. Big as he was, he could squeeze through a surprisingly tight place. The terrier reached the ledge and threw his tongue vociferously, then drove at the crevice. As he tried to enter, Gray's white fangs slashed his muzzle. Again and again Turk went to the attack, but Gray held the upper hand, and dealt out steady punishment. At last Gray turned and crept deeper amongst the stones. The terrier found another passage, and followed. Cracks and crannies finally stopped him and he had to confess defeat. Outside, the huntsman called his hounds away, and set off down the road that led towards

the kennels. An hour later Turk followed. There was blood on his
muzzle.

It was dusk when Gray left the rubbish heap.

from *Lakeland Gray, c.* 1936

Peter Beckford

Your country requires a good terrier. I should prefer the black or white
terrier: some there are so like a fox, that awkward people frequently
mistake one for the other. If you like terriers to run with your pack,
large ones, at times, are useful; but in an earth they do little good, as
they cannot always get up to a fox. You had better not enter a young
terrier at a badger. Young terriers have not the art of shifting like old
ones; and, should they be good for anything, most probably will go up
boldly to him at once, and get themselves most terribly bitten: for this
reason, you should enter them at young foxes when you can.

from *Thoughts upon Hunting, in a series of Familiar Letters,* 1781

Ring-Ouzel

Ay, see the hounds with frantic zeal
    The roots and earth uptear;
But the earth is strong and the roots are long,
    They cannot enter there.
Outspeaks the Squire, "Give room, I pray,
    And hie the terriers in;
The warriors of the fight are they,
    And every fight they win."

John Gay

See how the well-taught pointer leads the way;
The scent grows warm; he stops; he springs the prey;

The fluttering coveys from the stubble rise,
And on swift wing divide the sounding skies;
The scattering lead pursues the certain sight,
And death in thunder overtakes their flight. . . .

As in successive Toil the Seasons roll,
So various Pleasures recreate the Soul
The setting Dog, instructed to betray,
Rewards the Fowler with the Feather'd Prey.
Soon as the lab'ring Horse with swelling Veins,
Hath safely hous'd the Farmer's doubtful Gains,
To sweet Repast th' unwary Partridge flies,
At Ease amidst the scatter'd Harvest lies,
Wand'ring in Plenty, Danger he forgets,
Nor dreads the Slav'ry of entangling Nets.
The subtle Dog with sagacious nose
Scowres through the Field, and snuffs each Breeze that blows,
Against the wind he takes his prudent way,
While the strong Gale directs him to the Prey
Now the warm Scent assures the Covey near,
He treads with caution, and he points with Fear
Then lest some Sentry Fowl his Fraud descry,
And bid his Fellows from the Danger fly,
Close to the Ground in Expectation lies,
Till in the snare the fluttering Covey rise,
And on swift wing divide the sounding skies;
The scatt'ring lead pursues the certain sight,
And death in thunder overtakes the flight.

from *Rural Sports*, c. 1713

"Vincent"

My hasty meal dispatched, I seize my gun
And issue forth; from their clean kennels loos'd
My pointers meet me, and with unfeign'd joy
Around me bound impatient, as I trace
The rocky lane to yonder rising ground.

Near yonder hedge-row where high grass and ferns
The secret hollow shade, my pointers stand.
How beautiful they look! with outstretched tails,
With heads immovable and eyes fast fix'd,
One foreleg rais'd and bent, the other firm,
Advancing forward, presses the ground. . . .

In these rude solitudes diffuse a shade:
There loss not felt, while my observant eye
Follows my ranging setters. How they wind
Along the bending heath! and now they climb
The rocky ridge, where mid the broken crags
The whortle's purple berries peep. "Take heed!"
The pack is near at hand; the wary dogs
Draw slowly on. They stand immovable,
Backing the leader. Now my pulse beat quick
With expectation, but by practice trained
At once subsides, that coolness may assist
My steady aim. Meantime my well-trained dogs
Enjoy their sett: I hie them in: the birds
On sounding pinions rise, yet not so swift
But that the whistling shot o'ertake their flight. . . .

from *Fowling*, 1808

Nimrod (pseud.)

The old gentleman took the field in good style, being accompanied by
a servant to hold his horse when he dismounted, and two mounted
keepers in their green plush jackets and gold-laced hats. A leash of
highly bred red and white setters were let loose at a time, and beautifully
did they range the fields, quartering the ground in obedience to the
voice or the whistle. On the game being found, every dog was down,
with his belly close on the ground; and the net was unfurled, the
keepers advanced on a gentle trot, at a certain distance from each other,
and drew it over them and the covey at the same time.

from *Nimrod Sporting*, 1838

William Cobbett

A professed shot is, almost always, a very disagreeable brother sportsman. He must, in the first place, have a head rather of the emptiest to pride himself upon so poor a talent. Then he is always out of temper, if the game fail, or if he miss it. He never participates in that great delight which all sensible men enjoy at beholding the beautiful action, the docility, the zeal, the wonderful sagacity of the pointer and the setter. He is always thinking about himself; always anxious to surpass his companions. I remember that, once, Ewing and I had lost our dog. We were in a wood, and the dog had gone out and found a covey in a wheat stubble joining the wood. We had been whistling and calling him for, perhaps, half an hour or more. When we came out of the wood we saw him pointing with one foot up; and soon after, he, keeping his foot and body unmoved, gently turned round his head towards the spot where he heard us, turned his head back again. I was so delighted that I stopped to look in admiration. Ewing, astonished at my want of alacrity, pushed on, shot one of the partridges, and thought no more about the conduct of the dog than if the sagacious creature had had nothing at all to do with the matter.

from *Rural Rides,* 1830

Charles St John

Nothing is more trying to the constitution of a dog than this kind of shooting in winter; when the poor animal spends his time either in paddling about in half-frozen water, or in shivering at his master's feet whilst waiting for a fresh shot. The master perhaps has waterproof boots and a warm jacket on, a pipe in his mouth, and a mouthful of brandy to keep him warm; while the poor dog has none of these accompanying comforts, and is made to sit motionless on the wet or frozen ground with the water freezing on his coat. For my own part I administer as much as I can to the comfort of my canine companion, by always carrying him some biscuits, and by giving him either my plaid or a game-bag to lie upon. It is amusing to see a retriever wrapped up in a plaid, with only his head out of it, watching eagerly for the appearance of a flock of widgeon or ducks, which he often sees before I do myself.

from *Wild Sports and Natural History of the Highland*, 1919

Surtees

Mr Jorrocks not keeping any "sporting dogs," as the tax-papers call them, had borrowed a fat house-dog – a cross between a setter and a Dalmatian – of his friend Mr Evergreen, the greengrocer, which he had seen make a most undeniable point one morning in the Copenhagen Fields at a flock of pigeons in a beetroot garden. This valuable animal was now attached by a trash-cord through a ring in his collar to a leg of the sideboard, while a clean-licked dish at his side showed that Jorrocks had been trying to attach him to himself, by feeding him before starting.

"We'll take a coach to the Castle," said Jorrocks, "and then get a 'go-cart' or a cast somehow or other to Streatham, for we shall have walking enough when we get there. Browne is an excellent fellow, and will make us range every acre of his estate over half a dozen times before we give in." A coach was speedily summoned, into which Jorrocks, the dog Pompey, the Yorkshireman, and the guns were speedily placed, and away they drove to the Elephant and Castle.

from *Jorrocks's Jaunts and Jollities*, 1843

Dr John Henry Salter

I had a dog called Prince Rupert, a big, strong, curly, brown retriever, brother to King Koffee, who was the champion curly retriever in this country and the father of all the best for years. I kept Prince Rupert on the marsh because he was essentially a very strong dog and a marsh dog. He could stand any amount of work, like I was able to myself. . . .

It had been cold for several days, and was still freezing, but it was too rough for the ice to settle down on the water. In the dark I couldn't tell whether it was water or ice; I only knew that the keepers reported a good many fowl about in the morning, so I went down to see what I could get. They came over now and then, and I got seven or eight down. Some fell on to the water, and some on the land. It gradually got light, and then I saw that the water was covered with ice, but it could not be thick, because on the previous day there had been none, and it was now unduly thickened through the water's previous readiness to freeze.

Prince Rupert was a little out of condition, but he knew my signals, and when the time came to retrieve these birds there was a teal lying on the ice, about fifty yards out. I pointed it out to Prince, and he went for it. He dashed through the sedges, and made his way to the bird. The ice was not thin enough for him to swim through; he had to fight his way through it with his forelegs.

When within about a yard of it he was exhausted, but, craning his neck over the ice, he kept making futile attempts to get the bird. He would not turn back, but presently lay perfectly still on top of the water. My two keepers were coming up to join me, and they arrived at that moment. Of course, it meant drowning. I asked the men if they could suggest anything, and there was no rope, no boat, no anything. The water was deep. I was frantic. The poor dog was out there with not much of a kick left in him, yet even then he tried to crane his neck to get the bird.

"I'm d—d if I'm going to see the dog drown," I suddenly exclaimed. I chucked off my coat and waistcoat, and dashed into the sedges until I got to the edge of the ice. The first part of the ice broke by my trying to get on to it, but I went a little wide and to my great astonishment I succeeded in getting on an ice raft. It was floating, but it proved sufficient to bear me. I kept away from the rill the dog had made in going out and I bent down and gradually worked the floating ice by swaying my body until I got opposite to Prince. I then got hold of his topknot and walked back with him in just the same way.

When we got within a yard or two of the bank the whole contraption gave way, but of course I could struggle out. The dog was apparently dead. Coated with ice, he was an ice-dog – ice all over him in a great, big mass. We had to kick it off him. We carried him down to the decoy house, laid him in front of the fire, gave him brandy, kept rubbing him, of course – and he lived for years after.

There was another ice accident in which Prince Rupert figured.

We were shooting, and there was ice everywhere, and a rabbit got out of the sedge and went across the frozen water. I shot it some 25 yards out. The warmth of a rabbit or duck on thin ice very soon thaws it. Prince Rupert went after the rabbit, and would have got it out right enough, but it had lain just long enough to thaw the ice a little, and when Prince got to it he went right into the hole where the rabbit was lying. The ice proved too thick for him to break it, and there he was in the middle of a circle in which he kept spinning round with the rabbit in his mouth, fighting with his forelegs.

I broke the ice with my gun, and broke my gun in doing it. I made my friend Holmes come in, too, and together we rescued Prince Rupert.

from *Dr Salter . . . His Diary and Reminiscences, 1849 to 1932*

Surtees

Having cut himself some extremely substantial sandwiches, and filled his "monkey" full of sherry, our friend Jog slipped out the back way to loosen old Ponto, who acted the triple part of pointer, house-dog, and horse to Gustavus James. He was a great fat, black-and-white brute, with a head like a hat-box, a tail like a clothes-peg, and a back as broad as a well-fed sheep's. The brute was so frantic at the sight of his master in his green coat, and wide-awake to match, that he jumped and bounced, and barked, and rattled his chain, and set up such yells, that his noise sounded all over the house, and soon brought Mr Sponge to the scene of action, where stood our friend, loading his gun and looking consequential as possible.

"I shall only just take a (puff) stroll over moy (wheeze) ter-ri-to-ry," observed Jog, as Mr Sponge emerged at the back door.

Jog's pace was about two miles and a half an hour, stoppages included, and he thought it advisable to prepare Mr Sponge for the trial. He then shouldered his gun and waddled away, first over the stile into Farmer Stiffland's stubble, round which Ponto ranged in the most riotous, independent way, regardless of Jog's whistles and rates, and the crack of his little knotty whip. Jog then crossed the old pasture into Mr Lowland's turnips, into which Ponto dashed in the same energetic way, but these impediments to travelling soon told on his great buttermilk carcass, and brought him to a more subdued pace; still, the dog had a good deal more energy than his master. Round he went, sniffing and hunting, then dashing right through the middle of the field, as if he was out on his own account alone, and had nothing whatever to do with a master.

"Why, your dog'll spring all the birds out of shot," observed Mr Sponge; and, just as he spoke, whirr! rose a covey of partridges, eleven in number, quite at an impossible distance, but Jog blazed away all the same.

Mr Sponge's Sporting Tour, 1853

John Masefield

At half-past ten some lads on foot
Came to be beaters to a shoot
Of rabbits on the Warren Hill.
Rough sticks they had, and Hob and Jill
Their ferrets, in a bag, and netting.
They talked of dinner beer and betting,
And jeered at those who stood around.
They rolled their dogs upon the ground
And teased them: "Rats," they cried, "go fetch!"
"Go seek, good Roxer; 'z bite, good betch.
What dinner-beer'll they give us, lad?
Sex quarts the lot last years we had.
They'd ought to give us seven this.
Seek, Susan; what a betch it is."

Reynard the Fox, 1919

John W. Fortesque

"Why do you bring out a wild young dog?" I ask with asperity.

"Oh, she's nine or ten year old," he answers with a sweet smile; "and she isn't wild most times, but she's terrible hard of hearing. She'll be back in a minute, but I expect we'm best get on after her."

I think so too, and presently come upon her supremely busy on what is evidently a very faint line of scent.

"Looketh like a pheasant," says the keeper softly; "please to keep on after her, sir."

My Native Devon, 1924

Will H. Ogilvie

A-strain on your leashes, close coupled together,
Un-awed by the crowd, you come shouldering through
To carry our hearts with you straight to the heather
And out to the crag-tops that edge on the blue.
There sounds in the station a hill-torrent falling,
And birch-stem and boulder are wet with its spray;
Ben Lomond's awake and Schiehallion calling;
The peaks are all purple from Orchy to Spey.

There's a hill-track you'll climb by the side of the keepers
Before the first dewdrops have dried on the ling,
While out of the blaeberries flutter the cheepers,
And over the ridge go the strong on the wing.
You'll sniff the clean wind as it crosses the corrie
With scent of the moor on the breath of it blown,
And staunchly you'll stand on the line of your quarry
As still as the work of some sculptor in stone.

So waves the green flag, and farewell to you, setters!
What heart but must envy your path to the hills?
In gloom we return to our work-a-day fetters,
Our desks and our duty, our ink and our quills;
But night shall bring dreams of your heads in the heather
That surges and swings as you quarter it through;
Then gunshot — an echo — a floating brown feather —
And so shall we know that your dreams have come true!

"To a Brace of Setters. (Labelled for the North.)"
The Collected Sporting Verse of Will H Ogilvie, 1932

T. H. White

My setter bitch, though she scanned my face very closely, could never determine mood from expression. She waited for the tone of voice and, though I tested her with ferocious scowls and beaming smiles, drew no conclusions about the state of mind except by ear, or by recollection of painful or pleasant scenes in similar past circumstances. It was not so with Gos. Not only did he detect my feelings in my face, but by now I was able to detect at least two feelings in his.

from *The Goshawk*, 1951

Another of the higher country pleasures is associated with the shooting dog. The two best local dogs are Luke Fieldfare's Timmy, a golden cocker, and Fred Aytoun's Belle (or Mother) a black Labrador. Belle is ten years old, steady and nearly blind: Timmy is in his first season, constantly being smacked. Both are far more intelligent than a Christian, or at least than a clergyman. Sometimes, in a crisis, they are put on the same runner in a hedge: and then you can see Timmy working by inspiration, Belle by system. Timmy's small golden stump is wriggling with excitement, while Belle's blind old nose fades quietly up and down the ditch. When he finds the bird he takes it with a little pounce: when she gets the certain smell there is no acceleration. She walks on to it without a tremor, picks it like a gentle nursemaid, and delivers it to hand before you know it has been found.

from *England Have My Bones*, 1936

Jim Corbett

I never saw either of his parents. The Knight of the Broom I purchased him from someone who said he was a spaniel, that his name was Pincha, and that his father was a "keen gun dog". This is all I can tell you about his pedigree. I did not want a pup, and it was quite by accident that I happened to be with a friend when the litter of seven was decanted from a very filthy basket for her inspection. Pincha was the smallest and the thinnest of the litter, and it was quite evident he had reached the last ditch in his fight for survival. Leaving his little less miserable brothers and sisters, he walked once round me, and then curled himself up between my big feet. When I picked him up and put him inside my coat – it was a bitterly cold morning – he tried to show his gratitude by licking my face, and I tried to show him I was not aware of his appalling stench.

He was rising three months then, and I bought him for fifteen rupees. He is rising thirteen years now, and all the gold in India would not buy him. When I got him home, and he had made his first acquaintance with a square meal, warm water, and soap, we scrapped his kennel name of Pincha and rechristened him Robin, in memory of a faithful old collie who had saved my young brother, aged four, and myself, aged six, from the attack of an infuriated she-bear. Robin responded to regular meals as parched land does to rain, and after he had been with us for a few weeks, acting on the principle that a boy's and a pup's training cannot be started too early, I took him out one morning, intending to get a little away from him and fire a shot or two to get him used to the sound of gunfire. At the lower end of our estate there are some dense thorn bushes, and while I was skirting round them a peafowl got up and, forgetting all about Robin who was following at heel, I brought the bird fluttering down. It landed in the thorn bushes and Robin dashed in after it. The bushes were too thick and thorny for me to enter them, so I ran round to the far side where beyond the bushes was open ground, and beyond that again heavy tree and grass jungle which I knew the wounded bird would make for. The open ground was flooded with morning sunlight, and if I had been armed with a movie camera I should have had an opportunity of securing a unique picture. The peafowl, an old hen, with neck feathers stuck out at right angles and one wing broken, was making for the tree jungle, while Robin, with stern to the ground, was hanging on to her tail and being dragged along. Running forward I very foolishly caught the bird by the neck and lifted it clear of the ground, whereon it promptly lashed out with both legs and sent Robin heels-over-head. In a second he was up and on his feet again, and when I laid the dead bird down he danced round it making little dabs alternately at its head and tail. The lesson was over for that morning, and as we returned home it would have been difficult to say which of us was the more proud – Robin, at bringing home his first bird, or I, at having picked a winner out of a filthy basket. The shooting season was now drawing to a close, and for the next few days Robin was not given anything larger than a quail, doves, and an occasional partridge to retrieve.

We spent the summer on the hills, and on our annual migration to the foothills in November, at the end of a long fifteen-mile march, as we turned a sharp corner, one of a big troop of langurs jumped off the hillside and crossed the road a few inches in front of Robin's nose. Disregarding my whistle, Robin dashed down the khudside after the langur, which promptly sought safety in a tree. The ground was open, with a few trees here and there, and after going steeply down for thirty or forty yards flattened out for a few yards before going sharply down into the valley below. On the right-hand side of this flat ground there were a few bushes, with a deep channel scoured out by rainwater running through them. Robin had hardly entered these bushes when was on again, and with ears laid back and tail tucked in was running for dear life, with an enormous leopard bounding after him and gaining on him at every bound. I was unarmed, and all the assistance I could render was to "Ho" and "Har" at the full extent of my lungs. The men carrying M's dandy joined in lustily, the pandemonium reaching its climax when the hundred or more langurs added their alarm calls, in varying keys. For twenty-five or thirty yards the desperate and unequal race continued, and just as the leopard was within reach of Robin, it unaccountably swerved and disappeared into the valley, while Robin circled round a shoulder of the hill and rejoined us on the road. Two very useful lessons Robin learned from his hairsbreadth escape, which he never in after-life forgot. First, that it was dangerous to chase langurs, and, second, that the alarm-call of a langur denoted the presence of a leopard.

Robin resumed his training where it had been interrupted in spring, but it soon became apparent that his early neglect and starvation had affected his heart, for he fainted now after the least exertion.

There is nothing more disappointing for a gun dog than to be left at home when his master goes out, and as birdshooting was now taboo for Robin I started taking him with me when I went out after big game. He took to this new form of sport as readily as a duck takes to water, and from then on has accompanied me whenever I have been out with a rifle.

The method we employ is to go out early in the morning, pick up the tracks of a leopard or a tiger, and follow them. When the pug marls can be seen I do the tracking, and when the animal we are after takes to the jungle Robin does the tracking. In this way we have on occasions followed an animal for miles before coming up with it.

from *Man-eaters of Kumaon*, 1944

CHAPTER 6

Coarse Pastimes

I t is not easy for most dog owners to understand how anyone
with any degree of care for their dog should deliberately put it
to fight another. Yet there can be no doubt but that many dog
fighters have taken pride in the courage and prowess of their dogs
and exhibited towards them a degree of affection far warmer than
that shown by veterinary surgeons who breed dogs for laboratory
research. The gulf in understanding is not new and is unlikely ever to
be bridged. Attitudes towards dogs vary in time and place and are as
much influenced by religious doctrine as by the social environment
in which their owners live.

The first Queen Elizabeth was an ardent supporter of dog fighting
and of bull and bear baiting. The second Elizabeth undoubtedly has a
very different attitude.

It would, however, be quite wrong to suppose that the passage of
time alone has brought about more humane attitudes. Even while the
gladiatorial pastimes in which dogs engaged enjoyed support from the
highest in the land to the lowest, from both Church and State there
were people who gave voice to their reservations. Their efforts to
promote a more humanitarian attitude towards animals were often
frustrated. The Church was indifferent to the suffering of animals
because they had no souls, the State felt that the examples of bravery
and stoic suffering they were able to provide offered exemplars to
people who knew only too well that "human life is everywhere a state
in which much is to be endured, and little to be enjoyed". The
contemplation of courageously endured suffering worse than their
own was thought to help them to endure their own suffering.

There were four major bull and bear baiting pits in London. The earliest, patronized by Shakespeare, was Paris Gardens on Bankside not far from the Globe Theatre. During the reign of Queen Anne London had three bear gardens – at Hockley in Clerkenwell, in Marylebone Fields behind Soho Square, and in Tuttle Fields, Westminster.

The Paris Gardens had been built specifically to accommodate *bull*-baiting in 1546 by the Earl of Northumberland. It took its name from the owner of a house which stood on the site: Matthew de Paris.

On 15 January 1583 the theatre collapsed under the press of excited spectators, killing and maiming a great number. The theatre was rebuilt but again some of the tiered seating collapsed killing five men and two women. This succession of accidents were said to be the judgement of God on those who took pleasure in the sadistic spectacles.

The theatre was closed by Cromwell's Long Parliament in 1642. After the Restoration the spectacles were resumed. In 1687 they were transferred to a new venue at Hockley-in-the-Hole in Clerkenwell, London where baiting continued until 1754.

During the later years of the eighteenth century and on into the early years of the nineteenth century the two principal London venues were the Royal Pit in Birdcage Walk, much frequented by the boys of Westminster School, and the Westminster Pit, owned in its heyday by Charles Aistrop. Francis Ardrey took George Borrow, an employee of the Bible Society, to the Royal Pit. Robert Surtees, a lawyer, Justice of the Peace and High Sheriff of Durham, was also familiar with dog fighting after it had been made illegal; so too was Dr John Henry Salter, a general practitioner and Kennel Club Vice-Chairman who visited a pit in the company of some of his friends. Have times and attitudes changed quite as much as we might hope to believe is the case?

Robert Crowley

What follye is thys, to kepe wyth daunger,
A greate mastyfe dogge and a foule ouglye beare;
And to thys onelye ende, to se them two fyght,
With a terrible tearynge, a full ouglye syght.
And yet me thynke those men be mooste foles of all,

Whose store of money is but verye smale,
And yet everye Sondaye they will surelye spende
One penye or two, the bearwardes luuying to mende
At Paryse Garden eche Sondaye, a man shall not fayle
To fynde two or three hundredes, for the bearwardes vaile.

Of Bearbaytynge, 1550

John Bradford

The token of Gods judgement at hand for the contempt of the
Gospel, as that certain gentlemen upon the Sabbath day going in a
wherry to Paris Garden, to the bear baiting were drowned; and that a
dog was met at Ludgate carrying a piece of a dead child in his mouth.

Two Notable Sermons, 1574

Abraham Fleming

Of the mastivs or Bandogge called in Latine *Villaticus* or *Cathenarius*.

This kinde of Dogge called a mastyne or Bandogge is vaste, huge,
stubborne, ougly, and eager, of a hevy and burthenous body, and
therefore but of litle swiftnesse, terrible, and frightful to beholde, and
more fearce and fell then any *Arcadian* curre (not withstanding they
are sayd to have their generation of the violent Lion.) They are
called *Villatici*, because they are appoynted to watche and keepe
farme places and country cottages sequestered from common
recourse, and not abutting upon other houses by reason of
distaunce, when there is any fears conceved of theefes, robbers,
spoylers, and night wanderers. They are serviceable against the Foxe
and the Badger, to drive wilde and tame swyne out of Medowes,
pastures, glebelandes and places planted with fruite, to bayte and take
the bull by the ears, when occasion so requireth. One dogge or two
at the uttermost, sufficient for that purpose be the bull never so
monsterous, never so fearce, never so furious, never so stearne,
never so untameable. For it is a kinde of dogge capeable of courage,
violent and valiaunt, striking could feare into the harts of men, but

standing in feare of no man, in so much that no weapons will make him shrincke, nor abridge his boldnes. Our English men (to th' intent that theyr dogges might be the more fell and fearce) assist nature with arte, use, and custome, for they teach theyr dogges to baite the Beare, to baite the Bull and other such like cruell and bloudy beastes (appointing an overseer of the game) without any collar to defend theyr throtes, and oftentimes they traine them up in fighting and wrestling with a man having for the safeguard of his lyfe, eyther a Pikestaffe, a clubbe, or a sworde and by using them to such exercises as these, theyr dogges become more sturdy and strong. The force which is in them surmounteth all beleefe, the fast holde which they take with their teeth exceedeth all credit, three of them against a Beare, fowre against a Lyon are sufficient, both to try masteryes with them and uterly to overmatch them. Which *Henry* the seventh of that name, King of England (a Prince both politique & warlike) perceaving on a certaine time (as the report runneth) commaunded all suche dogges (how many soever they were in number) should be hanged, beyng deepely displeased, and conceaving great disdaine that an yll favred reascall curre should with such violent villany, assault the valiaunt Lyon king of all beastes. . . .

This dogge is called, in the maner, *Cathenarius, a Cathena*, of the chaine wherwith he is tyed at the gates, in ye daytime, least beyng lose he should doe much mischiefe and yet might give occasion of feare and terror by his bigge barcking.

from *Of Englishe Dogges*, 1576

Sir John Harington

He seeks to loose himselfe with sudden pangs:
He that hath seene a bull with mastiues chast,
That in his cares have fixt their cruell fangs,
How he doth runne, and rore, and with him bears,
The eager dogges, that still hold fast his ears. . . .

As a fell Mastive, whom a Grewnd [greyhound] more fell,
Hath tyrde, and in his throate now fastned hath
His cruell fangs, yet doth in vaine rebell,

Though under him, and seekes to do some skath:
For still the Grewnd prevailes, and doth excell
In force of breath, though not in rage and wrath:
So doth the cruell Pagan stive and straine,
To get from under him, but all in vaine.

from *Orlando Furioso,* 1591

Edmund Spenser

Like a wylde bull, that, being at bay,
Is bayted of a mastiffe and a hound
And a curre-dog, that doe him sharp assay
On every side, and beat about him round;
But most that curre, barking with bitter sownd,
And creeping still behinde, doth him incomber,
That in his chauffe he digs the trampled ground,
And threats his horns, and bellowes like the thonder.

from *The Faerie Queene,* 1596

Edward Guilpin

He'll cry oh rare! and scratch the elbow too
To see two Butchers curres fight; the cuckoo
Will cry oh rare! to see the champion bull,
Or the victorious mastife with crown'd skull:
And girlanded with flowers, passing along
From Paris garden.

from "Skiletheia", 1598

Sir John Davies

Publius, student at the common law,
Oft leaves his books, and for his recreation,

To Paris Garden doth himself withdraw,
Where he is ravisht with such delectation,
As down among the bears and dogs he goes,
Where, whilst he slipping cries, "To head! To head!"
His satin doublet and his velvet hose,
Are all with spittle from above be-spread,
Then is he like his father's country hall,
Stinking of dogges and muted all with hawkes.
And rightly too on him this filth doth fall
Which for such filthy sports his books forsakes,
Leaving old Plowden, Dyer, and Brooke alone,
To see old Harry Hunks and Sacarson.

from "The Scourge of Folly", 1611

John Evelyn

I went with — to Ye Bear Garden, where was cock-fighting, beare, dog-fighting, beare and bull baiting, it being a famous day for all those butcherley sports, or rather barbarous cruelties. The bulls did exceedingly well, but the *Irish* wolfe-dog exceeded, which was a tall greyhound, a stately creature indeede, who beate a cruell mastiff. One of the bulls toss'd a dog full into a lady's lap, as she sat in one of ye boxes at a considerable height from the arena. Two poore dogs were kill'd, and so all ended with the ape on horseback, and I most heartily weary of the rude and dirty pastime, which I had not seene, I think, in twenty years before.

from *Diary,* 16 June 1652

Revd Thomas Fuller

Pliny observes, that Britain breeds cowardly lions and courageous mastiffs, seems to me no wonder; the former being whelped in prison, the latter at liberty. An English mastiff, anno 1602, did in effect worst a lion, on the same token that Prince Henry allowed a kind of pension for his maintenance, and gave strict orders, that he that had fought with the king of beastes should never after encounter any inferior animals.

from *The History of the Worthies of England*, 1662

Samuel Pepys

After dinner, with my wife and Mercer to the Beare Garden, where I have not been, I think, of many years, and saw some good sport of the bull's tossing of the dogs: one into the very boxes. But it is a very rude and nasty pleasure. We had a great many hectors in the same box with us, and one very fine went into the pit, and played his dog for a wager, which was a strange sport for a gentleman.

from *Diary*, 14 August 1666

William Cavendish, Duke of Newcastle

I'll set up my bills, that gamesters of London, Horslydown, South-wark and Newmarket, may come in and bait him here before the ladies; but first, boy, go fetch me a bag-pipe; we will walk the streets in triumph, and give the people notice of our support.

It is a sport very pleasant to see the bear, with pink eyes learing after his enemies approach; the nimbleness and wait of the dog to take his advantage; and the force and experience of the bear again to avoid his assaults; if he were bitten in one place, how he would pinch in another to get free; that if he were taken once, then by what shift with biting, with clawing, with roaring, with tossing and tumbling, he would work and wind himself from them; and when he was loose, to shake his ears twice or thrice, with the blood and the slaver hanging about his physiognomy.

from *Humerous Lovers*, 1671

John Houghton

When he [the bull] is at full growth and strong, he is often baited almost to death; for that great exercise makes his flesh more tender; and so if waten in good time (before putrefaction, which he is more subject to than if not baited) he is tolerable good meat, altho' very red.

Some keep him on purpose for the sport of baiting, cutting off the tips of his horns, and with pitch, tow, and such-like matter, fasten upon them the great horns of oxen, with their tips cut off and covered with leather, lest they should hurt the dogs.

Because these papers go into several other countries, I'll say something on the manner of baiting the bull, which is by having a collar about his neck, fastened to a thick rope about three, four, or five yards long, hung to a hook, so fastened to a stake that it will turn round: with this the bull circulates to watch his enemy; which is a mastiff dog (commonly used to the sport) with a short nose, that his teeth may take the better hold. This dog, if right, will creep upon his belly, that he may, if possible, get the bull by the nose; which the bull as carefully strives to defend, by laying it close to the ground, where his horns are also ready to do what in them lies to toss the dog; and this is the true sport.

But if more dogs than one come at once, or they are cowardly and come under his legs, he will, if he can, stamp their guts out.

I believe I have seen a dog tossed by a bull thirty, if not forty feet high; and when they are tossed either higher or lower, the men about strive to catch them on their shoulders, lest the fall might mischief the dogs.

They commonly lay sand about, that it they fall upon the ground it may be the easier.

Notwithstanding this care, a great many dogs are killed, more have their limbs broke; and some hold so fast, that by the bulls swinging them, their teeth are often broke out.

To perfect the history of bull baiting, I must tell you, that the famed dogs have crosses or roses of various coloured ribbon stuck with pitch on their foreheads; and such like the ladies are very ready to bestow on dogs or bull that do valiantly; and when 'tis stuck on the bull's forehead, that dog is hollowed that fetches it off; tho' the true courage and art is to hold the bull by the nose 'till he roars; which a couragious bull scorns to do.

Often the men are tossed as well as the dogs; and men, bull, and dogs seem exceedingly pleas'd, and as earnest at the sport as it it were for both their lives or livelihoods. Many great wagers are laid on both sides; and great journeys will men and dogs go for such a diversion. I knew a gentleman that bought a bull in Hertfordshire on purpose to go a progress with him, at a great charge, into most of the great towns in the west of England.

This is a sport the English much delight in; and not only the baser sort, but the greatest lords and ladies.

from *A Collection for the Improvement of Husbandry and Trade,*
24 August 1694

Richard Brinsley Sheridan

Cruelty to the bull was not the only cruelty exercised on these occasions. What sort of moral lesson, for instance, was it to the child of the farmer, who brings his aged bull bitch, many years the faithful sentinel of his house and farm-yard, surrounded by her pups to prove at the bull-ring the staunchness of her breed? He brings her forward, sets her at the infuriated animal, she seizes him by the nose and pins him to the ground. But what is the reward from her owner, amidst the applause of the mob to his favourite animal? He calls for a hedging bill [hook], and to prove her breed, hews her to pieces without quitting her grip, while he sells her puppies at five guineas a piece.

House of Commons speech, 1802

Robert Southey

You may well conceive of what character the popular amusements needs must be, in a country where there is nothing to soften the manners or ameliorate the condition of the poor. The practice of bull-baiting is not merely permitted, it is even enjoined by the municipal law in some places. Attempts have twice been made in the legislature to suppress this barbarous custom: they were baffled and ridiculed, and some of the most distinguished members were absurd enough and hard-hearted enough to assert, that if such sports were abolished there would be an end of the national courage. Would to Heaven that this were true! that English courage had no better foundation than brutal ferocious cruelty! We should no longer be insulted in our ports, and our ships might defy their buccaneering cruisers. Do not suppose that this bull-baiting has any the smallest resemblance to our bull-feasts. – Even these I should agree with the Conde de Norana, and with the Church, in condemning as wicked and inhuman; but there is a splendour in the costume, a gaiety in the spectacle, a skill and a courage displayed in the action, which afford some apology for our countrymen, whereas this English sport is even more cowardly than bull-fights of the Portugueze. The men are exposed to no danger whatever; they fasten the animal to a ring, and the amusement is to see him toss the dogs, and the dogs lacerate his nostrils, till they are weary of torturing him, and then he is led to the slaughter-house to be butchered after their clumsy and cruel method. The bear and the badger are baited with the same barbarity; and if the rabble can get nothing else, they will divert themselves by worrying cats to death.

from *Letters from England,* 1807

Henry Thomas Alken

Dog fighting as a sport is the most captivating, the very crack of all others, not only to the butchers and drovers of the metropolis, but the whole herd of the lowest and the most infamous rabble of nackers, dogs-meat men, jackass drivers, prigs, kencrackers, rum kiddies, flash men, and knowing ones of most descriptions. The far greater part of the business is transacted in the fields, near the town, westward, and towards the east, beyond Battle-bridge, where, on every Sunday morning, great numbers of the most execrable miscreants, under heaven, are collected and allowed to perpetrate the most horrible cruelties on such unfortunate animals as may have been provided for the purpose, or may fall in their way. The poor cat, stolen from her home, is one of the most common victims. These are the great schools of barbarism and cruelty for the lower classes, and the best nurseries for thieves; and seem to be winked at in this reforming season, under the strange notion that we must not interfere with, or abridge the Sports of the lower people. Whatever policy there may be in such a proposition, it surely has not much morality to boast. The Sport, however, is conducted in a more regular way at the Westminster Pit, and at Rueben Martin's Pit in Tottenham Court Road. These meetings are usually attended by a class somewhat above those already described, and even by a few choice spirits of our Aristocracy.

from *The National Sports of Great Britain,* 1821

Anonymous

The Westminster Pit was crowded on Tuesday evening, Jan 18, with all the dog fanciers in the metropolis, to witness a battle between the celebrated dog Boney and a black novice called Gas, to whom the dog belongs. The stakes were forty sovereigns, and everything was arranged to the satisfaction of the amateurs. The pit was lighted with an elegant chandelier and a profusion of waxlights. The dogs were brought to scratch at eight o'clock in excellent condition, and were seconded by their respective masters. Boney was the favourite at 3 to 1, and so continued till within ten minutes of the termination of the contest – a confidence arising solely from his known bottom; for to the impartial spectator Gas took the lead throughout. The battle lasted an hour and fifty minutes, when Boney was carried out insensible. He was immediately bled and put in a warm bath. There were nearly 300 persons present.

Sporting Magazine, 1823

Anonymous

AN ITALIAN TURN-UP
Surprising Novelty in the Sporting Circle
On Tuesday next, September 5, at Seven o'clock in the Evening A
special grand Combat will be decided at the WESTMINSTER PIT FOR
ONE HUNDRED GUINEAS
Between that extraordinary and celebrated creature, the famed
Italian Monkey,
JACCO MACCACCO
of Hoxton, third cousin to the renowned Theodore Magocco, of
unrivalled fame, and a Dog of 20 lbs weight, the property of a
Nobleman, well-known in the circle.
N.B. The owner of the Monkey having purchased him at a great
expense, on account of his wonderful talents, begs to notice to his
friends of the Fancy that another person has started a match, with a
common Monkey, on the day preceding this match, with an attempt
to injure him and deceive the Public.
After which, a DOG-FIGHT, for Ten Pounds, between the
CAMBERWELL BLACK AND TANNED DOG; and the well-known
STRATFORD DOG; and a match between two Bitches, the property
of two Gentlemen well-known in the Fancy. To conclude with
BEAR-FIGHTING.
Regular Nights, Mondays and Wednesdays.

Advertisement, 1824

Anne Brontë

"That's my brave boy! – and Fergus – what have you been doing?"
  "Badger-baiting."
  And here he proceeded to give a particular account of his sport,
and the respective prowess evinced by the badger and the dogs; my
mother pretending to listen with deep attention, and watching his
animated countenance with a degree of maternal admiration I
though highly disproportionate to its object.

The Tenant of Wildfell Hall, 1848

George Borrow

Among other strange places to which Francis Ardry conducted me, was a place not far from the abbey church of Westminster.

Before we entered this place our ears were greeted by a confused hubbub of human voices, squealing of rats, barking of dogs, and the cries of various other animals. Here we beheld a kind of cock-pit, around which a great many people, seeming of all ranks, but chiefly of the lower, were gathered, and in it we saw a dog destroy a great many rats in a very small period; and when the dog had destroyed the rats, we saw a fight between a dog and a bear, then a fight between two dogs, then –

After the diversions of the day were over, my friend introduced me to the genius of the place, a small man of about five feet high, with a very sharp countenance, and dressed in a brown jockey coat, and top boots. "Joey," said he, "this is a friend of mine." Joey nodded to me with a patronising air. "Glad to see you, sir! – want a dog?"

"No," said I.

"You have one, then – want to match him?"

"We have a dog at home," said I, "in the country; but I can't say I should like to match him. Indeed, I do not like dog-fighting."

"Not like dog-fighting!" said the man staring.

"The truth is, Joe, that he is just come to town!"

"So I should think; he looks rather green – not like dog-fighting!"

"Nothing like it, is there, Joey?"

"I should think not; what is like it? A time will come, and that speedily, when folks will give up everything else, and follow dog-fighting."

"Do you think so?" said I.

"Think so? Let me ask what there is that a man wouldn't give up for it?"

"Why," said I, modestly, "there's religion."

"Religion! How you talk. Why, there's myself, bred and born an Independent, and intended to be a preacher, didn't I give up religion for dog-fighting? Religion, indeed! If it were not for the rascally law, my pit would fill better on Sundays than any other time. Who would go to church when they could come to my pit? Religion! why, the parsons themselves come to my pit; and I have now a letter in my pocket from one of them, asking me to send him a dog."

"Well, then, politics," said I.

"Politics! Why, the gemmen in the House would leave Pitt himself, if he were alive, to come to my pit. There were three of the best of them here to-night, all great horators. – Get on with you, what comes next?"

"Why, there's learning and letters."

"Pretty things, truly, to keep people from dog-fighting. Why, there's the young gentlemen from the Abbey School comes here in sholls, leaving books and letters, and masters too. To tell you the truth, I rather wish they would mind their letters, for a more precious set of young blackguards I never seed. It was only the other day I was thinking of calling in a constable for my own protection, for I thought my pit would be torn down by them."

Scarcely knowing what to say, I made an observation at random. "You show by your own conduct," said I, "that there are other things worth following besides dog-fighting. You practise rat-catching and badger-baiting as well."

The dog-fancier eyed me with supreme contempt.

"Your friend here," said he. "might well call you a new one. When I talks of dog-fighting, I of course means rat-catching and badger-baiting, ay, and bull-baiting too, just as when I speaks religiously, when I assays one I means three. And talking about religion puts me in mind that I have something else to do besides chaffing here, having a batch of dogs to send off by this night's packet to the Pope of Rome."

from *Lavengro*, 1851

Henry Mayhew

RAT-KILLER

In Brill-place, Somers'-town there is a variety of courts branching out into Chapel-street, and in one of the most angular and obscure of these is to be found a perfect nest of rat-catchers – not altogether professional rat-catchers, but for the most part sporting mechanics and costermongers. The court is not easily to be found, being inhabited by men not so well known in the immediate neighbourhood as perhaps a mile or two away, and only to be discovered by the aid and direction of the little girl at the neighbouring cat's-meat shop.

My first experience of this court was the usual disturbance at the entrance. I found one end or branch of it filled with a mob of eager listeners, principally women, all attracted to a particular house by the sounds of quarrelling. One man gave it as his opinion that the disturbers must have earned too much money yesterday; and a woman, speaking to another who had just come out, lifting up both her hands and laughing, said, 'Here they are – at it again!''

The rat-killer whom we were in search of was out at his stall in Chapel-street when we called, but his wife soon fetched him. He was a strong, sturdy-looking man, rather above the middle height, with light hair, ending in sandy whiskers, reaching under his chin, sharp deep-set eyes, a tight-skinned nose that looked as if the cuticle had been stretched to its utmost on its bridge. He was dressed in the ordinary corduroy costermonger habit, having, in addition, a dark blue Guernsey drawn over his waistcoat.

The man's first anxiety was to show us that rats were not his only diversion; and in consequence he took us into the yard of the house, where in a shed lay a bull-dog, a bull-bitch, and a litter of pups just a week old. They did not belong to him, but he said he did a good deal in the way of curing dogs when he could get 'em.

After I had satisfied him that I was not a collector of dog-tax, trying to find out how many animals he kept, he gave me what he evidently thought was "a treat" – a peep at his bull-dog, which he fetched from upstairs, and let it jump about the room with a most unpleasant liberty, informing me the while how he had given five pounds for him, and that one of the first pups he got by a bull he had got five pounds for, and that cleared him. "That Punch" (the bull-dog's name), he said, "is as quiet as a lamb – wouldn't hurt nobody; I frequently takes him through the streets without a lead. Sartainly he killed a cat the t'other afternoon, but he couldn't help that, 'cause the cat flew at him; though he took it as quietly as a man would a woman in a passion, and only went at her just to save his eyes. But you couldn't-easy get him off, master, when he once got a holt. He was a good one for rats, and, he believed, the stanchest and trickiest dog in London." . . .

"All my lifetime I've been a-dealing a little in rats" [he told me]; "but it was not till I come to London that I turned my mind fully to that sort of thing. My father always had a great notion of the same. We all like the sport. When any of us was in the country, and the farmers wanted us to, we'd do it. If anybody heerd tell of my being an activish chap like, in that sort of way, they'd get me to come for a day or so.

'If anybody has a place that's eaten up with rats, I goes and gets some ferruts, and takes a dog, if I've got one, and manages to kill em. Sometimes I keep my own ferruts, but mostly I borrows them. This young man that's with me, he'll sometimes have an order to go fifty or sixty mile into the country, and then he buys his ferruts, or gets them the best way he can. They charges a good sum for the loan of 'em — sometimes as much as you get for the job.

'You can buy ferruts at Leadenhall-market for 5s. or 7s. — it all depends; you can't get them all at one price, some of 'em is real cowards to what others is; some won't even kill a rat.

"I have kept ferruts for four or five months at a time, but they're nasty stinking things. I've had them get loose; but, bless you, they do no harm, they're as hinnocent as cats; they won't hurt nothink; you can play with them like a kitten. Some puts things down to ketch rats pots of pison, which is their secret — but I don't. I relies upon my dogs and ferruts, and nothink else.

"I went to destroy a few rats up at Russell-square; there was a shore come right along, and a few holes — they was swarmed with 'em there — and didn't know how it was; but the cleverest men in the world couldn't ketch many there, 'cause you see, master, they run down the hole into the shore, and no dog could get through a rat-hole.

"I couldn't get my living, though, at that business. If any gentleman comes to me and says he wants a dog cured, or a few rats destroyed, I does it.

"In the country they give you fourpence a rat, and you can kill sometimes as many in a farmyard as you can in London. The most I ever got for destroying rats was four bob, and then I filled up the brickwork and made the holes good, and there was no more come.

"I calls myself a coster; some calls theirselves general dealers, but I doesn't. I goes to market, and if one thing don't suit, why I buys another.

"I don't know whether you've heerd of it, master, or not, but I'm the man as they say kills rats – that's to say, I kills 'em like a dog. I'm almost ashamed to mention it, and I shall never do it any more, but I've killed rats for a wager often. You see it's only been done like for a lark; we've bin all together daring one another, and trying to do something nobody else could. I remember the first time I did it for a wager, it was up at—, where they've got a pit. There was a bull-dog a killing rats, so I says,

" 'Oh, that's a duffin' dog; any dog could kill quicker than him. I'd kill again him myself.'

"Well, then they chaffed me, and I warn't goin' to be done; so I says,

" 'I'll kill again that dog, for a sov'rin.'

"The sov'rin was staked. I went down to kill eight rats again the dog, and I beat him. I killed 'em I like a dog, with my teeth. I went down hands and knees and bit 'em. I've done it three times for a sov'rin, and I've won each time. I feels very much ashamed of it, though.

"On the hind part of my neck, as you may see, sir, there's a scar; that's where I was bit by one; the rat twisted himself round and held on like a vice. It was very bad, sir, for a long time; it festered, and broke out once or twice, but it's all right now."

from *London Labour and London Poor*, 1851

Dr John Henry Salter

We then adjourned to "the Pit," a crib upstairs, boarded high all round, in which the amusements of dog-fighting, ratting and badger hunting were accustomed to be held. Two huge dogs were first brought in, and I began to entertain some considerable trepidation lest the infuriated beasts should turn their attention from one another to the lookers-on, in which case a very poor chance any man would have had of getting off without serious bodily injury. However, they never seemed to dream of this – all their attention, energy, and fury were vented on one another, and a struggle ensued which a couple of lions could not have equalled. They were very nearly as large as lions. Frightful were the bites given and received on both sides, and blood streamed in all directions. 'Tis a brutal sport. The spectacle made me sick. Presently one of the brutes got such a hold upon the other's lower jaw that he must ultimately have killed him if not separated, for let go his hold he would not in spite of all the united efforts of the Pitmen, who walked about with the greatest unconcern in the interior of the pit, during the entire fight. By burning with the end of a cigar, and smoking into the dog's nostrils, the teeth were at last made to loose their hold, and the animals were taken to their boxes. Several other fights followed between smaller dogs, and then a badger-bait. The animal seemed almost accustomed to his work, for he was drawn continually by every dog set at him. The Pitman volunteered to "draw" him with his hand for a shilling and did so, but not without getting a most severe wound which lacerated his wrist in a frightful manner, dividing all the veins – but this was treated like everything else with the greatest nonchalance. After the badger-baiting some rats were turned in and killed, some scientifically, others by dogs never before tried. A complete slaughter-house the room became, and none of us was sorry when the last part of the entertainment was brought on, which was of the novelest and cruelest I ever beheld. Two cats were unbagged and set a-fighting; afterwards dogs were set on them to finish them, and this took an immense time to do, the struggles made by the poor cats being something fearful. I never before realised that "a cat has nine lives." It must be ninety-nine!

Dr Salter . . . His Diary and Reminiscences,
1849 to 1932, 18 February 1863

Anonymous

A Brutal Dog-Fight. Skip, of Long Island, and Jack of New York, Fight for $1,200 – Both Dogs Die in the Pit with Their Fangs in Each Other's Throats.

Early yesterday morning about two hundred roughs assembled at a dog-pit near Laurel Hill, Long Island, to witness a dog-fight, undoubtedly the most brutal one on record, between Jack of New

York, and Skip, of Long Island. The fight was for $1,200 and the conditions were that each dog should not weigh over twenty-six pounds. After the usual preliminaries on such occasions, a well-known New York sport was selected referee and the fight announced. Upon time being called, both dogs sprang from the arms of their respective handlers and with a ferocious snarl rushed at each other. Odds of $100 to $60 were freely offered on Skip, with few takers. Skip succeeded in fastening his fangs into his opponent's jaw and dragged him to the ground. Blood once drawn, the brutes became more ferocious, and began devouring one another in the most approved style. They had fought for nearly an hour when they had so lacerated one another as to be almost unrecognizable. The scene became so disgusting that a number of the spectators were obliged to retire. After an hour and ten minutes' fighting, both dogs showed signs of weakening, and it was plain that they could not continue longer. Urged by the cries of their respective backers, they tore each other's flesh. At last Skip seized his opponent by the throat and shook him as a terrier would a rat. Jack returned the compliment but was again seized by Skip. At this juncture the excitement became intense, and the crowd began to force themselves into the pit. The handlers seized their dogs and attempted to loosen their grip but not until life was extinct in both. The referee decided the fight was a draw, when a cry of foul was raised, and in an incredibly short time a general fight ensued, during which knives were freely used. One of the roughs residing in this City was stabbed in the abdomen and it has since been ascertained that the wound is likely to prove fatal. He was taken to his home by friends.

New York Times, 21 December 1876

Sir Jocelyn M. Lucas, Bart.

The Ilmer Sealyhams had two days in Lincolnshire recently – result five large badgers in under an hour and a half, no mean performance. The first dig was organised by Lady Charles Bentinck, and took place near Market Rasen. There was a choice of three earths, and the keeper suggested trying the nearest one first. "Only a single hole, an easy dig in sandy soil." The writer felt quite happy on putting terriers in to hear them find immediately. He felt rather less happy when they had moved on some yards downhill to see the keeper lying with his ear to the ground about sixty yards in the opposite direction. "Oh, I know this earth of old," said he, "it goes for miles." However, we drove our badger down hill, and by 2 o'clock had a trench about fifteen yards long and half-moon shaped, inside which we thought we had him cut off. Anyhow, everyone was full of optimism, when a digger called out, 'they are scuffling like anything, here, sir!' So they were, for they had slipped round the end to the main earth again. No use. So we tried another earth, but had to give up after dark in a thick fog, with Jack and Twinkle each on a badger. The pack on this occasion consisted of Jack, Bantam, Tim, Twinkle, Sally, Venom, Sheila, Pancake and Bracelet.

Having had this experience of Lincolnshire earths, we felt less confident when accepting the invitation of Mr J. St Vigor Fox to Girsby Manor. The first earth wasted little time, but Brock was not there; the second looked like a fox, so we did not try; the third, a good-sized one, was well worked. Accordingly Jack, Vic, Sheila, Pancake, Twinkle, Gipsey, Fish, and Sausage were slipped at various points, and all except Fish, who is young, got on right away. A shallow earth, three feet to four feet deep in most places, and sandy. For about twenty minutes they rattled round, now baying here, now there. Digging as yet would have done no good, but whenever a badger stopped to fight in the centre a few thuds overhead with the flat of a spade moved him on. Suddenly we heard a thumping noise away from the earth and a faint baying. We opened up well behind, and Jack, who appeared from another hole, was put in this. He spoke at once and went on a couple of yards or so. We dug down on top of him, to find the hole turned left-handed, and fear of the badgers getting back to the main earth was removed by hearing Sausage baying faintly through a wall of earth still farther to the left, and evidently facing us. Another yard of digging drove back the badgers, and, skipping six feet, we dug down again, only two feet deep now, the whole pack being up, with Jack leading. Here we found the first badger, which we drew with Jack and one or two others. Twinkle, who was buried in loose earth, was baying merrily a yard back, her tail being the only portion visible. Meanwhile another badger bolted, to be caught by Sausage and tailed by the writer, who passed it on to Mr Fox. Having transferred both these to sacks we uncovered Twinkle, to find her right up to one, and sent for Tim. He got another badger (great excitement). Sausage meanwhile, had got a catch-as-catch can grip on a fourth. It was not until we had dug her that we discovered that the badger had hold of her nose as well. She never whimpered once, and never let go, is an extraordinary bitch, and seems impervious to pain.

Four badgers seemed pretty good, but Bantam wanted a turn, and we had another one out of the loose earth inside three minutes. There were no more up either of these pipes, and we had probably rounded most of them up, if not all. The terriers were too excited to go down again in the same earth, so after lunch we went home with our bag of five. Jack and Sausage really shared the honours this time, but Twinkle scored heavily, as we owe the last three to her. Sheila is feeling very old just now, but is still as game as a pebble. We have two meets in Lincolnshire in January, and hope to go to Herefordshire, Oxfordshire and Bucks, as well as having local digs in Leicestershire.

"Badger Digging in Lincolnshire", *The Field,* 31 December 1921

Captain Lawrence Fitz-Barnard

Perhaps the most terrible fighting-dog that ever lived was a bitch named Bridget; she was unapproachable by man or beast, but a terrific fighter. They tell me she smashed a dog's skull in with her teeth. Her master, who went by the name of Billy the Barman, was a great sport − coursing, ratting, pigeon-shooting, boxing, dog-fighting were all one to him.

As you may guess by his name, he kept a pub, and, although it was in the heart of London, he had a duck-pond on his roof and a rabbit-warren in his cellar. When he was a little merry he would take two or three greyhounds and some ferrets down to his cellar, and course the rabbits as they dashed about the cellar.

He acquired Bridget in an unusual way. He and some friends were on a picnic in the country, and, I fear a little blotto. It was not unnatural that they should call on a sporting friend, who also kept a pub. This sportsman owned Bridget; she was kept tied up in a barn, and her food pushed to her at the end of a long stick. Being ready for a little fun, the owner offered to give Bridget to anyone who would unloose her. Billy – I fear he did not quite know what he was doing – walked straight up to her, patted her head, and let her loose. To everyone's surprise she did not eat him; probably Bridget was as surprised as anybody else. They took to each other, and he took her home, and they remained pals to her death.

It was sad, but he could never breed from Bridget. She had several litters of pups by good dogs, but after a day or two she would eat them. She did have one litter by mistake, by a little black and tan cur dog, and these were the only puppies she never ate. As they were Bridget's puppies, in spite of the cur blood, Billy bred from them, and some people say that this is how the black and tan colour came into the breed, and that it nearly ruined the fighting-dogs of London. It is a fact that most black and tan dogs are cowards, and they were fairly numerous some years ago.

Another great sport I knew in those days was great in more ways than one, for he weighed twenty-nine stone; there was just room for him in a hansom-cab.

One night at my place he ate five shillings' worth of sausage-rolls. I think this is the greatest feat I ever saw.

The same evening another dreadful thing happened. I was young then, and it was the reprehensible practice of my dear old brother and myself to invite some of the toughest nuts in London to our place after our people had gone to bed. Each brought his dog, and what with three or four turn-ups of twenty minutes or so, our pet badger, and a few dozen rats, we had some pleasant little evenings. The scene of action was the kitchen – this is where the sausage-rolls disappeared – and what we called our study, of which the most prominent article of furniture was the pit. There were double doors leading out to the garden, and when one was closed there was not a lot of room.

On the night in question our old trainer had gone out for something, and whilst we were thoroughly, if illegally enjoying ourselves, he returned, and we did not hear his knock. Being impatient, he thundered at the door in a quite unwarrantable manner. Someone said "Police!" Immediately there was a rush for the garden; a few escaped, but our big friend stuck in the door, and the frantic efforts of the prisoners to push him one way or the other was one of the drollest things imaginable. Seeing our retreat was cut off, I went to brave the police, opened the door, and there was old Deaffy. I returned and reassured the multitude, but found some of the party were missing. Now the garden terminated in a 9ft wall, with a mews at the back of it, and how they fled this wall causes me wonder to this day.

Unfortunately they happened to be some friends of ours who had dined with us earlier and stayed to see the fun. I had to round them up; and gentlemen strolling aimlessly about the streets in evening dress, with no hats or coats on, on a bitter cold night, caused a lot of speculation on the part of my friend, the bobby, on the corner.

He came up to me quite anxiously and asked me if there was a burglary, or what was the matter? I told him my friends were demons for fresh air; but we thought it wiser to wait till five o'clock in the morning, when the beats were changed – my old trainer was wise in the ways of coppers – then we floured the white dogs and sooted the dark ones and sent them home.

My brother and self had a big white dog then that was champion of London – we always said England; he made us quite famous, and we were known down East as "them young fellers what belongs to the big white dog."

He got loose one day whilst we were away, and, of course, set about the first dog he saw, who was naturally tied up. A maid we had then saw them and rushed out and pulled him off; true, she pulled the other dog's ear off as well, but I admire her to this day. I assure you few people would have gone near him, at all. Afterwards he did nearly kill two people, and the wretches I gave him to had him shot.

He was a dear old dog and as game as a pebble – one of the old sort. I have trod on his toe, and wondered what I was treading on till I looked down and saw him; he never said anything.

The first night I had him I tied him up in my study. I was reading a book after having admired him for some time, and, not thinking moved my foot suddenly; he claimed my boot in a moment. I was never so frightened in my life. I broke loose and seized an iron bar which happened to be handy, and we settled the question of superiority there and then. It wasn't fair, for he was tied up; but we never fell out again. Dear old chap, I am often sorry I hit him with that iron bar.

I had a little bitch at the same time who was quite different; she was as kind as a Christian. What a silly expression! She was far kinder than any Christian. She would turn away from a dog in the street and never look at a cat; but take her collar off and pick her up and she would have gone through hell to get at either. When our little shows were on she would know, though I used to tie her up at the top of the house. She would cry all night if she was left out; but if I fetched her she would give one little growl, and tremble with joy in my arms till I loosed her in the pit.

What dogs they were! They are dead and I am alive; the least worthy. I do not think they breed them now, but in my declining years I had a little fighting-dog who was the light of my eyes. Thinking only of myself, I never let her fight if I could help it; but she fought when she could, anything she could get her mouth on, and she was so small she seldom met anything near her size. At a few months old she killed a fox-hound, and amongst her trophies were a pony and a pig. Horses were not too big for her, and that her leg was broken by one did not stop her. She never fought an elephant, but that was because she never had the opportunity; the utter hopelessness of it would have been nothing to her dauntless heart; and, once she started, you might have called on the west wind to stop with as much hope of success.

For eleven years she was my pride and joy; for eleven years she slept at my feet. Even now the tears rise to my eyes. She was braver than any living thing, she was wiser than any man, and more faithful than a woman.

> She is dead; but her memory lives for ever in my heart.
> Nancy the Brave, the heart knew no fear;
> Courage too rich for use, for earth too dear.
> *Fighting Sports*, 1921

Arthur Blake Heinemann

Wherever in the kingdom vermin abounds there you will find terriers bred, trained and kept to wage war on the various beasts that are included in this category. These are the genuine working terriers, whose sole *raison d'être* is their utility, apart from the hold their deeds of derring-do have won them in their masters' affections. The Foxhunter wants a terrier to bolt his hunted fox, or in an unstopped and "hollow" country to eject a fresh one; the otter-hunter can do but little without a good terrier, when his hounds mark solid at some drain-mouth or tangled mass of tree-trunks and the badger-hunter, most difficult to please into a corner, keeping him to bay there, one of the hardest fighting beasts he is ever called to face underground. Punishment he must be prepared to take, however cautious and clever he is, and he must throw his tongue too, to tell the sturdy diggers where to sink down a trench to the scene of combat. As a rule a fox's bite is a mere nothing (though I have had a terrier's nose from snout to eye reduced to a pulp of broken bone by one), and little harm results, so it is with an otter's bite, both usually bite your terrier on the nose or top jaw. But the very serious wounds a badger inflicts are always disfiguring, often mortal, and require much attention afterwards in kennel, for days or even weeks before they are safely healed up. It is very amusing to anyone with experience of the gashes, especially on the under jaw, inflicted by a badger, to hear a man point proudly to some scar or scud on his terrier's nose inflicted by a fox or otter. Four badgers and a fox in one earth once put paid to a bitch of mine, and so mauled another that she was weeks recovering. Three badgers put four couple on the sick list for a month, and killed another bitch of mine. Another had a leg broken; another had an ear sheared clean off, and many have been subjected to very rough dental extractions by these formidable foes.

Some people think badger-digging makes terriers too hard for foxhunting, but I am not with them there; for I think a badger teaches them caution, and to throw their tongue, whereas a fox is but a soft beast for a plucky terrier to tackle, and he learns to take liberties. Also with fox a terrier thinks he is fighting another of his breed, whereas a badger's scent is something strange, and his growling and gruffings and charges very disconcerting. On the other hand, a terrier that is *hard* with a badger is too hard for a fox, but such a one is the boy to bolt an old otter.

I think for otter hunting you cannot have a terrier too hard, for a fox any yapping terrier of average pluck, and for a badger a very plucky one with discretion and tongue. The place for a working terrier is at work or resting on his master's bed or in his armchair, for no amount of comfort or coddling will make a good and proved terrier soft. He takes his work seriously and strenuously, and he likes his days off to be luxurious, and the closer the companionship between dog and master the more intelligent will the former become, and the greater individuality will he develop; and as to the latter, from whom will he better learn to be faithful and game to the death? . . .

In kennel, no man who values his terriers ever kennels them with the pack, and he deserves no sympathy if hounds kill them. I am also inclined to think terriers start kennel-fights. Heavily-marked terriers will often throw or beget all white puppies, and unless one breeds by the Mendelian theory, one can safely leave the colour fetich to languish with the rest of them all.

Returning to the question of size: for badger-digging you can use a bigger terrier in most earths, but a small one is useful when the badger is in loose grey shale or busy throwing up earth and sand behind him in his efforts to escape. In foxhunting a smaller terrier is necessary, especially for drains, but you want one (at least in moorland countries) who can keep up with hounds all day, and run the line, casting up some few minutes after hounds have marked their fox to ground. To do this he must have a certain length of leg and be built on galloping lines. For otter-hunting you cannot have a terrier too small or too game, and these combined are very difficult to get. They usually are the weakliest of each litter, and most difficult to bring to maturity, or those that have had a setback in their growth through illness.

Terriers never do well on kennel food, but scraps, and more liberty than hounds get. I think kennel life bores them to death. They want to be up and about and doing. As for gameness the hardest terriers to badger I have known have been no use in a dog-fight, wouldn't touch a cat (no test of a dog's gameness and very bad training), and one would only mumble a rat (but this was an exceptional case, I believe). Ratting and digging out rats for themselves with a little aid and any work beside the water is good training for underground terriers. But avoid rabbits, or one day your terriers will make you look foolish when you stand beside the diggers in the trench. Also be careful how you talk over the walnuts and wine about your terrier's prowess. Three very amusing experiences have fallen to my lot. Two "Show" men brought two fox-terriers to the West to try them out badger-digging. They patronized my team, praising their *natural* coats, and necks and shoulders, but saying they never saw such heads. They couldn't have pleased me more (but "I said nuffin," like Brer Rabbit). When we got to the earth they admitted at once that their dogs were too big; one looked like a miniature hound, perfect in make and shape, and the other was bigger. My two cornered their badger and were taken up, when the houndy-looking terrier went in so far, and did very well as far as went. He had pluck. The bigger terrier then tried an unoccupied earth, a big one as regarded size of hole, which pleased his master, but he would never have got through a rambling earth. They very kindly offered me a free £5 service of dog No. 1, which I declined, and asked me for a working certificate, which I made out according to what I had witnessed. So all went the same way home, and well-pleased.

Another time a lady brought down her team of white West Highland terriers, but they would not go to ground, find or bay a badger there, or join in a worry with a dead badger, and she said they didn't like the noise of the diggers shouting, and the noise of their spades and picks, nor the brambles at the mouth of the earth. A third time a youth brought some pretty Dandie-Dinmonts down, and told us yarns about their pluck. These next day would not go to ground, or look at a badger. Noise again! So all mine were kennelled, and in solemn silence a badger let go in view. I regret to say the Dandies wouldn't even hunt his line or go near him. Yet one more, if space admits: Two well-known working terrier men appeared at a big earth very freshly used by badgers. They had a Sealyham with a great reputation. So she went in first to find. "Nothing there," said her owner, but there was, for he was found by mine, and presently viewed, though not captured, and the Sealyham was found to have a gash on her seat of honour!!! But I am treading on good fellows' corns, and certainly on delicate ground; but a pound of practice is worth a ton of theory.

"Hunt Terriers", *The Foxhound*, October 1912

CHAPTER 7

Dogs as Pets

I n the United States and Canada there is roughly one dog for every five people, and in Australia one for every seven.

It is commonly supposed that the British have an unusually popular affection for dogs and, as a consequence, a higher population of dogs than many other countries or, indeed, perhaps any other country. It is also supposed that in Britain the dog population was, during the late 1980s and early 1990s, far higher than it had ever been. Both suppositions are wrong.

A survey carried out in 1990 by the European Consumer Protection Agency reveals that per head of human population France and Ireland have the highest populations of dogs in Europe: one for every six people. Then come Belgium, Portugal and the United Kingdom with one dog for every eight people, followed by Denmark and Italy, Netherlands, Spain, Germany and Greece. Luxembourg had the lowest canine population with one dog for every thirty-one people.

The dog population is now higher than it has ever been, though the growth rate has slowed and in some countries has been reversed as a consequence of years of economic depression.

The popularity of dogs as companions is remarkably enduring and for good reason. The relationship between dog and man is unique and uniquely close. Dogs, more than any other creature, have the ability as well as the desire to be close to man, to respond to his commands and even to anticipate them. A household dog offers affection, companionship, security, interest, a source of pride, a means of introduction to other dog owners, an inducement to take exercise and, with proper training, much more.

Doctors now recognize that dog owners are less likely to become ill and more likely to recover quickly and completely than are those who choose or are obliged to forgo the company of a dog.

Geoffrey Chaucer

And she had little dogs she would be feeding
With roasted flesh, or milk, or fine white bread.
Sorely she wept if one of them were dead
Or someone took a stick and made it smart.

from "Prologue" *The Canterbury Tales*, 1387

William Caxton

There was a lady that had two little dogs, and she loved them so took great pleasure in the sight and feeding of them. And every day she had dishes dressed for them with sops of milk and afterwards gave them meat. But there was a friar who said to her that it was not well done that the dogs should be fed and made so fat and the poor people so lean and famished for hunger. And the lady was wroth with him but she would not amend it.

And after she died there fell a wonder marvellous sight, for there were seen ever on her bed two little black dogs and as she lay dying they were about her mouth and licked it and when she was dead where the dogs had licked was all black as coal, as a gentlewoman told me that saw it, and named me the lady.

from *The Book of the Knight of La Tour Landry*, c. 1480

Ulisse Aldrovandi

Pet dogs, then, Blondus decided, ought to be classified into two species, because he observed that some have longer and some shorter hairs. The keepers of Maltese dogs here call those dogs that are full of the longer hairs "Nothi": for which reason we will give actual illustrations of both in this work. Blondus recommends those that are partly white, partly black, but at the present day the preference is for the red or the white. So then this dog, according to the theory of Blondus, is only a foot or half a foot long and commands a price all the greater when it is no larger than a mouse, and at its utmost magnitude it is of the size of the common weasel of the wood, which is technically called Viverra. In order to preserve its minute size, it is shut up in a basket, and is fed while in the basket, for if it is moved about quickly it grows to a disproportionate size. Another means by which the growth of these small animals is hindered, for there are naturalists who take the bark of the wild fig-tree which was newly formed, and apply it to the liver or the swelling spleen, and then hang it up in a heating-room until it is dry; they assert that while this process is going on the swelling of the stomach diminished.

from *Natural History, c.* 1570

Abraham Fleming

Of the delicate, neate, and pretty kind of dogges called the Spaniel gentle, or the comforter, in Latine *Melitaeusor Fotor.*

There is, besides those which wee have already delivered, another sort of gentle dogges in this our Englishe soyle but exempted from the order of the residue, the Dogges of this kinde doth *Callimachus* call *Melitoeos*, of the Iseland Melita, in the sea of *Siciliy*, (what at this day is named *Malta*) . . .

These dogges are litle, prety, proper, and fyne, and sought for to satisfie the delicatenesse of daintie dames, and wanton womens wills, instrumentes of folly for them to play and dally withall, to tryfle away the treasure of time, to withdraw their mindes from commendable exercises, and to content their corrupted concupiscences with vaine disport (A selly shift to shunne yrcksome ydlenesse.) These puppies the smaller they be, the more pleasure they provoke, as more meete play fellowes for minsing mistrisses to beare in their bosoms, to keepe company withal in their chambers, to soccour with sleepe in bed, and nourishe with meate at bourde, to lay in their lappes, and lick their lippes as they ryde in their waggons, and good reason it should be so, for coursenesse with fynenesse hath no felowship, but featnesse with neatnesse hath neighbourhood enough . . .

Notwithstanding many make much of these pretty puppies caled Spaniells gentle, yet if the question were demaunded what propertie in them they spye, which shulde make them so acceptable and precious in their sight, I doubt their answere would be long a coyning.

. . . And though some suppose that such dogges are fyt for no service, I dare say, by their leaves, they be in a wrong boxe. Among all other qualities therefore of nature, which be knowne . . . we find that these litle doges are good to asswage the sicknesse of the stomacke being oftentimes therunto applyed as a plaster preservative, or borne in the bosom of the diseased and weake person, which effect is performed by theyr moderate heate.

from *Of Englishe Dogges,* 1576

William Topsell

There is also at this day among us a new kinde of dog brought out of France (for we Englishmen are marveilous gredy gaping cormorants of things that be seldome, rare, strange and hard to get). And they be speckled all over with white and black, with mingled colours incline to a marble blew, which beautifies their skins and affordeth a seemely show of comlinesse. These are called French dogs as is above declared already.

from *Historie of the Foure-Footed Beastes,* 1607

John Marston

I was a scholar; seven useful springs
Did I deflower in quotations
Of cross'd opinions 'bout the soul of man:
The more I learnt, the more I learnt to doubt.
Delight, my spaniel, slept, whilst I baused leaves,
Tossed o'er the dunces, pored on the old print
Of titled words; and still my spaniel slept.
Whilst I wasted lamp-oil, baited my flesh,
Shrunk up my veins, and still my spaniel slept,
And still I held converse with Zabarell,

Aquinas, Scotus, and the musty saws
Of antique Donate: still my spaniel slept.
Still on went I; first, an sit anima;
Then, an 'twere mortal. O hold, hold! at that
They're at brain buffets, fell by the ears, amain
[Pell-mell] together: still my spaniel slept.
Then, whether 'twere corporeal, local, fixt,
Ex traduce; but whether 't had free will
Or no, hot philosophers
Stood banding factions, all so strongly propt,
I staggered, knew not which was firmer part;
But thought, quoted, read, observed, and pried,
Stuffed noting-books: and still my spaniel slept.
At length he waked, and yawned; and by yon sky
For aught I know, he knew as much as I!

"A Scholar and his Dog", c. 1620

Jonathan Swift

Happiest of the Spaniel race,
Painter, with thy colours grace;
Draw his forehead large and high,
Draw his blue and humid eye;
Draw his neck so smooth and round,
Little neck with ribands bound;
And the muscly swelling breast
Where the Loves and Graces rest;
And the spreading even back,
Soft, and sleek, and glossy black;
And the tail that gently twines,
Like the tendrils of the vines;
And the silky twisted hair,
Shadowing thick and velvety ear;

Velvet ears, which, hanging low,
O'er the veiney temples flow,
With a proper light and shade,

Let the winding hoop be laid;
And within that arching bower
(Secret circle, mystic power,)
In a downy slumber place
Happiest of the spaniel race.

"On Rover, a Lady's Spaniel,
Instructions to a painter," *c.* 1730

Thomas Gray

I was hindered in my last, and so could not give you all the trouble I would have done. The description of a road, which your coach wheels have so often honoured, it would be needless to give you: suffice it that I arrived safe at my uncle's, who is a great hunter in imagination; his dogs take up every chair in the house, so I am forced to stand at this present writing; and though the gout forbids him galloping after them in the field, yet he continues still to regale his ears and nose with their comfortable noise and stink.

Letter to Horace Walpole, c. 1760

William Hazlitt

A rough terrier dog, with the hair bristled and matted together, is picturesque. As we say, there is a decided character in it, a marked determination to an extreme point. A shock-dog is odd and disagreeable, but there is nothing picturesque in its appearance; it is a mere mass of flimsy confusion.

from "On the Picturesque and Ideal", *Table Talk,* 1821

James Orchard Halliwell-Philips

I had a little dog his name was Blue Bell,
I gave him some work, and he did very well;

I sent him up stairs to pick up a pin,
He stepped in the coal-scuttle up to his chin;
I sent him to the garden to pick some sage,
He tumbled down and fell in a rage;
I sent him to the cellar, to draw a pot of beer,
He came up again and said there was none there.

Children's Encyclopedia, 1842

Emily Brontë

I took a seat at the end of the hearthstone opposite that towards which my landlord advanced, and filled up an interval of silence by attempting to caress the canine mother, who had left her nursery, and was sneaking wolfishly to the back of my legs, her lip curled up, and her white teeth watering for a snatch. My caress provoked a long, guttural snarl.

"You'd better let the dog alone," growled Mr Heathcliff in unison, checking fiercer demonstrations with a punch of his foot. "She's not accustomed to be spoiled – not kept for a pet." Then, striding to a side door, he shouted again. "Joseph!"

Joseph mumbled indistinctly in the depths of the cellar, but gave no intimation of ascending; so his master dived down to him, leaving me vis-a-vis the ruffianly bitch and a pair of grim, shaggy sheep-dogs, who shared with her a jealous guardianship over all my movements. Not anxious to come in contact with their fangs, I sat still; but, imagining they would scarcely understand tacit insults, I unfortunately indulged in winking and making faces at the trio, and some turn of my physiognomy so irritated madam, that she suddenly broke into a fury and leaped on my knees. I flung her back, and hastened to interpose the table between us. This proceeding roused the whole hive; half a dozen four-footed fiends, of various sizes and ages, issued from hidden dens to the common centre. I felt my heels and coat-laps peculiar subjects of assault; and parrying off the larger combatants as effectually as I could with the poker, I was constrained to demand, aloud, assistance from some of the household in re-establishing peace.

Mr Heathcliff and his man climbed the cellar steps with vexatious phlegm: I don't think they moved one second faster than usual, though the hearth was an absolute tempest of worrying and yelping. Happily, an inhabitant of the kitchen made more despatch: a lusty dame, with tucked-up gown, bare arms, and fire-flushed cheeks, rushed into the midst of us flourishing a frying-pan – and used that weapon, and her tongue, to such purpose, that the storm subsided magically, and she only remained, heaving like a sea after a high wind, when her master entered on the scene.

"What the devil is the matter?" he asked, eyeing me in a manner that I could ill endure after this inhospitable treatment.

"What the devil, indeed!" I muttered. "The herd of possessed swine could have no worse spirits in them than those animals of yours, sir. You might as well leave a stranger with a brood of tigers."

"They don't meddle with persons who touch nothing," he remarked, putting the bottle before me, and restoring the displaced table. "The dogs do right to be vigilant. Take a glass of wine?"

"No, thank you."

"Not bitten, are you?"

"If I had been, I would have set my signet on the biter."

Heathcliff's countenance relaxed into a grin.

"Come, come," he said, "you are flurried, Mr Lockwood. Here, take a little wine. Guests are so exceedingly rare in this house that I and my dogs, I am willing to own, hardly know how to receive them. Your health, sir!"

from *Wuthering Heights*, 1847

Abraham Fleming

That plausible proverbe verified upon a Tyraunt, namely that he loved his sowe better then his sonne, may well be applyed to these kinde of people, who delight more in dogges that are deprived of all possibility of reason, then they doe in children that be capeable of wisdome and judgement. But this abuse peradventure raigneth where there hath bene long lacke of issue, or else where barrennes is the best blossome of bewty.

from *Of Englishe Dogges*, 1576

Jane Carlyle

O Lord! I forgot to tell you I have got a little dog, and Mr C. has accepted it with amiability. To be sure, when he comes down gloomy in the morning or comes in wearied from his walk, the infatuated little beast dances round him on its hind legs, as I ought to do and can't; and he feels flattered and surprised by such unwonted capers to his honour and glory.

Letter to John Forster, 1849

Revd J. G. Wood

I think that college dogs deserve to be reckoned as a separate class, like shepherd's dogs, for they, as a body, have certain peculiarities that distinguish them from all other dogs. It is said that almost any breed of dogs can be trained as shepherds' dogs, and it is quite certain that there is no living species of dog that has not led a collegiate life. Almost every resident member of the university possesses a dog and many possess several. Indeed, at my own college it was estimated that each member of the college had a dog and a third, while in another college two dogs and a quarter was the average.

from *The Illustrated Natural History,* 1853

Henry du Pré Labouchère

I do have feelings of guilt when I devour the friend of man, a dog. The other day I had a slice of spaniel, but it made me feel a cannibal. Dog epicures inform me that poodle is easily the best, and they recommend me not to eat bulldog, which is coarse and lacks all taste.

from *Diary of the Besieged Resident in Paris,* 1871

Richard Jefferies

There are dogs under the tables and chairs; dogs in the window-seat; dogs panting on the stone flags of the passage, after a sharp trot behind a trap, choosing the coolest spot to loll their red tongues out; dogs outside in the road; dogs standing on hind legs, and painfully lapping the water in the horse-trough; and there is a yapping of puppies in the distance. The cushions of the sofa are strewn with dogs' hairs, and once now and then a dog leisurely hops up the staircase.

Customers are served by the landlady, a decent body enough in her way: her son, the man of the house, is up in the "orchut" at the rear, feeding the dogs. Where the "orchut" ends in a paddock stands a small shed: in places the thatch on the roof has fallen through in the course of years and revealed the bare rafters. The bottom part of the door has decayed, and the long nose of a greyhound is thrust out sniffing through a hole. Dickon, the said son, is delighted to undo the padlock for a visitor who is "square." In an instant the long hounds leap up, half a dozen at a time, and I stagger backwards, forced by the sheer vigour of their caresses against the doorpost. Dickon cannot quell the uproarious pack: he kicks the door open, and away they scamper round and round the paddock at headlong speed.

What a joy it is to them to stretch their limbs! I forget the squalor of the kennel in watching their happy gambols. I cannot drink more than one tumbler of brown brandy and water; but Dickon overlooks that weakness, feeling that I admire his greyhounds.

from *The Amateur Poacher*, 1879

Jerome K. Jerome

What I've suffered from them this morning no tongue can tell. It began with Gustavus Adolphus. Gustavus Adolphus (they call him "Gusty" downstairs for short) is a very good sort of dog, when he is in the middle of a large field, or on a fairly extensive common, but I won't have him in-doors. He means well, but this house is not his size. He stretches himself, and over go two chairs and a what-not. He wags his tail, and the room looks as if a devastating army had marched through it. He breathes, and it puts the fire out.

At dinner-time, he creeps in under the table, lies there for a while, and then gets up suddenly; the first intimation we have of his movements being given by the table, which appears animated by a desire to turn somersaults. We all clutch at it frantically, and whereupon he struggles, he being under the impression that some wicked conspiracy is being hatched against him, becomes fearful, and the final picture presented is generally that of an overturned table and a smashed-up dinner, sandwiched between two sprawling layers of infuriated men and women.

He came in this morning in his usual style, which he appears to have founded on that of an American cyclone, and the first thing he did was to sweep my coffee cup off the table with his tail, sending the contents full into the middle of my waistcoat.

I rose from my chair, hurriedly, and remarking "—," approached him at a rapid rate. He preceded me in the direction of the door. At the door he met Eliza, coming in with the eggs. Eliza observed, "Ugh!" and sat down on the floor, the eggs took up different positions about the carpet, where they spread themselves out, and Gustavus Adolphus left the room. I called after him, strongly advising him to go straight downstairs, and not let me see him again for the next hour or so; and he, seeming to agree with me, dodged the coal-scoop, and went.

from *Idle Thoughts for an Idle Fellow*, 1889

Ambrose Bierce

He toils not, neither does he spin, yet Solomon in all his glory never lay upon a door-mat all day long, sun-soaked and fly-fed and fat, while his master worked for the means wherewith to purchase an idle wag of the Solomonic tail, seasoned with a look of tolerant recognition.

from *The Devil's Dictionary*, 1895

Somerville and Ross (pseud.)

Maria did pretty well as a lion: she hunted all dogs unmistakably smaller than herself, and whenever it was reasonably possible to do so she devoured the spoils of the chase, notably Jack Snipe. It was as a lamb that she failed; objectionable as I have no doubt a lamb would be as a domestic pet, it at least would not snatch the cold beef from the luncheon table, nor yet, if banished for its crimes, would it spend the night in scratching the paint off the hall door. Maria bit beggars (who valued their disgusting limbs at five shillings the square inch), she bullied the servants, she concealed duck's claws and fishes' backbones behind the sofa cushions, and yet, when she laid her brown snout upon my knee, and rolled her blackguard amber eyes upon me, it was impossible to remember her iniquities against her. On shooting mornings Maria ceased to be a buccaneer, a glutton, and a hypocrite. From the moment when I put my gun together, her breakfast stood untouched until it suffered the final degradation of being eaten by the cats, and now in the trap she was shivering with excitement, and agonizing in her soul lest she should yet be left behind.

from "Trinket's Colt", *Some Experiences of an Irish R. M.*, 1899

Jack London

When I was a very little lad, I had a very little dog called Punch. I saw to his feeding myself. Someone in the household had shot a lot of ducks, and we had a fine meat dinner. When I had finished, I prepared Punch's dinner – a large plateful of bones and tidbits. I went outside to give it to him. Now it happened that a visitor had ridden over from a neighbouring ranch, and with him had come a Newfoundland dog as big as a calf. I set the plate on the ground. Punch wagged his tail and began. He had before him a blissful half-hour at least. There was a sudden rush. Punch was brushed aside like a straw in the path of a cyclone, and that Newfoundland swooped down upon the plate. In spite of his huge maw he must have been trained to quick lunches, for, in the fleeting instant before he received the kick in the ribs I aimed at him, he completely engulfed the contents of the plate. He swept it clean. One last lingering lick of his tongue removed even the grease stains.

from "Pictures", *The Road*, 1907

William Henry Hudson

We kept eight dogs at that time; two were pointers, all the others just the common dog of the country, a smooth-haired animal about the size of a collie. Like all dogs allowed to exist in their own way, they formed a pack, the most powerful one being their leader and master. They spent most of their time lying stretched dog-fashion in the sun in some open space near the house, fast asleep. They had little to do except bark at strangers approaching the house and to hunt off the cattle that tried to force their way through the fences into the plantation. They would also go off on hunting expeditions of their own. Strange playmates and companions for Libby, as she was named, the pretty pet lamb with fleece as white as snow; yet so congenial did she find the dogs' society that by and by she passed her whole time with them, day and night. When they came to the door to bark and whine and wag their tails to call attention to their wants or to be noticed, the lamb would be with them but would not cross the threshold since the dogs were not permitted in the rooms. Nor would she come to her mistress when called, and having discovered that grass was her proper food she wanted nothing that human beings could give her. Not even a lump of sugar! She was no longer a pet lamb; she was one of the dogs. The dogs on their part, although much given to quarrels and fights among themselves, never growled or snapped at Libby; she never tried to snatch a bone from them, and she made them a comfortable pillow when they slept and slumbered for hours at a stretch.

from "Mary's Little Lamb," *The Book of a Naturalist*, 1919

Dornford Yates

The Bold was standing still at the head of the terrace steps, surveying his present dominion with the dignity of a lion. He resembled a little image that stands on a mantelpiece.

I bent my head to Nobby, under my arm.

"There he is," I whispered. "You see, he's very small, and, although he covers it up, I think he must feel very strange. So be gentle with him, old fellow."

Nobby put up his muzzle and licked my face.

The Bold descended the steps, as best he could. Happily, they were shallow; but I am inclined to think that they were the first he had used. But they had to be traversed, if he was to reach the grass – and The Bold knew how to behave.

I let him prove the lawn. Then I put Nobby down . . .

The meeting was well timed, for The Bold had just found that the lawn was uncomfortably big. After all, he was very tiny, and the sward must have seemed immense. Be that as it may, for the first time his tail went down, and he stood, a forlorn little figure, awed by his giant surroundings and plainly not at all sure of the way he had come. And then he turned to see Nobby, two paces away.

In a flash his tail was up and he faced the Sealyham squarely, as though he knew no fear. Nobby moved his tail and lay down – and The Bold came stumbling towards him and lay down, too.

from *The Berry Scene*, 1923

John Galsworthy

For it is by muteness that a dog becomes for one so utterly beyond value; with him one is at peace where words play no torturing tricks. When he just sits loving and knows that he is being loved, those are the moments that I think are precious to a dog; when, with his adoring soul coming through his eyes, he feels that you are really thinking of him.

Memories, 1924

Will H. Ogilvie

KIRKWHELPINGTON. — The signpost showed
A winding ribbon of moorland road;
And straightway I knew if I followed it through
I should come to a kingdom of puppy and pew.

I lay at ease on the thymy bank,
And deep of the springs of dreamland drank.
Then a parson came with a bag of meal
And a red-brown Border bitch at his heel,
And somehow I knew that a litter of four
Lay curled in a box at the vestry door;

"A Moorland Signpost",
The Collected Sporting Verse of Will H. Ogilvie, 1932

Katherine Mansfield

Connie came yesterday to see me carrying a baby Pekinese. Have
you ever seen a really baby one about the size of a fur glove —
covered with pale gold down with paws like minute seal flappers
— very impudent eyes and ears like fried potatoes? Good God!
What creatures they are. This one is a perfect complement to
Wing. We must have one. They are not in the least pampered or
fussy or spoilt. They are like fairy animals. This one sat on my
lap, cleaned both my hands really very carefully, polished the nails
then bit off careful each finger and thumb and then exhausted and
blown with eight fingers and two thumbs inside him gave a great
sigh and crossed his front paws and listened to the conversation.
He lives on beef steaks and loaf sugar. His partner in life when he
is at home is a pale blue satin bedroom slipper. Please let us have
one at the Heron.

Letter to John Middleton Murry, 23 January 1920

213

E. Arnot Robertson

Here is this admirable fellow, James Thurber: a delightful draughts-
man, the originator of The Seal in the Bedroom and The Secret Life
of Walter Mitty (for either of which I would be prepared to forgive
him almost anything, except his fawning attitude towards dogs), and
the only humorist I have ever met whom it is not a mistake to meet.
When he writes about dogs, masochism is rampant, he grovels to
them. Nine out of ten of Thurber's dogs, and he has owned over 50,
are, on the evidence of this book, nasty-natured, even by dog-loving
standards. The more they bite him, scorn him, embarrass him in
front of people, turn sick in his car and prefer to be fed by anyone
else, the more he appears to dote upon them.

Review of *Thurber's Dogs, The Spectator,* 16 December 1955

Ralph Wotherspoon

My home is a haven for one who enjoys
The clamour of children and ear-splitting noise
From a number of dogs who are always about,
And who want to come in and, once in, to go out.
Whenever I settle to read by the fire,
Some dog will develop an urge to retire,
And I'm constantly opening and shutting the door
For a dog to depart or, as mentioned before,
For a dog to arrive, who, politely admitted,
Will make a bee-line for the chair I've just quitted.
Our friends may be dumb, but my house is a riot,
Where I cannot sit still and can never be quiet.

"My Dumb Friends"

Gilbert Frankau

I have known some men, and some women also, who disliked Dog.
George Moore was one such. And my own mother happened to be
another of them.

But dog-haters are exceptional; I would almost write "freakish"; and their freakish hate is seldom inherited. The most fanatical dog-lover I ever knew, for instance, was a dog-hater's child – myself, deprived – the only deprivation I ever suffered by parental authority – of canine companionship.

Curiously, that deprivation lasted until I was four-and-twenty. Till then, barring a canary or so and a brace of doves (both of whom laid eggs for a surprised nursery), I had never owned any living thing of my own.

Yet stay. Am I quite right about this? Doesn't memory recall – even as these words flow from my pen – the wraith of a Fox-terrier in pursuit of that stripling who was myself, clad in an outrageous waistcoat of green checked with white and yellow, as he galloped the wild wet woods of Frankfurt-on-the-Main?

Yes, memory is right there. Such a Fox-terrier there was – and his name "X". He was called that in memory of the first paper for which I ever wrote (and which I also owned) at Eton in the long-ago days of the Great Queen.

That paper went the way of most Eton ephemerals; and its namesake did not return with me to England.

But how I came by my dog, "X", and to whom I gave him when I left Frankfurt, escapes me down the mists of the years.

Better do I remember his successor – a thin sad-faced Dane, bought all unwisely, who lingered but a little while before he licked my hand for the last time, and turned his head away, and passed to the Good Hunting and the Better Biscuits.

"Never again will I love Dog," I said to myself, as every dog-lover has said to himself on some such desolate day. Yet consolation came swiftly, and from that very mother who could not "abide the beasts" herself.

She left the choice to me – and that time, having a little more knowledge, I chose well.

Expensively too! Grandiosely! So that I shall never forget the commotion of that day when there presented himself to the astonished clerks of my City offices, the tiger-tamer from the North; and, following him, gentle as a lamb on his burnished chain, Dog of Dogs.

"Grim Tiger," his name was. "From Axwell Kennels by the northern main. Where the cropped Porthos throats a prizeless growl.

His line is traced through Redgrave's noblest strain," as you may read if you care for the lesser author.

And in appearance my "Grim Tiger" lived up to his name.

But for all his size – even at six months old he occupied most of the taxi in which he and I fared to the station – a less tigerish Brindle never lived. My Pamela and my Ursula, then mere babies, played with him from the first; and neither to them nor to any, baby or grown-up, did he ever do the least injury – though his python of a tail, merely beginning to wag, would often sweep my suburban tea-table clear; and on one occasion, walking and leaping his loose-box door early, he swiped the entire suburban butter-and-egg ration, standing tall as a man to the kitchen window-sill for the steal.

Those were the days before the dog-destroying motor-car.

"Grim" would accompany my walk to the station of a morning, find his way home alone, and alone return to meet me of an evening, waiting patently for me when I failed on those rare occasions to catch the 6.35 from Cannon Street. For he had a sense of time which is often not given to humans; and perhaps this made him doubly precious to one who has always lived by the clock.

Of a week-end we would roam together – five-and-thirty miles sometimes. And at holiday-time he was never far behind any horse's heels.

"Nick Carter and his blood-'ound," rude little boys of those days used to call after us. But for "Grim's" sake my vanity bore even with that.

I loved him you see! Yet I cannot pretend that my love for "Grim" was altogether shared in a modest household, whose sofa would only just accommodate his wet carcass stretched at doggy ease to dry perfumedly before the fire. Maybe also – and if so let it be a lesson to others – for the dog-bore can be even as the golf-bore to the wife of his bosom – I voiced my love too loudly and too often.

The cost of "Grim's" keep, moreover, was a constant bone of contention on "bill-nights". Neither did it escape wifely notice that the grooming of "Grim", with curry-comb, brush and shammy leather took time which a single-handed gardener might better have employed among his flowers.

Nevertheless, my passion for "Grim" remained unshakable until Fate again sent me from England; and I was forced to find him another home.

Only a temporary home, I hoped. But on my return to England, War came between.

He lived apart from me after that, to a ripe old age, and very happily as I am glad to think, in a great house which I still visit; and when his Time came, he, also, passed on.

"In Praise of Dog," an introduction to *Hutchinson's Dog Encyclopaedia*, 1934

Ogden Nash

For years we've had a little dog,
Last year we acquired a big dog;
He wasn't big when we got him,
He was littler than the dog we had.
We thought our little dog would love him,
Would help him to become a trig dog,
But the new dog got bigger,
And the old little dog got mad.

Now the big dog loves the little dog,
But the little dog hates the big dog,
The little dog is eleven years old,
And the big dog only one;
The little dog calls him Schweinhund,
The little dog calls him Pig-dog,
She grumbles broken curses
As she dreams in the August sun.

The big dog's teeth are terrible,
But he wouldn't bite the little dog;
The little dog wants to grind his bones,
But the little dog has no teeth;
The big dog is acrobatic,
The little dog is a brittle dog;
She leaps to grip his jugular,
And passes underneath.

The big dog clings to the little dog
Like glue and cement and mortar;
The little dog is his own true love;
But the big dog is to her
Like a scarlet rag to a Longhorn,
Or a suitcase to a porter;
The day he sat on the hornet
I distinctly heard her purr.

Well, how can you blame the little dog,
Who was once the household darling?
He romps like a young Adonis,
She droops like an old moustache;
No wonder she steals his corner,
No wonder she comes out snarling,
No wonder she calls him Cochon
And even Espèce de vache.

Yet once I wanted a sandwich,
Either caviare or cucumber,
When the sun had not yet risen
And the moon had not yet sank;
As I tiptoed through the hallway
The big dog lay in slumber,
And the little dog slept by the big dog,
And her head was on his flank.

"Two dogs have I",
The Private Dining Room, 1953

Roy Hattersley

There has only been one dog in my life: Dinah, an unintentional cross between a black Labrador and some sort of terrier. She was mine between my fifteenth birthday and the Tuesday on which I left home. Thereafter, she became part of the ever present past that I could comfortingly recreate whenever I returned to Sheffield. I have, of course, had other casual canine acquaintances. But Dinah was the one permanent relationship.

Before I was born, my mother and father brought with them from Mansfield an expert rat-catcher called Mick. Wire-haired, white, with a black patch over one eye and an ear permanently cocked for sounds in the undergrowth, Mick appears in many box Brownie snapshots taken by my father to immortalize his intended, not her dog. I still think of him as part of an age of short dresses, pleated skirts and cloche hats. Like the 1920s, he came to a bad end.

There are two interpretations of Mick's attempt to kill me. His defenders said he mistook me for one of the sleepy rodents whose necks he specialized in snapping with a single nip – a vole of some sort. His detractors attributed his intended infanticide to pure jealousy: the refusal to allow any other living thing to be patted or stroked. Whatever the reason, about three weeks after I began to compete with him for attention, he was apprehended with teeth bared and about to spring. It was agreed that one of us had to go. Having seen the faded sepia photographs of Mick and my mother sitting on Nottingham stiles and fences, I never dared ask how difficult the choice had been.

After Mick we turned to mongrels, in the belief that, like the working classes, what they lacked in breeding they made up in temperament. One called Teddy (after the bear of the same name) enjoyed a brief, brown existence before it died of a wasting illness. The decline, death and disposal of our furry liability proved such a trauma that, after burying it in the garden like Tess of the D'Urbervilles' horse, we decided that in future we would confine ourselves to rabbits.

Not that captive rabbits lie lightly on the consciences of suburban sentimentalists. Peter, a giant, black-and-white improvement on any of the pink-eyed monsters that Dürer ever painted, kept us in emotional turbulence for seven years. The first cause of concern was his claws, which grew into curved white talons of which a Manchu mandarin would have been proud. The second was the home-made hutch, which we always feared could not withstand the rigours of a Yorkshire winter. At the slightest sign of snow or rain we nailed an extra piece of lino on the roof. The result was a hutch capable of withstanding aerial bombardment and a rabbit shell shocked from a holocaust of hammering that preceded every wet and windy weather forecast.

But at least in winter Peter was declared to be in hibernation, and the decision that all he wanted was food and sleep at least absolved us from blame about his lack of exercise. In the summer we exorcised our guilt on Wednesdays and Sundays by unwinding a roll of wire netting and setting up a temporary corral on the piece of grass that was sometimes a parade ground but never lush enough to be a lawn.

Once coerced out of his hutch, Peter made great twitching leaps from side to side of his compound. Although we never associated the twitches with the psychosis of confinement, we did fear that the signs of joy on two days a week were indications of misery on the other five.

Peter died in advanced old age. He was pronounced dead by the butcher, whose previous opinions about his health we had accepted with a mixture of relief and cynicism. We wanted to believe that a sleek coat and clear eyes were a sign of contented good health. But we took the anthropomorphic view of domestic animals and the butcher, being a part-time farmer, thought of them as stock, not family. So we doubted his ability to understand a rabbit's inner emotions.

For some years after Peter's passing we directed all our surplus affection towards wild cats and stray dogs. The cats really were wild, the issue of vagabonds who had deserted the boiled fish of domesticity for the starlings and field-mice of the nearby church-yard. The dogs were almost always found before they were lost. They belonged to distant neighbours, who allowed them to wander from lamppost to lamppost. We always assumed such neighbours never seemed to mind.

So Bessy, a Cairn terrier from up the road, spent more time with us than at home. We tried to keep the fringe out of her eyes and we untangled the coat that naturally matted around the twigs and burrs she picked up from other people's gardens. Whisky — so-called because he came from Scotland rather than because of any resemblance to the pure-bred exquisites who advertise that substance — actually lived next door. Had his owners not decided to move to a flat from which animals were prohibited we would almost certainly have been prosecuted for abduction. When it was suggested that Whisky might be "put down" we stepped in. He went for rest and recuperation to elderly aunts in Worksop where, to my chagrin, he stayed — despite the indignity of initially being called Frisky, a name thought more suitable for the pet of two maiden ladies.

But all that was no more than preparation for Dinah. I do not recall why, after ten years of only making friends with dogs, we decided once more to have one in the family. All I remember is a freezing December journey across Sheffield, a change from tram to bus in Pond Street, and the farm of Mr Russell, farmer and part-time rabbit pathologist. Some weeks earlier one of Mr Russell's Labradors had escaped at quite the wrong time and formed a disastrous liaison with a notorious terrier which, to add insult to insatiability, "didn't even have a collar." The issue lay half asleep in front of a cast-iron outhouse stove.

With gentle encouragement from Mr Russell, three of the puppies got up, yawned, stretched their back legs and stumbled across the brick floor, exuding conscious, bewildered charm as if they knew that "a good home" went to the lucky winner. One took an incompetent bite in Mr Russell's direction and went back to sleep. Perversely, though not uncharacteristically, we decided that the dissident was our dog and Dinah was carried off between me and my blue gaberdine school raincoat.

If she ever took a bite at another human being we never heard of it. She bit every other sort of animal but not people. She even tried to bite a bumblebee. We saw her snap at it as it hovered above a marigold and shake her head as it began to buzz inside her mouth. Before we were out of the kitchen door the biter had been stung and was racing into forbidden territory beyond the front gate. It took us three days to find her. Eventually she was cornered and caught, and sent over to the RSPCA. My father reclaimed her and phoned home the message "that which was lost is found," and I stopped feeling guilty about going to the pictures on the previous night when I might have been out on the streets, shouting "Dinah" into disused shops and broken-down garages.

We loved her most simply because she was ours. But we loved her as well for her sheer irrational indomitability, the unreasonable hope and unjustified expectation that keeps animals going in tough times. On holiday, in Filey or Mablethorpe, she spent her days leaping a yard into the air, absolutely convinced that she was about to catch one of the seagulls that flew 50 feet over the beach.

The whole family lived in perpetual fear of attempted leaps across impassable gorges and improvident assaults upon Alsatians. But it was all worth it for the example that she set. Twenty years after Dinah was dead, on a sunny afternoon in Ipswich marketplace, a journalist asked me why I still believed that we could win the election. "Pathological optimism," I told him, with damaging accuracy. But I did not add that I learned it from a dog called Dinah.

"Me and my dogs"

Graham Greene

The woman wore an orange scarf which she had so twisted around her forehead that it looked like a toque of the twenties, and her voice bulldozed through all opposition – the speech of her two companions, the young motor-cyclist revving outside, even the clatter of soup plates in the kitchen of the small Antibes restaurant which was almost empty now that autumn had truly set in. Her face was familiar to me; I had seen it looking down from the balcony of one of the reconditioned houses on the ramparts, while she called endearments to someone or something invisible below. But I hadn't seen her since the summer sun had gone, and I thought she had departed with the other foreigners. She said, "I'll be in Vienna for Christmas. I just love it there. Those lovely white horses – and the little boys singing Bach."

Her companions were English; the man was struggling still to maintain the appearance of a summer visitor, but he shivered in secret every now and then in his blue cotton sports-shirt. He asked throatily, "We won't see you then in London?" and his wife, who was much younger than either of them, said, "Oh, but you simply must come."

"There are difficulties," she said. "But if you two dear people are going to be in Venice in the spring . . ."

"I don't suppose we'll have enough money, will we, darling, but we'd love to show you London. Wouldn't we, darling?"

"Of course," he said gloomily.

"I'm afraid that's quite, quite impossible, because of Beauty, you see."

I hadn't noticed Beauty until then because he was so well-behaved. He lay flat on the window-sill as inert as a cream bun on a counter. I think he was the most perfect Pekinese I have ever seen – although I can't pretend to know the points a judge ought to look for. He would have been as white as milk if a little coffee had not been added, but that was hardly an imperfection – it enhanced his beauty. His eyes from where I sat seemed deep black, like the centre of a flower, and they were completely undisturbed by thought. This was not a dog to respond to the word "rat" or to show a youthful enthusiasm if someone suggested a walk. Nothing less than his own image in a glass would rouse him, I imagined, to a flicker of interest. He was certainly well-fed enough to ignore the meal that the others had left unfinished, though perhaps he was accustomed to something richer than *langouste*.

"You couldn't leave him with a friend?" the younger woman asked.

"Leave Beauty?" The question didn't rate a reply. She ran her fingers through the long *café-au-lait* hair, but the dog made no motion with his tail as a common dog might have done. He gave a kind of grunt like an old man in a club who has been disturbed by the waiter. "All these laws of quarantine – why don't your congressmen do something about them?"

"We call them MPs," the man said with what I thought was hidden dislike.

"I don't care what you call them. They live in the Middle Ages. I can go to Paris, to Vienna, Venice – why, I could go to Moscow if I wanted, but I can't go to London without leaving Beauty in a horrible prison. With all kinds of undesirable dogs."

"I think he'd have," he hesitated with what I thought was admirable English courtesy as he weighed in the balance the correct term – cell? kennel? – "a room of his own."

"Think of the diseases he might pick up." She lifted him from the window-sill as easily as she might have lifted a stole of fur and pressed him resolutely against her left breast; he didn't even grunt. I had the sense of something completely possessed. A child at least would have rebelled . . . for a time. Poor child. I don't know why I couldn't pity the dog. Perhaps he was too beautiful.

She said, "Poor Beauty's thirsty."

"I'll get him some water," the man said.

"A half-bottle of Evian if you don't mind. I don't trust the tap-water."

It was then that I left them, because the cinema in the Place de Gaulle opened at nine.

It was after eleven that I emerged again, and, since the night was fine, except for a cold wind off the Alps, I made a circuit from the Place and, as the ramparts would be too exposed, I took the narrow dirty streets off the Place Nationale – the Rue de Sade, the Rue des Bains . . . The dustbins were all out and dogs had made ordure on the pavements and children had urinated in the gutters. A patch of white, which I first took to be a cat, moved stealthily along the house-fronts ahead of me, then paused, and as I approached snaked behind a dustbin. I stood amazed and watched. A pattern of light through the slats of a shutter striped the road in yellow tigerish bars and presently Beauty slid out again and looked at me with his pansy face and black expressionless eyes. I think he expected me to lift him up, and he showed his teeth in warning.

"Why, Beauty," I exclaimed. He gave his clubman grunt again and waited. Was he cautious because he found that I knew his name or did he recognize in my clothes and my smell that I belonged to the same class as the woman in the toque, that I was one who would disapprove of his nocturnal ramble? Suddenly he cocked an ear in the direction of the house on the ramparts; it was possible that he had heard a woman's voice calling. Certainly he looked dubiously up at me as though he wanted to see whether I had heard it too, and perhaps because I made no move he considered he was safe. He began to undulate down the pavement with a purpose, like the feather boa in the cabaret act which floats around seeking a top-hat. I followed at a discreet distance.

Was it memory or a keen sense of smell which affected him? Of all the dustbins in the mean street there was only one which had lost its cover – indescribable tendrils drooped over the top. Beauty – he ignored me as completely now as he would have ignored an inferior dog – stood on his hind legs with two delicately feathered paws holding the edge of the bin. He turned his head and looked at me, without expression, two pools of ink in which a soothsayer perhaps could have read an infinite series of predictions. He gave a scramble like an athlete raising himself on a parallel bar, and he was within the dustbin, and the feathered forepaws – I am sure I have read somewhere that the feathering is very important in a contest of

Pekinese – were rooting and delving among the old vegetables, the empty cartons, the squashy fragments in the bin. He became excited and his nose went down like a pig after truffles. Then his back paws got into play, discarding the rubbish behind – old fruit-skins fell on the pavement and rotten figs, fishheads . . . At last he had what he had come for – a long tube of intestine belonging to God knows what animal; he tossed it in the air, so that it curled round the milk-white throat. Then he abandoned the dustbin, and he galumphed down the street like a harlequin, trailing behind him the intestine which might have been a string of sausages.

I must admit I was wholly on his side. Surely anything was better than the embrace of a flat breast.

Round a turning he found a dark corner obviously more suited than all the others to gnawing an intestine because it contained a great splash of ordure. He tested the ordure first, like the clubman he was, with his nostrils, and then he rolled lavishly back on it, paws in the air, rubbing the *café-au-lait* fur in the dark shampoo, the intestines trailing from his mouth, while the satin eyes gazed imperturbably up at the great black Midi sky.

Curiosity took me back home, after all, by way of the ramparts, and there over the balcony the woman leant, trying, I suppose, to detect her dog in the shadows of the street below. "Beauty!" I heard her call wearily, "Beauty!" And then with growing impatience, "Beauty! Come home! You've done your wee-wee, Beauty. Where are you, Beauty, Beauty?" Such small things ruin our sense of compassion, for surely, if it had not been for that hideous orange toque, I would have felt some pity for the old sterile thing, perched up there, calling for lost Beauty.

"Beauty", *May We Borrow Your Husband and other Stories*, 1967

CHAPTER 8

Love Me, Love My Dog

Dogs go a long way towards destroying barriers to recognition and communication which too often exist between people. Dog owners often share a degree of camaraderie which is absent among other groups. Even those who don't own a dog, and may have no wish to do so, will often approach the owner of an attractive dog with enquiries as to its breed and age and will enjoy a brief moment fondling it. Such tendencies are made use of by doctors to communicate with withdrawn and autistic personalities, and to enable those whose institutionalized lives are lived outside normal society to experience the warmth of contact with other living creatures.

Not that dogs and their owners are or have been always welcomed. In 1618 the gentlemen of Royston were put to unwelcome expense by the frequent visits which their king, James I, made in order to hunt in Hertfordshire. It would not have been politic to inform the King directly but they managed to find a less direct means of letting the King know that he and his hounds had overstayed their welcome. They kidnapped one of the King's favourite hounds, Jowler, and only on the following day, when the King was becoming anxious for the hound's safety, was he returned with a message attached to his collar.

> Good Mr Jowler, we pray you speak to the (for he hears you every day and so doth not us) that it please his Majesty to go back to London, for else the country will be undone; all our provision is spent and we are not able to entertain him any longer.

The King was neither offended not affected by the petition. He appears to have regarded it as a joke and sufficient reason to extend his visit to Royston for a further two weeks.

Eventually Jowler came to a sad end when he was accidentally killed by a bolt from the Queen of Denmark's crossbow.

The King readily forgave his Queen's poor aim and alleviated her grief by the gift of a jewel worth £2,000 "pretending it was a legacy from his dear dead dog".

William Youatt

It may appear singular that in both the Old Testament and the New the dog was spoken of almost with abhorrence. He ranked among the unclean beasts. The traffic in him and the price of him were considered as an abomination and were forbidden to be offered in the sanctuary in the discharge of any vow.

One grand object in the institution of the Jewish ritual was to preserve the Israelites from the idolatry which at that time prevailed among every other people. Dogs were held in considerable veneration by the Egyptians, from whose tyranny the Israelites had just escaped. Figures of them appeared on the friezes of most of the temples, and they were regarded as emblems of the Divine Being. Herodotus, speaking of the sanctity in which some animals were held by the Egyptians, says that the people of every family in which a dog died, shaved themselves – their expression of mourning – and he adds that "this was a custom existing in his own time".

from *The Dog*, 1845

Petronius

Pelles put his hand to his mouth and made an excruciating sort of hissing, which he afterwards declared was Greek. Trimalchio, not to be outdone, made a noise like that of a trumpet and beckoned to his page, whom he called Croesus. The boy, a blear-eyed creature with horridly decayed teeth, was wrapping up a little black she-dog, disgustingly fat, in a green scarf, and was cramming her with a half-loaf which he had placed on the couch and which she, already satiated, was turning from with loathing. This put into Trimalchio's head the idea of sending for Scylax, his watchdog. The latter was very promptly brought in. He was a big dog with a chain round his neck. In answer to a kick from the doorkeeper this animal lay down in front of the table. Then Trimalchio threw him a piece of white bread, saying "No one in this house loves me better than this dog."

The boy, angry that such extravagant praise was bestowed on Scylax, put the little lap-dog on the ground and egged her on to fight. Scylax, as big dogs are wont to do, filled the dining-hall with a terrific barking and nearly tore Croesus's treasure to pieces. A quarrelsome uproar arose, and a candelabrum was upset over the table, and all the crystal vases were smashed, so that several of the feasters were splashed with scalding oil.

from *The Satyricon*

Martial

Issa is more piquant than Catullus' bullfinch. Issa is purer than the kiss of a dove. Issa is more tender than all the young maidens. Issa is more precious than the sapphires of India. The little Issa is Publius' heart's delight; when she gives a tiny whine you would have thought that she spoke, and she knows all her master's sorrows and his joys. She lies upon his neck, and sleeps without even a sigh escaping her, and if she finds herself in need there is no fear that she would ever sully the counterpane for by a little flutter of her paw she shows she wants to be set down, and after that she asks no more than to be gently cleaned. Such is the delicacy of the chaste little dog that she loves not at all, nor is there a spouse to be found who is worthy of a nymph so tender. So that death shall never quite take her from him, Publius has had a picture painted of her just as she really is. And when you look from Issa to the painting you think you see two Issas, or two portraits.

Epigrams, AD 86–98

Plutarch

Caesar once, seeing some wealthy strangers at Rome, carrying up and down with them in their arms and bosoms young puppy dogs and monkeys, embracing and making much of them, had occasion not unnaturally to ask whether the women in their country were not used to bear children; by that prince-like reprimand gravely reflecting upon persons who spend and lavish upon brute beasts that affection and kindness which nature has implanted in us to be bestowed on those of our own kind.

from *Symposiaca*, c. AD 100

Juvenal

Women see Alcestis on the stage sacrificing her life for her husband, but if they were in the like situation they would not do the same. Indeed, they would purchase the life of a favourite dog by the death of their husband.

Satire VI, c. AD 100–128

Jean Froissart

A grayhounde called Mithe, who always wayted upon the kynge, and woulde know no man els. For when so ever the kynge did ryde, he that kept the grayhounde dyd lette him lose, and he wolde streyght runne to the kynge and faune uppon hym, and leape with his fore fete uppon the kynge's shoulders. And, as the kynge and the Erle of Derby talked togyther in the courte, the grayhounde, who was wonte to leape uppon the kynge, left the kynge and came to the Erle of Derby, Duke of Lancastre; and made to him the same friendly continuance and chere as he was wonte to do the kynge. The duke, who knewe not the grayhounde, demanded of the kynge what the grayhounde wolde do? "Cousin," quod the kynge, "it is a greate goode token to you, and an evyl signe to me." "How knowe you that?" quod the duke. "I knowe it well," quod the kynge. "The grayhounde acknowledgeth you here this daye as Kynge of England, as ye shal be, and I shal be deposed; the grayhounde hath this knowledge naturally: therefore take hym to you, he wyll followe you and forsake me." The duke understood well those words, and cheryshed the grayhounde, who wolde never after followe kynge Richarde, but followed the Duke of Lancastre.

Chroniques, 1390, translated by John Bourchier

Agnes Sorel

And in the meanwhile we went out hunting the wild boar yesterday which little Robin, which you gave me, had found. And it turned out to be an unlucky hunt for little Robin because he was shot by a bolt which one of the huntsmen had let fly after the boar and now he is very ill. But I am going to look after him very carefully and I do hope he will get well.

Letter, c. 1430

Sir Thomas Malory

Then the Queen had always a little brachet [hound] with her, that Sir Tristram gave her the first time that ever she came into Cornwall, and never would the brachet depart from her but if Sir Tristram was nigh there as was La Beale Isoud; and this brachet was sent from the King's daughter of France unto Sir Tristram, for great love. And anon as this little brachet felt a savour of Sir Tristram, she leaped upon him, and licked his cheeks and his ears, and then she whined and quested, and she smelled at his feet and at his hands, and on all parts of his body that she might come to. Ah! my lady, said Dame Bragwaine unto La Beale Isoud, alas! alas! said she, I see it is mine own lord, Sir Tristram. And thereupon Isoud fell down in a swoon and so lay a great while; and when she might speak she said. "My lord, Sir Tristram, blessed be God ye have your life; and now I am sure ye shall be discovered by this little brachet for she will never leave you."

from *Le Morte D'Arthur*, 1478

231

Father Joseph de Acosta

Dogges have so multiplied in numbers and bignes that they are to this day the scourge and affliction of the Land for they eat the sheepe and go in troupes through the fields. Such that kill them are rewarded like to them that kill wolves in Spain. At the first there were no dogges in the Indies except some little dogges called "Alco". The Indians do so love these little dogges that they will spare their meate to feed them, so, as when they travel in the countrie they carry them with them upon their shoulders or in their bosomes, and when they are sicke they keep them with them, without any use, but, only for company.

from *Natural and Moral History of the Indies*, 1590

William Shakespeare

LAUNCE. When a man's servant shall play the cur with him, look you, it goes hard; one that I brought up of a puppy; one that I saved from drowning, when three or four of his blind brothers and sisters went to it. I have taught him even as one would say precisely, "Thus would I teach a dog." I was sent to deliver him as a present to Mistress Silvia from my master, and I came no sooner into the dining-chamber but he steps me to her trencher and steals her capon's leg. O! 'tis a foul thing when a cur cannot keep himself in all companies. I would have, as one should say, one that takes upon him to be a dog indeed, to be, as it were, a dog at all things. If I had not had more with than he, to take a fault upon me that he did, I think verily he had been hanged for't: sure as I live, he had suffered for't: you shall judge. He thrusts me himself into the company of three or four gentleman-like dogs under the duke's table: he had not been there – bless the mark – a pissing-wile, but all the chamber smelt him. "Out with the dog," says one; "What cur is that?" says another; "Whip him out," says the third; "Hang him up," says the duke. I having been aquainted with the smell before, knew it was Crab, and goes me to the fellow that whips the dogs: "Friend," quoth I, "you mean to whip the dog?" "Ay, marry, do I," quoth he. "You do him the more wrong," quoth I; "'twas I did the thing you wot of." He makes me no more ado, but whips me out of the chamber. How many masters would do this for his servant? Nay, I'll be sworn, I have sat in the stocks for puddings he hath stolen, otherwise he had been executed; I have stood on the pillory for geese he hath killed, otherwise he had suffered for't; thou thinkest not of this now. Nay, I remember the trick you served me when I took my leave of Madam Silvia: did not I bid thee still mark me and do as I do? When didst thou see me heave up my leg and make water against a gentle-woman's farthingale? Didst thou ever see me do such a trick?

from *Two Gentlemen of Verona*, 1591

Francis Bacon

For take an Example of a Dog: And mark what a Generosity and Courage he will put on, when he findes himselfe maintained by a Man; who to him is in stead of a God, or Melior Natura; which courage is manifestly such as that creature, without that confidence of a better Nature then his owne, could never attaine.

from *Essay on Atheisme*, c. 1597

Sir John Harington

Your little Dog that bark'd as I came by,
I strake by hap so hard, I made him cry,
And straight you put your finger in your eye
And low'ring sate, I ask'd the reason why.
"Love me and love my Dog," thou didst reply:
"Love, as both should be lov'd." "I will," said I,
And seal'd it with a kisse. Then by and by
Clear'd were the clods of thy faire frowning skie;
Thus small events great masteries may try.
For I by this do at their meaning guesse,
That beat a whelpe afore a lyonesse!

"To his wife for striking her dog", c. 1600

233

Sir John Harington

May it please your Highnesse to accept in as goode sorte what I nowe offer, as it hath done aforetyme; and I may saie I pedo fausto; but, havinge goode reason to thinke your Highnesse had good will and likinge to reade what others have tolde of my rare Dogge, I will even give a brief histories of his good deedes and straunge feats: and herein will I not plaie the curr myselfe, but in goode soothe relate what is no more nor lesse than bare verity. Although I mean not to disparage the deedes of Alexanders horse, I will match my Dogge against him for good carriage, for, if he did not bear a great Prince on his back, I am bolde to saie he did often bear the sweete wordes of a greater Princesse on his necke.

I did once relate to your Highnesse after what sorte his tacklinge was wherewithe he did sojourn from my house at the Bathe to Greenwiche Palace, and deliver up to the Courte there such matters as were entrusted to his care. This he hathe often done, and came safe to the Bathe, or my howse at Kelstone, with goodlie returnes from such Nobilitie as were pleasede to emploie him; nor was it ever tolde our Ladie Queene, that this Messenger did ever blab ought concerninge his highe truste, as others have done in more special matters. Neither must it with two charges of sack wines from the Bathe to my howse, by my man Combe; and on his way the cordage did slackene, but my trustie bearer did now beare himselfe so wisely as to covertly hide one flasket in the rushes, and take the other in his teethe to the howse, after whiche he wente for the first, and returnede with the other parte of his burden to dinner: hereat yr Highnesse may marvele and doubte, but we have livinge testimonie of those who wroughte in the fieldes and espiede his worke, and now live to tell they did muche longe to plaie the Dogge and give stowage to the wine themselves; but they did refrain, and watchede the passinge of this whole businesse.

I neede not saie how muche I did once grieve at missing this Dogge, for, on my journiee towardes Londone, some idle pastimers did diverte themselves withe hunting mallards in a ponde, and conveyd him to the Spanish Ambassadors, where in a happie houre after six weekes I did heare of him; but suche was the courte did he play the Don, that he was no lesse in good likinge there than at

234

home. Nor did the householde listen to my claim, or challenge, till I rested my suite on the Dogges own proofes, and made him perform such feats before the Nobles assembled, as put it past doubt that I was his Master. I did send him to the hall in the time of dinner, and made him bringe thence a pheasant out of the dish which created much mirthe; but much more when he returnede at my commandment to the table again, and put it again in the same cover. Herewith the companie was well content to allowe me my claim, and we bothe were well content to accept it, and came homewardes.

I coud dwell more on this matter, but jubes renovare dolorem; I will now saie in what manner he died: As we traveld towrdes the Bathe, he leapede on my horses necke, and was more earneste in fawninge and courtinge my notice, than what I had observed for some time backe; and, after my chidinge his disturbinge my passinge forwardes, he gave me some glances of such affection as movede me to cajole him; but, alas, he crept suddenly into a thorny brake, and died in such a short time. Thus I have strove to rehearse such of his diedes as maie suggest much more to yr Highnesse thought of this Dogge. But, havinge saide so much of him in profe, I will say somewhat too in verse, as may finde hereafter at the close of this historie.

Now let Ulysses praise his Dogge Argus, or Tobite be led by that Dogge whose name doth not appear: yet coud I say such things of my BUNGEY, for so was he styled, as might shame them both, either for good faith, clear wit, or wonderful deedes; to say no more than I have said of his bearing letters to London and Greenwiche, more than a hundred miles. As I doubte not but your Highnesse woulde love my Dogge, if not myselfe, I have been thus tedious in his storie; and againe saie that, of all the Dogges near your father's Courte, not one hathe more love, more diligence to please, or less pay for pleasinge, than him I write of; for verily a bone will contente my servante, when some expecte greater matters, or will knavishly find oute a bone of contension.

I now reste your Highnesse friend in all service that maye suite him.

Letter to Prince Henry, 14 June, 1608

James I

Sweete hairte blessing blessing blessing on my sweete tome badgers hairte rootes and all his, for brieding me so fyne a kennel of yong howndes, some of thaime so faire and well shaped, and some of thaime so fine prettie litle ones as thaye are worthie to lye on Steenie and Kates bedde; and all of thaime runne together as a lumpe, both at sente and uewe, and God thanke the maister of the horse, for provyding I with a numbre of faire usefull horsis, fitte for my hande; in a worde I proteste I was never maister of suche horses and howndes; the bearare will tell you quhat fyne running we hadde yesterdaye. Remember now to take the aire discreitlie and peece and peece, and for Gods saike and myne, keepe thyselfe verrie warme, especially thy heade and thy showlders, putte thy parke of Bewlie to an ende, and love me still and still, and so God blesse thee and my sweete daughter and god-daughter, to the comforte of thy deare dade,

James R.

P. S. – Thy olde purveyoure sent thee yesternight six Partridges and two levrettis. I am now going to hawke the pheasant.

Letter to Lord Buckingham, c. 1620

Samuel Pepys

At home, my wife's brother brought her a pretty black dog which I liked very well, and went away again.

8 February, 1660

My wife and I had some high words upon my telling her that I would fling the dog which her brother gave her out of the window if he pissed the house any more.

12 February, 1660

In the morning my wife tell me that the bich hath whelped four young ones and is very well after it, my wife having had a great fear that she would die thereof, the dog that got them being very big.

19 February, 1660

At night my wife and I did fall out about the dog's being put down in the Sellar, which I had a mind to have done because of his fouling the house, and I would have my will; and so we went to bed and lay all night in a Quarrel.

Diary, 6 November, 1660

Samuel Butler

Agrippa kept a Stygian Pug
I' th' Garb and Habit of a Dog,
That was his Tutor, and the Cur
Read to th' occult Philosopher,
And taught him subt'ly to maintain
All other Sciences are vain.
  To this, quoth Sidrophel, "Oh! Sir,
Agrippa was no conjurer,
Nor Paracelsus, no nor Behmen,
Nor was the Dog a Cacodaemon,
But a true Dog that would show Tricks
For th' Emperor, and leap o'er Sticks;
Would fetch and carry, was more civil
Than other Dogs, but yet no Devil:
And whatsoe'er he's said to do,
He went the self-same way we go.

from *Hudibras*, 1664

Samuel Pepys

All I observed was the silliness of the King, playing with his dogs all the while and not minding the business.

Diary, September, 1666

Sir Richard Steele

They both of them sit by my fire every Evening and wait with Impatience; and, at my Entrance, never fail of running up to me, and bidding me Welcome, each of them in its proper Language. As they have been bred up together from Infancy, and have seen no other Company, they have acquired each other's Manners; so that the Dog gives himself the Airs of a Cat, and the Cat, in several of her Motions and Gestures, affects the Behaviour of the little Dog,

The Tatler, 1711

I would not be thought in all this to hate such honest Creatures as Dogs; I am only unhappy that I cannot partake in their Diversions. But I love them so well, as Dogs, That I often go with my Pockets stuffed with Bread to dispense my Favours, or make my Way through them at Neighbours' Houses. There is in particular a young Hound of great Expectation, Vivacity, and Enterprize, that attends and Flights where-ever he spies me. This Creature observes my Countenance, and behaves himself accordingly. His Mirth, his Frolick, and Joy upon the Sight of me has been observed, and I have been gravely desired not to encourage him so much, for it spoils his Parts; but I think he shews them sufficiently in the several Boundings, Friskings, and Scourings, when he makes his Court to me: But I foresee in a little time he and I must keep Company with one another only, for we are fit for no other in these Parts.

The Spectator, 12 September 1712

Allan Ramsay

My Bawty is a cur I dearly like,
Till he yowled fair she strak the poor dumb tyke;

If I had filled a nook within her breast,
She wad have shawn fair kindness to my beast.

from *Lover's Logic*, 1724

Alexander Pope

You are to know then, that as it is likeness that begets affection, so my favourite dog is a little one, a lean one, and none of the finest shaped. He is not much spaniel in his fawning, but has (what might be worth any man's while to imitate him in) a dumb, surly sort of kindness that rather shows itself when he thinks me ill-used by others, than when we walk quietly or peaceably by ourselves. If it be the chief point of friendship to comply with a friend's motions and inclinations, he possesses this in an eminent degree: he lies down when I sit, and walks when I walk, which is more than many good friends can pretend to.

c. 1730

Alexander Pope

I am his Highness' dog at Kew;
Pray tell me, Sir, whose dog are you?

Epigram. "Engraved on the collar of a Dog,
which I gave to His Royal Highness,"
c. 1737

Christopher Smart

A snub nosed dog, to fat inclined,
Of the true hogan-mogan kind,
The favourite of an English dame,
Mynheer Van Trumpo was his name.
Met honest Towzer on the 'Change;

239

And whom have we got here, I beg?
Quoth he, and lifted up his leg:
An English dog can't take an airing,
But foreign scoundrels must be staring.
I'd have your French dogs, and your Spanish
And all your Dutch, and all your Danish,
By which our species is confounded
Be hanged, be poisoned, or be drowned;
No mercy on the race suspected,
Greyhounds from Italy excepted:
By them my dames ne'er prove big-bellied,
For they, poor toads, are Farrinellied.
Well, of all our dogs, it stands confessed,
Your English bulldogs are the best;
I say it, and will set my hand to't;
Cambden records it, and I'll stand to't.

from Poems on Several Occasions, 1732

Tobias Smollett

The only object within doors upon which she bestows any marks of affection, in the usual style, is her dog Chowder; a filthy cur from Newfoundland, which she had in a present from the wife of a skipper in Swansey. One would imagine she had distinguished this beast with her favour on account of his ugliness and ill-nature; if it was not, indeed, an instinctive sympathy between his disposition and her own. Certain it is, she caresses him without ceasing; and even harasses the family in the service of this cursed animal, which, indeed, has proved the proximate cause of her breach with Sir Ulic Mackilligut.

from Humphrey Clinker, 1771

Robert Burns

O wha my babie-clouts will buy?
O wha will tent me when I cry?

Wha will kiss me whare I lie?
The rantin' dog the daddie o't.

from "The Rantin Dog,
The Daddie O't", *c.* 1785

William Cowper

I must tell you a feat of my dog Beau. Walking by the river side, I
observed some water-lilies floating at a little distance from the bank.
They are a large white flower, with an orange-coloured eye, very
beautiful. I had a desire to gather one, and, having your long cane in
my hand, by the help of it endeavoured to bring one of them within
my reach. But the attempt proved vain, and I walked forward. Beau
had all the while observed me very attentively. Returning soon after
toward the same place, I observed him plunge into the river, while I
was about forty yards distant from him; and, when I had reached the
spot, he swam to land with a lily in his mouth, which he came and
laid at my foot.

Letter to Lady Hesketh, 1787

Edmund Blunden

And through the park come gentlemen riding,
And behind the glossy horses Newfoundland dogs follow.
Says one dog to the other, "This park, Sir, is mine Sir."
The reply is not wanting: hoarse clashing and mouthing
Arouses the masters
The Colonel Montgomery, of the Life Guards, dismounts,
"Whose dog is this?" The reply is not wanting,
From Captain Macnamara, Royal Navy: "My dog."
"Then call your dog off, or by God he'll go sprawling."
"If my dog goes sprawling, you must knock me down after."

"Incident in Hyde Park, 1803"

William Wordsworth

Among the favourites which it pleased me well
To see again, was one by ancient right
Our inmate, a rough terrier of the hills;
By birth and call of nature pre-ordained
To hunt the badger and unearth the fox
Among the imperious crags, but having been
From youth our own adopted, he has passed
Into a gentler service. And when first
The boyish spirit flagged, and day by day
Along my veins I kindled with the stir,
The fermentation and the vernal; heat
Of poesy, affecting private shades
Like a sick lover, then the dog was used
To watch me, an attendant and a friend,
Obsequious to my steps early and late,
Though often of such dilatory walk
Tired, and uneasy at the halts I made.
A hundred times when roving high and low,
I have been harassed with the toil of verse,
Much pains and little progress, and at once
Some lovely image in the song rose up
Full-formed, like Venus rising from the sea;
Then have I darted forwards to let loose
My hand upon his back with stormy joy,
Caressing him again and yet again.
And when at evening on the public way
I sauntered, like a river murmuring
And talking to itself when all things else
Are still, the creature trotted on before;
Such was his custom; but whene'er he met
A passenger approaching, he would turn
To give me timely notice.

from *The Prelude*, 1805

Robert Southey

The wild rose is called a dog-rose; the scentless violet, dog-violet. Jolly dog, is the highest convivial encomium which a man can receive from his companions; honest dog, is when he is a reprobate; dog is the word of endearment which an Englishman uses to his child, and it is what he calls his servant when he is angry; puppy, is the term of contempt for a coxcomb; and bitch, the worst appellation which can be applied to the worst of women. A flatterer is called a spaniel, a ruffian is called a bull-dog, an ill-looking fellow an ugly hound; whelp, cur, and mongrel, are terms of contemptuous reproach to a young man; and if a young woman's nose turns upwards she is certainly called pug.

from *Letters from England,* 1807

Revd William B. Daniel

Charles II was famous for a partiality for a particular breed, and came generally accompanied to the Council Board with a favourite Spaniel. His successor, James II, had a similar attachment, and it is reported of him by Bishop Burnet that being once in a dangerous storm at sea and obliged to quit the ship to save his life, he vociferated with impassioned accents as his principal concern: "Save the Dogs . . . and Col. Churchill."

from *Rural Sports* 1807–13

Alfred, Lord Tennyson

As the husband is, the wife is: thou art mated with a clown,
And the grossness of his nature will have weight to drag thee down.
He will hold thee, when his passion shall have spent its novel force,
Something better than his dog, a little dearer than his horse.

from *Locksley Hall,* 1833

243

Thomas Moore

Byron's fondness for dogs accompanied him throughout life. Of his favourite Boatswain, traits are told indicative not only of intelligence, but of a generosity of spirit which might well win for him the affections of such a master as Byron.

Mrs Byron had a fox-terrier, called Gilpin, with whom her son's dog, Boatswain, was perpetually at war, taking every opportunity of attacking and worrying him so violently, that it was very much apprehended he would kill the animal. Mrs Byron therefore sent off her terrier to a tenant at Newstead; and on the departure of Lord Byron for Cambridge, his "friend" Boatswain, with two other dogs, was intrusted to the care of a servant till his return. One morning the servant was much alarmed by the disappearance of Boatswain, and throughout the whole of the day he could hear no tidings of him. At last, towards evening, the stray dog arrived, accompanied by Gilpin, whom he led immediately to the kitchen fire, licking him and lavishing upon him every possible demonstration of joy. The fact was, he had been all the way to Newstead to fetch him; and having now established his former foe under the roof once more, agreed so perfectly well with him ever after, that he even protected him against the insults of his master (a task which the quarrelsomeness of the little terrier rendered no sinecure), and, if he but heard Gilpin's voice in distress, would fly instantly to his rescue.

from *Letters and Journals of Lord Byron, with notices of his life,* 1830

Thomas Campbell

On the green banks of Shannon, when Sheelah was nigh,
No blithe Irish lad was as happy as I;
No harp like my own could so cheerily play,
And wherever I went was my poor dog Tray,
When at last I was forced from my Sheelah to part
She said – while the sorrow was big at her heart;
"Oh! remember your Sheelah, when far, far away,

And be kind, my dear Pat, to our poor dog Tray.'
Poor dog! he was faithful, and kind, to be sure,
And he constantly loved me, although I was poor;
When the sour-looking folks sent me heartless way,
I had always a friend in my poor dog Tray.
When the road was so dark, and the night was so cold,
And Pat and his dog were grown weary and old,
How snugly we slept in my old coat of grey,
And he licked me for kindness – my poor dog Tray.
Though my wallet was scant, I remembered his case,
Nor refused my last crust to his pitiful face;
But he died at my feet one cold winter's day,
And I played a sad lament for my poor dog Tray.
Where now shall I go, poor, forsaken, and blind?
Can I find one to guide me, so faithful and kind?
To my native village, so far, far away
I can never more return with my poor dog Tray.

from "The Irish Harper", c1835

Ebenezer Elliott

Acres eats his tax on bread,
   Acres loves the plough, man;
Acres' dogs are better fed,
   Beggar's slave! than thou, man.
Acres' feeder pays his debts,
   Waxes thin and pale, man,
Harder works and poorer gets,
   Pays his debts in jail, man.
Acres in a palace lives,
   While his feder pines, man;
Palaced beggar ne'er forgives
   Dog on whom he dines, man.

from "Drone v. Worker", c 1830

Thomas Babington Macaulay

How odd that people of sense should find any pleasure in being accompanied by a beast who is always spoiling conversation.

from Life and Letters

Septimus Winner

Oh where, oh where ish mine lit-tle dog gone;
Oh where, oh where can he be . . .
His ears cut short und his tail cut long:
Oh where, oh where ish he . . .

I loves mine la-ger tish ve-ry goot beer,
Oh where, of where can he be . . .
But mit no mon-ey I can-not drink here,
Oh where, oh where ish he . . .

A-cross the o-cean in Ger-man-ie
Of where, oh where can he be . . .
Der depicters dog ish der best com-pan-ie
Of where, oh where ish he . . .

Un sausage ish goot, bo-lo-nie of course,
Oh where, oh where can he be . . .
Dey makes un mit dog und dey makes em mit horse,
I guess dey makes em mit he . . .

"Der Deutchers' Dog," 1864

Senator George Graham Vest

Gentlemen of the Jury: The best friend a man has in this world may turn against him and become his enemy. His son or daughter that he has reared with loving care may prove ungrateful. Those who are nearest and dearest to us, those whom we trust with our happiness and our good name, may become traitors to their faith. The money that a man has, he may lose. It flies away from him, perhaps when he needs it the most. A man's reputation may be sacrificed in a moment of ill-considered action. The people who are prone to fall on their knees to do us honour when success is with us may be the first to throw the stone of malice when failure settles its cloud upon our heads. The one absolutely unselfish friend that a man can have in this selfish world, the one that never deserts him and the one that never proves ungrateful or treacherous is his dog.

Gentlemen of the Jury, a man's dog stands by him in prosperity and in poverty, in health and in sickness. He will sleep on the cold ground, where the wintery winds blow and the snow drives fiercely, if only he may be near his master's side. He will kiss the hand that has no food to offer, he will lick the wounds and sores that come in encounters with the roughness of the world. He guards the sleep of his pauper master as if he were a prince. When all other friends desert he remains. When riches take wings and reputation falls to pieces, he is constant in his love as the sun in its journey through the heavens. If fortune drives the master forth an outcast in the world, friendless and homeless, the faithful dog asks no higher privilege than that of accompanying him to guard against danger, to fight his enemies, and when the last scene of all comes, and death takes the master in his embrace and his body is laid away in the cold ground, there by his graveside will the noble dog be found, his head between his paws, his eyes sad but open in alert watchfulness, faithful and true even to death.

> Inscription on a monument to Old Drum, a Coonhound, at Warrensburg, Missouri. The dog was killed by a neighbour and the inscription records Vest's statement to the court which considered the offence, 1870

John Ruskin

> I have a dog of Blenheim birth
> With fine long ears and full of mirth;
> And sometimes, running o'er the plain,

He tumbles on his nose:
But, quickly jumping up again,
Like lightening he goes!
'Tis queer to watch his gambols gay:
He's very loving – in his way:
He even wants to lick your face,
But that is somewhat out of place.
But Dash is not content with this!
Howe'er, let all his faults be past,
I'll praise him to the very last.

"My dog Dash", *c.*1880

Sir Walter Alexander Raleigh

Two slim, grim, well-dressed youths had a large dog whom they seized repeatedly by the fore and hind paws and after a preliminary swing flung him into the water. As the dog weighed about five stone they could not fling him far, and he always came down thus in a foot of water, and scrambled out muddy and dripping to submit to a repetition. He took his encores with a cheerful submissiveness that puts our best actors to shame. I remember a gentleman who lost his temper because I and a few friends refused to allow the play of "Hamlet" to proceed until we had encored his death as the King. Yet this thud in falling was scarcely louder. The joint owners of the dog (they must have been owners) went through the business with a mechanical and depressed devotion that affected me much.

Letter to Lucie Jackson, 3 August 1888

Jerome K. Jerome

He is very imprudent, a dog is. He never makes it his business to inquire whether you are in the right or in the wrong, never bothers as to whether you are going up or down life's ladder, never asks whether you are rich or poor, silly or wise, sinner or saint. You are his pal. That is enough for him, and come luck or misfortune, good repute or bad, honour or shame, he is going to stick to you, to comfort you, guard you, give his life for you, if need be – foolish, brainless, soulless dog!

I wish people could love animals without getting maudlin over them, as so many do. Women are the most hardened offenders in such respect, but even our intellectual sex often degrade pets into nuisances by absurd idolatry. There are the gushing young ladies who, having read "David Copperfield", have thereupon sought out a small, long-haired dog of nondescript breed, possessed of an irritating habit of criticising a man's trousers, and of finally commenting upon the same by a sniff, indicative of contempt and disgust. They talk sweet girlish prattle to this animal (when there is anyone near enough to overhear them), and they kiss its nose, and put its unwashed head up against their cheek in a most touching manner; though I have noticed that these caresses are principally performed when there are young men hanging about.

Then there are the old ladies who worship a fat poodle, scant of breath and full of fleas. I knew a couple of elderly spinsters once who had a sort of German sausage on legs which they called a dog between them. They used to wash its face with warm water every morning. It had a mutton cutlet regularly for breakfast; and on Sundays, when one of the ladies went to church, the other always stopped at home to keep the dog company.

There are many families where the whole interest of life is centred upon the dog.

from *Idle Thoughts for an Idle Fellow*, 1889

August Strindberg

I loathe people who keep dogs. They are cowards who haven't got the guts to bite people themselves.

from *Inferno*, 1898

Rudolph Chambers Lehmann

Rufus, a bright New Year! A savoury stew,
Bone, broth, and biscuits, is prepared for you.
See how it steams in your enamelled dish,
Mixed in each part according to your wish.
Hide in your straw the bones you cannot crunch —
They'll come in handy for to-morrow's lunch;
Abstract with care each tasty scrap of meat,
Remove each biscuit to a fresh retreat
(A dog, I judge, would deem himself disgraced
Who ate a biscuit where he found it placed);
Then nuzzle round and make your final sweep,
And sleep, replete, your after-dinner sleep.
High in your hall we've piled the fire with logs
For you, the doyen of all our corps of dogs.
There, when the stroll that health demands is done,
Your right to ease by due exertion won,
There shall you come, and on your long-haired mat,
Thrice turning round, shall tread the jungle flat,
And, rhythmically snoring, dream away
The peaceful even of your New Year's Day.

Rufus! there are who hesitate to be won
Merits, they say, your master sees alone.
They judge you stupid, for you show no bent
To any poodle-dog accomplishment.
Your stubborn nature never stooped to learn
Tricks by which mumming dogs their biscuits earn.
Men mostly find you, if they change their seat,
Couchant obnoxious to their blundering feet;
Then, when a door is closed, you steadily
Misjudge the side on which you ought to be;
Yelping outside when all your friends are in,
You raise the echoes with your ceaseless din,
Or, always wrong, but turn and turn about,
Howling inside when all the world is out.
They scorn your gestures and interpret ill

Your humble signs of friendship and goodwill.
Laugh at your gambols, and pursue with jeers
The ringlets clustered on your spreading ears;
See without sympathy your sore distress
When Ray obtains the coveted caress,
And you, a jealous lump of growl and glare,
Hide from the world your head beneath a chair.

They say your legs are bandy — so they are!
Nature so formed them that they might go far;
They cannot brook your music; they assail
The joyful quiverings of your stumpy tail —
In short, in one anathema confound
Shape, mind and heart, and all my little hound.
Well, let them rail. If, since your life began,
Beyond the customary lot of man
Staunchness was yours; if of your faithful heart
Malice and scorn could never claim a apart;
If in your master, loving while you live,
You own no fault or own it to forgive;
If, as you lay your head upon my knee,
Your deep-drawn sighs proclaim your sympathy;
If faith and friendship, growing with your age,
Speak through your eyes, and all his love engage;
If by that master's wish your life you rule —
If this be folly, Rufus, you're a fool.

Old dog, content you; Rufus, have no fear:
While life is yours and mine your place is here.
And when the day shall come, as come it must,
When Rufus goes to mingle with the dust
(If fate ordains that you shall pass before
To the abhorred and sunless Stygian shore),
I think old Charon, punting through the dark,
Will hear a sudden friendly little bark;
And on the shore he'll mark without a frown
A flap-eared doggie, bandy-legged and brown.
He'll take you in; since watermen are kind,
He'd ask no obol, but instal you there

On Styx's further bank without a fare.
There shall you sniff his cargoes as they come,
And droop your head, and turn, and still be dumb —
Till one fine day, half joyful, half in fear,
You run and prick a recognizing ear,
And last, oh, rapture! leaping to his hand,
Salute your master as he steps to land.

"To Rufus: A Spaniel"

Mark Twain (pseud.)

Dogs are incapable of blushing, a fact which has given rise to the suggestion that they are incapable of shame. Even if dogs could blush this would pass unnoticed on a black dog. Man is the Only Animal that Blushes. Or needs to.

from *Following the Equator*, 1897

O. Henry (pseud.)

I don't suppose it will knock any of you people off your perch to read a contribution from an animal. Mr Kipling and a good many others have demonstrated the fact that animals can express themselves in remunerative English, and no magazine goes to press nowadays without an animal story in it, except the old-style monthlies that are still running pictures of Bryan and the Mont Pelée horror.

But you needn't look for any stuck-up literature in my piece, such as Bearoo, the bear, and Snakoo, the snake, and Tammanoo, the tiger, talk in the jungle books. A yellow dog that's spent most of his life in a cheap New York flat, sleeping in a corner on an old sateen underskirt (the one she spilled port wine on at the Lady Long-shoremen's banquet), mustn't be expected to perform any tricks with the art of speech.

I was born a yellow pup: date, locality, pedigree and weight unknown. The first thing I can recollect, an old woman had me in a basket at Broadway and Twenty-third trying to sell me to a fat lady. Old Mother Hubbard was boosting me to beat the band as a genuine Pomeranian – Hambletonian – Red – Irish – Cochin-China Stoke-Pogis fox terrier. The fat lady chased a V around among the samples of gros grain flannelette in her shopping bag till she cornered it, and gave up. From that moment I was a pet – a mamma's own wootsey squidlums. Say, gentle reader, did you ever have a 200-pound woman breathing a flavour of Camembert cheese and Peau d'Espagne pick you up and wallop her nose all over you, remarking all the time in an Emma Eames tone of voice: "Oh, oo's um oodlum, doodlum, woodlum, toodlum, bitsy-witsy skoodlums?"

From a pedigreed yellow pup I grew up to be an anonymous yellow cur looking like a cross between an Angora cat and a box of lemons. But my mistress never tumbled. She thought that the two primeval pups that Noah chased into the ark were but a collateral branch of my ancestors. It took two policemen to keep her from entering me at the Madison Square Garden for the Siberian bloodhound prize.

I'll tell you about that flat. The house was the ordinary thing in New York, paved with Parian marble in the entrance hall and cobblestones above the first floor. Our flat was three fl – well, not flights – climbs up. My mistress rented it unfurnished, and put in the regular things – 1903 antique upholstered parlour set, oil chromo of geishas in a Harlem tea house, rubber plant and husband.

By Sirius! there was a biped I felt sorry for. He was a little man with sandy hair and whiskers a good deal like mine. Henpecked? – well, toucans and flamingoes and pelicans all had their bills in him. He wiped the dishes and listened to my mistress tell about the cheap, ragged things the lady with the squirrel-skin coat on the second floor hung out on her line to dry. And every evening while she was getting supper she made him take me out on the end of a string to walk.

If men knew how women pass the time when they are alone they'd never marry. Laura Lean Jibbey, peanut brittle, a little almond cream on the neck muscles, dishes unwashed, half an hour's talk with the iceman, reading a package of old letters, a couple of pickles and two bottles of malt extract, one hour peeking through a hole in the window shade into a flat across the air-shaft – that's about all there is to it. Twenty minutes before time for him to come home from work she straightens up the house, fixes a rent so it won't show, and gets out lots of sewing for a ten-minute bluff.

I led a dog's life in that flat. Most all day I lay there in my corner watching the fat woman kill time. I slept sometimes and had pipe dreams about being out chasing cats into basements and growling at old ladies with black mittens, as a dog was intended to do. Then she would pounce upon me with a lot of drivelling poodle palaver and kiss me on the nose – but what could I do? A dog can't chew cloves.

I began to feel sorry for Hubby, dog my cats if I didn't. We looked so much alike that people noticed it when we went out; so we shook the streets that Morgan's cab drives down, and took to climbing the piles of last December's snow on the streets where cheap people live.

One evening when we were thus promenading, and I was trying to look like a prize St Bernard, and the old man was trying to look like he wouldn't have murdered the first organgrinder he heard play Mendelssohn's wedding-march, I looked up at him and said, in my way:

"What are you looking so sour about, you oakum trimmed lobster? She don't kiss you. You don't have to sit on her lap and listen to talk that would make the book of a musical comedy sound like the maxims of Epictetus. You ought to be thankful you're not a dog. Brace up, Benedick, and bid the blues begone."

The matrimonial mishap looked down at me with almost canine intelligence in his face.

"Why, doggie," says he, "good doggie. You almost look like you could speak. What is it, doggie – Cats?"

Cats! Could speak!

But, of course, he couldn't understand. Humans were denied the speech of animals. The only common ground of communication upon with dogs and men can get together is in fiction.

In the flat across the hall from us lived a lady with a black-and-tan terrier. Her husband strung it and took it out every evening, but he always came home cheerful and whistling. One day I touched noses with the black-and-tan in the hall, and I struck him for an elucidation.

"See, here, Wiggle-and-Skip", I says, "you know that it ain't the nature of a real man to play dry nurse to a dog in public. I never saw one leashed to a bow-wow yet that didn't look like he'd like to lick every other man that looked at him. But your boss comes in every day as perky and set up as an amateur prestidigitator doing the egg trick. How does he do it? Don't tell me he likes it."

"Him?" says the black-and-tan. "Why, he uses Nature's Own Remedy. He gets spifflicated. At first when we go out he's as shy as the man on the steamer who would rather play pedro when they make 'em all jackpots. By the time we've been in eight saloons he don't care whether the thing on the end of his line is a dog or a catfish. I've lost two inches of my tail trying to sidestep those swinging doors."

The pointer I got from the terrier – vaudeville please copy – set me thinking.

One evening about six o'clock my mistress ordered him to get busy and do the ozone act for Lovey. I have concealed it until now, but that is what she called me: The black-and-tan was called "Tweetness." I consider that I have the bulge on him as far as you could chase a rabbit. Still "Lovey" is something of a nomenclatural tin can on the tail of one's self-respect.

At a quiet place on a safe street I tightened the line of my custodian in front of an attractive, refined saloon. I made a dead-ahead scramble for the doors, whining like a dog in the press despatches that lets the family know that little Alice is bogged while gathering lillies in the brook.

"Why, darn my eye if the saffron-coloured son of a seltzer lemonade ain't asking me to take a drink. Lemme see – how long's it been since I saved leather by keeping one foot on the foot-rest? I believe I'll – "

I knew I had him. Hot Scotches he took, sitting at a table. For an hour he kept the Campbells coming. I sat by his side rapping for the waiter with my tail, and eating free lunch such as a mamma in her flat never equalled with her homemade truck bought at a delicatessen store eight minutes before papa comes home.

When the products of Scotland were all exhausted except the rye bread the old man unwound me from the table leg and played me outside like a fisherman plays a salmon. Out there he took off my collar and threw it into the street.

"Poor doggie," says he; "good doggie. She shan't kiss you any more. 'S a darned shame. Good doggie, go away and get run over by a street car and be happy."

I refused to leave. I leaped and frisked around the old man's legs happy as a pug on a rug.

"You old flea-headed woodchuck-chaser," I said to him – "you moon-baying, rabbit-pointing, egg-stealing old beagle, can't you see that I don't want to leave you? Can't you see that we're both Pups in the Wood and the missus is the cruel uncle after you with a dish towel and me with the flea liniment and a pink bow tie on my tail. Why not cut that all out and be pards for evermore?"

Maybe you'll say he didn't understand – maybe he didn't. But he kind of got a grip on the Hot Scotches, and stood still for a minute, thinking.

"Doggie," says he finally, "we don't live more than a dozen lives on this earth, and very few of us live to be more than 300. If I ever see that flat any more I'm a flat, and if you do you're a flatter; and that's no flattery. I'm offering 60 to that Westward Ho wins out by the length of a dachshund."

There was no string, but I frolicked along with my master to the Twenty-third Street ferry. And the cats on the route saw reason to give thanks that prehensile claws had been given them.

On the Jersey side my master said to a stranger who stood eating a currant bun:

"Me and my doggie, we are bound for the Rocky Mountains."

But what pleased me most was when my old man pulled both of my ears until I howled and said:

"You common, monkey-headed, rat-tailed, sulphur-coloured son of a door mat, do you know what I'm going to call you?"

I thought of "Lovey," and I whined dolefully.

"I'm going to call you 'Pete'," says my master; and if I'd had five tails I couldn't have done enough wagging to do justice to the occasion.

from "Memoirs of a yellow dog", *The Four Million*, 1906

Jack London

I have sometimes held forth (facetiously, so my listeners believed) that the chief distinguishing trait between man and the other animals is that man is the only animal that maltreats the females of his kind. It is something of which no wolf nor cowardly coyote is ever guilty. It is something that even the dog, degenerated by domestication, will not do. The dog retains the wild instinct in this matter, while man has lost most of his wild instincts – at least, most of the good ones.

from "Pictures," *The Road*, 1907

Anonymous

SATURDAY. My Mama left for America – beastly country – too far off. I cried a good deal at dinner time – dinner cold and damp. Walked in the Park – bit a Park Keeper – Park Keeper tasted of tobacco. Must speak to Pom about this.

SUNDAY. Awoke early – walked in Charles Street – bit a Bishop going to Church – Bishop High Church and thin – tasted poor. Dinner hot and good.

MONDAY. Very wet and muddy – drove in Piccadilly and walked in Green Park – killed an inferior Pekingese. Bit a waiter (German) – tasted of soup.

TUESDAY, Walked in Berkeley Square – met Lord R—y – wagged tail – no notice taken – bit Lord R—y – too much notice taken – very sore and cross. Dinner a consolation. Mem. Lord R. has a neutral taste.

WEDNESDAY. Had a tooth-ache – no fun! no dinner!! no bites!!

THURSDAY. Wish my Mama would return. Very dull without her. Fear she will bring another dog back from America. Dreadful thought. Bit a man with a wooden leg – no taste at all!

FRIDAY. Read in the "Dogs' Gazette" that Ll—d G—e is to tax Pekingese £100 each. Walked to Westminster – bit Ll—d G—e – tasted like Welsh Rabitt.

"Diary of a Demon", *The Kennel*, 1910

Harding Cox

Randy's wind was up, after his affair with the billy goat of Innistorwhele. I think he had a hunch to swim over to the island,

and take it out of the surviving hill climbers; as he was ever gazing over the water to the distant islet. But, apparently, thinking better of it, he eschewed goat flesh, and chewed mutton in the shape of an innocent lamb, which, having lost its dam, was being brought up by hand at a local cottager's. Naturally the owner waxed exceeding wrath and put in an excited appearance, bearing what remained (mostly wool and gore) of his cherished lambkin in his arms.

'Aw, yer 'anner," gasped Terry Milligan – for such was his name – "see phwat yez dirthy, shark-faced son av a disgraceful mother has done teu me poor, helpless lamd – bad cess to 'im for a mangy, squint-eyed, three cornered cur dog – teu Hell wid'm!"

There was no gainsaying the transgression; for Randy had been caught flagrante delicto, and was rendered parti-coloured by tell-tale crimson stains and slavering jaws.

I was furious! I had never known my favourite bull terrier to be guilty of such truculent rascality before. My first impulse was to belabour him within an inch of his life; but after careful considera-tion I fell back on what I hoped might prove a far more efficacious punishment, and one which I hoped would give the backslider furiously to think before venturing on any similar atrocity. I tied what remained of the unfortunate lambkin to his neck, gave him a sharp reminder with an ash plant and shut him up in an outhouse.

At intervals I visited him, and each time admonished him with tongue and stick; with the consequence that he became utterly fed up with the too intimate company of his victim's corpse. When at last he was released from durance vile and the adhesive incubus, he was exalted with joy and thanksgiving, and signified the same in the usual canine manner. The Ancient Mariner could hardly have felt more relieved when the bindings of the defunct albatross slid from his neck.

As for Terry Millighan, he was solaced with a five pound note (there were such pleasant pledges of the Bank of England in those days).

"The Holly Saints bless yer 'anner!" he exclaimed fervently. "Faith an' ut's meself phway whill be havin' another lamb seun; an' if so be, yer 'anner and yer anner's iligant dog whill be wantin' moore spoort, be gob, ye're welcome – more power teu yez both!"

Now I did not appreciate being identified as an accomplice of Randy's crime, either as an accessory before or after the fact; but what was the use of arguing the matter with an ignoramus such as Terry. I just let it pass!

It is said that when once a dog has taken to mutton mauling the obsession is incurable; but I can vouch for it, that "Mr Champion Streatham Monarch II" never again molested a sheep. He couldn't bear the sight of one; nor would he partake of the flesh thereof; unless camouflaged by culinary art. So that was that!

from *A Sportsman at Large*, c. 1925

Harold Monro

O little friend, your nose is ready; you sniff,
Asking for that expected walk,
(Your nostrils full of the happy rabbit-whiff)
And almost talk.

And so the moment becomes a moving force;
Coats glide down from their pegs in the humble dark;

You scamper the stairs,
Your body informed with the scent and the track and the mark
Of stoats and weasels, moles and badgers and hares.

We are going OUT. You know the pitch of the word,
Probing the tone of thought as it comes through fog
And reaches by devious means (half-smelt, half-heard)
The four-legged brain of a walk-ecstatic dog.

OUT through the garden your head is already low.
You are going your walk, you know,
And your limbs will draw
Joy from the earth through the touch of your padded paw.

Now, sending a little look to us behind,
Who follow slowly the track of your lovely play,
You fetch our bodies forward away from mind
Into light and fun of your useless day.

Thus, for our walk, we took ourselves, and went
Out by the hedge, and tree, to the open ground.
You ran, in delightful strata of wafted scent,
Over the hill without seeing the view;
Beauty is hinted through primitive smells to you:
And that ultimate Beauty you track is but rarely found.

Home . . . and further joy will be waiting there:
Supper full of the taste of bone.
You lift up your nose again, and sniff, and stare
For the rapture known

Of the quick wild gorge of food, then the still lie-down;
While your people will talk above you in the light
Of candles, and your dreams will merge and drown
Into the bed-delicious hours of night.

"Dog", *c.* 1925

Edward Verrall Lucas

If I had been called in to assist in the making of man I should have
deprived him of the wish to smoke. Tobacco and I will never
agree. (It's funny, by the way, about pipes. When I first saw His I
thought it was a bone, still burning, with a very odd smell. It was
quite a shock to find it was made of wood and contained fire.) I
should also have seen to it that man was less restless. That is his
principal fault. He has many merits; he likes us, he is warm to lie
against, he provides bones, he wants to see rats exterminated, he
goes long walks, he keeps a car in which it is pleasant to ride, he
marries weak women who can be easily coaxed into what They call
spoiling us. But at the same time he has no steadiness. He is always
doing something else.

from *The Book of Aberdeen, c.* 1930

Patrick Chalmers

Puppy dog, rough as a bramble,
   Eyed like a saint
Beggar to slobber and gambol,
   Corky and quaint,
Chasing your tail like a fubsy turbillion,
Plaguing a playmate with fuss of a million
   Gnats,
But keen as a kestrel
   And fierce as a stoat is,
A-thrill to ancestral
   Furies at notice
   Of rats,
Rats, little hound of Beelzebub, rats!

And as you sleep off a surfeit,
   Mischief and tea,
Prone on the summer warm turf, it
   Surely must be
(Rapturous whimper and tremulant twitching),
Somewhere or other there's hunting bewitching:
   That's
More blessed than biscuit;
   I'll lay, through your slumbers,
They squeak and they frisk it
   In shadowy numbers,
   R-r-rats,
Rats, little hound of Beelzebub, rats!

"Patsy, Green Days and Blue Days", *c.* 1935

Jean-Paul Sartre

Liking children and dogs too much, is a substitution for loving
adults.

from *Words*, 1964

George Orwell (pseud.)

Although its [pet keeping] worst follies are committed by upper-class women, the animal cult runs right through the nation and is probably bound up with the decay of agriculture and the dwindled birthrate. Several years of stringent rationing have failed to reduce the dog and cat population.

from *The English People*

P. G. Wodehouse

It was at this moment that there emerged from the clubhouse where it had been having a saucer of tea and a slice of cake, a Pekinese dog of hard-boiled aspect. It strolled on to the green, and approaching Agnes's ball subjected it to a pop-eyed scrutiny.

There is a vein of eccentricity in all Pekes. Here, one would have said, was a ball with little about it to arrest the attention of a thoughtful dog. It was just a regulation blue dot, slightly battered. Yet it was obvious immediately that it had touched a chord. The animal sniffed at it with every evidence of interest and pleasure. It patted it with its paw. It smelled it. Then, lying down, it took it in its mouth and began to chew meditatively.

To Agnes the mere spectacle of a dog on a green had been a thing of horror. Brought up from childhood to reverence the rules of Greens Committees, she had shuddered violently from head to foot. Recovering herself with a powerful effort, she advanced and said "Shoo!" The Peke rolled its eyes sideways, inspected her, dismissed her as of no importance or entertainment value, and resumed its fletcherizing. Agnes advanced another step, and the schoolmistress for the second time broke her Trappist vows.

"You can't move that dog," she said. "It's a hazard."

"Nonsense."

"I beg your pardon, it is. If you get into casual water, you don't mop it up with a brush and pail, do you? Certainly you don't. You play out of it. Same thing when you get into a casual dog."

They train these schoolmistresses to reason clearly. Agnes halted, baffled. Then her eye fell on Captain Jack Fosdyke, and she saw the way out.

"There's nothing in the rules to prevent a spectator, meeting a dog on the course, from picking it up and fondling it."

It was the schoolmistress' turn to be baffled. She bit her lip in chagrined silence.

"Jack, dear," said Agnes, "pick up that dog and fondle it. And," she added, for she was a quick-thinking girl, "when doing so, hold its head over the hole."

It was a behest which one might have supposed that any knight, eager to win the lady's favour, would have leaped to fulfil. But Captain Jack Fosdyke did not leap. There was a dubious look on his handsome face, and he scratched his chin pensively.

"Just a moment," he said. "This is a thing you want to look at from every angle. Pekes are awfully nippy, you know. They make sudden darts at your ankles."

"Well, you like a spice of danger."

"Within reason, dear lady, within reason."

"You once killed a lion with a sardine opener."

"Ah, but I first quelled him with the power of the human eye. The trouble with Pekes is, they're so short-sighted, they can't see the human eye, so you can't quell them with it."

from *Nothing Serious*, c. 1936

Damon Runyon

Well, by and by Marvin Clay gets the doll in the taxicab, and away they go, and it is all quiet again on Broadway, and Regret and I stand there speaking of this and that, and one thing and another, when along comes a very strange-looking guy leading two very strange-looking dogs. The guy is so thin I figure he must be about two pounds lighter than a stack of wheats. He has a long nose, and a sad face, and he is wearing a floppy old black felt hat, and he has on a flannel shirt, and baggy corduroy pants, and a see-more coat, which is a coat that lets you see more hip pockets than coat.

Personally, I never see a stranger-looking guy on Broadway, and I wish to say I see some very strange-looking guys on Broadway in my day. But if the guy is strange-looking, the dogs are even stranger-looking, because they have big heads, and jowls that hang down like an old-time faro bank dealer's, and long ears the size of bed sheets. Furthermore, they have wrinkled faces, and big, round eyes that seem so sad I half expect to see them burst out crying.

The dogs are a sort of black and yellow colour, and have long tails, and they are so thin you can see their ribs sticking out of their hides. I can see at once that the dogs and the guy leading them can use a few Hamburgers very nicely, but then so can a lot of other guys on Broadway at this time, leaving out dogs.

Well, Regret is much interested in the dogs right away, because he is a guy who is very fond of animals of all kinds, and nothing will do but he must stop the guy and start asking questions about what sort of dogs they are, and in fact I am also anxious to hear myself, because while I see many a pooch in my time I never see anything like these.

"They is bloodhounds," the sad-looking guy says in a very sad voice, and with one of these accents such as Southern guys always have. "They is man-tracking bloodhounds from Georgia."

Now of course both Regret and me know what bloodhounds are because we see such animals chasing Eliza across the ice in Uncle Tom's Cabin when we are young squirts, but this is the first time either of us meet up with any bloodhounds personally, especially on Broadway. So we get to talking quite a bit to the guy, and his story is as sad as his face, and makes us both feel very sorry for him.

In fact, the first thing we know we have him and the bloodhounds in Mindy's and are feeding one and all big steaks, although Mindy puts up an awful squawk about us bringing the dogs in, and asks us what we think he is running, anyway. When Regret starts to tell him, Mindy says never mind, but not to bring any more Shetland ponies into his joint again as long as we live. Well, it seems that the sad-looking guy's name is John Wangle, and he comes from a town down in Georgia where his uncle is the high sheriff, and one of the bloodhound's name is Nip, and the other is Tuck, and they are both trained from infancy to track down guys such as lags who escape from the county pokey, and bad niggers, and one thing and another, and after John Wangle gets the kinks out of his belly on Mindy's steaks, and starts talking good, you must either figure him a high-class liar, or the hounds the greatest man-trackers the world ever sees.

Now, looking at the dogs after they swallow six big sirloins apiece, and a lot of matzoths, which Mindy has left over from the Jewish holidays, and a job lot of goulash from the dinner bill, and some other odds and ends, the best I can figure them is hearty eaters, because they are now lying down on the floor with their faces hidden behind their ears, and are snoring so loud you can scarcely hear yourself think.

How John Wangle comes to be in New York with these bloodhounds is quite a story, indeed. It seems that a New York guy drifts into John's old home town in Georgia when the bloodhounds are tracking down a bad nigger, and this guy figures it will be a wonderful idea to take John Wangle and the dogs to New York and hire them out to the movies to track down the villains in the pictures. But when they get to New York, it seems the movies have other arrangements for tracking down their villains, and the guy runs out of scratch and blows away, leaving John Wangle and the bloodhounds stranded.

So here John Wangle is with Nip and Tuck in New York, and they are all living together in one room in a tenement house over in West Forty-ninth Street, and things are pretty tough with them, because John does not know how to get back to Georgia unless he walks, and he hears the walking is no good south of Roanoke. When I ask him why he does not write to his uncle, the high sheriff down there in Georgia, John Wangle says there are two reasons, one being that he cannot write, and the other that his uncle cannot read.

Then I ask him why he does not sell the bloodhounds, and he says it is because the market for bloodhounds is very quiet in New York, and furthermore if he goes back to Georgia without the bloodhounds his uncle is apt to knock his ears down. Anyway, John Wangle says he personally loves Nip and Tuck very dearly, and in fact he says it is only his great love for them that keeps him from eating one or the other, and maybe both, the past week, when his hunger is very great indeed.

Well, I never before see Regret so much interested in any situation as he is in John Wangle and the bloodhounds, but personally I am getting very tired of them, because the one that is called Nip finally wakes up and starts chewing my leg, thinking it is maybe a steak, and when I kick him in the snoot, John Wangle scowls at me, and Regret says only very mean guys are unkind to dumb animals.

But to show you that John Wangle and his bloodhounds are not so dumb, they come moseying along past Mindy's every morning after this at about the same time, and Regret is always there ready to feed them, although he now has to take the grub out on the sidewalk as Mindy will not allow the hounds in the joint again. Naturally Nip and Tuck become very fond of Regret, but they are by no means as fond of him as John Wangle, because John is commencing to fat up very nicely, and the bloodhounds are also taking on weight.

from "The Bloodhounds of Broadway," *More than Somewhat*, 1937

Roy Campbell

I hate "Humanity" and all such abstracts: but I love people. Lovers of "Humanity" generally hate people and children, and keep parrots or puppy dogs.

Light on a Dark Horse, 1951

Richard Milhous Nixon

A man down in Texas heard Pat on the radio mention the fact that our two daughters would like to have a dog. And, believe it or not, the day before we left on this campaign trip we got a message from Union Station in Baltimore saying they had a package for us. We went down to get it. You know what it was? It was a little cocker spaniel dog in a crate that he sent all the way from Texas. Black and white spotted. And our little girl Tricia, the six year old, named it Checkers. And you know, the kids love the dog, and I just want to say this right now, that regardless of what they say about it, we're gonna keep it.

Comment after being accused of accepting improper gifts, 1952

Arnold Toynbee

America is a large, friendly dog in a very small room. Every time it wags its tail it knocks over a chair.

Broadcast, 14 July 1954

Gerald Durrell

Every evening Mother would go for a walk with the dogs, and the family would derive much amusement from watching her progress down the hill. Roger, as senior dog, would lead the procession, followed by Widdle and Puke. Then came Mother, wearing an enormous straw hat, which made her look like an animated mushroom, clutching in one hand a large trowel with which to dig any interesting wild plants she found. Dodo would waddle behind, eyes protruding and tongue flapping, and Sophia would bring up the rear, pacing along solemnly, carrying the imperial puppy on its cushion. Mother's Circus, Larry called it.

from My Family and Other Animals, 1956

T. H. White

People in those days had rather different ideas about the training of dogs to what we have today. They did it more by love than strictness. Imagine a modern MFH going to bed with his hounds, yet Flavius Arrianus says that it is "Best of all if they can sleep with a person because it makes them more human and because they rejoice in the company of human beings: also if they have had a restless night or been internally upset, you will know of it and will not use them to hunt next day." In Sir Ector's kennel there was a special boy, called the Dog Boy, who lived with the hounds night and day. He was a sort of head hound, and it was his business to take them out every day for walks, to pull thorns out of their feet, keep cankers out of their ears, bind the smaller bones that got dislocated, dose them for worms, isolate and nurse them in distemper, arbitrate in their quarrels and to sleep curled up among them at night. If one more learned quotation may be excused, this is how, later on, the Duke of York who was killed at Agincourt described such a boy in his *Master of Game*: "Also I will teach the child to lead out the hounds to scrombre twice a day in the morning and in the evening, so that the sun be up, especially in winter. Then should he let them run and play long in a meadow in the sun, and then comb every hound after the other, and wipe them with a great wisp of straw, and this he shall do every morning. And then he shall lead them into some fair place where tender grass grows as corn and other things, that therewith they may feed themselves as it is medicine for them." Thus, since the boy's "heart and his business be with the hounds," the hounds themselves become "goodly and kindly and clean, glad and joyful and playful, and goodly to all manner of folks save to the wild beasts to whom they should be fierce, eager and spiteful."

Sir Ector's dog boy was none other than the one who had his nose bitten off by the terrible Wat. Not having a nose like a human, and being, moreover, subjected to stone-throwing by the other village children, he had become more comfortable with animals. He talked to them, not in baby-talk like a maiden lady, but correctly in their own growls and barks. They all loved him very much, and revered him for taking thorns out of their toes, and came to him with their troubles at once. He always understood immediately what was wrong, and generally he could put it right. It was nice for the dogs to have their god with them, in visible form.

The Wart was fond of the Dog Boy, and thought him very clever to be able to do these things with animals – for he could make them do almost anything just by moving his hands – while the Dog Boy loved the Wart in much the same way as his dogs loved him, and thought the Wart was almost holy because he could read and write. They spent much of their time together, rolling about with the dogs in the kennel.

The kennel was on the ground floor, near the mews, with a loft above it, so that it should be cool in summer and warm in winter. The hounds were alaunts, gaze-hounds, lymers and braches. They were called Clumsy, Trowneer, Phoebe, Colle, Gerland, Talbot, Luath, Luffra, Apollon, Orthros, Bran, Gelert, Bounce, Boy, Lion, Bungey, Toby, and Diamond. The Wart's own special one was called Cavall, and he happened to be licking Cavall's nose – not the other way about – when Merlyn came in and found him.

"That will come to be regarded as an insanitary habit," said Merlyn, "though I cannot see it myself. After all, God made the creature's nose just as well as he made your tongue.

"If not better," added the philosopher pensively.

from *The Once and Future King,* 1958

John Steinbeck

Charley likes to get up early, and he likes me to get up early too. And why shouldn't he? Right after his breakfast he goes back to sleep. Over the years he has developed a number of innocent-appearing ways to get me up. He can shake himself and his collar loud enough to wake the dead. If that doesn't work he gets a sneezing fit. But perhaps his most irritating method is to sit quietly beside the bed and stare into my face with a sweet and forgiving look on his face; I come out of deep sleep with the feeling of being looked at. But I have learned to keep my eyes tight shut. If I even blink he sneezes and stretches, and the night's sleep is over for me. Often the war of wills goes on for quite a time, I squinching my eyes shut and he forgiving me, but he nearly always wins. He liked travelling so much he wanted to get started early, and early for Charley is the first tempering of darkness with the dawn.

from *Travels with Charley,* 1962

Robert Garioch

I kicked an Edinbro dug-luver's dug,
leastweys I tried; my timing wes owre late.
It stopped whit it wes daein til my gate
and skelpit aff to find some ither mug.

Whit a sensation! If a clockwark thug
suid croun ye wi a brolly owre yir pate,

the Embro folk wad leave ye til yir fate;
it's you, maist like, wad get a flee in yir lug.

But kick the Friend of Man! Or hae a try!
The Friend of Wummin, even, that's faur waur
a felony, mair dangerous forbye.

Meddle wi puir dumb craiturs gin ye daur;
that maks ye a richt cruel bruitt, my! my!
And whit d'ye think yir braw front yett is for?

"Nemo canem impune lacessit",
Selected Poems, 1966

Sir Stanley Spencer

I no more like people personally than I like dogs. When I meet then
I am only apprehensive whether they will bite me, which is
reasonable and sensible.

Quoted in Maurice Collis, *Stanley Spencer, a Biography*

Alan Bennett

It [the dog] is the one species I wouldn't mind seeing vanish from the
face of the earth. I wish they were like the White Rhino – six of
them left in the Serengeti National Park, and all males.

Getting On, 1972

John Sparrow

That indefatigable and unsavoury engine of pollution, the dog.

Letter to *The Times,* 30 September 1975

270

John Tickner

All dogs consider themselves to be Man's Best Friend. They show this by treating him with kindness and understanding, showing how to hunt things and above all, training him to do everything for the comfort and well-being of Dog.

Small dogs are undoubted experts at being Man's Best Friend and never stop saying so. They are strong supporters of the theory that "Small is Beautiful". Terriers are quite convinced that all terriers are not only beautiful but are the most expert of all because they know that to get the best out of Man they must not only be kind but also be firm and therefore handle Man with a very firm paw indeed – the little steel paw in the little velvet glove and sometimes with the help of the little steel teeth as well.

All terriers are jolly little dogs because they make quite sure that everything in life is planned for their jollity and comfort. They smile in a jolly way when they are sleeping in Man's favourite armchair and helping themselves to Man's favourite food and are especially noisily jolly when they are biting things like foxes and rabbits, other dogs and even Man himself.

There is no doubt that, of all breeds, terriers have the greatest sense of humour, even if it sometimes seems to all other creatures that their sense of humour is a bit twisted. It is by no means always clear to anyone else what is going on inside a tiny terrier-type mind.

Terriers are happiest indoors when they are making themselves comfortable, which is almost always, and they are happiest outdoors when they are making other creatures uncomfortable which is as often as possible. They are natural hunting dogs and are jolliest of all when worrying someone or something. If they can't find anything more interesting they worry Man himself. This appeals so much to their sense of humour that they laugh long, loudly and piercingly as anyone who lives within earshot of a terrier – and that means within a considerable mileage – is constantly reminded.

As their name implies, terriers were invented, probably by terriers themselves, to be earth dogs. This means that they went underground whenever and wherever they could and they still do. They have great fun going underground in fox earths and hurling abuse down the front passages or even in at the back door.

They also follow their underground instincts by going to ground at home under cushions and furniture and bedclothes and anywhere else where they can lurk, waiting to bite anything that moves, such as ankles and legs and things.

Tickner's Terriers, 1977

Anonymous

No one would know, to look at me, that I live like a rat in a sewer, shunned by friends and relatives alike.

They would never dream that the smart, elegant woman they admire is too ashamed to invite anyone into the stinking pig-sty that is her home.

There is only me to see the squalor in which I live – me and the fourteen dogs who created it and who are my obsession, one that has cost me the respect of my grown-up children, any money I ever had, a court conviction and even a marriage.

When my second husband issued an ultimatum and said either the dogs had to go or he would, my choice was inevitable. I even helped him to pack.

My neighbours hate my dogs and have even tried to poison them, but luckily the dogs have been trained to eat only what I give them.

One neighbour even reported me to the RSPCA, but the officers who came round said they had never seen dogs in better condition. It was my condition that worried them. Another neighbour had me served with a noise abatement summons, and I was given 12 months' probation for keeping barking dogs.

Last year, when the rest of my family was celebrating the birth of my grand-daughter, I spent the day in tears mourning the anniversary of the death of one of my best-loved dogs. Naturally my daughter never brings the child to see me. Neither she nor my son will ever set foot in my house, with the result that I have not seen my son for five years, nor have I ever seen his child.

My own daughter has threatened finally to disown me if I breed another dog, yet breeding and exhibiting is my life. I've travelled all over the country and abroad, as a sought-after judge and the UK's foremost authority on my particular breed.

I write for magazines and foreign journals on the subject, and last year at Cruft's, no fewer than five overseas enthusiasts sought me out. People always flock to talk to me at dog shows.

I have always been so consumed by my obsession that I barely even noticed when my children left home to move into homes of their own. I was always too eagerly expecting yet another litter of puppies to appreciate that they had simply grown too ashamed of the house in which they grew up to stay any longer.

My dogs have always lived indoors, you see, I could never keep them outside in kennels, as they were somehow part of the family. The result was that over the years, the house grew more and more shabby, as the dogs chewed chair legs and ripped wallpaper. And, with the disintegration of the kitchen lino and the erosion of the plaster from the walls, came the children's growing embarrassment at the state of the place and their reluctance to bring friends back.

By the time the children left home, I was exhibiting or judging every weekend. My family of dogs, which had begun with one when I got married, had grown to 10 by then, as I could never bear to sell any. None of the people who turned up to buy them ever seemed quite good enough to own one of my dogs.

The years rolled by, and it wasn't until every one of my diminishing circle of friends refused to dog-sit in the stinking hole that was my home, so that I could judge an important show abroad, that it really hit me what had happened to my life. And yet I didn't do anything about it.

I could never see the satisfaction of keeping a cabinet full of china or inviting people to look at all the housework I'd done. The squalor depressed me, of course it did, but never enough to change my way of life. Now as a pensioner I live on £65 a week, more than £20 of which is swallowed up on dog food and vets' bills. I walk miles every day exercising the dogs, and sometimes it all gets so much I have to get away.

I drive up on to the moors and spend hours looking at the magnificent views. Then I'm fine again, and I can't wait to get home to my dogs.

When I look back on my life, I feel stupid and exasperated. I have so many regrets, but there's no help, and certainly no sympathy, for people like me – and believe me, my case is not unique.

I know there's only one way I'm ever going to get out of this obsession – and that's in a coffin.

> "Love that took my cash, respect and marriage",
> *Manchester Evening News,* 9 October 1995

Frank Jackson

The company were agreed that the subject of our discussion was a twenty-two carat puffed-up, overweening buffoon.

One of our number, more kind than the rest of us, was anxious that something good should be said of our victim.

"Yes, but you've got to agree he's a dogman."

Tom was having none of it but isn't one to discourage good intentions.

"What is a dogman?"

We looked at one another and thought while the debris of a substantial repast was cleared from our table and our drinks were replenished. Tom asked permission of the ladies to light his pipe. Permission was granted graciously.

The discussion kept us going until the landlord insisted that it was long past his bedtime.

We quickly agreed that "dogman" included both sexes, though Tom was not happy at our acceptance that there may be more than two. We dismissed the politically correct suggestion that we ought to be attempting to define "dog-person". I sheepishly admitted that I couldn't remember how the term was defined in my dictionary or even if it was defined – it is. We were in no doubt but that being a dogman was an ancient and honourable estate, a title to be worn with pride, preserved with respect and jealously guarded. Just as the title travelled without sexual baggage so it was equally applicable to all races, creeds and classes. We were agreed that the title was hard earned and bestowed only by one's peers, never, among people of proper upbringing and susceptibilities, was it self-bestowed.

"That", said Sally, "would be like judging dogs with painted fingernails – you know what I mean!" "Or wearing silly clothes and hats just so that you will be recognised." "Or wearing sandals," said Tom. "Or drinking lager," said Alan. "Or picking one's nose in public," said Jimmy, who has an unfortunate tendency to be coarse.

It was apparent that the conversation was running off the rails so I told my Tristam Hillier story. He was returning from France and was stopped by customs. His passport said he was a painter but inspection of his luggage revealed a quantity of works of undoubted art.

"Where did you get these?" "I painted them." "So you're an artist not a painter." "It's very kind of you to say so but I couldn't possibly make such a claim."

The story enabled the company to give the principal subject more thought. We were agreed that an absolute requirement of a dogman was that home must be shared with at least one dog and that dogs should provide many of the enjoyments of life.

Tom told his tatler's tale of the man walking up New Hall Lane pushing an empty wheelbarrow. "Nah then, Jimmy, what's up?" "Nowt much, lad, but mi pup's badly and a chap feels a fool walkin' abaat by hissel."

By this time the landlord had returned from giving his dogs their pre-bedtime scamper. Sue finished Alan's crisps and Brownie looked at Tom with eyes glowing with adoration. Tom had bred her, named her after Tim White's beloved dog, trained her and remained her god.

Tom gave the landlord a résumé of our discussion while the rest of us attended to our comfort and Jimmy got the drinks. When we returned the landlord suggested that dogmen drank a lot and were reluctant to go to bed. This was uncalled for and we told him so. He apologised without conviction.

"Isn't dogman the same as fancier?" asked the landlord, inadvertently further agitating already troubled waters. We thought not, though all dogmen are fanciers not all fanciers are dogmen. A fancier is simply someone with an interest in dogs but who may or may not share his home with dogs. Interest may involve participation in canine activities, he may write about dogs, buy and sell them or even steal them – Mayhew is adamant that dog thieves were an important part of "The Fancy". "Fancier" is a term which may be self-bestowed, though connotations of possible dishonesty and skulduggery make this unlikely. We agreed that the subject who had led us into the debate was undoubtedly a Fancier. Indeed we could not readily think of anyone more fancy.

Tom brought us back to our main topic.

We were adamant that there was no such thing as a vicarious dogman, though some have tried what they thought was the back door. I recalled that a member of the General Committee once had to borrow a dog in order to present the required image. "Happily," I said, "the General Committee now contains some genuine examples of the article." The company gave me a funny look and Sally snorted in a most unladylike manner. I felt uncomfortable.

Ann must have realised that the Sabbath had begun and asked if dogmen could go to Heaven. I know she regretted the question because I told one of Ronnie's jokes, that which is generally regarded as the funniest of the two.

It seems that a wee Scottish dogman died. In life he had swapped appointments, put up his friends and pulled his tongue out at the Chairman. He went to Hell. After some years of torture and agony in the fiery furnace he happened to look up and saw God looking down at him: "Oh, Lord. I didna' ken." The Lord, in his infinite wisdom and mercy replied: "Well, ye ken noo."

I don't know whether familiarity, lack of sympathy with Ronnie's alleged sense of humour or religious residues make Alan dislike the story.

"St Roch refused to enter Heaven without his dog, he was a dogman."

She told us that St Patrick was not a dogman. It seems the venerable gent had been given a bowl of soup by a charitable lady. He drank the soup only to discover a dog's paw at the bottom of the dish. Overcome with remorse he restored the dog to life, where-upon it leapt out of the dish and rushed down the road biting people. St Patrick ran after it, caught it and with a single dreadful blow killed it stone dead.

The names of St Bernard, St Colmcille, St Francis, St Hubert were invoked without advancing the discussion. When Jimmy added St Partridge and St Vulpes to the list we decided against continuing the religious theme.

We were in no doubt but that dogmanship cannot be attained by reading or writing about dogs, not even by judging them, only by living with them and having fun with them. Alan said that dogmen don't denigrate other people's dogs. We all heartily agreed with that. We didn't regard commercial breeders and puppy farmers as dogmen. Dogmen don't exploit dogs. I suggested, not without a degree of seriousness, that all dogmen are adept with a yard brush and hosepipe. The suggestion was contemptuously dismissed by Ann who insisted that she never cleaned her lounge, still less her bedroom, with yard brush and hosepipe.

Our glasses were empty and the landlord was getting restive. It was time to sum up. Tom did the honours, succinctly as ever. "Surely a dogman is someone who feels undressed when he hasn't got his dogs with him."

We all agreed with that and the company evaporated into the night. We all went home happily knowing that our own dogs were waiting to welcome us.

"The Company in Session", *Our Dogs Annual*, 1995

CHAPTER 9

Curs & Mongrels

Dictionaries may not always be reliable sources of information about dogs. *The Concise Oxford Dictionary*'s definition of cur as a "worthless, low-bred, or snappish dog" is, at best, less than adequate and at worst misleading. For them, the word derives from "kur-dogge", which in turn derives from Middle Dutch *korre* and perhaps ultimately from the Old Norse *kurra* to grumble or growl. But there is more to their history.

Curs have, indeed, always been dogs which were without value to sportsmen, but they were certainly not without value to farmers and herdsmen. Low-bred, whatever that term may mean, perhaps, but certainly not without value.

"Cur", Captain Grose's *Dictionary of the Vulgar Tongue* (1811) states: "A cut or curtailed dog. According to the forest laws, a man who had no right to the privilege of the chase, was obliged to cut or law his dog: among other modes of disabling him from disturbing the game, one was by depriving him of his tail: a dog so cut was called a cut or curtailed dog, and by contraction a cur. A cur is figuratively used to signify a surly fellow."

Perhaps the temptation to associate "cur" with "curtail" should be resisted? Even though a curtal was a docked horse, the association appears to be tenuous.

A "curtail-dog" was originally a dog belonging to an unqualified person, and, under Forest Laws, it had to have its tail cut short, partly for identification purposes, but also because having a tail increases speed and agility, both necessary when harassing deer. Later on, "curtail-dog" was applied to any dog not intended for sport, and eventually, huntsmen used the word "cur" to refer disparagingly to any dog other than the hunt's own hounds or terriers.

So perhaps "cur" is no more than a diminutive of "curtail-dog".

"Cur" might also derive from "currour", a forest-keeper during the reign of eleventh-century Robert I. Part of the duties of a currour would be to ensure that dogs which were allowed in the forest had a right to be there either because they belonged to people entitled to hunt or because they had been "curtailed", probably by the currour himself.

In *The British Dog* Carson Ritchie speculates that the Welsh *ki-taeog* might well be the origin of the word "cur". Some other historians have also pointed to a Welsh connection, and found three types of cur, among the eight breeds – *gellgi, milgi, olrhead, bytheuad, cholwyn, bugeilgi, ki-taeog* and *callawet* – defined in Howell's Code. However, Howell's Code is a forgery, produced long after its purported date, at a time when "cur" was a term in common use for non-sporting dogs. Abraham Fleming, writing in 1576, frequently used "cur" when referring to mongrels, guard dogs, draft dogs and dogs from overseas, but never to any type of sporting dog.

The three Welsh curs were the watch cur, the house cur and the shepherd's or herdsman's cur. The suggestion that *ki-taeog* not only gave rise to "corgi" but also to "cur" is fanciful, though it may well be possible that corgi is a corruption of *cur-gi*, cur dog. (The Welsh for dog is "*ci*", with variations; *chi, nghi* or, *gi. Cor* is Welsh for dwarf.) Corgi is more likely to be a dwarf dog, than a dog which lacks a tail.

While in Britain "cur" has never been applied to dogs used for sport, in the United States its old meaning is being eroded: the word has been adopted for some breeds developed for sporting purposes, such as the Black Mouth Cur, the Mountain Cur, and the Leopard Cur.

Abraham Fleming

Of such dogges as keep not their kinde, of such as are mingled out of sundry sortes not imitating the conditions of some one certaine spice, because they resemble no notable shape, nor exercise any worthy property of the true perfect and gentle kind, it is not necessarye that I write any more of them, but to banishe them as unprofitable implements, out of the boundes of my Booke, unprofitable I say for any use that is commendable, except to intertaine strangers with their barcking in the day time, giving warnying to them of the house, that such & such be newly come, whereupon wee call them admonishing Dogges, because in that point they performe theyr office . . .

There is comprehended, under the curres of the coursest kinde, a certaine dogge in kytchen service excellent. For when any meate is to bee roasted they go into a wheele which they turning rounde about with the waight of their bodies, so diligently looke to their businesse, that no druge nor skullion can doe the feate more cunningly. Whom the popular sort hereupon cal Turnespets [Turnspit].

Of the Dogge called the Daunser, in Latine *Saltator or Tympanista*.

There be also dogges among us of a mungrell kind which are taught and exervcised to daunce in measure at the musicall sounde of an instrument, as, at the just stroke of the drombe, at the sweete accent of the Cyterne, & tuned strings of the harmonious Harpe showing many pretty trickes by the gesture of their bodies. As to stand bolte upright, to lye flat upon the grounde, to turne rounde as a ringe holding their tailes in their teeth, to begge for theyr meate, and sundry such properties, which they learne of theyr vagabundicall masters, whose instruments they are to gather gaine, withall in Citie, Country, Towne, and Village. As some which carry olde apes on their shoulders in coloured jackets to move men to laughter for a little lucre . . .

Of other dogges . . .

The first bred of a bytch and a wolfe, in Latine *Lyciscus*.

The second of a bytche and a foxe. In Latine *Lacoena*.

The third of a beare and a bandogge. In Latine *Urcanus*.

Of the first we have none naturally bred within the borders of England. The reason is for the want of wolfes, without whom no such kinde of dog can bee ingendred . . .

Of the second sort we are not utterly voyde of some, because this our Englishe soyle is not free from foxes (for in deede we are not without a multitude of them in so much as diverse keepe, foster, and feede them in their houses among their houndes and dogges, eyther for some maldie of mind, or for some sicknesse of body,) which peradventure the savour of that subtill beast would either mitigate or expell.

The thirde kinde which is bred of a Beare and a Bandogge we want not heare in England, (A straunge and wonderfull efect, that cruell enimyes should enter into ye worke of copulation & bring forth so savage a curre.) Undoubtedly it is even so as we have reported, for the fyery heate of theyr fleshe, or rather the pricking thorne, or most of all, the tyckling lust of lechery, beareth such swinge and sway in them, that there is no contrairietie for the time, but of constraint they must joyne to ingender. And why should not this bee consonant to thruth? why shoulde not these beastes breede in this lande, as well as in other forreigne nations? For wee reede that Tigers and dogges in *Hircania*, that Lyons and Dogges in *Arcadia*, and that wolfes and dogges in *Francia*, couple and procreate . . . The *Urcane* which bred of a beare and a dogge,

> Is fearce, is fell, is stoute and stronge,
> And byteth sore to fleshe and bone,
> His furious force indureth longe
> In rage he will be rul'de of none.

That I may use the wordes of the Poet *Gratius*. This dogge exceedeth all other in cruell conditions, his leering and fleering lookes, his strearene and savage vissage, maketh him in sight feareful and terrible, he is violent in fighting, & wheresoever he setteth his tenterhooke teeth, he taketh such sure & fast holde, that a man may sooner teare and rende him in sunder, then lose him and seperate his chappes. He passeth not for the Wolfe, the Beare, the Lyon, nor the Bulle and may wortherly (as I think,) be companion with *Alexanders* dogge which came out of *India*.

from *Of Englishe Dogges*, 1576

Michael Drayton

Then Ball, my cut-tailed cur, and I begin to play.
He o'er my sheep-hook leaps, now th'one, now th'other way,
Then on his hinder feet he doth himself advance,
I tune, and to my note my lively dog will dance.

"Dancing Dog"

I. Walsh

'Tis pitty poor Barnet a Vigilant, Vigilant Curr,
That us'd for to bark, if a mouse, if a mouse did but stirr,
Should being grown old, and unable, unable to bark,
Be doom'd by a Priest, be doom'd by a Priest, to be hang'd
 by his clark,
I prey good Sir therefore, weigh right well, right well his Case,
And save us poor Barnet, Hang cleric, hang cleric, hang cleric
 in place.

> from "The Jovial Companions", 1709

Dr Alexander Pennycuik

Howl and Lament, ye Newland Tykes and Currs,
Ye who for Lesser Matters make great Sturrs,
Bark with a Hideous Noise and direful Moan,
For Tories Turk your Captain's dead and gone,
The Trusty Punler of the Newland Pease,
Lyes Breathless, Ah, and none knew his Disease.

His Awful Looks the Traveller did Afright,
The Vagabond by Day, the Thief by Night.
With Vigilence and Care he kept the Store,
And seldom wandered from his Master's Door.
No Beggar, yea no Laird durst make his Entry,
Without Leave asked of this Valient Sentry.

Hell's Porter Cerberus, though Fierce and Cruel,
Durst never face this Hero at a Duell,
Now he is past both Phisick Oyl and Plaister,
And Murdered lyes by his too Cruel Master.
Who yet may vow and swear to his last Breath,
He had no hand in his kind Mastiff's Death.

> from *Geographical Historical Description
> of the Shire of Tweeddale*, 1715

Alexander Pope

Whate'er of dunce in College or in Town
Sneers at another, in toupee or gown;
Whate'er of mongrel no one class admits,
A wit with dunces, and a dunce with wits.

from *The Dunciad, Book IV,* 1728

Thomas Bewick

I cannot help thinking, that if the same pains were taken in breeding
man-kind, that Gentlemen have bestowed upon the breeding of
their Dogs, Horses & game Cocks, that human nature might, as it
were, be new modelled – hereditary diseases banished, & such a race
of Mankind might people the country as we can form no true
conception of, and instead of a nation of mongrels, there would, in
time, appear a nation of "Admirable Crichtons."

from *A Memoir, c.* 1828

George Eliot

"Well, well, Vixen, you foolish wench, what is it, what is it? I must
go in, must I? Ay, ay, I'm never to have a will o' my own any more.
And those pups, what do you think I'm to do with 'em, when
they're twice as big as you – for I'm pretty sure the father was that
hulking bull-terrier of Will Baker's – wasn't he now, eh, you sly
hussy?" (Here Vixen tucked her tail between her legs, and ran
forward into the house. Subjects are sometimes broached which a
well-bred female will ignore.)

from *Adam Bede,* 1859

Anonymous

EXTRAORDINARY CURIOSITY. – A SUBJECT FOR NATURALISTS.
We had submitted to our inspection on Friday last two hybrid animals, whose existence certainly is an incontestable answer to the question which has often been mooted by naturalists, – "Can or will animals of the canine and feline race breed together?" The animals to which we allude are the produce of a lioness and a true English mastiff. They are a dog and a bitch, and are about seven weeks old. The bitch presents no extraordinary feature, and at first glance would be taken for a mongrel, while the dog at once catches the eye as something uncommon. He has all the true colour of the African lion, has a black stripe down his back, and a species of black fringe under the howl, which has all the appearance of an incipient mane. Both animals have the power of extending and retracting the claws like a cat; and their movements, especially those of the male, when playing together and when feeding, partake more to the feline than the canine method. The male stands nearly a foot high, the female not quite so large; their limbs are immensely powerful, and their general appearance assures one that, when full grown, they will be most formidable customers. That they are really what they are represented to us is a matter of certainty and not speculation. The mother was brought to this country four years back by Captain W. H. Patten-Saunders, and given to his mother, in whose possession she has been ever since. The sire, a fine mastiff, has also been in that lady's possession for the same period. They have constantly occupied the same yard, but have generally been chained up. The lioness has never seen a lion since her arrival in this country, and no animal except the mastiff can have had access to her. These curiosities will, no doubt, create great speculation among naturalists, and the discussion will tend to enliven the coming dull season, if no more useful end will be answered.

Bell's Life, November 1862

Idstone (pseud.)

The first cross between two separate breeds is an undoubted "mongrel," a shapeless nondescript, blending generally in its malformations the faults of both types. A glance at the likeness of Mr Hanley's "Half-and-Half," figured in Stonehenge's book on the Dog, will show the truth of this assertion; and in a subsequent engraving of "Hystericks," the fourth cross from the Bulldogs ("Half-and Half" being the first, as her name implies), the Bulldog strain is evident to a practical eye.

In the first cross it would require consummate judgement to discover any trace of Greyhound in these days – I say advisedly in these days – for thirty years ago the first cross was to be seen on every highway and thoroughfare, the half-and-half being the best truck-dog the itinerant costermonger or nut-barrow man could purchase, and such dogs were brewed and broken to harness as a livelihood by dealers in harness-dogs in the neighbourhood of Manchester and Liverpool.

Crossing undoubtedly adds to the dog's intelligence. The highest-bred dogs are, as a rule, wanting in this faculty. This is the result of in-breeding. The whole system becomes enfeebled; the constitution is more liable to disease, and soon succumbs; the brain is weak; the circulation slow. Palsy, fits, dropsy, tumours, rickets, malformation of the limbs, cancer, every variety of disease attacks high-bred favourites, from which the tinker's mongrel escapes.

Many of these calamities occur from the close confinement, the pampering, and high feeding to which these valuable strains are subjected; but most of them are the result of that constitutional infirmity and scrofulous habit which is the curse of inbred or prize animals.

Judicious crossing can only be be successful when done with judgement and patience. We must wait for years to obtain the result, and we may be disappointed in the end.

The mongrel, in the common acceptation of the title, is the dog of the poor man or the ignorant one, who breeds by accident, or takes what is given him and is satisfied. It is aimless, of course. It may be between Spaniel and Terrier – one which no time will ever set right; or Newfoundland and Setter, which is equally disastrous; but supposing it to be between English white Terrier and Bulldog, that first production is valueless, and ought to be kept only to get by degrees the proper and accepted formation of head and jaws, which will declare itself in the course of generations.

It is difficult to imagine how beautiful and talented a race or races of dogs might be produced by practical, patient, and thoughtful breeders. It is painful to think how little care and attention has been given to the subject, and how rude the hands and ignorant the heads of those who have until lately given attention to breeding. The form, the colour, the perseverance, the sense, the dash of the Foxhound – to whose culture many men who would have been eminent in any walk of life have bent all their energies – these brilliant qualities show us how much remains as yet undeveloped in the canine race, and how much has been accomplished.

Mongrels, however, constitute the large majority of what I must take the liberty of calling the canine population, and these wayfarers imperil the purity of many a kennel, and what is more, the safety of many a household. To them we may trace the spread of hydrophobia (a disease utterly incurable), the destruction of game, especially in the nesting season, and those depredations committed under the trials of hunger, for which, often unjustly, foxes are made answerable.

The five-shilling duty has not materially diminished the number of these vagrant curs, nor has it influenced the breeding of the dog in any way. The middle classes will seldom take a dog from each other, except as a gift, and there is no encouragement to those who breed dogs to begin with pure, and, consequently, expensive parents.

Possibly want of education as to the dog's form and breeding is the fertile cause of this love of underbred animals, for artisans in manufacturing towns, if they keep or breed dogs at all, soon become celebrated for their "strain."

from *The Dog: with Simple Directions for his Treatment and notices of the best dogs of the day and their breeders or exhibitors*, 1872

Sir Arthur Conan Doyle

"Rouse old Sherman up, and tell him with my compliments that I want Toby here at once. You will bring Toby back in the cab with you."

"A dog, I suppose?"

"Yes, a queer mongrel, with a most amazing power of scent. I would rather have Toby's help than that of the whole detective force of London."

from *The Sign of Four*, 1890

Jerome K. Jerome

I endeavoured to obtain possession of a lame dog, but failed. A one-eyed dealer in Seven Dials, to whom, as a last resource, I applied, offered to lame one for me for an extra five shillings, but this suggestion I declined. I came across an uncanny-looking mongrel late one night. He was not lame, but he seemed pretty sick; and, feeling I was not robbing anybody of anything very valuable, I lured him home and nursed him. I fancy I must have over-nursed him. He got so healthy in the end, there was no doing anything with him. He was an ill-conditioned cur, and he was too old to be taught. He became the curse of the neighbourhood. His idea of sport was killing chickens and sneaking rabbits from outside poulterers' shops. For recreation he killed cats and frightened small children by yelping round their legs. There were times when I could have lamed him myself, if only I could have got hold of him. I made nothing by running that dog – nothing what-ever. People, instead of admiring me for nursing him back to life, called me a fool, and said that if I didn't drown the brute they would.

from *Second Thoughts of an Idle Fellow*, 1898

Alfred Ollivant

The Tailless Tyke had now grown into a huge Cerberus. Deep-chested as a barrel; legs like Gothic arches; great bullhead; lower jaw reaching perpetually forward as if for prey; eyes scowling always askance; cropped ears perking mouse-like on a round bald skull; a coat like coir; and back running from shoulder to loins, abruptly terminated by the knob-like tail; and when he regarded you his eyes rolled and his head moved not at all. In all, he looked like the Satan of a dog's Hell.

from *Owd Bob, the Grey Dog of Kenmuir*, 1898

Edmond Rostand

No, but I have several dogs in my make-up. I fight a bit.
The spaniel part of me gets excited at the sound of gun-fire,
But then my memory of being a poodle
Evokes a bloody wing, the eye of a dying hind,
I remember what a rabbit puts into its last look
And I feel stirring within me my heart of a Saint Bernard.

from *Patou*, c.1900

Sir Percy Fitzpatrick

There were six puppies, and as the waggons were empty we fixed up a roomy nest in one of them for Jess and her family. There was no trouble with Jess; nobody interfered with her, and she interfered with nobody. The boys kept clear of her; but we used to take a look at her and the puppies as we walked along with the waggons; so by degrees she got to know that we would not harm them, and she no longer wanted to eat us alive if we went near and talked to her.

Five of the puppies were fat strong yellow little chaps with dark muzzles — just like their father, as Ted said; and their father was an imported dog, and was always spoken of as the best dog of the breed that had ever been in the country. I never saw him, so I do not really know what he was like — perhaps he was not a yellow dog at all; but, whatever he was, he had at that time a great reputation because he was "imported", and there were not half a dozen imported dogs in the whole of the Transvaal then. Many people used to ask what breed the puppies were — I suppose it was because poor cross faithful old Jess was not much to look at, and because no one had a very high opinion of yellow dogs in general, and nobody seemed to remember any famous yellow bull-terriers. They used to smile in a queer way when they asked the question, as if they were going to get off a joke; but when we answered "Just like their father – Buchanan's imported dog," the smile disappeared, and they would give a whistle of surprise and say "By Jove!" and immediately begin to examine the five yellow puppies, remark upon their ears and noses and legs, and praise them up until we were all as proud as if they had belonged to us.

Jess looked after her puppies and knew nothing about the remarks that were made, so that they did not worry her, but I often looked at the faithful old thing with her dark brindled face, cross-looking eyes and always moving ears, and thought it jolly hard lines that nobody had a good word for her; it seemed rough on her that everyone should be glad there was only one puppy at all like the mother – the sixth one, a poor miserable little rat of a thing about half the size of the others. He was not yellow like them, nor dark brindled like Jess, but a sort of dirty pale half-and-half colour with some dark faint wavy lines all over him, as if he had tried to be brindled and failed; and he had a dark sharp wizened little muzzle that looked shrivelled up with age.

Most of the fellows said it would be a good thing to drown the odd one because he spoilt the litter and made them look as though they were not really thoroughbred, and because he was such a miserable little rat that he was not worth saving anyhow; but in the end he was allowed to live. I believe no one fancied the job of taking one of Jess's puppies away from her; moreover, as any dog was better than none, I had offered to take him rather than let him be drowned. Ted had old friends to whom he had already promised the pick of the puppies, so when I came along it was too late, and all he could promise me was that if there should be one over I might have it.

As they grew older and were able to crawl about they were taken off the waggons when we outspanned and put on the ground. Jess got to understand this at once, and she used to watch us quite quietly as we took them in our hands to put them down or lift them back again. When they were two or three weeks old a man came to the waggons who talked a great deal about dogs, and appeared to know what had to be done. He said that the puppies' tails ought to be docked, and that a bull-terrier would be no class at all with a long tail, but you should on no account clip his ears. I thought he was speaking of fox-terriers, and that with bull-terriers the position was the other way round, at that time; but as he said it was "the thing" in England, and nobody contradicted him, I shut up. We found out afterwards that he had made a mistake; but it was too late then, and Jess's puppies started life as bull-terriers up to date, with long ears and short tails.

I felt sure from the beginning that all the yellow puppies would be claimed and that I should have to take the odd one, or none at all; so I began to look upon him as mine already, and to take an interest in him and look after him. A long time ago somebody wrote that "the sense of possession turns sand into gold," and it is one of the truest things ever said. Until it seemed that this queer-looking odd puppy was going to be mine I used to think and say very much what the others did but with this difference, that I always felt sorry for him, and sorry for Jess too, because he was like her and not like the father. I used to think that perhaps if he were given a chance he might grow up like poor old Jess herself, ugly, cross and unpopular, but brave and faithful. I felt sorry for him, too, because he was small and weak, and tottering, the other puppies used to push him away from his food and trample on him; and when they were old enough to play they used to pull him about by his ears and pack on to him – three or four to one – and bully him horribly. Many a time I rescued him, and many a time gave him a little preserved milk and water with bread soaked in it when the others had shouldered him out and eaten everything.

After a little while, when my chance of getting one of the good puppies seemed hopeless and I got used to the idea that I would have to take the odd one, I began to notice little things about him that no one else noticed, and got to be quite fond of the little beggar – in a kind of way. Perhaps I was turning my sand into gold, and my geese into swans; perhaps I grew fond of him simply because, finding him lonely and with no one else to depend on, I befriended him; and perhaps it was because he was always cheerful and plucky and it seemed as if there might be some good stuff in him after all. Those were the things I used to think of sometimes when feeding the little outcast. The other puppies would tumble him over and take his food from him; they would bump into him when he was stooping over the dish of milk and porridge, and his head was so big and his legs so weak that he would tip up and go heels over head into the dish. We were always picking him out of the food and scraping it off him: half the time he was wet and sticky, and the other half covered with porridge and sand baked hard by the sun.

One day just after the waggons had started, as I took a final look round the outspan place to see if anything had been forgotten, I found the little chap – who was only about four inches high – struggling to walk through the long grass. He was not big enough or strong enough to push his way – even the stems of the down-trodden grass tripped him – and he stumbled and floundered at every step, but he got up again each time with his little tail standing straight up, his head erect, and his ears cocked. He looked such a ridiculous sight that his little tragedy of "lost in the veld" was forgotten – one could only laugh.

What he thought he was doing, goodness only knows; he looked as proud and important as if he owned the whole world and knew that everyone in it was watching him. The poor little chap could not see a yard in that grass; and in any case he was not old enough to see much, or understand anything, for his eyes still had that bluish blind look that all very young puppies have, but he was marching along as full of confidence as a general at the head of his army. How he fell out of the waggon no one knew; perhaps the big puppies tumbled him out, or he may have tried to follow Jess, or have climbed over the tail-board to see what was the other side, for he was always going off exploring by himself. His little world was small, it may be – only the bedplank of the waggon and the few square yards of the ground on which they were dumped at the outspans – but he took it as seriously as any explorer who ever tackled a continent.

The others were a bit more softened towards the odd puppy when I caught up to the waggons and told them of his valiant struggle to follow; and the man who had docked the puppies' tails allowed, "I believe the rat's got pluck, whatever else is the matter with him, for he was the only one that didn't howl when I snipped them. The little cuss just gave a grunt, and turned round as if he wanted to eat me. I think he'd 'a' been terrible angry if he hadn't been so s'prised. Pity he's such an awful-looking mongrel."

But no one else said a good word for him: he was really beneath notice, and if ever they had to speak about him they called him "The Rat". There is no doubt about it he was extremely ugly, and instead of improving as he grew older, he became worse; yet, I could not help liking him and looking after him, sometimes feeling sorry for him, sometimes being tremendously amused, and sometimes – wonderful to relate – really admiring him. He was extraordinarily silent; while the others barked at nothing, howled when lonely, and yelled when frightened or hurt, the odd puppy did none of these things; in fact, he began to show many of Jess's peculiarities; he hardly ever barked, and when he did it was not a wild excited string of barks but little suppressed muffled noises, half bark and half growl, and just one or two at a time; and he did not appear to be afraid of anything, so one could not tell what he would do if he was.

One day one of the oxen, sniffing about the outspan, caught sight of him all alone, and filled with curiosity came up to examine him, as a hulking silly old tame ox will do. It moved towards him slowly and heavily with its ears spreadwide and its head down, giving great big sniffs at this new object, trying to make out what it was. "The Rat" stood quite still with his stumpy tail cocked up and his head a little on one side, and when the huge ox's nose was about a foot from him he gave one of those funny abrupt little barks. It was as if the object had suddenly "gone off" like a cracker, and the ox nearly tumbled over with fright; but even when the great mountain of a thing gave a clumsy plunge round and trotted off, "The Rat" was not the least frightened; he was startled, and his tail and ears flickered for a second, but stiffened up again instantly, and with another of those little barks he took a couple of steps forward and cocked his head on the other side. That was his way.

He was not a bit like the other puppies; if anyone fired off a gun or cracked one of the big whips the whole five would yell at the top of their voices and, wherever they were, would start running, scrambling and floundering as fast as they could towards the waggon without once looking back to see what they were running away from. The odd puppy would drop his bone with a start or would jump round; his ears and tail would flicker up and down for a second; then he would slowly bristle up all over, and with his head cocked first on one side and then on the other, stare hard with his half-blind bluish puppy eyes in the direction of the noise; but he never ran away.

And so, little by little, I got to like him in spite of his awful ugliness. And it really was awful! The other puppies grew big all over, but the odd one at that time seemed to grow only in one part – his tummy! The poor little chap was born small and weak; he had always been bullied and crowded out by the others, and the truth is he was half starved. The natural consequence of this was that as soon as he could walk about and pick up things for himself he made up for lost time, and filled up his middle piece to an alarming size before the other parts of his body had time to grow; at that time he looked more like a big tock-tockic beetle than a dog.

Besides the balloon-like tummy he had stick-out bandy-legs, very like a beetle's too, and a neck so thin that it made the head look enormous, and you wondered how the neck ever held it up. But what made him so supremely ridiculous was that he evidently did not know he was ugly; he walked about as if he was always thinking of his dignity, and he had that puffed-out and stuckup air of importance that you only see in small people and bantam cocks who are always trying to appear an inch taller than they really are.

When the puppies were about a month old, and could feed on porridge or bread soaked in soup or gravy, they got to be too much for Jess, and she used to leave them for hours at a time and hide in the grass so as to have a little peace and sleep. Puppies are always hungry, so they soon began to hunt about for themselves, and would find scraps of meat and porridge or old bones; and if they could not get anything else, would try to eat the raw-hide nekstrops and reins. Then the fights began. As soon as one puppy saw another busy on anything, he would walk over towards him and, if strong enough, fight him for it. All day long it was nothing but wrangle, snarl, bark and yelp. Sometimes four or five would be at it in one scrum; because as soon as one heard a row going on he would trot up hoping to steal the bone while the others were busy fighting.

It was then that I noticed other things about the odd puppy: no matter how many packed on to him, or how they bit or pulled him, he never once let out a yelp; with four or five on top of him you would see him on his back, snapping right and left with bare white teeth, gripping and worrying them when he got a good hold of anything, and all the time growling and snarling with a fierceness that was really comical. It sounded as a lion fight might sound in a toy phonograph.

Before many days passed, it was clear that some of the other puppies were inclined to leave "The Rat" alone, and that only two of them – the two biggest – seemed anxious to fight him and could take his bones away. The reason soon became apparent: instead of wasting his breath in making a noise, or wasting strength in trying to tumble the others over "The Rat" simply bit hard and hung on; noses, ears, lips, cheeks, feet and even tails – all came handy to him; anything he could get hold of and hang on to was good enough, and the result generally was that in about half a minute the other puppy would leave everything and clear off yelling, and probably holding up one paw or hanging its head on one side to ease a chewed ear.

When either of the big puppies tackled the little fellow the fight lasted much longer. Even if he were tumbled over at once – as generally happened – and the other one stood over him barking and growling, that did not end the fight: as soon as the other chap got off him he would struggle up and begin again; he would not give in. The other puppies seemed to think there was some sort of rule like the "count out" in boxing, or that once you were tumbled over you ought to give up the bone; but the odd puppy apparently did not care about rules; as far as I could see, he had just one rule: "Stick to it," so it was not very long before even the two big fellows gave up interfering with him. The bites from his little white teeth – sharp as needles – which punctured noses and feet and tore ears, were most unpleasant. But apart from that, they found there was nothing to be gained by fighting him: they might roll him over time after time, but he came back again and worried them so persistently that it was quite impossible to enjoy the bone – they had to keep on fighting for it.

At first I drew attention to these things, but there was no encouragement from the others; they merely laughed at the attempt to make the best of a bad job. Sometimes owners of other puppies were nettled by having their beauties compared with "The Rat", or were annoyed because he had the cheek to fight for his own and beat them. Once, when I had described how well he had stood up to Billy's pup, Robbie caught up "The Rat", and placed him on the table, said: "Hats off to the Duke of Wellington on the field of Waterloo." That seemed to me the poorest sort of joke to send five grown men into fits of laughter. He stood there on the table with his head on one side, one ear standing up, and his stumpy tail twiggling – an absurd picture of friendliness, pride and confidence; yet he was so ugly and ridiculous that my heart sank, and I whisked him away. They made fun of him, and he did not mind; but it was making fun of me too, and I could not help knowing why; it was only necessary to put the puppies together to see the reason.

After that I stopped talking about him, and made the most of the good points he showed, and tried to discover more. It was the only consolation for having to take the leavings of the litter.

Then there came a day when something happened which might easily have turned out very differently, and there would have been no stories and no Jock to tell about; and the best dog in the world would never have been my friend and companion. The puppies had been behaving very badly, and had stolen several nekstrops and chewed up parts of one or two big whips; the, drivers were grumbling about all the damage done and the extra work it gave them; and Ted, exasperated by the worry of it all, announced that the puppies were quite old enough to be taken away, and that those who had picked puppies must take them at once and look after them, or let some one else have them. When I heard him say that my heart gave a little thump from excitement, for I knew the day had come when the great question would be settled once and for all. Here was a glorious and unexpected chance; perhaps one of the others would not or could not take his, and I might get one of the good ones . . . Of course the two big ones would be snapped up: that was certain; for, even if the men who had picked them could not take them, others had been promised puppies before me would exchange those they had already chosen for the better ones. Still, there were other chances; and I thought of very little else all day long, wondering if any of the good ones would be left; and if so, which?

In the afternoon Ted came up to where we were all lying in the shade and startled us with the momentous announcement:.

"Billy Griffiths can't take his pup!"

Every man of us sat up. Billy's pup was the first pick, the champion of the litter, the biggest and strongest of the lot. Several of the others said at once that they would exchange theirs for this one; but Ted smiled and shook his head.

"No," he said, "you had a good pick in the beginning." Then he turned to me, and added: "You've only had leavings." Someone said "The Rat", and there was a shout of laughter, but Ted went on: "You can have Billy's pup."

It seemed too good to be true; not even in my wildest imaginings had I fancied myself getting the pick of the lot. I hardly waited to thank Ted before going off to look at my champion. I had seen and admired him times out of number, but it seemed as if he must look different now that he belonged to me. He was a fine big fellow, well built and strong, and looked as if he could beat all the rest put together. His legs were straight; his neck sturdy; his muzzle dark and shapely; his ears equal and well carried; and in the sunlight his yellow coat looked quite bright, with occasional glints of gold in it. He was indeed a handsome fellow.

As I put him back again with the others the odd puppy, who had stood up and sniffed at me when I came, licked my hand and twiddled his tail with the friendliest and most independent air, as if he knew me quite well and was glad to see me, and I patted the poor little chap as he waddled up. I had forgotten him in the excitement of getting Billy's pup; but the sight of him made me think of his funny ways, his pluck and independence, and of how he had not a friend in the world except Jess and me; and I felt downright sorry for him. I picked him up and talked to him; and when his wizened little face was close to mine, he opened his mouth as if laughing, and shooting out his red tongue dabbed me right on the tip of my nose in pure friendliness. The poor little fellow looked more ludicrous than ever: he had been feeding again and was as tight as a drum; his skin was so tight one could not help thinking that if he walked over a mimosa thorn and got a scratch on the tummy he would burst like a toy balloon.

I put him back with the other puppies and returned to the tree where Ted and the rest were sitting. As I came up there was a shout of laughter, and turning round to see what had provoked it – I found "The Rat" at my heels. He had followed me and was trotting and stumbling along, tripping every yard or so, but getting up again with head erect, ears cocked and his stumpy tail twiddling away just as pleased and proud as if he thought he had really started in life and was doing what only a "really and truly" grown-up dog is supposed to do – that is, follow his master wherever he goes.

All the old chaff and jokes were fired off at me again, and I had no peace for quite a time. They all had something to say: "He won't swap you off!" "I'll back 'The Rat'!" "He is going to take care of you " "He is afraid you'll get lost " and so on; and they were still chaffing about it when I grabbed "The Rat" and took him back again.

Billy's failure to take his puppy was so entirely unexpected and so important that the subject kept cropping up all the evening. It was very amusing then to see how each of those who had wanted to get him succeeded in finding good reasons for thinking that his own puppy was really better than Billy's. However they differed in their estimates of each other's dogs, they all agreed that the best judge in the world could not be certain of picking out the best dog in a good litter until the puppies were several months old; and they all gave instances in which the best looking puppy had turned out the worst dog, and others in which the one no one would look at had grown up to be the champion. Goodness knows how long this would have gone on if Robbie had not mischievously suggested that "perhaps 'The Rat' was going to beat the whole lot". There was such a chorus of guffaws at this that no one told any more stories.

The poor little friendless Rat! It was unfortunate, but the truth is that he was uglier than before; and yet I could not help liking him. I fell asleep that night thinking of the two puppies – the best and the worst in the litter. No sooner had I gone over the splendid points in Billy's pup and made up my mind that he was certainly the finest I had ever seen, than the friendly wizened little face, the half-cocked ears and head on one side, the cocky little stump of a tail, and the comical dignified plucky look of the odd puppy would all come back to me. The thought of how he had licked my hand and twiddled his tail at me, and how he dabbed me on the nose, and then the manful way in which he had struggled after me through the grass, all made my heart go soft towards him, and I fell asleep not knowing what to do.

When I woke up in the morning, my first thought was of the odd puppy – how he looked to me as his only friend, and what he would feel like if, after looking on me as really belonging to him and as the one person that he was going to take care of all his life, he knew he was to be left behind or given away to anyone who would take him. It would never have entered his head that he required someone to look after him; from the way he had followed me the night before it was clear he was looking after me; and the other fellows thought the same thing. His whole manner had plainly said: "Never mind, old man! Don't you worry: I am here."

We used to make our first trek at about three o'clock in the morning, so as to be outspanned by sunrise; and walking along during that morning trek I recalled all the stories that the others had told of miserable puppies having grown into wonderful dogs, and of great men who had been very ordinary children; and at breakfast I took the plunge.

"Ted," I said, bracing myself for the laughter, "if you don't mind, I'll stick to 'The Rat'."

from *Jock of the Bushveld*, 1907

Thomas Hardy

In Havenpool Harbour the ebb was strong,
And a man with a dog drew near and hung,
And taxpaying day was coming along,
   So the mongrel had to be drowned.
The man threw a stick from the paved wharf-side
Into the midst of the ebbing tide,
And the dog jumped after with ardent pride
   To bring the stick aground.

But no: the steady suck of the flood
To seaward needed, to be withstood,
More than the strength of mongrelhood
   To fight its treacherous trend.
So, swimming for life with desperate will,
The struggler with all his natant skill
Kept buoyant in front of his master, still
   There standing to wait the end.

The loving eyes of the dog inclined
To the man he held as a god enshrined,
With no suspicion in his mind
   That this had all been meant.
Till the effort not to drift from shore
Of his little legs grew slower and slower,
And, the tide still outing with brookless power
   Outward the dog, too, went.

Just ere his sinking what does one see
Break on the face of that devotee?
A weakening to the treachery
   He had loved with love so blind?
The Faith that had shone in that mongrel's eyes
That his owner would save him by and by
Turned to much like a curse as he sank to die,
   And a loathing of mankind.

"The Mongrel", c.1915

Matthew Arnold

Max and Kaiser we to-day
Greet upon the lawn at play;
Max a dachshound without blot –
Kaiser should be, but is not.
Max, with shining yellow coat,
Prinking ears and dewlap throat –
Kaiser, with his collie face,
Penitent for want of race.

c. 1910

Jaraslov Hašek

"Do you know how to treat animals? Are you really fond of them?"

"Well, sir," said Schweik, "I like dogs best, because it's a paying game if you know how to sell them. It's not in my line, because I'm too honest, but people used to come bothering me, all the same, because they said I sold them a pup, as you might say, sir, instead of a sound, thorough-bred dog. As if all dogs can be sound and thorough-bred. And then they always wanted a pedigree, so I had to have pedigrees printed and turn a mongrel, that was born in a brickworks, into a pure-bred pedigree dog. Oh, you'd be surprised, sir, at the way all the big dog fanciers swindle their customers over pedigrees. Of course, there ain't many dogs that could truthfully call themselves out-and-out thoroughbreds. Sometimes the mother or the grandmother got mixed up with some mongrel or other, or maybe several, and then the animal takes after each of them. Ears from one, tail from another, whiskers from another, jowls from a fourth, bandy legs from a fifth, size from a sixth; and if a dog had a dozen connections of that sort, you can just imagine, sir, what he looks like. I once bought a dog like that, Balaban his name was, and he had so many parents he was that ugly that all the other dogs kept out of his way, and I only bought him because I was sorry for the animal being deserted, like. And he used to squat at home all day long in a corner, and he was always so down in the mouth that I had to sell him as a fox terrier. What gave me the most trouble was dyeing him to make him piebald. The man who bought him took him away to Moravia, and I haven't laid eyes on him since.

The Good Soldier Schweik, 1920–3

W. H. Hudson

I am able to recover a distinct picture of the state of things in the pre-muzzling times [pre-1897–9]. It is a very different state from that of to-day. One thing that was a cause of surprise to me in those days was the large number of dogs, mostly mongrels and curs, to be seen roaming masterless about the streets [of London]. They were all classed as pariahs, although they all, no doubt, had their homes in the mean streets and courts, just as the ownerless pariah dogs in Eastern towns have their homes – their yard or pavement or spot of waste ground where they live and bask in the sun when not roaming in quest of food and adventures. Many of these London pariahs were wretched-looking objects, full of sores and old scars, some like skeletons and others with half their hair off from mange and other skin diseases. They were to be seen all over London, always hunting for food, hanging about the areas, like the bone- and bottle-buyers, looking for an open dust-bin where something might be found to comfort their stomachs. They also haunted butchers' shops, where the butcher kept a jealous eye on their movements and sent them away with a kick and a curse whenever he got the chance. Most, if not all, of these poor dogs had owners who gave them shelter but no food or very little, and probably in most cases succeeded in evading the licence duty.

There is no doubt that in the past the dog population of London was always largely composed of animals of this kind – "curs of low degree," and a great variety of mongrels, mostly living in their wits. An account of the dogs of London of two or three or four centuries ago would have an extra-ordinary interest for us now, but, unfortunately, no person took the pains to write it . . .

That the bond uniting man and dog in all instances when the poor brute was obliged to fend for himself in the inhospitable streets of London was an exceedingly frail one was plainly seen when the muzzling order of 1897 was made. An extraordinary number of apparently ownerless dogs, unmuzzled and collarless, were found roaming about the streets and taken by hundreds every week to the lethal chamber. In thirty months the dog population of the metropolis had decreased by about one hundred thousand. The mongrels and dogs of the "rascall sort" had all but vanished, and this was how the improvement in the character of the dog population came about immediately. But a far more important change had been going on at the same time – the change in the temper of our dogs; and it may here be well to remark that this change in disposition was not the result of the weeding-out process I have described. The better breeds are not more amiable than the curs of low degree. The man who has made a friend and companion of the cur will tell you that he is as nice-tempered, affectionate, faithful, and intelligent as the nobler kinds, the dogs of "notable shape".

Let us now go back to the muzzling time of 1897–9, and I will give here the substance of the notes I made at the time . . .

The dog-muzzling question (I wrote) does not interest me personally, since I keep no dog, nor love to see so intelligent and serviceable a beast degraded to the position of a mere pet or plaything – a creature that has lost or been robbed of its true place in the scheme of things. Looking at the matter from the outside, simply as a student of the ways of animals, especially here in London, there is so great a multitude of quite useless animals. No doubt a large majority of the dogs of the metropolis are household pets, pure and simple, living indoors in the same rooms as their owners, in spite of their inconvenient instincts. On this subject I have had my say in an article on "The Great Dog Superstition", for which I have been well abused; the only instinct of the dog with which I am concerned at present is that of pugnacity. This is like his love of certain smells disgusting to us, part and parcel of his being, so that for a dog to be perfectly gentle and without temper that barks and bites must be taken as evidence of its decadence – not of the individual but of the race or breed or variety. Whether this fact is known or only dimly surmised by dog-lovers, more especially by those who set the fashion in dogs, we see that in recent years there has been a distinct reaction against the more degenerate kinds★ – those in whose natures the jackal and the wild-dog writing has quite or all but faded out – the numerous small toy terriers; the Italian greyhound, shivering like an aspen leaf; the drawing-room pug, ugliest of man's (the breeder's) many inventions; the pathetic Blenheim and the King Charles spaniels, the Maltese, the Pomeranian, and all the others that have, so to speak, rubbed themsleves out by acquiring a white liver to please their owners' fantastic tastes. A more vigorous beast is now in favour, and one of the most popular is undoubtedly the fox-terrier. This is assuredly the doggiest dog we possess, the most aggressive, born to trouble as the sparks fly upward. From my own point of view it is only right that fox-terriers and all other good fighters should have liberty to go out daily into the streets in their thousands in search of shindies, to strive with and worry one another to their hearts' content; then to skulk home, smelling abominably of carrion and carnage, and, hiding under their master's sofa, or other dark place, to spend the time licking their wounds until they are well again and ready to go out in search of fresh adventures. For God hath made them so.

But this is by no means the view of the gentle ladies and mild-tempered gentlemen who own them, nor, I dare say, any canophilist, whether the owner of a dog or not. What these people want is that their canine friends shall have the same liberty to enjoy themselves to make use of our streets and parks without risk of injury or insult; that they shall be free to notice or not the salutations

---

★ Alas! since these notes were made, fourteen years ago, there has been a recrudescence of the purely woman's drawing-room pet dog. The wretched griffon, looking like a mean cheap copy of the little Yorkshire – one of the few small pet animals which has not wholly lost its soul – appears to have vanished. But the country has now been flooded with the Pekinese, and one is made to loathe it from the constant sight of it in every drawing-room and railway carriage and motor-car and omnibus, clasped in a woman's arms.

and advances of others of their kind; to graciously accept or contemptuously refuse, with nose in the air, according to the mood they happen to be in or to the state of their digestive organs, an invitation to a game of romps. This liberty and safety they do now undoubtedly enjoy, thanks to the much-abused muzzling order.

from "Dogs in London", *The Book of a Naturalist,* 1919

Sauntering along a lane-like road between Charterhouse Hinton and Woolverton, in the West Country, I spied a small red dog trotting along some distance behind me. He was in the middle of the road, but seeing that he was observed he sheered off to the other side, and when nearly abreast of me paused suspiciously, sniffed the air to get the exact smell, then made a dash past, and after going about twenty or thirty yards full speed, dropped once more into his travelling trot, to vanish from sight at the next bend in the road.

Though alone, I laughed, for he was a very old acquaintance of mine. I knew him well, although he did not know me, and regarding me as a stranger he very naturally associated my appearance with that well-aimed stone or half-brick which had doubtless registered an impression on his small brain. I knew him because he is a common type, widely distributed on the earth; I doubt if there are many countries where you will not meet him – a degenerate or dwarf variety of the universal cur, smaller than a fox-terrier and shorter-legged; the low stature, long body, small ears, and blunt nose giving him a somewhat stoaty or even reptilian appearance among the canines. His red colour is, indeed, the commonest hue of the common dog, or cur, wherever found. It is rarely a bright red, like that of the Irish setter, or any pleasing shade of red, as in the dingo, the fox, and the South American maned wolf; it is dull, often inclining to yellow, sometimes mixed with grey as in the jackal, sometimes with a dash of ginger in it. The unbeautiful yellowish-red is the prevailing hue of the pariah dog. At all events that is the impression one gets from the few of the numberless travellers in the East who have condescended to tell us anything about this low-down animal.

Where the cur or pariah flourishes, there you are sure to find the small red dog, and perhaps wonder at his ability to maintain his existence. He is certainly placed at a great disadvantage. If he finds or steals a bone, the first big dog he meets will say to him, "Drop it!" And he will drop it at once, knowing that if he refuses to do so it will be taken from him, and his own poor little bones perhaps get crunched in the process. As compensation he has, I fancy, a somewhat quicker intelligence, a subtler cunning. His brains weigh less by a great deal than those of the bulldog or big cur, but – like ladies' brains compared with men's – they are of a finer quality.

When I encountered this animal in the quiet Somerset road, and laughed to see him and exclaimed mentally, "There he goes, the same old little red dog, suspicious and sneaky as ever, and very brisk and busy although his years must be well-nigh as many as my own," I was thinking of the far past, and the sight of him brought back a memory of one of the first of the small red dogs I have known intimately. I was a boy then, and my home was in the pampas of Buenos Ayres. I had a young sister, a bright, lively girl, and I remember that a poor native woman who lived in a smoky hovel a few miles away was fond of her, and that she came one day with a present for her – something precious wrapped up in a shawl – a little red pup, one of a litter which her own beloved dog had brought forth. My sister accepted the present joyfully, for though we possessed fourteen or fifteen dogs at the time, these all belonged to the house; they were everybody's and nobody's in particular, and she was delighted to have one that would be her very own. It grew into a common red dog, rather better-looking than most of its kind, having a bushier tail, longer and brighter-coloured hair, and a somewhat foxy head and face. In spite of these good points, we boys never tired of laughing at her little Reddie, as he was called, and his intense devotion to his young mistress and faith in her power to protect him only made him seem more ludicrous. When we all walked together on the grass plain, my brother and I used to think it great fun to separate Reddie from his mistress by making a sudden dash, and then hunt him over the turf. Away he would go, performing a wide circuit, then, doubling back, would fly to her for safety. She, stooping and holding out her hands to him, would wait his coming, and at the end, with one flying leap, he would land himself in her arms, almost capsizing her with the force of the impact, and from that refuge look back reproachfully at us.

The cunning little ways of the small red dog were learned later when I came to know him in the city of Buenos Ayres. Loitering at the water-side one day, I became aware of an animal of this kind following me, and no sooner did he catch my eye than he came up, wagging, wriggling, and grinning, smiling, so to speak, all over his body; and I, thinking he had lost home and friends and touched by his appeal, allowed him to follow me through the streets to the house of relations where I was staying. I told them I intended keeping the outcast a while to see what could be done with him. My friends did not welcome him warmly, and they even made some disparaging remarks about the little red dogs in general; but they gave him his dinner — a big plateful of meat — which he devoured greedily, and then, very much at home, he stretched himself out on the hearth-rug and went fast asleep. When he woke an hour later he jumped up and ran to the hall, and, finding the street-door closed, made a great row, howling and scratching at the panels. I hurried out and opened the door, and out and off he went, without so much as a thank-you. He had found a fool and had succeeded in getting something out of him, and his business with me was ended. There was no hesitation; he was going straight home, and knew his way quite well.

Years afterwards it was a surprise to me to find that the little red dog was an inhabitant of London. There was no muzzling order then, in the 'seventies, and quite a common sight was the independent dog, usually a cur, roaming the streets in search of stray scraps of food. He shared the sparrows' broken bread; he turned over the rubbish heaps left by the road-sweepers; he sniffed about areas, on the look-out for an open dust-bin; and he hung persistently about the butchers' shop, where a jealous eye was kept on his movements. These dogs doubtless had owners, who paid the yearly tax; but it is probable that in most cases they found for themselves. Probably, too, the adventurous life of the streets, where carrion was not too plentiful, had the effect of sharpening their wits. Here, at all events, I was witness of an action on the part of a small red dog which fairly astonished me; that confidence trick the little Argentinian beast had practised on me was nothing to it.

In Regent Street, of all places, one bright winter morning, I caught sight of a dog lying on the pavement close to the wall, hungrily gnawing at a big beef bone which he had stolen or picked out of a neighbouring dust-hole. He was a miserable-looking object, a sort of lurcher, of a dirty red colour, with ribs showing like the bars of a grid-iron through his mangy side. Even in those pre-muzzling days, when we still had the pariah, it was a little strange to see him gnawing his bone at that spot, just by Peter Robinson's, where the broad pavement was full of shopping ladies; and I stood still to watch him. Presently a small red dog came trotting along the pavement from the direction of the Circus, and catching sight of the mangy lurcher with the bone he was instantly struck motionless, and crouching low as if to make a dash at the other, his tail stiff, his hair bristling, he continued gazing for some moments; and then, just when I thought the rush and struggle was about to take place, up jumped this little red cur and rushed back towards the Circus, uttering a succession of excited shrieky barks. The contagion was irresistible. Off went the lurcher, furiously barking too, and quickly overtaking the small dog dashed on and away to the middle of the Circus to see what all the noise was about. It was something tremendously important to dogs in general, no doubt. But the little red dog, the little liar, had no sooner been overtaken and passed by the other, than back he ran, and picking up the bone, made off with it in the opposite direction. Very soon the lurcher returned and appeared astonished and puzzled at the disappearance of his bone. There I left him, still looking for it and sniffing at the open shop doors. He perhaps thought in his simplicity that some kind lady had picked it up and left it with one of the shopmen to be claimed by its rightful owner.

I had heard of such actions on the part of dogs before, but always with a smile; for we know the people who tell this kind of story — the dog-worshippers, or canophilists as they are sometimes called, a people weak in their intellectuals, and as a rule unveracious, although probably not consciously so. But now I had myself witnessed this thing, which, when read, will perhaps cause others to smile in their turn.

But what is one to say of such an action? Just now we are all of us, philosophers included, in a muddle over the questions of mind and intellect in the lower animals, and just how much of each element goes to the composition of any one act; but probably most persons would say at once that the action of the little red dog in Regent

Street was purely intelligent. I am not sure. The swiftness, smoothness, and certainty with which the whole thing was carried out gave it the appearance of a series of automatic movements rather than a reasoned act which had never been rehearsed.

Recently during my country rambles I have been on the look-out for the small red dog, and have met with several interesting examples in the southern counties. One, in Hampshire, moved me to laughter like that small animal at Charterhouse Hinton.

This was at Sway, a village near Lymington. A boy, mounted on a creaking old bike, was driving some cows to the common, and had the greatest difficulty in keeping on while following behind the lazy beasts on a rough track among the furze bushes; and behind the boy at a distance of ten yards trotted the little red dog, tongue out, looking as happy and proud as possible. As I passed him he looked back at me as if to make sure that I had seen him and noted that he formed part of that important procession. On another day I went to the village and renewed my acquaintance with the little fellow and heard his history. Everybody praised him for his affectionate disposition and his value as a watch-dog by night, and I was told that his mother, now dead, had been greatly prized, and was the smallest red dog ever seen in that part of Hampshire.

Some day one of the thousand writers on "man's friend" will conceive the happy idea of a chapter or two on the dog – the universal cur – and he will then perhaps find it necessary to go abroad to study this well-marked dwarf variety, for with us he has fallen on evil days. There is no doubt that the muzzling order profoundly affected the character of our dog population, since it went far towards the destruction of the cur and mongrels – the races already imperilled by the extraordinary predominance of the fox-terrier. The change was most marked in the metropolis, and after Mr Long's campaign I came to the conclusion that here at all events the little red dog had been extirpated. He, with other varieties of the cur, was the dog of the poor, and when the muzzle deprived him of the power to fend for himself, he became a burden to his master. But I was mistaken; he is still with us, even here in London, though he is very rare.

from "The Little Red Dog", *The Book of a Naturalist,* 1919

Harding Cox

My love of dogs was, to a certain extent, an inborn trait; owing its origin to the laws of heredity; for The Dads was sure possessed of this amiable idiosyncrasy.

The first dog I ever recognized as such was a cherished animal belonging to my parent, which he averred was a Clumber spaniel, but which would have been hardly rated by anyone possessing even the most elementary knowledge of the breed.

His name was Dash. I have no knowledge of the days of his youth, but I remember him as a rather plethoric and blear-eyed specimen of the canine race. According to his doting master, he had been a marvel on any and every species of game in his time, which was not mine! He was a kindly soul enough, but by way of testing his amiability I loosed off a gin-trap, teeth downwards, on the small of his back, whereupon he proceeded to bite me – good and hard.

With loud lamentations and according to custom, I fled to the arms of Old Mary and sobbed out my tale of woe. The tragic tale was conveyed to Grannie, and she, in turn, recited it to her son, conjuring him to have the offensive Dash executed there and then. The Dads was adamant, however, and was callous enough to declare that my lesion served me right. When I had thought it well over, I was magnanimous enough to agree, for my affection for the old dog was real enough.

But a compromise was arrived at. Dash was to be awarded C. B., chained to a kennel in the yard.

Then a feud arose between him and an aggressive old Cochin cock, lord of a harem of half-a-dozen barn-door hens. This vulgar bird used to marshal his seraglio, and descend on Dash's food. When the latter made a sortie from his entrenched position, with blood-curdling growls and gnashing of teeth, the cowardly birds would retreat until they were just beyond the length of his tether, and then the rooster would flap his wings and indulge in ill-timed crowing and struttings.

This struck me as unreasonable, so I watched my opportunity, unfastened the old dog's bonds, and bidding him take up his position in his kennel and lie low, I awaited developments.

Issue was soon joined.

The enemy descended on the flesh-pots as usual, but when Dash, with no restraining chain, dashed out, there was a rare to-do. The retreat became a rout, and the blatant Cochin and his entourage were only just in time to escape dire disaster by hustling through the trap-door of the hen-run, where the enemy could not follow. But the raiders were not to be thus easily debarred from their forays. Their C. O., relying on the aforesaid trap-door, repeated the manoeuvre, leaving Dash, thoroughly disgruntled, snarling defiance through the wire netting of the hen-run. Again human intelligence, as exemplified by a simple little child, was brought into play. This time I waited until the feathered felons were close to their objective, and then slipped over to their retreat and lowered the trap-door of their legitimate quarters; consequently, when Dash made his assault, their haven of safety was debarred them, and the gallant old dog had the time of his life! Such a clucking and squawking you never heard. Murder would surely have ensued had not Old Mary, at the head of her scullions, caused a diversion. As it was, the bumptious rooster was a sorry sight to behold, having lost the whole of his tail feathers and a goodly mouthful of lesser plumes. Thenceforth Dash was left in peace; but his hatred of the whole chicken tribe (except when cooked and garnished) remained unabated.

Dear little old Grannie was wont to say that Dash would eat up an old boot rather than that the fowls should have it.

Being of an inquiring and experimental turn of mind, I decided to put this theory to the test.

I dismembered a worn-out shooting boot belonging to The Dads and strewed the pieces in front of the old dog's kennel, calling out "Coup! coup!" and whistling, after the fashion of the ancient servitor whose job it was to minister to the fowls. Sure enough, Dash did devour the leather, to the last piece; but instead of being lauded for my investigation I was severely reprimanded, whilst Dash was subjected to a course of emetics and castor oil, with (be it happily said) satisfactory and obvious results!

When brother Irwin came down from Magdalene, Cambridge, he brought with him a black-and-tan terrier bitch, which he had possessed himself of at alma mater, not at all a bad specimen, probably provided by the then dog dealer of Parker's Peace. In my time the man in possession was named Callaby.

An ill-assorted union was arranged between Dido (for so she was called) and the ancient Dash, the result being a most ungodly nondescript which was called Toby. I adopted this humble mongrel from puppyhood, and grew to love him with an exceeding great love.

"Handsome is as handsome does" was sure exemplified in the case of Tobias, for he became one of the best aids to the gun I ever chanced across. Nothing came amiss to him; he was dead keen on fur and feather, had a wonderful nose and a faculty for exploiting it to the best advantage of the shooter; moreover, he was death on all vermin, and game as a pebble. He was a black and white and weighed about sixteen pounds only. One day he was accidentally shot by one of my cousins and seemed in a bad way. The Dads, who also loved him, brought him home in his arms. The poor little fellow was bleeding profusely and appeared very weak and limp.

I let myself go in a passion of grief, I snatched the patient from my father, when the undaunted and affectionate Toby rallied to lick my face with glad wishes.

Happily his injuries were not so severe as they looked, and in less than a week my little pal was up and about again.

from *A Sportsman at Large*, c.1925

Sir Hugh Walpole

I heard that "something" give a shrill squeal; I crossed and discovered a very small, dirty, bleeding and dishevelled puppy. Raging as though I were myself the puppy, I abused the ruffian, whereat he laughed and said I could have the perishing dog if I so wished. The "perishing dog" was Hamlet.

He was exactly as he is described in the "Jeremy" books. He lived with me for ten years in the village of Polperro in Cornwall, and died during the War of an incurable eczema caught from his obstinate and greedy feeding on unsavoury fish. I have owned a great many dogs, some of them very finely bred, very aristocratic, very intelligent, but none of them have ever approached Hamlet (Jacob was his actual name) for wisdom, conceit, self-reliance and true affection. He was a ghastly mongrel – I tremble to think of the many different breeds of dogs that have gone into his making – but he had Character, he had Heart, he had an unconquerable zest for life.

interview in *John o'London's Weekly*

Rudyard Kipling

"Mongrels are always smartest," said Mr Randolph half defiantly.

"Don't call 'em mongrels." The Commander tweaked Lil's impudent little ear. "Mike was a bit that way. Call 'em 'mixed'. There's a difference."

from *A Sea Dog*

Wyndham Lewis

Now, when you cut me dead and say that I'm
Not kennel-bred, nor pure of pedigree,
I'll think how often that old
Mongrel, Time,
Has cocked a leg against your Family Tree.

from *Dumb Friends' Corner*

Shannon Garst

Dogs were of supreme importance in Alaska. During the nine months of winter they were the sole means of transportation. Men could not be dependent upon the remarkable animals that served them so well without becoming intensely attached to them.

In Nome dogs were the chief source of conversation. Wherever men gathered the talk was of dogs. Everyone was sure that his dog was the most intelligent, the most loyal, the strongest, swiftest, best. Sometimes the arguments led to violent quarrels. It was the same among the school children. Nearly every family owned at least one good husky or malemute, or just plain dog, but every boy was positive that his was the best.

Scotty Allan's little boy, George, finally suggested a way to settle an argument. They would hold a kid's dog-team race to decide which dogs in Nome were really champions.

George, who had, in a manner of speaking, been reared on dogs and who looked like a small edition of his dad, was almost as dog-wise as his father. Some of his earliest recollections were of Dubby's constant companionship. The famous leader had been retired from active work now. He helped train the pups of Scotty's kennel for sledge work; he guarded the meat room of the kennel and acted as nurse for George when he was small. The boy used to ride him like a horse, or the dog would pull his small sled. There was one matter, however, upon which the boy and the dog had trouble. George had a Teddy bear of which he was very fond. He was in the habit of taking it to bed with him. Dubby also liked the toy and would steal it from under the covers and hide it. George finally gave in and allowed the dog to have the Teddy bear for his own.

George took a great liking to a mongrel-looking dog around the town named Baldy and he tried to persuade his father to buy it for the kennel.

Scotty shook his head. "I thought I'd brought you up to hae better dog sense than that. I'm trying to collect good dogs – dogs with promise. Baldy hae good legs and chest, but nae other good points of an Alaskan dog."

"I don't care about points," George insisted. "I like him. And the man who owns him isn't good to him."

So Scotty bought the dog.

George Allan was only six when he got the idea of the kid's dog-team race, and started a vogue that soon became an institution.

from *Scotty Allan, King of the Dog-team Drivers*, 1948

H. C. Barkley

I have often bred aristocratic dogs, dogs descended from great prize-winners and with long pedigrees, and among them I have had some good ones, honest and true; but as a rule I must say my experience proves that the shorter the pedigree the better the dog, and now if I could get them I should like to keep dogs that never had a father. Some people I know call me a cad, a clod, a chaw-bacon, etc., and they call my dogs curs and mongrels. Such men talk nonsense and should be kept specially to make speeches during the recess. I don't care to defend myself., but I must stand up for my dogs against all comers; and I assert boldly that, nine times out of ten, a dog with no pedigree is worth two with a long one. When I get a new dog I never ask who he is, or who his father was, but I go by his looks and his performance.

Rat-catching for the use of schools, 1960

CHAPTER 10

Extra Senses

I t is an indisputable fact that dogs have senses which are far more acute than those which we superior beings enjoy. Their sense of smell, of hearing and in some breeds of sight are such as we can scarcely imagine. Recent research has also revealed a battery of other senses which, once recognized by man, can be utilized to his advantage.

Perhaps one of the most exciting is the ability to detect the onset of epileptic seizures and to warn the victim even before he or she has become aware of the imminent fit, and thus enable them either to take whatever steps may be possible to divert the seizure or to reach a place of safety before its onset. The means by which dogs detect the onset of seizures is not yet fully understood, but of their ability to do so there is no doubt.

There are numerous cases of the unusual behaviour of dogs which seemed to be provoked by some impending event. Many of these tend to be dismissed as the product of wishful thinking on the part of fond owners. Some, however, cannot be quite so easily dismissed.

There is a story which tells how a delicate sense of smell, some degree of prescience or perhaps just good fortune led to a fortunate discovery.

In 1608 the churchwardens of St Mary, Lambeth paid two shillings "for a panel of glass for the window where the picture of the pedlar stands."

The picture showed a pedlar carrying his pack, with his dog at his heels, and refers to a story the likely truth of which each must decide for himself.

It seems that a pedlar and his dog were walking along the bank of the Thames in Lambeth when the dog, perhaps in a search for something edible, dug up a crock of gold. The pedlar, realizing that the gold belonged to the owner of the land reinterred it before opening negotiations with the churchwardens for the purchase of the land. This was achieved for the sum of two shillings and sixpence and when the transaction was complete the pedlar, doubtless with suitable expressions of feigned surprise and genuine delight, once more exhumed the crock of gold.

He was now a rich man but not an ungrateful one. He endowed the church of St Mary with an acre of the surrounding lands, though only on condition that the church exhibit a picture of him and his dog. The picture was replaced by a window in 1703.

John Ray

That the Soul of Brutes is material, and the whole Animal, Soul and Body, but a meer Machine, is the Opinion publickly own'd and declar'd of Descartes, Gassendus, Dr Willis and others; the same is also necessarily consequent upon the Doctrine of the Peripateticks, viz. That the sensitive Soul is educed out of the Power of the Matter, for nothing can be educed out of the air, but what was there before, which must be either Matter or some Modification of it. And therefore they cannot grant it to be a spiritual Substance, unless they will assert it to be educed out of nothing. This Opinion, I say, I can hardly digest. I should rather think Animals to be endu'd with a lowe Degree of Reason, than that they are mere Machines. I could instance in many Actions of Brutes that are hardly to be accounted for without Reason and Argumentation; as that commonly noted of Dogs, that running before their Masters they will stop at a divarication of the way, 'till they see which Hand their Masters will take; and that when they have gotten a Prey, which they fear their Masters will take from them, they will run away and hide it, and afterwards return to it. What account can be given why a Dog, being to leap upon a Table, which he sees to be too high for him to reach at once, if a Stool or Chair happens to stand near it, doth first mount up that, and from thence the Table? If he were a Machine or Piece of

Clockwork, and this motion caus'd by the striking of a Spring, there is no reason imaginable why the Spring being set to work, should not carry the Machine in a right line towards the Object that put it in motion, as well when the Table is high as when it is low: whereas I have often observ'd the first leap that the Creature hath taken up the stool, not to be directly toward the Table, but in a line oblique and much declining from the Object that mov'd it, or that part of the Table on which it stood.

from *Wisdom of God Manifested in the Works of the Creation*, 1691

Claudius Aelianus

And I have before now been informed of a Sicilian dog that was an enemy of adulterers and most hostile to the tribe. The guilty wife, hearing that her husband was coming back from abroad, had hidden her lover in her house and believed him to be safely concealed, for the servants too were concealing the guilt of their mistress and the servants at the door had been bribed, and the thief felt confident that everything was going all right. But it did not turn out so at all, far from it, for the pet dog, where the thief was, howled and scratched with his feet against the door and roused his master, who soon became conscious that something or other was wrong, he broke the door and caught the offender. He found he was armed with a sword and was waiting until night to kill him and then marry his wife.

from *De Natura Animalum, c.* AD 200

Ulisse Aldrovandi

Other persons in selecting a well-bred dog create a circle of flame and place all the pups in the middle of it, and they believe that one to be the best which the mother first runs up to save.

Others make observations of puppies while they are sucking milk; and for this reason, if any of them adhere to those dugs of the mother that are nearer the heart, these they judge the better on account of that position and to be more spirited . . .

from *Natural History, c.* 1560

Matthew Hopkins

The Discoverer never travelled far for it, but in March 1644, he had
some seven or eight of that horrible sect of Witches living in the
Towne where he lived, a Towne in Essex called Maningtree, with
divers other adjacent Witches of other towns, who every six weeks
in the night (being always on the Friday night) had their meeting
close by his house, and had their severall solemne sacrifices there
offered to the Devill, one of which this discoverer heard speaking to
her Imps one night, and bid them goe to another Witch, who was
thereupon apprehended, and searched by women who had for many
years knowne the Devills marks, and found to have three teats about
her, which honest women have not: so upon command from the
Justice, they were to keep her from sleep two or three nights,
expecting in that time to see her familiars, which the fourth night she
called in by their severall names, and told them what shapes, a
quarter of an houre before they came in, there being ten of us in the
roome, the first she called was

1. Holt, who came in like a white kitling.

2. Jarmara, who came in like a fat Spaniel without any legs at all,
she said she kept him fat, for she clapt her hand on her belly, and said
he suckt good blood from her body.

3. Vinegar Tom, who was like a long-legg'd Greyhound, with an
head like an Oxe, with a long taile and broad eyes, who when this
discoverer spoke to, and bade him goe to the place provided for him
and his Angels, immediately transformed himselfe into the shape of a
child of foure yeeres old without a head, and gave halfe a dozen
turnes about the house, and vanished at the doore.

4. Sack and Sugar, like a black Rabbet.

from *The Discovery of Witches,* 1647

Joseph Addison

It is well known by the Learned, that there was a Temple upon
Mount Aetna dedicated to Vulcan, which was guarded by Dogs of
so exquisite a Smell, (say the Historians) that they could discern

whether the Persons who came thither were Chast or otherwise. They used to meet and faun upon such as were Chast, caressing them as the Friends of the Master Vulcan; but flew at those who were polluted, and never ceased barking at them till they had driven them from the Temple.

My Manuscript gives the following Account of these Dogs and was probably designed as a Comment upon this Story.

These Dogs were given to Vulcan by his sister Diana, the Goddess of Hunting and Chastity, having bred them out of some of her Hounds, in which she had observed this natural Instinct and Sagacity. It was thought she did it in Spight to Venus, who, upon her Return home, always found her Husband in a good or bad Humour, according to the Reception which she met with from his Dogs. They lived in the Temple several Years, but were such snappish Curs that they frighted away most of the Votaries. The Women of Sicily made a solemn Deputation to the Priest, by which they aquainted him, that they would not come up to the Temple with their annual Offerings unless he muzzled his Mastiffs; and at last compromised the Matter with him, that Offering should always be brought by a Chorus of young Girls, who were none of them above seven Years old. It was wonderful (says the Author) to see how different the Treatment was which the Dogs gave to these little Misses, from that which they had shown to their Mothers. It is said that Prince of Syracuse, having married a young Lady, and being naturally of a jealous Temper, made such an Interest with the Priests of the Temple, that he procured a Whelp from them of this famous breed. The young Puppy was very troublesome to the fair Lady at first, insomuch that she sollicited her Husband to send him away, but the good Man cut her short with the old Sicilian Proverb, Love me, love my Dog. From which Time she lived peaceably with both of them. The Ladies of Syracuse were very much annoyed with him, and several of very good Reputation refused to come to Court till he was discarded. There were indeed some of them that defied his Sagacity, but it was observed, tho' he did not actually bite them, he would growle at them most confoundedly. To return to the Dogs of the Temple: After they had lived here in great Repute for several Years, it so happened, that as one of the Priests, who was making a charitable Visit to a Widow who lived on the

Promontory of Lilybeum, returned home pretty late in the Evening, the Dogs flew at him with so much Fury, that they would have worried him if his Brethren had not come in to his Assistance: Upon which, says my Author, the Dogs were all of them hanged, as having lost their original instinct.

I cannot conclude this Paper without wishing, that we had some of this Breed of Dogs in Great Britain, which would certainly do Justice, I should say Honour, to the Ladies of our Country, and shew the World the difference between Pagan Women and those who are instructed in sounder Principles of Virtue and Religion.

The Spectator, 11 August 1714

Samuel Rogers

    Anselm, higher up,
Just where it drifts, a dog howls loud and long,
And now, as guided by a voice from heaven,
Digs with its feet. That noble vehemence –
Whose can it be, but His who never erred?
A man lies underneath. Let us to work!
But who descends Mont Vealn? 'Tis La Croix.
Away, away! if not, alas! too late.
Homeward he drags an old man and a boy,
Faltering and falling, and, but half awaked,
Asking to sleep again.

from *Italy,* 1822–8

William Taplin

The souls of deceased bailiffs and common constables are in the bodies of setting dogs and pointers; the terriers are inhabited by trading justices: the bloodhounds were formerly a set of informers, thief takers, and false evidences; the spaniels were heretofore courtiers, hangers-on of administration and hack-journal writers, all of whom preserve their primitive qualities of fawning on their feeders, licking their hands, and snarling and snapping at all who offer to offend their masters. A former train of gamblers and blacklegs are now embodied in that particular species denominated lurchers; bulldogs and mastiffs were once butchers and drovers; grey-hounds and hounds owe their animation to country squires and masters of foxhounds; while whistling, useless lap-dogs draw their existence from the quondam beau; macaronies and gentlemen of the tiffy, still being the playthings of the ladies, and used for their diversion. There are also a set of sad dogs derived from attornies; and puppies who were in past times attornies' clerks, shopmen to retail haberdashers, men-milliners, etc., etc. Turnspits are animated old aldermen who still enjoy the smell of roast meat; that droning, snarling species stiled Dutch pugs have been fellows of colleges; and that faithful, useful tribe of shepherds' dogs were in days of yore, members of parliament who guarded the flock, and protected the sheep from the wolves and thieves, although indeed, of late, some have turned sheep-biters, and worried those they ought to have defended.

from *The Sportsman's Cabinet, or a Correct Delineation of the Various Dogs used in the Sports of the Field; including the Canine Race in general,* 1803

Revd William B. Daniel

As the Doctor was travelling from Midhurst into Hampshire, the dogs, as usual in country places, ran out barking as he was passing through a village, and amongst them he observed an ugly little cur, that was particularly eager to ingratiate himself with a setter bitch that accompanied the Doctor: whilst stopping to water his horse, he remarked how amorous the cur continued, and how courteous the setter seemed to her admirer. Provoked to see a creature of Dido's high blood so obsequious to such mean addresses, the Doctor drew one of his pistols and shot the cur; he then had the bitch carried on horseback for several miles: from that day, however, she lost her appetite, ate little or nothing, had no inclination to go abroad with her master, or attend to his call, but seemed to repine like a creature in love, and express sensible concern for the loss of her gallant.

Partridge season came, but Dido had no nose. Some time after she was coupled to a setter of great excellence, which with no small difficulty had been procured to have a breed from, and all the caution that even the Doctor himself could take was strictly exerted, that the pups might be pure and unmixed; yet not a puppy did Dido bring forth but what was the picture and colour of the cur, that he had so many months before destroyed. The Doctor fumed, and had he not personally paid such attention to preserve the intercourse uncontaminated, would have suspected that some negligence had occasioned the disappointment: but his views were in many subsequent litters also defeated, for Dido never produced a whelp which was not exactly similar to the unfortunate Cur who was her first and murdered lover.

from *Rural Sports*, 1807–13

Percy Bysshe Shelley

I met Murder on the way –
He had a mask like Castlereagh –
Very smooth he looked, yet grim;
Seven blood-hounds followed him:

All were fat; and well they might
Be in admirable plight,
For one by one, and two by two,
He tossed them human hearts to chew
Which from his cloak he drew.

from *The Mask of Anarchy:
Written on the Occasion of the
Massacre at Manchester*, 1819

Robert Fitzroy

Towards ten o'clock in the morning screaming swarms of sea birds darkened the sky above the town of Concepcion on the Pacific

Coast of Chile. At 11.30 the dogs fled out of the houses. Ten minutes later an earthquake destroyed the town.

Report, 1835

Revd Richard Barham

A great big dog runs loose in the yard,
And a horse-shoe is nail'd on the threshold sill, –
To keep out aught that savours of ill, –
But, alack! the chimney-pot's open still!
– That great big dog begins to quail,
Between his hind-legs he drops his tail.
Crouch'd on the ground, the terrified hound
Gives vent to a very odd sort of sound;
It is not a bark, loud, open, and free,
As an honest old watch-dog's bark should be;
It is not a yelp, it is not a growl,
But a something between a whine and a howl;
And, hark! – a sound from a window high
Responds to the watch-dog's pitiful cry.

from "The Witches' Frolic", 1840

Mary Russell Mitford

My beautiful, white greyhound, Mayflower, for instance, is as whimsical as the finest lady in the land. Among her other fancies, she has taken a violent affection for a most hideous stray dog, who made his appearance here about six months ago, and contrived to pick up a living in the village, one can hardly tell how. Now appealing to the charity of old Rachael Strong, the laundress – a dog-lover by profession; now inning a meal from the light-footed and open-hearted lasses at the Rose; now standing on his hind-legs, to exhort by sheer beggary a scanty morsel from some pair of "drouthy cronies", or solitary drover, discussing his dinner or supper on the alehouse bench; now catching a mouthful, flung to him in pure contempt by some scornful gentleman of the shoulder-knot, mounted on his throne, the coach-box, whose notice he had attracted by dint of ugliness; now sharing the commons of Master Keep the shoemaker's pigs; now succeeding to the reversion of the well-gnawed bone of Master Brown the shopkeeper's fierce house-dog; now filching the skimmilk of Dame Wheeler's cat – spat at by the cat; worried by the mastiff; chased by the pigs; screamed at by the dame; stormed at by the shoemaker; flogged by the shop-keeper; teased by all the children, and scouted by all the animals of the parish – but yet living through his griefs, and bearing them patently, "for suffrance is the badge of all his tribe" – and even seeming to find, in an occasional full meal, or a gleam of sunshine, or a wisp of dry straw on which to repose his sorry carcase, some comfort in his disconsolate condition.

In this plight he was found by May, the most high-blooded and aristocratic of greyhounds; and from this plight did May rescue him – invited him into her territory, the stable; resisted all attempts to turn him out; reinstated him there, in spite of maid and boy, mistress and master; wore out everybody's opposition, by the activity of her protection, and the pertinacity of her self-will; made him sharer of her bed and of her mess; and finally established him as one of the family as firmly as herself.

from *Our Village*, 1832

The Druid (pseud)

Cribb would fight a redhot poker till it became cold; his jawbone was quite bare; there was not a bit of under-lip, and he'd put out a fire with his feet. That's why they called him "The Fire Eater". You had only to say "Kill that cat", and it was done. Still he would bear any amount of teasing, and never fought till I told him. I kept him two years after he was blind; he would make his bed at the badger's door, and get in next morning and go creeping along by the wall to find his head. He was a biggish eighteen pound dog, and he'd draw a cover beautifully. They would go to his cry. I have got Jack, a great grandson of his, now, and he'll draw and find foxes with any hound. Never speaks to riot. Jack threw his tongue last season, and out came a hare. Mr Hall was there, "Oh! Jack, Jack!" he said, "you've made a mistake." Then out came a fox close under the hedge.

from *Scott and Sebright,* 1842

Charles St John

The dog that lives with his master constantly, sleeping before his fire, instead of in the kennel, and hearing and seeing all that passes, learns, if at all quick-witted, to understand not only the meaning of what he sees going on, but also, frequently, in the most wonderful manner, all that is talked of.

*

A shepherd once, to prove the quickness of his dog, which was lying before the fire in the house where we were talking, said to me, in the middle of a sentence concerning something else – "I'm thinking, Sir, the cow is in the potatoes." Though he purposely laid no stress on these words, and said them in a quiet, unconcerned tone of voice, the dog, which appeared to be asleep, immediately jumped up, and leaping through the open window, scrambled up the turf roof of the house, from which he could see the potato-field. He then (not seeing the cow there) ran and looked into the byre where she was, and finding that all was right, came back to the house. After a short time the shepherd said the same words again, and the dog repeated his look-out; but on the false alarm being a third time given, the dog got up, and wagging his tail, looked his master in the face with so comical an expression of interrogation, that we could not help laughing aloud at him, on which, with a slight growl, he laid himself down in his warm corner, with an offended air, and as if determined not to be made a fool of again.

from *Wild Sports and Natural History of the Highlands,* 1846

George Borrow

The weather had been propitious: a slight frost had rendered the ground firm to the tread, and the skies were clear; but now a change came over the scene, the skies darkened, and a heavy snow-storm came on; the road then lay straight through a bog, and was bounded by a deep trench on both sides; I was making the best of my way, keeping as nearly as I could in the middle of the road, lest, blinded by the snow which was frequently borne into my eyes by the wind, I might fall into the dyke, when all at once I heard a shout to windward, and turning my eyes I saw the figure of a man, and what appeared to be an animal of some kind, coming across the bog with great speed, in the direction of myself; the nature of the ground seemed to offer but little impediment to these beings, both clearing the holes and abysses which lay in their way with surprising agility; the animal was, however, some slight way in advance, and, bounding over the dyke, appeared on the road before me. It was a dog, of what species I cannot tell, never having seen the like before or since; the head was large and round; the ears so tiny as scarcely to be discernible; the eyes a fiery red: in size it was rather small than large; and the coat, which was remarkably smooth, as white as the falling flakes. It placed itself directly in my path, and showing its teeth, and bristling its coat, appeared determined to prevent my progress. I had an ashen stick in my hand, with which I threatened it; this, however, only served to increase its fury; it rushed upon me, and I had the utmost difficulty to preserve myself from its fangs.

"What are you doing with the dog, the fairy dog?" said the man, who at this time likewise cleared the dyke at a bound.

He was a very tall man, rather well dressed as it should seem; his garments, however, were like my own, so covered with snow that I could scarcely discern their quality.

"What are ye doing with the dog of peace?"

"I wish he would show himself one," said I; "I said nothing to him, but he placed himself in my road, and would not let me pass."

"Of course he would not be letting you till he knew where ye were going."

"He's not much of a fairy," said I, "or he would know that without asking."

from Lavengro, 1851

George Sand (pseud.)

We have a tradition for you. When people wish to make a good watch-dog they have him pounded. Did you know that? This is the way they proceed. Auguste the carpenter, who is a sorcerer and a dog-pounder, went on a very dark night to Millochau's at the latter's request in order to pound Millochau's dog. The night was so dark that Auguste had to crawl over the bridge on all fours in order not to drown himself, so he says; but that, perhaps, was also part of the conjugation; although he does not confess it. The dog was three or four days old. It is necessary that the dog should not have seen the light when subjected to the operation; he is put in a mortar and pounded with a pestle. Auguste says that the dog does not take any harm thereby; but I am rather inclined that he first crushes it, and that, thanks to his art, restores it to life again. While he pounds him he repeats three times the following formula:

> My good dog, I pound thee;
> Thou shalt know neither neighbour nor neighbouress,
> Except myself who pound thee.

I now resume the story of Millochau's dog. The said dog became so bad (that is, so good) that it used to devour people and beasts. He knew nobody but Auguste; but as he used to go and worry the sheep even in the pen, Millochau was obliged to kill him. It appears that Auguste had pounded him a little more than necessary.

Letter to Maurice Dupin, January 1854

Lewis Carroll (pseud.)

"Take a bone from a dog: What remains?"

Alice considered. "The bone wouldn't remain of course, if I took it – and the dog wouldn't remain, it would come to bite me – and I'm sure *I* shouldn't remain."

"Then you think nothing would remain?" said the Red Queen.

"I think that's the answer."

"Wrong as usual," said the Red Queen: "the dog's temper would remain"

"But I don't see how —"

"Why, look here!" the Red Queen cried: "the dog would lose its temper, wouldn't it?"

"Perhaps it would," Alice replied cautiously.

"Then if the dog went away, its temper would remain!" the Queen exclaimed triumphantly.

from *Through the Looking Glass and What Alice Found There*, 1871

Robert Louis Stevenson

The leading distinction between dog and man, after and perhaps before the different duration of their lives, is that one can speak and the other cannot. The absence of the power of speech confines the dog in the development of his intellect. It hinders him from many speculations, for words are the beginning of metaphysic. At the same blow it saves him from many superstitions, and his silence has won for him a higher name of virtue than his conduct justifies. The faults of the dog are many. He is vainer than man, singularly greedy of notice, singularly intolerant of ridicule, suspicious like the deaf, jealous to the degree of frenzy, and radically devoid of truth. The day of an intelligent small dog is passed in the manufacture and the laborious communication of falsehood; he lies with his tail, he lies with his eye, he lies with his protesting paw; and when he rattles his dish or scratches at the door his purpose is other than appears.

from *The Character of Dogs*, c.1885

Anonymous

At the disruption in 1843 the bulk of the shepherds (in the Vale of Yarrow, in the Scottish Border land) joined in the Free Kirk. But one collie held by the Establishment principle and refused to "come out." Every Sabbath he went alone to the Establishment Church, where he had been wont to accompany his owner. His master refused to coerce him. "Na, na," he said, "He's a wise dawg; I'll no meddle wi' his convictions." The collie's adherence to the Establishment had, however, a disastrous end. He was accustomed to lie during the sermon on the pulpit stairs, no doubt the better to hear the discourse. Below him were placed the stove-pipe hats of the elders. On one unfortunate day he fell asleep, rolled off his step, and managed to get his head firmly fixed inside one of the hats. Bitterly mortified, the dog fled from the kirk, and ever afterwards, as his master said, "had nae trokins wi' releegion."

from *The Spectator*, 1904

Anonymous

Sir Rider Haggard relates that he was sleeping peacefully at one o'clock in the morning of the 10th of July. One hour afterwards Lady Haggard, who was sleeping in the same room, heard her husband groaning and emitting queer noises like a wounded animal. Nervously she called him. Sir Rider Haggard heard her voice like a dream but could not quite get rid of the nightmare which was pressing him. When he actually awoke he told his wife he had dreamt of Bob, an old Pointer belonging to Miss Haggard. He has seen him struggling in a terrible manner as if he were going to die. This dream had two distinct issues; the novelist remembers having felt a sensation of suffocation as if he had been drowning; the time he heard his wife's voice till the time he awoke completely up the dream took a more precise form. Sir Rider Haggard said, "I saw old Bob, the Pointer, among the reeds of a pond. It appeared to me that my personality seemed to come from the dog's body who put his head against mine in a strange way. Bob tried to speak to me and as he could not speak with his voice tried to transmit to me in an indefinite manner the idea that he was about to die."

Sir Rider Haggard went to sleep again and the novelist had no further trouble. Next morning at breakfast he related to his daughters what he had dreamt, and laughed with them at their mother's fright – he thought the nightmare was the result of indigestion.

As regards Bob, nobody bothered about him since the afternoon before he was seen with the other dogs, and had been with his mistress. Only when the dinner hour came without Bob's appearance Miss Haggard commenced to be a bit uneasy, and the novelist suspected that the dream had come true. Search parties were sent out. On the fourth day Sir Rider Haggard himself found the poor dog floating in the water of a pond among the reeds two miles from the house. His skull and feet were broken. On first examination by a veterinary surgeon it looked as if the animal had been caught in a snare, but afterwards there were indisputable traces that the dog had been run over by a train and that someone had thrown him into the pond. On July 9th a railwayman had found the bloody collar of Bob and there is not the slightest doubt that the dog was killed on the night of the dream. By chance that night an express excursion train, which did not usually pass, had passed that way a few minutes before midnight, which had been the cause of the accident. All these circumstances are proved by the novelist in a series of documents. According to the veterinary surgeon, death was almost instantaneous, and it preceded by two hours the dream of Sir Rider Haggard.

Letter to the *Journal of Psychic Research,* 1904

Andrew Lang

Dear Professor,

Recently in your article in the "Morning Post" you quoted the case of a thing being seen simultaneously by a lady and a dog. I think my experience might interest you. I was reading in front of the fire in my drawing-room. The door was shut. My dog, Dan, was sleeping on the floor; all of a sudden I was roused from my reading by the dog who had commenced to growl. I bent over and caressed him but he got worse, then I looked in the same direction that the animal was looking, and to my astonishment I saw the form of a woman dressed in grey near the door. I could not distinguish her face which was hidden by some plants on the table. I thought it was my sister and called her by name, asking her why she had returned so early and how she had come through the door without making any noise, but I remembered I had bolted the door; then I got up terrified while Dan hurled himself against the invisible intruder who disappeared although the door of the drawing-room was still shut. The dog showed signs of rage and terror, his head was low and his fur was up, he appeared to have seen a real person because when I opened the door he barked furiously and went down the stairs looking everywhere for somebody, although he could not find anyone. I was by myself in the house and I experienced a great feeling of relief when in a short time afterwards my sister arrived. I have no theory to explain this but I am absolutely sure that both I and the dog perceived something.

Letter to the Society for Psychical Research, 19 February 1909

Mark Twain

They continued to whisper for some little time. Presently a dog set up a long, lugubrious howl just outside – within ten feet of them. The boys clasped each other suddenly, in an agony of fright.

"Which of us does he mean?" gasped Huckleberry.

"I dono – peep through the crack. Quick!"

"No, you, Tom!"

"I can't – I can't do it. Huck!"

"Please, Tom. There 'tis again!"

"Oh, lordy, I'm thankful!" whispered Tom. "I know his voice. It's Bull Harbison."

"Oh, that's good – I tell you, Tom, I was most scared to death; I'd 'a' bet anything it was a stray dog."

The dog howled again. The boys' hearts sank once more.

"Oh, my! that ain't no Bull Harbison!" whispered Huckleberry. "Do, Tom!"

Tom, quaking with fear, yielded, and put his eye to the crack. His whisper was hardly audible when he said:

"Oh, Huck, it's a stray dog!"

"Quick, Tom, quick! Who does he mean?"

"Huck, he must mean us both – we're right together."

"Oh, Tom, I reckon we're goners. I reckon there ain't no mistake 'bout where I'll go to. I been so wicked."

from *The Adventures of Tom Sawyer*, 1876

Raymond Queneau

The traveller was once more left alone for a time, resonant chunks of water were running down the window panes. His glass was empty now. He looked about him.

One of the doors which led into the café was, at a certain given moment, pushed; the traveller didn't see anyone come in; he leant over the table to investigate and perceived a dog who had just come in.

The dog, an undeniable mongrel, more like a fox-terrier than anything else and with a tolerably brown coat, inspected the legs of two or three tables or chairs, sniffing, turned round in circles two or three times, then, in a manner which was not intrusive, approached the newcomer, sideways. The man made little whistling sounds with his mouth, a way of making up to the animal; which animal, with a sure and supple movement, jumped on to the chair opposite the traveller and sat down.

Each looked at the other.

"You'd like a lump of sugar, eh, my dog?" said the traveller.

"I am not your dog," replied the quadruped. "I don't belong to anyone but myself. I am not just the dog that goes with the house; if the proprietor of the house supposes that to be the case, then he is making a grave mistake. As for sugar, I appreciate it, and I should not disdain a piece. Indeed, over there, on the sideboard, there is a full sugar basin; without offending you or inconveniencing you, that would be an opportunity of doing me a kindness."

The traveller remained motionless and silent for a moment, without however the features of his face presenting the stigmata of astonishment or terror. He got up before long and went to fetch a piece of sugar, gave it to the dog who munched it.

After having licked his chops, the dog said:

"I'm called Dino. That's my name: Dino."

"Delighted," said the traveller, "I am Amédée Gubernatis, the youngest deputy in France."

"Very honoured," said the dog. "Are you of Italian origin?"

"Like many good Frenchmen," replied the deputy.

"Please don't be offended, Monsieur Amédée," said the dog, "I am not by any means a racialist, even though on my father's side I can lay claim to a fine pedigree."

He smiled; and, seriously, added:

"You must be bored here."

"I? Not in the least," said Amédée. "I'm never bored."

"It's only animals who are never bored," said the dog. "Or people who are only very little removed from a natural life. But if that were the case with a deputy, I should be amazed."

"I've always got some project I'm thinking over," said Amédée, "some plan, some scheme, law, decree."

"You must be overworked," said the dog, shaking his head.

"I don't know the meaning of the word, overworked. Why, I've been working ever since I was thirteen, and between twelve and sixteen hours a day."

"You give me the shivers," said the dog. "Would you mind inconveniencing yourself once more and going to fetch me a piece of sugar?"

"With great pleasure," said Amédée.

The sugar munched, the conversation continued.

"Why work so hard?" asked the dog.

"I'm a specialist. A specialist in budgetary and financial questions. I am not only a Doctor of Laws and a graduate of Political Science, I am also a Bachelor of Science. That has never been known to happen before, so that's where my strength lies — part of my strength."

"You're ambitious, what," said the dog, finishing licking his chops.

"Ambitious . . . ambitious . . . that's easy to say . . . ambitious."

"Do you think of the good of the people? Of the people under your jurisdiction?"

"Certainly. It was for their benefit that I became a specialist. After all, everyone can't be as erudite as I: it's for their good that I accumulate so much power. I fight for them with the aid of these weapons."

"By yourself?"

"For the time being. I parted company with a friend on the way. I'm on a walking tour of this district. It's very instructive. And what souvenirs!"

The dog yawned and jumped down from his chair. He walked

round in circles two or three times, sniffed at two or three things and went away, pushing another door, without a parting word.

from *At the Edge of the Forest*, 1956

Robert Bernen

I did look at Toby, many times a day, but his good qualities eluded me. Skeletal, mangy, frightened and dull, he showed no interest at all in sheep. The first time I took him around the inland pasture with me – on a lead, because he wouldn't come otherwise – the ewes moved away from him in alarm, but by the next day they were all fully aware of his harmless nature, and ignored him. I soon discovered, in fact, that he was thoroughly afraid of them.

But that was natural enough for a dog in that starving and feeble condition. As soon as I got him home, I tied him up in a corner of the byre with some straw to bed down on, and brought him a dish of bread and milk. It was a middling portion – I did not want to feed him too much all at once. Toby swallowed the food in great gulps that were like inhalations. He didn't stop to chew or taste, his aim was to get the mush into his stomach as instantly as he could. Then he quickly licked the yellow plastic dish. Then he belched once or twice and vomited up most of the meal. He ate that again almost as quickly as he had the first time, and then vomited it again. As he was eating it a third time, I left him alone. When I came back a few hours later, he was snoozing on the pile of straw I had left there for him, just as I had left it, not rearranged or pawed about at all. After a few meals he stopped vomiting, but his appetite remained ferocious. One morning I found he had chewed up and eaten a large chunk of his yellow plastic dish.

The next day I took him out with me, a long line of grass rope tied to his neck and trailing behind him. The precaution was not needed. Toby walked slowly, without enthusiasm or spring. It was May, and I was cutting turf for the first time in my life. It was an agonizing effort. I couldn't understand how it was possible for one man to cut enough turf to last a whole year. While I worked, Toby would lie on the bank near me, his eyes directed blindly away, his head slightly raised towards the sun, or else he would lie on his side and sleep. He seemed to be deliberately trying to drink in the hazy sun, as I remembered myself further south often lying in the sun on the first warm days of May, trying to absorb sun and warmth after the winter. So he lay there, day after day, dozing in the weak sun that filtered through the high clouds. From time to time I would look over at him, hoping to see him shift and stir, make a few half turns and coil freshly into a new position, but he never did. He lay, still and extended on his side, soaking up such sun as he could get. I wondered if he would ever sit up and watch the sheep the way the mother dog did. He paid no attention to them when they wandered by, and they ignored his presence. I noticed that his pale, yellow eyes did not seem to be focused on anything at all.

For several weeks Toby showed no inclination to run, much less jump. It was only after two weeks that I saw him take his first leap, and that a short one. But gradually he began to grow more alert, as the vitamin pills and liberal feeding took effect. His coat began to thicken and grow smoother, his eyes brightened and his step became brisker and more flexible. He began to lie not on his side, as before, but on his belly, his paws out straight before him, his head raised to the sun. I had had him for a month when I first felt sure that there was a real improvement in his condition. The fur had not returned to the bare spots, but he was less bony and walked with a livelier, padding step. And it was then, when he was just getting on his feet, that the qualities of the dog as I was later to know them, the first signs of his character, which till then had been smothered by debility, began to appear.

Toby took to wandering off without notice, and though I had taught him to come in when called or whistled to, he would often disappear while I was working at turf, and refuse to return. At such times, I often found him lurking hidden behind a bank of turf not more than a few feet away, listening to me whistle and call, as loud as I could, hunting for him in every direction. From time to time I noticed Toby staring at me, while I worked, with a peculiar intensity, a kind of interest, it seemed to me, and puzzlement too, as if he understood what an enormous effort I was making to get out the year's turf, and wondered what I was at. There was a kind of pitying look in his eyes, I sometimes thought, or a mocking one. What fools these mortals are, he seemed to be thinking. And then when he saw me observing him in return, he would turn his head away, settle his chin on his paws, and resume his snooze in the sun.

It was that way of lying and watching, seeming to reflect, or even meditate, while he was observing me all the while, that first made me improve my opinion of the dog. "There must be something to this dog," I thought. I know now that he really was observing me, and from time to time he evidently came to conclusions. That came out sharply one day in July. Jimmy Burke had come to cut turf for us. With his usual energy, he had started at ten in the morning, and at six in the evening he still showed no signs of flagging. He was on his third bank of turf, and it was becoming clear that he meant to cut half a winter's supply of fuel for us before he stopped. It was up to me to spread the turf as he cut it – every one of the thousands of pieces – that was what Jimmy expected, and it would have been too much to let him down, in the face of all his own work that day. Pride kept me at the work, though my back and arms were painful and stiff.

Suddenly, standing on the brow of the bank of turf, I looked about and realized that Toby had gone. I had kept him in sight all day, but now he had slipped away. I began to whistle, then call. Jimmy stopped his work and looked on curiously. His face showed his amused expectation of learning something – about the dog, no doubt, and about me as well. Our eyes reached out across the landscape in every direction. Bits of rough heather, spots that some kind of blight had touched and turned brown, caught our eyes, and tufts of rough, red grass. I looked for any movement of red or brown in among the areas of green, or for signs of uneasiness among the sheep grazing the meadows below us, but saw nothing. All was still. I whistled again.

"Funny he don't come in when he hears you whistling him," Jimmy remarked, "and you feeding him like that."

He put the turf spade in position to begin work again.

"He'll soon come back," he said. "He's not far off."

I decided to give one last whistle, as loud as I could. Then, as the pieces of turf began flying on to the bank again, I saw Toby at last. He was lying perfectly still behind a clump of tall, heavy rushes, not twenty feet away, peering through them with an expression of intense, bemused curiosity. I saw in his eyes at once that he had made a great discovery. He was still just taking in the fact that I could fail to see him, even when he was face to face with me. He had discovered his own protective camouflage. But he had discovered something more important – that he was shrewder than me, and that there were ways he could fool me when he wanted to.

from "The Yellow Dog", *Tales from the Blue Stacks*, 1978

Proteus (pseud.)

Except for the children asleep upstairs, the evening of a great storm found me alone in the house. My wife was attending that *sine qua non* of village life, a performance of *Blithe Spirit* in the Reading Room. Darkness had fallen and nobody else remained. I drank a little whisky and considered the next move. Would it be preferable to regale myself with Beethoven or Mozart? Or neither, but listen instead to the wilder music of the wind as it eddied in the chimney and set the television aerial thrumming? In the event the record-player stayed silent. A new and mesmeric presence intervened.

Sitting on the arm of my chair, I realized, was the senior terrier. Her eyes were directed towards my face. It is three years since she saw me. Rising ten, she became suddenly and finally blind; and being a fox terrier with all her lineage of courage and self-sufficiency, carried on much as usual. After nearly thirteen years together we have small need nowadays of formal communication. We meet briefly at seven a.m. when, after ceremonial yawning and stretching of stiffening limbs, she takes her first airing before Reveille sounds for the younger and more hobbledehoy gundogs. We seldom meet again until, all others having retired to bed or bath, I sit with a nightcap and think the thoughts that come with the ending of the day.

The senior terrier sits on the arm of the chair to think them with me. Tonight she was paying an unscheduled visit. She well knew that the evening was young because the junior terrier, not yet harboured in the kitchen, still slept post-prandially on the rug. Broken routine made the occasion special. Ears cocked, she held the salute with her sightless eyes. I returned her gaze, then stroked her neck. That she did not move represented an eloquent speech. She is a fastidious person and, though friendly to authorized strangers, disdains their touch. Neither will she encourage mine if there is an eye-witness to the familiarity. By remaining, she made this a telepathic moment. So we shared thoughts soundless, as one can with very old friends.

337

Her face, once bright tan with a blaze, is whitened now. The grey slash from eye to muzzle, left by a fox in her active-service days, has become invisible, merging with the sign of advancing years, just as the incident itself has been cut down to size by the other happenings of a long, full life. Old lady, I thought, you are nearer the end than the beginning. And realization came late that the same applied to me. Inevitably my mind turned to the business of growing old gracefully, untroubling to others. When the time comes, I hope I manage it as well as she does. In particular, I hope I shall be as meticulous as she is at keeping friendships green, and at evolving a design for living to fit declining powers.

She does not take much exercise nowadays. She even gave up the summer evening's stroll along the chalk track between the barley fields when asked to share it with a spaniel who, though well-meaning, had loutish manners. But she has no prejudice against youth in general. She chaperones the junior terrier with dignity, and is treated in response with the respect both given and taken by members of their patrician breed. She is in full possession of her faculties, as newspapers say of centenarians. Three rats learned this in the exodus at harvest. They will learn nothing else. What we haven't, we'll do without is good terrier philosophy, and the senior terrier demonstrates that if you cannot see them you can still catch them. Sometimes a turning ear and a growl indicate that she has heard a cat stamping its feet on the lawn; nobody else can.

She is teaching her successor to adopt a superior air towards the gundogs. This old-fashioned social barrier fits her generation. The gundogs are working class. Terriers are members of the household. Not only the fact but the spirit of this distinction must be maintained, and will be while there is breath in her body.

Perhaps this will not be for very long. We have shared much together, times of ecstasy and desolation, but chiefly of bright contentment. She has cheered me by some of her triumphs and adventures, and I have wished I could have done something to inspire her in return. We have dug and hunted together, I have known the pleasures of her children, and she has given her heart to mine. When we part she will leave me incomplete, but richer for her comradeship.

One can think too much of the future.

from "A Lady of seniority", *The Changing Year*, September, 1973

Michael Murray

"Pipsqueak", my Border Terrier, having survived being drowned at birth, shot at and abandoned in the bush between Mombasa and Nairobi during her first year of life, soon established herself as my constant companion and guardian on the tea plantation where I lived on the edge of the "Mau" forest in Western Kenya.

I was alone in the living-room of my shack one evening listening to a gramophone record of Paul Robeson singing "Ol' Man River". Pipsqueak (who was inclined to howl along with any music) had retired to her basket in the kitchen and the other dogs were in a kennel outside. Halfway through the song there was a sullen commotion from the direction of the kitchen, as of objects being thrown about or falling on the floor. No barks, just a lot of bumps; and knowing Kiprigoin (my kitchen toto) had long since retired to his hut, I grabbed the pressure lamp which was my only source of light and hurried through to investigate. I opened the kitchen door to find Pipsqueak half crouching in the middle of the floor, surrounded by logs which had apparently fallen from a small pile stacked against one wall. She never gave me a glance but just stood there, tail quivering, head cocked on one side with her eyes riveted on a shadowy corner by the stove. "It must be a rat –" I thought – "or maybe just a stupid cockroach" (which were a plague in that house); and I moved forward with my lamp to have a look, picking up a log as I went, cursing Pipsqueak for the mess.

The next moment, I froze with terror. What I had thought was a large, rather lumpy log, suddenly moved and spread – and rising up from its middle was the unmistakable head of a cobra. The memory of what followed is slightly blurred, but I recall hearing an extra sharp hiss from my lamp or was it the snake, and Pipsqueak darting forward snarling. The cobra's uncoiled length seemed to fly across the floor; I just watched, helplessly, as the dog grabbed, shook and threw it around the kitchen as if she was playing with a piece of old rope, or her favourite toy, in a macabre sort of dance. After a while, I noticed that the "toy" no longer seemed to be writhing of its own accord and dared to believe one of Pipsqueak's bites had severed something vital. Meanwhile, the night watchman (Kiprigoin's uncle), who had been asleep outside, had been woken up by the commotion and was now hammering on the door. Between us, we prised Pipsqueak away from her kill which turned out to be a "Spitting Cobra" over three feet long. Its venom, which can blind and paralyse its victim if directed at the eyes, had, we discovered, been spat with deadly accuracy at the mantle of my pressure lamp.

With daylight . . . we quickly spotted the cause of Pipsqueaks's unusual behaviour in the night, for clearly visible in the damp earth close to the tent, indeed all around the tent, were the pad-marks of a very large cat. Dick Platt, who had made a study of animal spoor, was convinced it was a leopard, and with this rather chilling discovery, we decided it was time to move camp, quickly. So we began packing up the tent and loading the Land-Rover, without even thinking of breakfast. I thought Pipsqueak was in the front of the Land-Rover with Peggy while we were doing that, but suddenly realized she wasn't, when the sound of frantic high-pitched barking came from the direction of the road, some way back from the river. Piling into the vehicle, we drove towards the sound but as we reached the muddy track that passed for a road in those parts, the barking ceased and there was no sign of Pipsqueak. We searched fruitlessly for a few minutes on either side of the road and then it started again – but further away, fainter and oddly muffled as though she was down a burrow and it was more a cross between a growl and a whimper. We found her eventually and she was right under the road, halfway along a narrow concrete culvert, her head just visible in the dark recess about half a metre from the entrance. She took a lot of persuading to come out – in fact I had to reach in and pull her the last few inches. Her reason for being there and her reluctance to come out then became clear. Her muzzle was torn and bleeding and all around the entrance to the culvert there were tufts of fur and spots of blood, and the same large pad-marks we had seen by the tent. So it seemed that Pipsqueak had had another lucky escape – though a small dog, she had the intelligence to go backwards down a culvert and so outwit a leopard. She surely deserved her luck.

from "A Pipsqueak with the heart of a lion. The further adventures of a Border Terrier in East Africa, Northern Border Lines," 1995

* * *

Arrian

The Celts have a variety of dog no less clever at hunting on scent than the Carian and Cretan, but in shape sorry brutes. In pursuit these give tongue with a clanging howl like the yelping Carians, but are more eager, when they catch the scent. Sometimes indeed they gladden so outrageously, even on a stale trail that I have rated them for their excessive barking, alike on every scent, whether it be of the hare going to form, or at speed. In pursuing and recovering her, when started, they are not inferior to the Carians or Cretans, save in the one point of speed.

It is good sport, if they kill but a single hare in the winter season, so much resting-time do they give her in the chase; unless, by being frightened out of her wits at the tumultuous uproar of the pack she becomes an easy prey.

The dogs are called Segusians, deriving their name from a Celtic people, amongst whom, I suppose, they were first bred and held repute. But all that can be said about them has been anticipated by the Elder Xenophon. For they manifest nothing different from others in their mode of finding or hunting their game, having no peculiarity, unless one were to speak of their shape, which I scarce think worth while, except merely to say that they are shaggy and ugly, and such as are most high-bred are most unsightly. So that the comparison of them to mendicants on the highways is popular with the Celts. For their voice is dolorous and pitiful, and they do not bark on scent of their game, as if eager and savage, but as if plaintively whining after it.

Cynegeticus, c. AD 150

Gace de la Vigne

Then there is heard a sound
Such that no living man
Ever heard so fine a melody.
No response or alleluia
In the fine chapel of the King

Ever gave such pleasure
As hearing such a hunt.
Some sing a motet as they go;
Others sing a double hocket.
The biggest sing the tenor part;
Others sing the countertenor;
Those with the sharper voice
Sing treble with a will;
The smallest sing the quadruplum,
Making a fifth on the duplum.
Some sing a minor semitone;
Others a major semitone;
Diapente, diapason,
And the rest diatessaron.

from *Poème sur la Chasse*, 1359

William Shakespeare

THESEUS: Go, one of you, find out the forester;
    For now our observation is performed;
    And since we have the vaward of the day,
    My love shall hear the music of my hounds.
    Uncouple in the western valley; let them go:
    Despatch, I say, and find the forester.
    We will, fair Queen, up to the mountain's top,
    And mark the musical confusion
    Of hounds and echo in conjunction.
HIPPOLYTA: I was with Hercules and Cadmus once,
    When in a wood in Crete they bay'd the bear
    With hounds of Sparta; never did I hear
    Such gallant chiding; for, besides the groves,
    The skies, the fountains, every region near
    Seem'd all one mutual cry: I never heard
    So musical a discord, such sweet thunder.
THESEUS: My hounds are bred out of the Spartan kind,
    So flew'd, so sanded; and their heads are hung
    With ears that sweep away the morning dew;

Crook-knee'd, and dew-lapp'd like Thessalian bulls;
Slow in pursuit, but match'd in mouth like bells,
Each under each. A cry more tunable
Was never holla'd to, nor cheer'd with horn,
In Crete, in Sparta, nor in Thessaly:
Judge when you hear.

from *A Midsummer Night's Dream*, c. 1600

Gervase Markham

If you would have your Kennel for sweetness of cry, then you must compound it of some large dogs, that have deep solemn Mouths, and are swift in spending, which must as it were bear the base in the consort; then a double number of roaring, and loud-ringing Mouthes, which must bear the counter-tenor; then some hollow plain sweet Mouths, which must bear the mean or middle part; and so with these three parts of Musick, you shall ever make your cry perfect: and herein you shall observe, that these Hounds thus mixt, do run just and even together, and not hang loose off from one another, which is the vilest sight that may be; and you shall understand, that this composition is best to be made of the swiftest and largest deep-mouthed dogs, the slowest and middle-siz'd dog, and the shortest-legg'd slender dog, amongst these you may cats in a couple or two small single Beagles which as small trebles may warble amongst them: the cry will be a great deal more sweet.

If you would have your Kennel for loudness of Mouth, you shall not then choose the hollow deep Mouth, but the loud clanging Mouth, which spendeth freely and sharply, and as it were redoubleth in utterance: and if you mix with them the Mouth that roareth, and the mouth that whineth, the cry will be both louder and smarter; and these Hounds are for the most part of the middle size, neither extream tall, nor extream deep flewed, such as for the most part your *Shrop-shire*, and pure *Worcester-shire* dogs are, and the more equally you compound these mouths, having as many Roarers as Spenders, and as many Whiners, as of either of the other, the lowder and pleasanter your cry will be, especially if it be in sounding tall woods, or under the echo of Rocks.

If you would have your Kennel for depth of mouth, then you shall compound it of the largest dogs which have the greatest mouths and deepest flews, such as your *West-Countrey, Cheshire*, and *Lancashire* dogs are, and to five or six base couple of mouths, shall not add above two couple of Counter-tenors, as many means, and not above one couple of Roarers, which being heard but now and then, as at the opening or hitting of a scent, will give much sweetness to the solemness, and graveness of the cry, and the Musick thereof will be much more delightful to the ears of the beholder.

And now to return to my purpose; your Kennel thus composed of the swiftest Hounds, you shall as nigh as you can, sort their Mouths into three equal parts of Musick, that is to say, Base, Counter-tenor, and Mean; the Base are those mouths which are most deep and solemn, and are spent out plain and freely, without redoubling: the Counter-tenor are those which are most loud and ringing, whose sharp sounds pass so swift, that they seem to dole and make division; and the mean are those which are soft sweet mouths, that though plain, and a little hollow, yet are spent smooth and freely; yet so distinctly that a man may count the notes as they open. Of these three sorts of mouths, if your Kennel be (as near as you can) equally compounded, you shall find it most perfect and delectable: for though they have not the thunder and loudness of the great dogs, which may be compared to the high wind-instruments, yet they will have the tunable sweetness of the best compounded consorts; and sure a man may find as much Art and delight in a Lute, as in an Organ.

from *Countrey Contentments . . .*, 1631

Izaak Walton

And for the dogs that we use, who can commend their excellency to that height which they deserve? How perfect is the hound at smelling, who never leaves or forsakes his first scent, but follows it through so many changes and varieties of other scents, even over, and in, the water, and into the earth! What music doth a pack of dogs then make to any man, whose heart and ears are so happy as to be set to the tune of such instruments! How will a right Greyhound fix his eye on the best Buck in a herd, single him out, and follow him, and him only, through a whole herd of rascal game, and still know and then kill him! For my hounds, I know the language of them, and they know the language and meaning of one another, as perfectly as we know the voices of those with whom we discourse daily.

from *The Compleat Angler*, 1653

Joseph Addison

Sir Roger being at present too old for Fox-hunting, to keep himself in Action, has disposed of his Beagles and got a Pack of Stop-Hounds. What these want in Speed, he endeavours to make Amends for by the Deepness of their Mouths and the Variety of their Notes, which are suited in such Manner to each other, that the whole Cry makes up a compleat Consort. He is so nice in this Particular, that a Gentleman having made him a Present of a very fine Hound the other Day, the Knight return'd it by a Servant with a great many Expressions of Civility; but desired him to tell his Master, that the Dog he had sent was indeed a most excellent Base, but that at present he only wanted a Counter-Tenor. Could I believe my Friend had ever read Shakespear, I should certainly conclude he had taken the Hint from Theseus in the Midsummer-Night's Dream.

from *The Spectator*, 13 July 1711

Anonymous

To Mr H—y's GREAT DOG, on the west-side of Portman-square.
BRINDLED SIR, —
I give you this genteel appellation, though you really deserve to be addressed in a manner less elevated. I have a high veneration for your species, but you are so ill-tempered and noisy, that you are become an arrant nuisance to the neighbourhood. I take up a pen against you instead of a stick, which might be a better weapon, in behalf of several eminent fair ones, whose repose you disturb, some of whom possibly have not reclined their aching heads on the soft,

downy, reconciling pillow, above five minutes, before you begin your confounded, discordant orisons. If you mean to shine conspicuous in the Isle of Dogs, you must fawn and flatter like your diminutive brothers, and you would soon be exalted from the step of the area you now stand on to the sofa in the drawing-room. I have spared you hitherto in compassion to your youth; but if you do not soften your notes a little, by barking in a flattering key, I shall be very sharp with you. That you may long live a hearty, jolly, but withal peaceful dog, is the wish of
Brindled Sir,
Your Anonymous Adviser.

Morning Post, 1775

Anonymous

The physiological effect of music is beyond dispute very powerful. Probably its most prominent influence is over the nervous system, and consequently over the brain. In the old fables we are told how music could not only tame wild animals, but move trees and rocks. Leaving aside this last clause, which must be interpreted allegorically, there is no room for doubt that wild and domestic animals are deeply affected by music. In no case is this more noticeable than with man's best friend, the dog. In a curious book published more than a century ago by the learned friend of old Samuel Johnson, Dr Richard Brocklesby, a member of the Royal Society, a series of quaint experiments and observations on the behaviour of dogs and other animals under the influence of music are given. Dr Hector Chomet, a Frenchman, also carried out a series of experiments of the same kind some hundred years later. In all cases it has been proved that dogs really possess an ear for music. It is true that at first dogs do not exactly love music. They are influenced by it, and manifest fear, uneasiness, or dislike in more or less marked manner. But dogs soon become educated; their awe, fear, or uneasiness quickly changes to interest and apparently love of music. One thing is peculiarly interesting; key instruments seem to act on their nerves in a disagreeable way, and as a rule it takes much longer to accustom a nervous, frightened dog to the notes of a cornet, trombone, or even the flute. As far as we can judge, music acts on the unsophisticated dog as a mysterious outside power for which they cannot account, and which overawes them by its mysterious influencing of their nervous centres. Wind instruments act on a larger volume of air, and the nerves are affected by swifter or key instruments sets the air waves in motion. This may account for the fact that dogs are often partial to martial strains when they would howl at the sweetest ditty scraped on the violin, or the softest lullaby banged out of a piano. Dogs, however, are quickly educated in a musical way, as in most and it is wonderful to see what a true knowledge of the musical art they soon acquire. Learned dogs and circus dogs are too well known to need any long notice. We all know how they can be taught to dance, play tricks, and go through long and intricate performances without word of command, but merely guided by music. The clown of dogdom, the poodle, has always been associated with the fiddle and flute. Toby, too, understands the signals conveyed by his master's drum and fife. Educated or uneducated, a dog possesses an even finer ear than man. The slightest musical discord acts like an electric shock on his nerves, he jumps and wildly protests. This sensitiveness seems to exist in all animals, more especially when in a wild state, but it can be singularly refined and intensified. Only two years ago, there was a learned dog at Darmstadt who had become the terror of all bad musicians. He belonged to a musical family, and having been present during the training of a numerous family by a stern father, he gradually acquired a most extraordinarily acute ear. No matter where this dog was, whatever instrument was being played, he at once detected the slightest false note or discord, and protested loudly until silenced by his master. This dog was introduced into theatres, concerts, and musical "at-homes", and he proved such an exacting critic, so absolutely accurate and without prejudice, that a dead set was made against him, and he had speedily to retire into private life, for many a professional and amateur thirsted for his blood. But as I have said before, this acuteness in detecting discords is common with the dog tribes. Only last year a series of most interesting experiments were made by a violinist on the animals in the London Zoological Gardens. Bears, lions, elephants, etc., were all sensibly influenced by the music. What most directly interests us, however, is the behaviour of the wolves, foxes, and wild dogs. The

European wolf manifested unmistakable dislike. He set up his back, held his tail between his legs, and showed its teeth by drawing back its lips in a nervous and fixed sneer. The Indian wolf was terrified; it trembled, crouched down with its fur erect, and slunk away; then attracted by unconquerable curiosity it came forward with every symptom of extreme fear. Curiously enough, the jackals and some of the foxes did not show quite so much alarm as the wolves. Female jackals simply ran back to their dens, and refused to come out. The male stood its ground better. With fur erect, they crept backwards and forwards with sneering lips, and uttered growls on any discord being struck. Meanwhile, the prairie wolves, African jackals, and a vast number of different kinds of foxes, sat up in their cages, or lay on their ledges, looking at the musicians, listening to the strains, but all quickly manifested their horror of discords. Many of the larger foxes and the dingoes came forward to listen to the music, their fear being dominated by the curiosity, and apparent by an irresistible, half painful, half pleasurably attraction. It is a pity that the experiment was only made with a violin. But, I believe, that on the days when the military band plays close by the Zoo, the animals do not manifest any fear, though some of them show curiosity, and either become excited or lie down quietly, listening intently. Scotch shepherds' dogs manifest no dislike, but, on the contrary, a real appreciation of that most strange of instruments, the bagpipes. It is a well-known fact that cavalry horses soon learn the meaning of trumpet signals, and will perform all the most intricate evolutions when riderless, or even when mounted by ignorant recruits. Regimental dogs show the same aptitude for acquiring a knowledge of the meaning of bugle signals. It may be less generally known that dogs have been trained by smugglers and thieves to act on hearing musical and whistling sigarrisons in continental towns where bands play in the open air, it is quite amusing to see how dogs congregate round the band stand, and dance about, having romps and games of hide-and-seek among themselves to the strains of the band. No attention, however, seems to have been paid to the behaviour of dogs on hearing music when they are ill. If any dog lover or learned professor has noted incidents under these latter circumstances it would be interesting to hear about them; also whether dogs can really be made to sleep under the influence of music. This last matter is of some importance, as it would help towards an understanding of the way in which music acts on the animal economy, a question which has always been more or less in dispute, and which has recently been revived in academical and medical circles.

"Dogs and Music", *The British Fancier*, 20 May 1892

Will H. Ogilvie

When the opal lights in the West had died
   And night was wrapping the red ferns round,
As I came home by the woodland side
   I heard the cry of a single hound.

The huntsman had gathered his pack and gone;
   The last late hoof had echoed away;
The horn was twanging a long way on
   For the only hound that was still astray.

While, heedless of all but the work in hand,
   Up through the brake where the brambles twine,
Crying his joy to a drowsy land
   Javelin drove on a burning line.

The air was sharp with a touch of frost,
   The moon came up like a wheel of gold;
The wall at the end of the woods he crossed
   And flung away on the open wold.

And long as I listened beside the stile
   The larches echoed that eerie sound:
Steady and tireless, mile on mile,
   The hunting cry of a single hound.

"A Single Hound",
The Collected Sporting Verse of Will H Ogilvie, 1932

Robert Falcon Scott

For it is on such nights that the dogs lift up their voices and join in a chant which disturbs the most restful sleepers. What lingering instinct of bygone ages can impel them to this extra-ordinary custom is beyond guessing; but on these calm, clear, moonlight nights, when all are coiled down placidly sleeping, one will suddenly raise his head, and from the depths of his throat send forth a prolonged, dismal wail, utterly unlike any sound he can produce on ordinary occasions.

As the sound dies away another animal takes it up, and then another and another, until the hills re-echo with the same unutterably dreary plaint. There is no undue haste, and no snapping or snarling, which makes it evident that this is a solemn function – some sacred rite which must be performed in these circumstances. If one is sentimentally inclined, this chorus almost seems to possess the woes of ages; as an accompaniment to the vast desolation without, it touches the lowest depths of sadness.

from *The Voyage of the Discovery*, 1905

Irene McLeod

I'm a lean dog, a keen dog, a wild dog, and lone;
I'm a rough dog, a tough dog, hunting on my own;
I'm a bad dog, a mad dog, teasing silly sheep;
I love to sit and bay at the moon, to keep fat souls from sleep.

from "Lone Dog", *Songs to Save a Soul*, 1915

Frederick Watson

Hounds, like all real artists, sing on the smallest possible provocation, but they prefer the night before a hunt because they have not dined, and feel – quite naturally – extremely aesthetic.

Hound singing has been resolutely ignored by musical authorities.

Even the bagpipes have had their own dismayed literature; and there are, one may presume, handbooks on the triangle. But although serious-minded representatives of the BBC have lain in English dew to connect up Bridge parties all over the place with the hesitant and rather niggardly transports of the nightingale, the solid, sustained and purely Slavonic symphony of foxhounds has been deliberately ignored.

If the night is clear, and so painfully still that strangers in "The Pig and Turnip" can listen without opening the bedroom windows, well-bred hounds feel it a religious duty to acquaint all subscribers, members, farmers, villagers, foxes, and vagrants, within a radius of three miles, that there will be a bit of sport in the morning. That, in fact, was happening when this chronicle opens.

As the clock struck 1 a.m. and everybody was nicely asleep all along the Muchley valley, little Wistful (who being harrier-bred was a promising soprano) rose dutifully on the sleeping-bench and, with a preliminary tuning note or two, quavered an opening bar. It rose and melted away. Her brother, Wayfarer, blinking with ignoble slumber, threw in his throaty alto. Two mournful voices rose with anguished but limited cadence. Hubert, the disillusioned kennel tom-cat, twitched his abandoned whiskers as he crouched by the boiler-house door, but what were two harriers in the empty moonlight? Ravisher and Comely, Crinoline and Trespass — a little late but in excellent voice. Then Cosy, Warrior, Tapster and Vanity, Bouncer, Ranger, Damsel and Hornet. The mournful chant went up, quavered, wavered, and as those fine basses Warlock, Samson, Harper and Lawless came in, the chord fell an octave, the harmonies blended, the full chorus grew and sounded, melted a little and was sustained. But here was not finality. That came with old Conqueror, whose hollow note, like a sonorous dinner-gong, effulgent and deafening, gave a sense of high tide before the ebb. There was Welsh in the pack — too much by half as Owen (who had come from Sussex) said — and where there is Welsh the range of voice is operatic.

The moonlight shed its pale radiance on the ecstatic faces, the shuttered eyes, forlorn muzzles and quivering throats. The whole kennel was in it now. Twenty couple altogether. The night had been soundless and, with ever-extending consternation, the valley was more and more aware that, according to their old law and heritage, hounds were singing . . .

from *In the Pink,* 1932

G. K. Chesterton

But all can hark at the dark of even
The bells that bay like the hounds of heaven,
Tolling and telling that over and under,
In the ways of the air like a wandering thunder,
The hunt is up over hills untrod:
For the wind is the way of the dogs of God: . . .
And we poor men stand under the steeple
Drawing the cords that can draw the people
And in our leash like the leaping dogs
Are God's most deafening demagogues.

"The Bell Ringers", 1933

CHAPTER 11

Breeding

As with so many canine activities breeding exists at a number of
different levels and for a number of different purposes. Those
ill used dogs which conceive on street corners and subsequently, to the consternation of their feckless owners, produce
puppies are the source of many of the problems for which all dogs are
often held to be responsible. At the other end of the scale are the packs
of foxhounds, some bred for more than two hundred years and
matched for speed, nose, voice, colour and ability in a way which
has not been equalled by any other breed. The best of these packs
represent the pinnacle of the breeder's art. Of more recent origin are
the highly successful and carefully planned breeding programmes,
both in Britain and America, which produce dogs capable of accepting
the demanding training required to produce guides for the blind.

The best breeders produce dogs with a particular purpose in
mind. Their aim may be to produce dogs capable of winning in the
show ring, winning on the track or the coursing field, performing
well to the gun, carrying out pastoral duties or undertaking any one
of the myriad services which dogs perform in the service of man.

Breeding dogs is an endlessly enthralling and demanding activity
which captivates people in all walks of life. Her Majesty Queen
Elizabeth II breeds dogs, though it is not so much for her famous
Corgis that she enjoys the respect of fellow breeders but for the strain
of Labradors which, for many years, have so successfully carried her
Sandringham affix.

Of course there are breeders who are just as capable of deluding themselves about the quality of their puppies as they are of

deluding potential purchasers. Optimism may be the most important quality required by breeders. Some may allow optimism to turn into belief and belief into claims which cannot be substantiated. This small minority has attracted the attention of writers sometimes with hilarious and occasionally uncomfortable results.

Charles Darwin

How strongly these domestic instincts, habits, and dispositions are inherited, and how curiously they become mingled, is well shown when different breeds of dogs are crossed. Thus it is known that a cross with a bulldog has affected for many generations the courage and obstinacy of greyhounds; and a cross with a greyhound has given a whole family of shepherd-dogs a tendency to hunt hares. These domestic instincts, when thus tested by crossing, resemble natural instincts, which in a like manner become curiously blended together, and for a long period exhibit traces of the instincts of either parent: for example, Le Roy describes a dog, whose great-grandfather was a wolf, and this dog showed a trace of its wild parentage only in one way, by not coming in a straight line to his master when called.

from *On the Origin of Species by means of Natural Selection*, 1859

With Greyhounds also there has been much close interbreeding, but the best breeders agree that it may be carried too far. Sir J. Sebright declares that by breeding in-and-in, by which he means matching brothers and sisters, he has actually seen the offspring of strong spaniels degenerate into weak and diminutive lapdogs. The Rev. W. D. Fox has communicated to me the case of a small lot of bloodhounds, long kept in the same family, which became very bad breeders, and nearly all had a bony enlargement in the tail. A single cross with a distinct strain of bloodhounds restored their fertility, and drove away the tendency to malformation in the tail. I have heard the particulars of another case with bloodhounds, in which the female had to be held to the male. Considering how rapid is the natural increase of the dog, it is difficult to understand the large price of all highly improved breeds, which almost implies long-continued close inter-breeding, except on the belief that this process lessens fertility and increases liability to distemper and other diseases.

from *The Variation of Animals and Plants under Domestication*, 1867

Nimrod (pseud.)

It sometimes strikes me that, as hounds improve in beauty, which they certainly do, they lose other more necessary qualities. This is certainly the case, unless they are bred from the very best blood. I conclude this part of my subject, then, by assuring you that, if you attempt to form a pack of fox-hounds yourself, you must not, clever fellow as you are, expect perfection under ten years, and that makes a hole even in a young man's life. I can only say it cost me that time to form what I considered a steady and stout pack. Some sorts prove vicious, however highly bred; some unsound, some delicate; and, forasmuch as it requires three years to find out the results of any cross, how favourable soever may be the expectation from it, the breeder of hounds is too often, if not working in the dark, involved in uncertainties and perplexities to no small amount. As is the case with breeding horses, faults of generations back, on one side or the other, will appear; and with hounds, even should the cross suit the first time, there is perplexity again; the produce must be three years old before their real goodness can be verified; and their sire must be at least five or six, as no man would breed from a hound much under three years standing in his work. Should the cross nick, however, spare no pains to continue it, if circumstances will enable you to do so – that is to say, if the dog and the bitch are within 500 miles of each other.

from *Life of a Sportsman*, 1832

Isaac Bell

It has become noticeable that a number of the hounds were knuckled over at the knee. At that time many people did not object to this stance; in fact many admired it, looking on it as associated with extra straightness. This knuckling over was often associated with "turned in toes" (pigeon-toed is I believe the expression), in some cases to such a degree that the hound was actually standing on the outer side of his feet. So fashionable did this basically unsound stance become among the breeders of foxhounds that it became known as the Peterborough stance and it took the combined influence of highly respected judges of hounds, the Duke of Beaufort, Captain Maurice Barclay. Colonel Peach Borwick and Captain Tom Wickham Boynton, to prick the bubble on which the fashion was based. Nor was this knuckling over the only deleterious fashion to pervade foxhounds. What Ikey Bell described as "a craze for lumber", a desire for excessive bone often, it seemed, for its own sake and in spite of the way in which heavy bone reduced a hound's agility and stamina, produced hounds which satisfied the prevailing fashion but which were far less efficient in the hunting field than Frank Freeman's light boned packs had been, though their appearance was often disparaged by those who placed appearance before function.

"The main lesson we have learned throughout these changes," said Bell, "is that we should not be led away by extravagances, which do not actually improve the working capacity of our hounds."

from *Foxiana, c.* 1930

Captain Lawrence Fitz-Barnard

The fighting-dog was derived by crossing the Bulldog with a terrier. The terrier is not known, but it was probably the Old English terrier, a white dog, and I believe the breed is now extinct.

The gameness comes from the Bulldog, which has always stood as the emblem of British courage. When I say Bulldog, I do not refer to the modern monstrosity of that name, which the showbench has transformed into a useless cur, but the old Bulldog who was kept for use, and was a very different animal from its present namesake. He was used to catch and hold bulls for the butcher, and also for bull-baiting.

Useful as he was for these purposes, the Bulldog was too slow for fighting, although originally used for this sport. His bulky body and short face were excellent for seizing a large object and hanging on, but he could not get a mouth on quickly. Again, you must not confuse him with the modern creation, for man has so improved the short nose that these poor brutes can now hardly pick up their own food.

The Bulldog, then, was too slow and too short in the face for quick work, and some genius crossed him with a terrier, which made the produce lighter in the body and longer in the head – in short a quicker dog – and he retained the courage of the Bulldog. By selection in breeding he even overdid his ancestors in this requisite, and became the gamest thing in the world.

This cross was originally the bull-and-terrier, which has become shortened to Bull-terrier.

Again the showman has stepped in and made a breed of his own, also useless, and called it the Bull-terrier. The show-ring is the death-knell of usefulness for all animals; I need only mention the show hunter, the carrier-pigeon, and the show greyhound.

from *Fighting Sports*, 1921

Anonymous

EXTRAORDINARY BIRTH. – A bitch, belonging to Mr C. R. Peck, of Ware, Herts. (partly Newfoundland,) produced last week, at one litter, and by one dog, the extraordinary number of seventeen puppies. Three were still-born, eight she has since smothered by over laying them, three have been drowned, and three are now alive; she was two days in her trouble. When she was about two years old she had fourteen puppies by one dog. She is now about four years old, and has never had puppies but twice.

from *American Turf Register and Sporting Magazine*, February 1834

CHAPTER 12

In Competition

G iven man's delight in inventing games, and then elevating them to such a status that national prestige depends upon them, it is likely that competitions involving dogs go back a very long way. Given man's competitive nature it could not have been long after one man and his dog emerged from their cave to find themselves confronted by their neighbour and his dog.

The first recorded dog show was in 1603 when the Holy Roman Emperor, Rudolf II, helped form the Society of Experienced Hunters which, for a five-year period, met weekly in the Emperor's private chambers at Hradčany Castle in Prague. As compensation when his seventeen-year-old daughter refused to marry the 51-year-old Rudolf, the Duke of Bavaria sent him a gift of twelve hunting dogs which so captivated the emperor that he organized a field trial in the Castle grounds over an eight-day period, in which 480 dogs competed, some coming from as far away as Spain. This is the first record we have found of a competitive event involving dogs.

Another show, this time exclusively devoted to Schipperkes, took place on the Grande Place, Brussels in 1690. This event appears to have been one of a regular series organized by Brussels shoemakers to show off their dogs in their ornate, intricately worked metal collars.

In 1791 Ignaz Cernov and Father Martin Pelcl visited a dog show which took place in Prague – in Josef Emanuel Malabatla Canal's garden. It lasted three days. The dogs were judged in a twelve-foot-square fenced run. There were 128 dogs on exhibition, 28 Pyrenees

Shepherds, 18 Spitz, 16 Butcher dogs, 14 Dachshunds, 12 Mountain Dogs, 10 Poodles, 9 Pugs, 7 Pyrenees, 8 Russian Wolfhounds and 6 St Bernards.

Dog shows in Britain had been taking place at least since 1776, when John Warde, widely regarded as the father of British Foxhunting, held the first of a series of hound shows at his home at Squerries near Westerham, in Kent. Urban shows were being advertised at least from 1834 when Charley Aistrop, the notorious proprietor of the equally notorious Westminster Pit, ran a show for toy spaniels.

In the February 1834 issue of the *Sporting Magazine* the following advertisement ran: "The show, of 9 lb spaniels for a silver cream jug will take place at Charley Aistrop's, the Elephant and Castle, on Wednesday." The advert, included along with other items of interest to the "Canine Fancy", was flanked by a challenge from "Thomas Williams of Liverpool, (who) will match a dog, of 18½ lbs weight, against the Birmingham dog, of the same weight, for £10, £20 or £50. His money is ready at the Newmarket Tavern, Maddox-street, Liverpool." Below this announcement was a report of an "Extraordinary birth! at which a bitch belonging to Mr C. R. Peck of Ware, Herts. (partly Newfoundland) produced last week, at one litter, and by one dog the extraordinary number of seventeen puppies."

In 1823 the *Sporting Magazine* had published a report about Charley Aistrop's activities and it was during that year that Billy, a cross-bred Bulldog, bred by Aistrop's father, sold to Charley Dew and purchased, after Dew's death in 1822, by Charley Aistrop, killed 100 rats in 5½ minutes. Charles Williams' *Dogs and their Ways* records that: "Over the door of a parlour of a public house in Denmark Street, St Giles', is a glass case, inclosing the stuffed remains of 'Billy', an extraordinary animal of rat-killing notoriety." Sadly Billy's remains have disappeared without trace.

However in the late 1820s the public's attitude towards baiting sports changed: it found them unacceptably cruel. Furthermore Aistrop's wife was killed, when feeding the bears baited at the Westminster Pit.

So Charles Aistrop, Charley's son, changed tack: he started the first dog club, but Jemmy Shaw and Jack Brown (both pugilists of no great consequence) were quick to follow his lead.

Like Aistrop Jemmy Shaw's fame rests on the exploits of one, or perhaps, two dogs. He was the owner of the "Wonder Tiny", an Old English Terrier which achieved fame by killing 200 rats in 54 minutes, and of Jacko which killed 1,000 rats in 1 hour 40 minutes, though the killing was spread over a ten-week period, 100 rats being killed each week, the final lot being killed on 1 May 1862. Until 1852, he was landlord of the Blue Anchor, Bunhill Row, St Lukes. In 1853 he took over the Queen's Head, Windmill Street, Haymarket, following the death of its landlord, Jem Burns. Jem Burns had run shows for Bulldogs of which he was a well-known breeder. A dog show, which took place in 1855 when Shaw had become mine host at the Queen's Head, is the subject of a painting which now hangs in the Kennel Club Smoke Room. It contains portraits of both Jemmy Shaw and Charley Aistrop and records the often sordid events with which both were so closely associated.

By 1857 the shows held at the Eight Bells in London and at public houses in various cities were well established and increasingly well supported by breeders and exhibitors of non-sporting breeds. The sporting breeds seem to have become rather neglected. However during the next two years correspondence in *The Field* began to explore the possibility and the advisability of running a show for sporting breeds.

The show eventually took place on 28 and 29 June 1859 as part of a well-established poultry show held at the Corn Market, Newcastle-upon-Tyne. The event has since erroneously come to be regarded as the first dog show, but its significance is as the first dog show to attract a high proportion of its entries from far afield, something which had become possible with the advent of the railway.

As the longest surviving member of those who promoted the show William Pape later laid claim to credit both for the idea and for promoting the event. In fact three men each deserve a share of it: William Pape, a well-known Newcastle gunsmith, was certainly one. John Shorthose, a noted Pointer and Setter breeder who worked for the brewers, Bass & Co, who were persuaded to sponsor the event, and Richard Brailsford, Lord Derby's senior kennel man was the third and possibly the most important.

"To Mr W. R. Pape", in 1908, in a report which relied entirely on evidence provided by Pape himself, who was by then the only surviving member of the partnership, *Our Dogs*, with a fine disregard for the truth, said, "belongs the honour of conceiving and carrying to a successful issue the first dog show . . . Mr Pape saw earlier than any other breeder that uniformity of type in the different varieties of dog could only be brought about by competitive shows – in other words, in order to arrive at a common understanding of the points required it was necessary that breeders should have opportunities to compare their dogs, and that the only means of doing this was, as Mr Pape saw clearly, by providing prizes for competition and appointing men to judge who knew what was required, and whose decisions would be respected."

A more accurate account appeared in the *Newcastle Courant* for Friday, 1 July 1859. "The new feature of the addition of Sporting Dogs to the show of Poultry was a great attraction, and tended in no slight degree to the success of the meeting. The arrangements were admirably carried out: litters, with proper divisions, round three sides of a spacious building were set apart from the dogs, which were chained and sufficiently protected by barriers from any chance of injuring or alarming the visitors, and in this section the prizes given, two valuable guns, from the manufacture of Mr Pape, gunmaker, of this town, were probably a sufficient inducement to produce twenty-three entries for Pointers and thirty-seven for Setters, many being from different parts of the kingdom . . ."

In August there was yet another development, the Cleveland Agricultural Society, tried a few classes for hounds, after being persuaded by Thomas Parrington, a Yorkshire farmer, and MFH for the Sinnington hunt. Within a very few years over 60 packs were represented at the event, and the show moved to Redcar, Malton, Beverley and York, and finally, in 1877, to Peterborough where it remains, as the world's most important show for working hounds.

In November, 1859 Richard Brailsford ran a show in Birmingham. An appreciation of his efforts was published later in *The British Fancier*: "Mr Richard Brailsford", they said, "was an old man in the early part of the 'sixties' and to him is ascribed the initiation of the great National Show at Birmingham. He was an enthusiast in dogs, especially pointers and setters, and well known throughout the country not only as a scientific breeder, but as a splendid handler of dogs. He came mostly to the front while in the employment of the

Earl of Derby, and for more than fifty years was noted as one of the most celebrated of dogmen. He also lived with Lord Chesterfield. After many years trying to arrange public competitions for dogs, he was successful. He persevered, and at last succeeded in getting up the National Show of Sporting Dogs at Birmingham."

The United States took an active part in developing dog shows. The first Westminster Kennel Club show, called "The First Annual New York Bench Show of Dogs" was held at Gilmore's Gardens, New York from 8 to 11 May 1877. It attracted an entry of 1,177 dogs which were judged by a panel of five judges, one of whom came from England. Among the entries were two Deerhounds bred by Queen Victoria. They were valued by their American owners at £19,000 each. A St Bernard, bred in the Swiss hospice, was also entered. The show was reported by Shirley Dare in the *Spirit of the Times*.

After the initial work had been done by Warde and Aistrop, Brailsford, perhaps more than anyone else, paved the way for Charles Cruft whose energy, flair and showmanship would transform dog shows into a major public attraction, which also provided a source of interest and enjoyment for dog enthusiasts all over the world. During his lifetime Cruft was compared to the great American showmen, Phineas T. Barnum.

It is apparent that by the end of the nineteenth century dog shows were being organized very much on the lines we would recognize today. In Britain nowadays well over 5,000 take place each year and the largest of these, Cruft's, attracts more than 20,000 entries.

Coursing

The pursuit of hares by a brace of greyhounds whose performances are marked to decide the winner dates at least from the reign of King James I of England (1566–1625). In later years Shakespeare was himself familiar with the principal coursing grounds and sufficiently interested in the sport to cause his characters to enquire as to the progress of their friends' hounds. It was not, however, until 1776, when Lord Orford founded the famous Swaffham Club and his friend the Duke of Norfolk set down the rules under which coursing should be conducted (basically unchanged to the present day) that coursing was put on to a formal basis.

The sport's premier competition, the Waterloo Cup, has been run annually since 1836 when it consisted of an eight-dog competition, increased to 16 in the following year and to 64 dogs when the winner was King Lear. The sport has produced dogs which have found their way into legend and into literature. The first such was Lord Lurgan's Master MacGrath who was the winner in 1868, 1869 and 1871. Even this scarcely credible achievement, however, was eclipsed by Colonel North's Fullerton, who shared first place in 1889 with his kennel mate, Troughend, and then went on to win in 1890, 1891 and 1892. It is unlikely that Fullerton's achievement will ever be equalled, let alone surpassed.

Racing Sled Dogs, Terriers, Sheepdog Trials

Sewallis Shirley, who had founded the Kennel Club in 1873, organized the first sheepdog trials to be held at Rhiwlas, Bala on the 64,000 acre Welsh estate of Richard John Lloyd-Price. The two were friends as well as sporting companions and also shared a wide interest in dogs of all sorts. Lloyd-Price was a committee member of the first Crystal Palace Show held in 1870. He was also a member of the Kennel Club's first committee.

The first Bala sheepdog trial was organized by the Rhiwlas Field Trial Committee, whose experience of gundog trials doubtless stood them in good stead with their new venture. The event, "open to the world", was judged by a panel of local worthies who had the assistance of an "experienced and trusted shepherd".

After an aborted effort to arrange the trial for 9 August the event eventually took place on 9 October at Garth Goch, a short distance from Bala. Ten dogs were entered, the 10s. entrance fee perhaps being rather more than shepherds were prepared to pay to enter what the organizers had described as a "novelty" event. It was won by William Thomson, a Scotsman resident in Wales. Three hundred people attended the trials. By 1875 the number had grown to 2,000 who watched 30 dogs competing.

The Bala event was eventually outclassed by its rival at Llangollen and the two merged in 1878. Even so Sewellis Shirley had made his mark in yet another canine arena.

Competitions which test the prowess of dogs become ever more varied and ever more demanding. Sled-dog races now take place almost everywhere snow is to be found and even, using wheeled vehicles, where there is no snow.

For almost almost 10,000 years the Eskimo peoples have relied on sled dogs for their very survival. Arctic exploration, which began in the 1700s and has continued ever since, relied heavily on the strength and endurance of sled dogs, until and even beyond Captain Sir Vivian Fuch's expedition in 1957, though by this time mechanized snow tractors were replacing dogs.

Races began in 1908 after Allan "Scotty" Allan, who, along with Leonard Seppala, was to become a legendary figure in the history of sled dogs, proposed a one-off race to discover who had the best team. During the previous year the Nome Kennel Club had been founded with the express purpose of organizing the race and devising its rules. The initial All Alaska Sweepstakes was won by Albert Fink's team driven by John Hegness, but it was Scotty Allan and Leonhard Seppala who were to dominate the race in succeeding years.

It was, however, in 1925 that Seppala and his dog achieved their most enduring claim to fame.

Diphtheria, one of several lethal diseases which civilization has brought to the Eskimos, threatened the population of Nome. The community's meagre supply of vaccine was quickly exhausted and the nearest source of more was in Anchorage, 955 miles away. The railway could carry the vaccine to Nenana but the remaining 658 miles would have to be covered by dog teams which, in January weather, normally took US mail teams 25 days. Within that time the outbreak would have become an epidemic.

Leonard Seppala was in Nome and it was arranged that he would meet a team travelling from Nenana carrying supplies of vaccine. The plan was that on his outward journey he would leave dogs at various Eskimo villages and use these to replenish his team during his return journey.

Seppala made the journey to Shaktolik in four days, meeting the incoming driver and his cargo of serum. He had just crossed the 43-

mile wide frozen Norton Sound, by far the most treacherous part of his journey, even so he turned his team round and repeated the journey through the Arctic night arriving at Issac's Point after a journey of more than 90 miles. It was afternoon before he and his team arrived in Cheenik from where Gunnar Kasson's fresh team continued the journey, reaching Nome on the morning of 2 February 1925.

The entire trip from Nenana to Nome had been accomplished in just five and a half days. Leonhard Seppala and his team had covered 340 miles. No other team had covered more than 53.

The Congressional record of the truly epic journey records that "men had thought that the limit of speed and endurance had been reached in the gruelling races of Alaska, but a race for sport and money proved to have far less stimulus than this contest, in which humanity was the urge and life was the prize."

Anonymous

CANINE FANCY

SPANIEL SHOW. – The show of 9lb spaniels for a silver cream jug will take place at Charley Alstrop's, the Elephant and Castle, Peter-street, Westminster, on Wednesday.

A part of Lord Chesterfield's racing and hunting stud passed through St Albans and Barnet on Thursday, on their way to town, to be sold at Tattersall's.

American Turf Register and Sporting Magazine, February 1834

Anonymous

My father came from Limerick,
  My mother came from York,
A half bred Yorkshire, blue and tan,
  They hailed me as from Cork.
An Irish Terrier I was called
  And sent on bench to show,

But oh! how little they believed
   I should cause such a row.
Short legs, long legs, lean head and small,
   Heavy heads, short heads, or anything at all,
I was fated at the show my future lot to see,
   And consider 'at a class' what should become of me.
Would Committees be so kind as our fate to leave
Until as to points we are perfectly agreed?

The Livestock Journal, 1876

Shirley Dare

Speaking out of the depths of native ignorance, I assert that the extremely high-bred dogs of the bench show were the ugliest of their kind. Indeed, like coaches and trotting horses and gentlemen's dress, and every thing in which English style is pattern, the standard seems to be a select and formulated ugliness.

The St Bernards quite destroyed the romance attaching to their names by proving, one and all, uncompromising red and yellow dogs, with a savage cast of countenance, perhaps of disgust in life taking part in a show with scores of insignificant terriers looking for all the world as if they had been dry picked. I should think that anyone lost in snow, finding one of these monster St Bernards pawing over him with its usual expression, would immediately expect to be saved from freezing by being eaten alive.

I have a devout thankfulness that I was not the owner of some of these dogs. The great Siberians, for instance, brindled like tigers, with their ears cut short, images of cruel despotic power, their enormous heads, thick as if hewn square, a cold savagery in their eyes as if they had eaten convicts till all that hate and despair of the lost had concentrated itself in that dreadful regard.

Spirit of the Times, 1877

Anonymous

The world of "Canaille", or "Doggery", as Mr Carlyle translates the word – which is only disparaging and contemptuous when it is applied to a human community – exemplifies a great many varieties of animal life and character in the one canine species . . .

There is, indeed, no distinct species of animal including varieties differing so much from one another in size, form, colour, faculties of sense, habits and capabilities of training for different purposes, and in their disposition towards the human "lords of creation", our noble selves, who from time immemorial have found in the docile and affectionate dog an agreeable companion and a faithful and useful servant. . . . A general Dog Show . . . including all or many worthy kinds, is a spectacle of peculiar interest to a thoughtful observer of natural history. But, even in an exhibition limited to the varieties of terriers, of those dogs whose instincts and faculties lead them to pursue their prey by tearing up the surface of the soil or penetrating holes in the earth, there is a wonderful diversity of appearance. Our readers . . . will perhaps also bestow a little reflection upon these manifold aspects of the canine race, at least within the terrier denomination.

The Royal Aquarium, Westminster, which has on many occasions been the scene of dog shows of various kinds – of collies, bull-dogs, toy-dogs, and pugs, last week made a "new departure", when the first exhibition of terriers was opened to the public for three days. This show presented all the best features to which visitors of older exhibitions of a similar description are accustomed. The entries were over five hundred and fifty in number, and the animals, divided into fifty-seven classes, were a most creditable collection. All the arrangements, including those for benching and feeding, were excellent; ample space was provided in the judging-rings; the wide avenues between rows of benches allowed visitors to move about and examine the dogs with freedom and comfort; and the ventilation and lighting were good. The general arrangements, in the hands of Mr C. Crufts, left nothing to be desired, except that at one period of the afternoon, owing to the influx of visitors, the stock of catalogues was temporarily exhausted. In the fifty-seven classes were represented all the terrier classes of the British Isles. English fox-terriers, smooth and rough coated, Airedales, Bedlingtons, bull-terriers, Scotch Dandie Dinmonts, Skyes and prick-eared terriers, red and wheaten-coloured Irish specimens, the Welsh type, black-and-tans, and toy terriers found place and the quality throughout was of a very high order.

"Terrier Show at the Aquarium", *The Illustrated London News,* 20 March 1886

David McLachan

As I was an exhibitor of Irish Terriers at Ayr yesterday, and as I was very much disappointed with the awards, I feel it a duty to demand an explanation from you for acting in the manner you did. In the dog class you gave Garryford first, which was right enough, provided Garryford had a right to be there, which is very doubt-ful, he being a champion dog. Were it not that Garryford's new owner is a direct descendant of "King Agrippa" he would not have been there, as no gentleman would send a champion dog to compete in such classes. As for Gifford – had it not been that his chain was in Mr Lumsden's left hand, he would not have been looked at, as no man who knows anything about an Irish Terrier would look at him. You gave third to a dog with nothing but legs to look at; whereas Fagan got fourth – a dog that has been first in England before a competent judge. Either you know nothing about an Irish Terrier, or, if you do, it was evident that it was the owner and not the dog, that got the prize.

In the bitch class you placed Randy fourth after being changed from fifth – a bitch that was second at Glasgow in a class of twenty dogs. You put her first at Wishaw and gave nothing to Erin; yesterday you gave Erin second over the same bitch Randy, and made the lame excuse that you did not know Erin – a bitch wide in chest and with a very bad leg, and has a face like a monkey. You told me in the ring that Randy's coat was soft; there was no difference in her coat from Wishaw show. I have bred fox, Skyes and Irish Terriers before you knew what a dog was. I should like to know how you have the audacity to pose before the public as a judge of Irish Terriers. Did you ever breed or own one? Do you know anything about their points? If you do, the trust reposed in you was sadly misdirected. Do you imagine for a moment that I am going to be sat upon by an amateur like you. I have no objection to other people paying for your education, but I do not intend to do so. I made careful search yesterday after I got my dogs on their benches, for the purpose of having an explanation from you. You may consider yourself very lucky I did not find you – and future exhibitors of Irish Terriers were unfortunate that I did not – as I would have given you a few practical hints that you would have remembered every time you saw an Irish Terrier. However I will make it my special study to see you on the subject. Meantime I demand an explanation from you. I do not intend to speak behind your back, as you did of me in the ring yesterday, but to inform you that I intend to write to the "Stockkeeper" and other papers on the subject.

You told Mr Lumsden yesterday that you had made a mess of it – so Mr Lumsden told me. Well, it is my turn now. And explanation I demand at once.

Letter to the *Scottish Fancier and Rural Gazette,* May 1887

Charles Dickens

In that great canine competition which drew crowds some week or two ago, to Islington, there were furnished many wonderful opportunities for moralizing on humanity. It was difficult to keep fancy within bounds. With regard to the prize dogs for instance (to plunge into the subject at once), was there not something of the quiet triumph of human success about their aspect? Was there not something of human malice and disappointment about the look of the unsuccessful competitors? Was there not a tendency in these last to turn their backs upon the winners, and to assume an indifference which they did not feel? There was a certain prize retriever, and a more beautiful animal never wagged tail . . .

Great monster boar-hound, alone worth a moderate journey to get a sight of; gigantic neighbour of the pomeranian with your deep chest, your pointed nose, and your sable fur; sweet-faced muff from St Bernard, whose small intellect is what might be expected of a race living on the top of a mountain with only monks for company; small shadowy-faced Maltese terrier; supple fox-hound; beloved pug; detested greyhound of Italy; otter-hounds that look like north country gamekeepers – each and all I bid you farewell.

from *All the Year Round*

Anonymous

Who the man with the white waistcoat was who offered a bribe of a fiver to one of the judges at Cruft's?

"Things we want to know," *The British Fancier*, 26 February 1892

Anonymous

From the *Kennel Gazette* of April we gather that Mr Sydney Smith, fancy dealer and importer, of Victoria-street, Bristol – not Mr Councillor Sydney W. Smith, the highly respected St Bernard breeder and exhibitor of Leeds, we would have our readers to know – has at least earned for himself notoriety, for the advent of his initiation into the exhibition world has been celebrated by his being "warned off" the Show Ring and Field Trial Course by the Kennel Club, and this "for life," for an alleged attempt to bribe a judge and other discreditable conduct on the very threshold of his induction. A correspondent, after Cruft's Show, asked in our "Things we want to know" column, who the man with the white waistcoat was? and it will now be dangerous to wear such an article of apparel at shows, its spotlessness and emblem of purity notwithstanding. From the manner in which Mr Sydney Smith appears to have commenced his exhibition career it would be dangerous to hazard an opinion as to what pitch of proficiency he might have reached if allowed to continue in the eccentric, as it was reprehensible, course which he seems, with the guileless innocence almost, to have, by some strange notion of the fitness of things, been prompted to pursue.

"Kennel Notes," *The British Fancier*, 22 April 1892

Anonymous

The two following communications have recently been received from the above now notorious fancier, and as they are both sent for publication, we reproduce them verbatim, or as nearly so as is possible.

Dr Edditor

will you kindley Publish the Fowling. Seeing in your last weeks British Fancer something tuching my name i might tell the Collie Club and the Kennel Club that i am very well pleased to hear the Dession they came to For it will be a great saving to me i had a perfect right to try a Judge and a Judge had a perfect right to denigh me But as i wase Deturmon to go straight through and not apolegise knowning that i was perfectly right i an satesfied to know now what i beleved before i have proved all i wanted to prove For had i conued the Dog Line whare would my last Days Ended i am you Humble Servent

SIDNEY SMITH,

92, Victoria st Bristol.

Manager

My Dr Sir as i have parted with my Collies you will kindly stop it comming out again in your British Fanciour And i Most Hartely than you For such liberal Turms you have aforded me. For it is entirely through your paper that i have sold them. You may use this Letter in anny way two your advantage if it will do you aney service i am yours truly,

SIDNEY SMITH,

92 Victoria st Bristol.

Mr Sidney Smith and "The British Fancier", *The British Fancier*, 20 May 1892

Rawdon Briggs Lee

I have known a man act as a judge of foxterriers who had never bred one in his life, had never seen a fox in front of hounds, had never seen a terrier go to ground, had never seen either otter, weasel, or foumart outside the glass case in which they rested on the wall in a bar parlour, and had not even seen a terrier chase a rabbit. His slight experience of working a terrier had been obtained at a surreptitious badger bait in the stable of a beer house, and a violent attack on a dozen mangy rats by a mongrel terrier in an improvised pit in the bedroom of the landlord of the same hostel.

from *Modern Dogs*, 1893

Dr John Henry Salter

They take (or took) everything very easily in Russia. A dog show, for instance, didn't last a day or two – it lasted a week or two, or as long as they seemed to like.

I was taken down to the show at the Manege (with the largest unsupported roof in the world) and asked how I would like to judge. I said, "How do you judge?" They explained that there were only three prizes in each class – gold, silver and bronze medals. The dogs would be brought up singly into a little side room, weighed and measured, and gone thoroughly over, and then His Imperial Highness the Czar would have the gold medal, His Imperial Highness the Grand Duke Nicholas the silver medal, and another Imperial Highness the bronze, with everybody else nowhere.

I told them I looked on that as a farce, so they asked me to judge according to our English fashion – the Czar wished it, and we were to show them how to do it.

So, looking at the big place, I saw a large stage at one end, most elaborately and extravagantly got up, with stuffed bears and birds and all kinds of things all round, and I was told that that was "for the band." But I explained that in England we judged everything out in the open, and we would make the stage into the judging place there, putting the band away on the other side of the building.

And we did so. The Russians were delighted with the whole thing. They could see what was being done; they watched the judging with great interest, and we made quite a new era in dog shows in Russia. You can't think what kudos England got out of it.

It had formerly been the custom to take each dog singly before the judge, who inspected him critically, took his measure, inquired the name of the owner, and asked any question about him that possessed any interest to him; but our practice of having the dogs in each class brought before us in one ring at the same time, weeding out the bad ones, carefully eliminating the best, and then most critically making our final awards, without any knowledge of owner or pedigree, evidently created much interest, and gave greater satisfaction – so much so that it was adopted at all future shows.

We had seventy or more dogs in the ring at a time, separated the indifferent ones from the good ones till we were quite certain about the inferior ones, which we then turned out. It took a whole day to judge a class, and in the end I had given the Czar a bronze medal and some much inferior person the gold medal, thus showing our English independence. The Grand Duke Nicholas came into the ring and told me they would never have any but English judges – and seemed much tickled because I gave the Czar a small bronze! Some jewels were struck off in commemoration of this show – six only. Three were presented to the three Grand Dukes Nicholas, Serge and Vladimir, and three to the English judges, Shirley, Jones and myself. Prince Shirinsky was the giver.

from *Diary and Reminiscences, 1849 to 1932*, 26 January 1898

Francis Dillon (Ed.)

WILLIAM ASPDEN: Talking of trials, I've heard it said that they are all right for a day's entertainment, but that they have no practical value. TOM THOMAS: That's quite wrong. You want a car that goes well at forty miles per hour, and you've got to experiment till you get one that goes well at eighty. And it's the same with dogs. If you can handle a dog in international trials, you'll work more smoothly and efficiently with your dogs at home. The aim, you see, in international trials is to get your dog to do exactly what he's got to do at home, only do it better. You send him off, for instance, to fetch sheep that may be out of sight in trials. You do that at home, don't you? Then he's got to do that in trials again, bring them in quietly and steadily. It isn't the dog that does best time that gets most marks, oh dear! no. The good dog always works at a distance and then he doesn't hurry the sheep. By the way, it's a mistake to have a dog with too keen an eye: it mesmerises the sheep and everything's at a standstill. Then he's got to keep his sheep together, as he would on the mountain side; and that's no easy matter because sheep have got character just like dogs. There's the Glamorgan Welsh sheep. You know Cwmpadest, how defiant they are and how they'll break hedges and wander, they're not timid like the Cheviots. I've seen them defying the dog and retreating backwards into the pen, stamping their feet with anger. Then after the penning-in trials you have got to single, that is, separate one sheep, marked with a red ribbon, from the rest. That's not easy because you know how sheep will follow one another. I've seen competitors driving this one sheep towards the remaining nineteen and command the dog to hold her; and he does. Of course he mustn't bite, that disqualifies him.

And you know it isn't only the collie that makes a sheep-dog. Here's a story, and it's true. Old Ann Rhydowen had a fox-terrier. The police found that she had no licence for the dog and brought her to court. She told the magistrates that her fox-terrier was a sheep-dog. They laughed at that, so she took them into a field and got her little terrier to fetch the sheep as neatly as could be. There was no fine.

Country Magazine, 1949

Judith Anne Lytton, Baroness Wentworth

Exhibitors have to reckon with many kinds of judges.

1. The weak-minded, well-meaning man, who never can make up his mind and gets hot and flustered and nervous, and makes the exhibitors cross and takes all the life out of the exhibits by having them lifted up and down and sent round and round the ring fifty times where once would suffice. This kind of judge almost invariably ends up by awarding the prizes to the wrong dogs because, by looking at them too long, he loses the invaluable general impression of shape, style, and outline, and eventually makes his decision on questions of minute detail, which are thus given an importance

beyond their actual value. Looking long and too closely at a thing is a bad system as it tends to destroy all sense of proportion. I once saw an old gentleman come into a picture gallery. He did not look at the pictures in the ordinary way, but examined several canvases with a magnifying glass. Some judges seem to judge dogs much in the same way.

2. The old hand who is open to alter his decisions, according to the advantage he thinks he is likely to get, either in hard cash or in other ways.

3. The equally old hand who has a kink in his temper, who will put you up to-day and down to-morrow, out of pure spleen and biliousness, who is insulted if he is bribed and more insulted if he is not.

4. The sensationalist, who likes to turn everything topsy turvy.

5. The ostentatious and self-righteous prig who is always blowing his own trumpet.

6. The rare judge, who knows his business, who is firm, courteous, and dignified in the ring, and punctual in getting there, who is rapid and decided in his awards, and perfectly consistent and reliable.

7. The jovial, happy-go-lucky man, who is always late, arrives in breathless haste, with a flushed face and eager eye and has to catch an early train home. He hurries through his classes, loses his pencil, mislays his judging book, awards the stud dog prize to a bitch, gives the Pomeranian championship to a Pug, and the open challenge cup to a litter, addresses the secretary as "My lad", shakes hands with total strangers, thanks everybody profusely, and vanishes in a whirl of flurry, taking the slips of the last class with him, and leaving everybody bewildered and gasping.

8. The bully who swears at the ring steward, insults the secretary, orders the exhibitors out of the ring if they dare so much as sneeze without leave, frightens the dogs, reduces novices to hysterics, awards the prizes to the right dogs, and departs saying he never saw such a cussed lot of wastrels in his life.

Perhaps the meanest of all judges is the man who tries hard to buy a dog for himself and on failing to get it pegs the dog back at every opportunity. No man who is capable of this is fit to judge at all. Of course a man who acts as agent for others may try to buy a dog by special request of a client and may not like the dog himself. I am not, however, referring here to dog brokers, but to people who are independent of dog selling as a trade.

from *Toy Dogs and their Ancestors,* 1911

Dr John Henry Salter

With a little judgement you can do a great deal. I had a telegram from France one Monday morning from a man who signed himself Paul Caillaird. He was a great contractor in Paris, very wealthy, having big estates, and he also tried to become a sportsman quickly. I knew nothing of him at the time. The telegram asked me if I would send him six dogs of different breeds, all famous in this country as having the best. If I would send him a specimen of each of these breeds to exhibit in Paris on the following Sunday he would have a chance of winning.

I thought this just like a crazy Frenchman to telegraph to a stranger an impossible problem.

But I thought it over, and rather liked the venture, and I determined to have a cut at it.

I telegraphed to Shirley, the Chairman of the Kennel Club, saying, "What will you take for your retriever to be delivered by special messenger at Liverpool Street Station on Friday afternoon, if in good condition?" I similarly telegraphed to a man named Bullead down in Devonshire in regard to a pointer, and to O'Callaghan, who had the best Irish setters; to somebody else about an English setter, and so on.

On Friday afternoon I went to Liverpool Street, telling old Baines to meet me there.

There were the six dogs and the men with them. They were in tip-top condition. I said to Barnes, "You take these dogs across to France and deliver them there to somebody who will be waiting for you at Calais. Get his receipt for them, and come back."

On the Monday morning I got a telegram from M. Caillaird: "I have won first prize with every dog you sent me and the gold medal for the Championship of the Exhibition. Thank you very much."

What was the result of that? He got what he wanted – notoriety as being the greatest breeder of sporting dogs in France! His reputation was made as a sportsman. With the ownership of these dogs he was able to constitute himself a judge, and he had the most beautiful estate in Cape Finisterre.

from *Diary and Reminiscences, 1849 to 1932*

Sir Peter Jeffrey Mackie

It is not necessary, in a work of this kind, to discuss the vexed question of the influence of canine exhibitions on the sporting dog. Much good has been done by these; but, alas! also much evil. The sporting dog, however, has suffered less than most other breeds, and on the whole, in the writer's opinion, distinct benefit has accrued, except in the case of the spaniel breed. This is due to the fact that dogs of other breeds have not been tampered with to the same extent as the spaniel has been by "fanciers," whose handiwork is seen in the numerous grotesque creatures which appear on the bench, and, with considerable difficulty, are able to walk a few times round the judge's ring. With these, however, the gamekeeper has nothing to do. The breed is right enough, but by selection a non-sporting class has produced animals unfitted for work owing to the exhibitors' want of knowledge and the apathy of the other classes. One must remember however, that those are selected specimens, and that it is possible to find animals of the same breed which are quite fit and able for field-work.

The majority of our sporting dogs men are men who are good sportsmen, and who judge the animals from a working point of view. So also are the majority of the exhibitors of sporting dogs. For this reason, the type of our best animals which win on the bench is an improvement on the dog of thirty years ago, and there is undoubtedly greater uniformity. We would therefore advise the discerning reader to attend these exhibitions – not to walk round when the dogs are benched, but to make a point of being present at the judging, to plant himself stolidly down opposite the ring, and to scrutinise carefully every animal in it.

from *The Keeper's Book, A Guide to the Duties of a Gamekeeper*, 1904

Arthur Blake Heinemann

To-day it is fashionable to hold classes for working terriers at Dog Shows, and specialize in various breeds or strains, each vying with the other for press-puffs and paragraphs, and capping each others' fairy-tales as to their terrier's exploits; for, tell it not in Gath, this is a profitable game, and as one judge and breeder of the latest candidates for fashion's favour said to me, "I know they're no use except at home among themselves, but what would you do? I can sell them like hot cakes." Another judge and breeder of a rival strain also shown of late years, said, "Be careful when you are buying one, for half of them are no use at all." "Deeds not words" should be the working-terrier's motto, and just as good wine needs no bush, so his record in the Badger-club season's booklet, or the foxes or otters he has bolted for the local packs duly chronicled by the hunting journalist, should prove a better passport to favour than any award at a dog-show, where practical and actual trials are entirely out of the question.

Also it is impossible to judge by appearances, for a dead-game dog may bear a scar, while a more useful and cautious one with tongue may not. I once judged a working-class, of course two ladies were among the competitors, for they dearly love dog shows, and like the late Lord Granville Gordon, I was tempted to give the prize to the best-looking lady; but being out for business, I asked what each terrier had done. Well, one of them had killed twenty moles in one night, and the other was made to sit and beg, when I discovered he was one I had bred and drafted as the ugly duckling of my litter! In this class the terrier I gave first prize to was utterly useless next week to badger, while an unplaced one was the very best a man could wish to work. All of which shows I am a very bad judge; if not, what a farce it all is.

Forbidden fruit is always sweetest, and breeders of show terriers are never tired of dinning into one's ears that their dogs are workers as well, and bred on the right lines for make and shape, but they lose sight of the fact that while they have been breeding them for straightness, they have acquired a giraffe-like length of leg, and while breeding them for appearance and show-points they have lost all their individuality, intelligence and stamina. Pluck, I admit, they still have left them, but it is rare and usually developed in the wrong direction of quarrelsomeness. The long-punishing jaw one hears so much of is gained at the expense of brain-pan, and is itself a misnomer. Turn to Nature's handiwork, and you will find the badger and otter with their short, puggy jaws give more punishing bites than the longer-jawed fox, whose brain-pan behind it is larger than a modern show terrier's.

Then as to coat; buy a show terrier, and do nothing to his coat, and in six months' time you will think your kennelman dishonest, for in the Teddy Bear he leads out for your inspection you will fail to recognize the pin-wire coated champion of Cruft's or the Crystal Palace. Now, breeders of working terriers are bitten with the craze for show-bench honours, and are fast making themselves ridiculous, to say nothing of spoiling the fruits of the labours of long years' breeding. Type is all very well, but it's "dogged as does it." And if you have a big badger-sett to tackle or an old dog otter in a wet drain, why! type won't help you much.

Again, the working terrier men rush to extremes and breed short legs at the expense of straightness and narrow chests; and gameness at the expense of tongue. Moderation and sound judgement are what is wanted, and away with the old fetich of weight. A big dog fox weighs but 16 lbs, and he is taller than any terrier, yet he goes to ground where a lower-legged badger who weighs 25 lbs cannot draw himself in. Who would buy a terrier weighing 30 lb, as a badger often does? or one standing as high on the leg as a fox who weighs 14 lbs less? It is the broad chests that cloddy dogs have and loaded shoulders that stop them, not *moderate* length of leg if the heart is there. As for coats, *natural* coats, hard as bristles on a dandy-brush, with plenty of undercoat, are what you want and can get, too, if you have the right blood, and, generally speaking, a rough-coated terrier is more likely to turn a worker than a smooth one, but if you get a smooth one good he is usually dead game. These smooth ones that keep cropping up in our litter no doubt point to the very remote cross of bull in them, to my mind the only admissible cross with the true working fox terrier, which gives them gameness, dogged perseverance and nose, but rather militates against tongue, and wants very careful elimination or tempering judiciously.

In turn these smooth ones often beget or throw rough pups with hard coats. A soft, silky-coated dog is usually too game and quarrelsome, and probably has a cross of Dandie or Bedlington. All terriers that run with hounds should be white in colour or have white about them. Hounds when closing in often maul unintentionally the terriers, covered as they are with mud and blood, but have better chance to discriminate between quarry and auxiliary if the latter is white or whitish. This especially applies to otter packs, where a coloured terrier is often tallied by ignorant or excited members of the field for an otter, and where the terrier often pulls out an otter all among the pack. Terriers should always be picked up at a worry of fox or otter whenever possible, for they stand no earthly chance in a hound's jaws.

"Hunt Terriers", *The Foxhound*, October 1912

Edith Somerville

Some years ago an opportunity came to me to visit a great, grave Dog Show. This took place in Bath, and it was, I am sure, a model of the best possible arrangements. I was a visitor to Bath and knew no one there. I wandered, solitary and friendless, through aisles and corridors, resounding with the protests of the exhibits. Their despairing chorus seemed to turn to hatred as I strayed by. I felt that they regarded me as a lone Irish wolf, and that if their restraining chains gave way, I should immediately be torn in pieces.

With this in mind I found myself in a palatial chamber, lined all round with Labradors, whose angry eyes were fixed on me. Keeping carefully in the centre of the gangway, I was aware of a long black arm outstretched as if to stop me. It belonged to a very large, shining, black bitch. I paused at a cautious distance, but her yellow eyes implored me.

"Hold my hand!" they said, "Be kind to me!"

Thus, in a South Carolina Slave-market, might some forlorn Aunt Cloe or Topsy have supplicated a passer-by. I took the great paw that she extended to me and held it, and comforted her as best I could. I hated having to let go and leave her. But, (as I said to her), "Since there's no help, come, let us kiss and part."

As I passed on into the free sunlight that she could see but could not share, I heard a heart-broken cry. I hurried away.

Happy Days, 1917

A. G. Sturgeon

There is an old axiom, "An exhibitor's business is to hide his dog's faults and a judge's to find them," but do not infer from that saying anyone is entitled to fake his dog. There is just an ordinary ring-craft sense required, and if the dog being shown has a particular fault, the exhibitor will learn in time to make so much of the dog's good qualities that the fault in question is more or less lost sight of by the judge.

If the exhibitor is a sportsman there is no need for me to dwell on the advice, "Keep smiling – win or lose." But unfortunately there is a class of exhibitor whose idea of dog-showing is covered by the words, "Win, tie or wrangle," and to such people there is only one course suggested, which is, either change their methods or keep out altogether. This class of exhibitor, unless placed at the top, either rags the judge openly or crawls round the show hinting at all sorts of low-down ulterior motives.

If an exhibitor cannot both win and lose decently, his place is at home. To shy one's hat in the air and behave otherwise like an exuberant puppy with a bone, when one wins, and to give way to pettish temper with malicious mouthings when one loses, is to declare one's-self absolutely outside the pale in any sport.

from *Bulldogdom,* 1919

Frederick Watson

Every Hunt must have A Puppy Show because that is how a Master has his young entry kept and fed and taught incurable habits for nothing. Puppies enter to fox in the cubbing season. As they have hitherto entered to everything else it is quite a new thrill for them. The Puppy Show is held in order that the simpletons who have walked a puppy, or even a couple, may put on their Sunday clothes and realize how much better their puppy looks than the other people's.

Puppies are destructive, expensive, homicidal, and full of sorrow. Fortunately not all live. It is rumoured that some busybody has invented a vaccine which will preserve them from distemper. That is, we suppose, what short-sighted people call Progress. Do we speak too strongly? Without a surplus of puppies there will be no puppy walkers, and without puppy walkers no Puppy Show. Don't forget that a fifty to one chance for a prize, a dish of tea and the Master's speech, is about all the farmer's wife gets out of the Hunt. And if the farmer's wife loses interest, what then? What indeed! Where's your precious vaccine now?

It is customary at a Puppy Show for the Master to invite two or three fellow Masters to come over and judge his puppies. With derisive smiles these Masters accept. They arrive and put on kennel coats, and have little books, and look very knowing indeed. In a ring, where all the walkers can see their puppies dragged and propelled about, the judging goes on for hours and hours. The only other function comparable to it in length of time, solemnity, and absence of all spiritual or physical compensations is the pibroch playing at a Highland gathering.

After the judging is over, the whole party, with hosts of members, strangers, farmers, and all their friends, troop towards the tea-tent. Here the Master – whose smile has never fluctuated throughout the day – is surrounded by his fellow-Masters of all kinds – even of beagles and otter hounds, so broken down are social distinctions on that great day.

After tea – with which cold beef and ham may be eaten if the Master can run to it – the prizes are presented. Then come the speeches. These are always given by the same people at every Hunt because it is absolutely essential that the right thing is said every year. After the most coherent Master has congratulated the Hunt on such an unusually fine show of puppies, old Mr Dumbleday gets up to speak for the farmers. There is one of his sort in every Hunt. He has retired long enough to forget what farming is really like, or possibly he has lived so long he goes back before the bad times, or he mayn't have been a farmer at all. But apart from that he has spent an hour with the Hunt Secretary, who writes all the speeches anyhow, for fear they won't stop. Mr Cracklethorpe, the Field Master's gamekeeper (who either has a fox in the home coverts or concocts his own advertisement for *The Field*, then deprecates the notions of some keepers who blame the fox for their own lack of knowledge. He recalls instances of vixens adopting pheasant poults who had.

From *Hunting Pie*, 1931

Don Marquis

i have just come from a swell
dog show he said i have
been lunching off a dog that was
worth at least one hundred
dollars a pound

from "the merry flea",
maxims of archy,
archy and mehitabel, 1931

Lady Kitty Ritson

Then I had to make tracks for New York, where I was judging Alsatians at the Westminster show.

I found to my horror that I was scheduled to begin at eight o'clock in the evening, a moment when I am generally thinking of my bed. This was the second time in my life that I have been really frightened in the show-ring, when I stood there really quite alone in a huge ring with hundreds of seats around, many of them filled with women in furs and wearing diamonds. Somebody kindly gave me a clap, and then everybody clapped – a friendly demonstration towards a shivering stranger which did do quite a bit towards heartening me.

That is a magnificent show, and the organization is wonderful. The dogs are kept below and brought upstairs for their classes when wanted by means of telephone messages. The rings are scrupulously clean and there is hardly any noise. I have judged three times in America, once at the "Garden" (Westminster) and twice at Mrs Dodge's show, the Morris and Essex. The latter is a fairyland show, held in May, out of doors, in blazing sunshine on a ground which is bright with flags and coloured chairs. Last time there was an entry of 2,000 individual dogs, and a "gate" of 25,000 people.

But to return to the New York show. I was inwardly shaking with fright in that great ring, until I had looked over the first puppy dog, and then I was only interested. If you know your job you haven't time to be frightened, and you can say that you know your job without being conceited. You may judge well or badly, but you can still know your job. At the end of the day you are fully cognisant of whether you have just judged "according to Cocker" or whether you have been blessed with that wonderful spirit of inspiration which every judge sometimes gets.

I enjoyed myself that evening, and I was looking forwards to doing the bitches the next day ("the females", as most people in America call them, or "the matrons"). They still fight a bit shy of that controversial word "bitch".

Classes in America are rather different from England, as at the very end of all things there is a supreme class entitled "Not For Competition in the Classes" where the champions all parade. This provides intense excitement all round. So far, a little bitch had carried everything before her. She had won her classes, she was "Best of Winners" and now she was to meet all the giants in keen combat.

Dear little "Lola", I shall never forget her with her lovely feminine outline, and her perfect dignity. It was chock-a-block with well-known German imported champions, many of them old friends that I knew well. Amongst them, the celebrated "Utz v. Hauschutting", a dog who was supposed to be the marvel of the age, and the latest German Grand Champion.

I paraded them round, I gazed at them, I weighed them up, and then I looked again at Lola – Lola so sound, so quiet, so typical, with none of the exaggerations which have ruined the breed. I walked forward and gave her handler, Simpson, the coveted purple and gold ribbon. Little Lola had beaten all the champions, and beaten them rightly.

from *Me and My Dogs,* 1933

D. Nunn

This is the Show
That Cruft built:
These are the dogs
Who wanted a prize,
So went to the Show
That Cruft built.

These are the maids
Who groomed the dogs
Who wanted a prize,
So went to the Show
That Cruft built.

This is the cock
That crowed in the morn
To wake the maidens, all forlorn,
To take the dogs –
Some hairy, some shorn –
Who wanted a prize
For their style and size,
To be won at the Show
That Cruft built.

These are the judges,
Some tall of form,
Who had to get up
In the early dawn,
To watch the maidens, all forlorn,
Bring in their dogs –
Some hairy, some shorn;
Dogs that got brushed
From daylight to dusk,
To win in the Show
That Cruft built.

This is the Greyhound,
Champion of all,
Who won the cup,
Over large and small
And went so happily
Back to his stall.
The best in the Show
That Cruft built.

"The Show that Cruft Built",
Our Dogs, 9 March 1934

D. P. Todd

Now there's many a song about hunting,
Packs and huntsmen are honoured by name,
But there isn't a song about terriers
Which in Lakeland have gained lasting fame.

So always remember your terriers,
Protect them from wet and from cold,
For the love of a tyke for his master
Can never be measured in gold.

Whether it's Fury or Trixie or Nellie,
Or Rock, Jock or Turk it's the same,
One quality you'll find among them,
And dalesfolk call it "dead game".
And whether he's rough or smooth-coated,
He'll tackle badger, otter or fox,
Run a drain or creep into a soil-hole,
Or squeeze through a grike in the rocks.

He'll yield not one inch though they maul him,
He'll fight to the death on his own,
Though sometimes he'll be imprisoned
By a rush-in of soil or of stone.
And then the brave lads of the valleys

To save him will toil day and night,
And join in a Hallo of triumph
As he blinks back to God's blessed light.

Now at Cruft's famous show down in London,
They have Lakelands that aren't worth the name.
If you showed 'em a fox or an otter
They'd fly for their lives without shame.
They're not built to creep or to battle,
But to sit on a chair in a house,
And they do say that one recent champion
Was chased down the road by a mouse!

So here's to our gallant laal workers,
Not beauties, perhaps, but they'll do.
With gameness they've also affection,
And make you a pall good and true.
And when your terrier, in old age, is dying,
And the world all about you seems sad,
A lick on the hand will console you,
For a truer friend man never had.

The Terrier Song, 1935

Lt Col. G. H. Badcock

I shall never cease to inveigh against what I consider to be the iniquity of allowing some judges to issue challenge certificates to breeds they have never bred or owned and know nothing about, while those who have kept and won championships in such breeds are debarred from so doing, and yet that goes on as merrily as ever and nobody seems to care.

None but a self-elected body would be so blind as to what must ultimately be their own fate in debarring women from their full share in their councils. It is a pity they don't take a lesson from real life and see what happened through trying to stop women having the vote.

Self-elected bodies are the last to learn a lesson obvious to all others.

I have been to one or two shows lately, and am shocked at the pace at which the ruin of the various breeds of gun dogs is proceeding. A great many Springers I have seen on the bench of late have the same vacant look affecting most of the modern-day show Cockers and Red Setters, and the sporting instinct is fast becoming bred out of both.

I hardly know an honest breed of gun dogs left in the show world other than the Labrador, and that the poison of looks as opposed to utility will invade them before long is practically a certainty.

I suppose really I am a Pharisee – I who keep a commercial kennel, criticizing others for treating a show-ring as a commercial enterprise. At least I have kept and lived with sporting dogs all my life, and my love for them is not based on what I can make out of them commercially. To reform a difficult dog of any breed, and the training of a gun dog, is more to me than what they bring me in cash. I wonder though very much, and very often, how many people who now show and come under the category of dog-lovers, would keep a dog at all if the commercial side were non-existent. That is where the deterioration comes in. Dog shows are simply commercialism run riot, and I doubt whether twenty per cent of those engaged in them have any deep love for a dog at all.

Just the same commercial spirit pervades field trials. The same dogs go the round of the trials, and most of the same people judge every year.

In whichever direction you turn you will find the same spirit of commercialism ruining everything. The point-to-point I used to ride in as a boy is a thing of the past, and steeplechasers just go out to qualify as hunters. International polo is a question of who can, and will, pay the longest price for ponies. International cricket and football are almost on a par with a declaration of war, and though I live far away from that world, I am told that much the same spirit pervades the Olympic Games.

from *The Understanding of a Dog,* 1935

James Thurber

At one of the last dog shows in which she [Medve] was entered with two or three of her best male pups, she was reluctant to get up on the bench assigned to her and her family, and so I got up on it myself, on all fours, to entice her to follow. She was surprised and amused, but not interested, and this was also true of my wife, who kept walking past the bench, saying, out of the corner of her mouth, "Get off that bench, for the love of heaven!"

from "And so to Medve", Thurber's Dogs, 1955

Montague H. Horn

It has been a long, cold miserable day with the rain ceasing for only short intervals, and it has been a blank day too. Hounds have travelled a long way beside the rising river, but at last the master calls a halt at the bridge, and among the few who have remained with him until the end is a young woman, leading a weary little Border Terrier.

The master leans upon his pole and tells her that he is sorry sport has been poor, he would have liked to have tried her terrier. He tells her it looks game, and sticking his pole into the sodden ground he runs his hand down its back, spans it behind the shoulders, its head in the palm of his hand, just like judges do in a show ring.

He remarks what is very obvious that the dog has a grand head, and she informs him that it is a very noted winner, and she says how sorry she is that neither she nor her dog can join them on the North Heddon, where hounds meet on Saturday. Well, it's not his fault that it was a wet day, but he's a decent chap, and has to overcome a lot of worries himself, so he draws a capacious wallet from his pocket and scribbles a few lines on the back of an old envelope and hands them to the girl. Reading them, she smiles. "How awfully nice of you," she says.

"Not at all," he replies, "it has been a great honour to meet such a famous little dog. I hope your luck continues." The little dog picks his way behind his owner's heels, through the wet grass, now eligible for the class for exhibits holding a working certificate.

from "On the Working-Terrier Class",
Our Dogs, 17 December 1954

John Tickner

As we remarked, the progeny of a terrier love-match arranged by a terrier without human advice, can be embarrassing. Short-legged Deerhounds or Border Terrier bodies running about on Greyhound legs are apt to attract attention and provoke astonishing comments from astonished passers-by. On the other hand, you can obtain some very pleasing results indeed by forgetting to close the right door at the right time if you own the sort of terrier that the Kennel Club wouldn't look at and your neighbour is the proud owner of a pedigree show-winning dog.

from *Tickner's Terriers*, 1977

Frank Jackson

I admitted that I was interested in dogs and a wary look came into his eyes. I recognized the look, having seen it before in other eyes when the subject of dogs surfaced in a conversation. The look told me that I looked normal enough and seemed normal enough, but that since I expressed an interest in dogs I couldn't possibly be normal.

"Really?" he said. "How interesting and how many dogs have you got?"

"Six," I lied, we had fourteen at that moment but we always pretend, even to ourselves, to have six. A look of sheer panic crossed his face. I began to pity him, Fancy having to make conversation with a lunatic who lived with six dogs. Heroically he pulled himself together and pressed on with the next inevitable question.

"What sort are they?"

"Border Terriers."

"Oh yes, they're nice dogs, very pretty." I knew that he hadn't the faintest idea what a Border Terrier looked like and that he was probably thinking of a Border Collie with which he thought himself well acquainted because of the *Lassie* films. It was going to be a long hard evening and I tried to change the subject.

"Do you have any hobbies?"

"I enjoy ballroom dancing and a pipe of tobacco in the evening."
I had a picture of him swathed in yards of tulle encrusted with hand-
sewn sequins doing a tango while knocking the dottle from his pipe
into his partner's wig. He pressed on.

"Tell me, aren't you worried about the health problems? You do
have children you know". An impulse to admit to some vague
recollection of having children was sternly squashed.

"What health problems do you mean?"

"Well you know, worms and all that. They can make people go
blind." Control slipped.

"It's surprising now what people believe can make you go blind. I
notice that you wear glasses."

"No, I mean dogs really are a serious health hazard, everyone
knows that they are. Aren't you worried about your children?"

"My father was brought up with dogs and not very well kept ones
at that. He's twice your age and at a rough guess I would say his
eyesight is about twice as good. Do you think it might be the
dancing or the pipe that's affected yours? I was brought up with dogs
and so were my kids, our health seems OK." I had gone too far and
again tried to change the subject.

"Talking of health, how's your son?"

"Oh he's a little better the doctor says. He was referred to a
psychiatrist you know but he's only seeing him once a month now."

"Has he started playing hockey again?"

"Well no. He wanted to and the doctor said he ought to take
more exercise but we didn't want him to overtax himself."

"Why don't you buy him a dog. He would enjoy its company
and exercising it would do him good."

"That's what the doctor suggested but I'm worried about his
health. I'm surprised that you show dogs though, I mean it's an odd
sort of hobby. They are all peculiar people aren't they? I've seen
Cruft's on the television and once went to a show at my youngest's
school and most of the people really are a bit strange." I could feel
that he had me against the ropes. There have been times when only
inane good manners have prevented me from remarking on the
peculiar appearance and eccentric foibles of my fellow exhibitors.
However loyalty came to the fore.

"Oh I don't know, you must remember that people who do any
activity look peculiar to those who do something else or nothing at

all. Also people who show dogs are drawn from all age groups and from all sections of the community. In fact that is one of the game's strengths, it doesn't depend on youthful vigour or agility or speed or strength. It depends on knowledge and skill both of which are improved with experience."

He hadn't expected such a spirited defence and our positions on the ropes were now reverted, I pressed home the advantage.

"Can you think of any other competitive hobby which allows teenagers and octogenarians to compete against one another on equal terms?"

"Well no, but surely you aren't claiming it's a healthy hobby."

"Look, I was a reasonably proficient competitive swimmer and like to think that I was a bit better at judo. Are they healthy occupations?"

"Yes, of course, very."

"Well swimming has left me with a chronic set of sinuses which have done my hearing no good whilst judo has left me with rheumatics in assorted broken bones. On top of which by the time I was 20 I was going down hill in both sports and had nothing to look forward to except slowly getting worse."

"Well what about golf then, old people can play that. I've seen them."

"Of course they can but not well and if you've done anything well it's hard to accept and harder to enjoy doing it less well. If you show dogs you can look forward to getting better, your next dog may be the best ever. And do you know what it costs to join a good golf club and to buy a set of clubs which you can't even breed from?"

He gave me a funny look and started on another tack.

"What do you actually get out of dogs? You sell them for a good price, I suppose."

I knew that Catch 22 had arrived. If I claimed to make a profit from dogs I would be sane in his eyes but a sane, callous profiteer. If on the other hand I admitted to paying handsomely for the privilege of sharing my home with six insanitary brutes without at least trying to make money by selling their offspring I would be indelibly branded as insane. I don't know what came over me but I told the truth.

"It probably costs us more to produce a puppy than we get by selling it."

"How do you mean? It can't cost you anything. Surely the mother rears her pups?"

"Not entirely and she has to be fed extra to do it and the pups need good food and plenty of it. Then there are stud fees, transport, housing, heating, vets' fees, registration fees and . . ."

I stopped, it was evident that he wasn't listening. Anyone who lived with six dogs must be peculiar but anyone who lost money from the exercise was obviously totally mad. He seemed to want to humour me. Perhaps to ward off any violent manifestation of my madness.

"Would you like a drink?"

"Thank you, I'd like half of shandy, please."

I had lied again. Half of shandy was not what I wanted and was certainly not what I needed, However to ask for anything stronger would only confirm his belief that breeding dogs was the most unhealthy and degrading interest ever.

"Cheers, and thank you."

He looked pleased with himself.

"Cheers. I did well out of that. Gave him a pound and he gave me change for a fiver."

"Oh."

"Tell me doesn't all the dishonesty in dogs nauseate you? All the back biting and things.'

"I'm sorry, I'm not really with you. I've not noticed much dishonesty and I've found most of the people to be very friendly and genuine, certainly there's no more back biting in dogs than there is anywhere else." He didn't believe me and gave me a look which said, "Perhaps not dishonest by your standards". He had read all about the dishonesty and the cheating, he knew that it was widespread. It had been in the papers.

"Come now, you know darned well that people cheat like mad. They nobble other people's dogs, and they do all sorts of things to their own to make them look better than they really are."

"Oh really, what sort of things?"

"Well they dye the dog's coat and powder them to change the colour. They put stuff on them to make the coats stand up or lie down and look shiny and feel better. They curl them and perm them. Dogs are given drugs to make them show better or to grow or to stop them from growing. There are all sorts of things going on as you must know."

"Anyone who was caught doing any of those things would be hauled up before the Kennel Club, just like a trainer would be before the Jockey Club, and they would be for the high jump I can assure you."

"Oh the Kennel Club knows that it's all going on but they do nothing about it. Perhaps they are doing it themselves or they turn a blind eye to it because of the money involved."

I was getting on to shaky ground but said, "I'm sure that you're wrong."

"Well then what about the judges? You can't tell me that they are honest."

"I'm a judge." This revelation confirmed rather than refuted his opinion, but he was getting distinctly edgy.

"Ah come now, if you're a judge" . . . I suppose I should in the circumstances have been grateful for the doubt, "You must know about all the fiddling and I hope that you're not going to try to tell me that you're not making money out of it." It had become obvious that I couldn't tell him anything. He wasn't programmed to receive anything that might disturb his own weird misconceptions. Owning dogs is insanitary, being interested in them is peculiar, breeding them without showing a profit is insane, showing them is dishonest and judging them is far worse.

"Well," he said, "you needn't tell me that you don't make money out of judging and there must be quite a few other advantages for a judge." He didn't actually nudge me or even wink but his meaning was clear: judges were not only dishonest but also immoral. I must have looked annoyed because he quickly seemed to remember that he was not only in company with a lunatic but an unhealthy, criminal, immoral lunatic. For his own safety he had better humour me.

"Would you like another shandy?" I didn't think that the barman could afford it and so I refused, politely I hope. He tried another tack.

"Do you show at Cruft's?"

"Yes."

"Have you ever had a Cruft's Champion?" It would have been a waste of time and effort to try to explain that there was no such thing as a Cruft's Champion except in the uninformed minds of journalists. I lied again.

"Yes."

His eyes lit up. He had hit the jackpot.

"I'll bet that you made a lot of money out of that."

At this stage we were joined by a friend of mine. My friend is a soccer referee. I introduced the two and went off to get some drinks. Large whiskies for myself and my friend, a shandy for him, and a drink for the barman. As I walked away he was talking to my friend.

"Soccer," he said, "now there's a dirty game."

"Dirty Dog", *Our Dogs Christmas Annual*, 1977

Les Barker

Row upon row upon row of Retrievers!
Wave after wave of Weimeraners!
A host of Golden Labradors,
Like a big barking bunch of bananas!

There were fifteen thousand of us there,
This was our time to take power,
For dogkind to finally take over,
O Rover, now is your hour!
A spate of Spaniels (Irish Water),
(Cocker), (Springer), (Sussex) and (Clumber)
There were Pointers in every direction,
O Dogdom, arise from thy slumber!

I went down their ranks and harangued them,
Being the only intellectual there,
I tried to whippet up hysteria,
But the Groenendaels groaned in despair.

Masses and masses and masses of Bassets!
The Borzois were back in town,

Greyhounds and Elkhounds and Wolfhounds abounding!
This was our chance, would mankind be brought down?

I lectured on Barxist philosophy,
I gave talk after talk after talk,
Arise from your sleep, O ye Westies
You have nothing to lose but your chalk!

Collies and Keeshonds and Corgis and Cairns!
No more need the Chow Chow kowtow,
Remember the Boxer Rebellion!
O Shih Tzu, your moment is now!

In folly, I called the Collies to follow,
They stayed, like the Malamutes, mute,
Deerhounds stood around looking doubtful,
And the Yorkies just tried to look cute.

Single-handed, I stormed a petfood stand,
And brandished a tin of Chum,
Someone shouted: "Where's your tin opener,
And where's your opposable thumb?"

Row after row of hyenas!
The Chihuahuas just made me feel small,
They say it was a good year for Setters,
I'm sorry I went there at all.

"Mrs Ackroyd's retreat from Cruft's",
Our Dogs, February 1988

Miles Kington

The major surprise at Cruft's Dog Show this Friday will be the
unveiling of a totally new breed of dog – the Crufts. Bred in secret as
the ultimate in show dogs, the Crufts will have all the features that

make a pedigree prize-winner: long legs, a short body, hair which sweeps down over the eyes to the ground, powerful forequarters, spacious hind-quarters, a small kitchen and planning permission for an extension behind.

"The beauty of the Cruft," says top breeder Mr or Mrs Shirley Coppice, "is that not only does it look like all the best breeds rolled into one, it also behaves like them. It will unroll a lavatory paper pack at top speed and wag its tail when shown a tin or anything needed for a TV commercial. It will stand motionless for hours, or walk round and round in a circle. When you throw a stick for it, it stays right where it is."

One of the most unusual features of the Cruft is that it can be hooked up to any computer terminal and linked to a database, which will give it immediate on-line information about dog-shows held anywhere in the world, traffic conditions near Earls Court and discount offers on dog food within 100 miles.

Some experts, however, have disputed whether the Cruft can legally be defined as a dog at all: an animal which is controlled by a mini-computer and powered by a small electrical engine is not recognizably the same kind of animal as a Yorkshire terrier. But Shirley Coppice indignantly rebuts this line of thought.

"As dogs evolve, so does our definition of a dog. What we are seeing now is the third-generation dog of the computer age, the dog which thinks for its owner. We are working towards the fourth generation, one which thinks for itself, and there are even plans for the fifth-generation dog, one which is too intelligent to want to go in for pedigree dog shows.

"Sir! (writes Major Crupper of Chunk-on-the-Wold)

It is absolutely typical of a trendy media person like Miles Kingston to make ignorant fun of a vital British institution like Cruft's, which has given enjoyment to thousands of people and probably been enjoyed by the odd dog or two. Every day in my kennels I perfect two or three new models of dog which are exported all over the world to bring priceless foreign earnings to Britain.

Incidentally, may I take this opportunity of saying that the Derbyshire terrier which we started exporting in late 1984 has developed a fault in the front off-shoulder, and we are with-drawing all examples of this model for rectification? Thank you.

Yours,

Sir (writes Champion Champagne Charlie)

As a prize-winning dog of many years' standing, and lots of walking around as well, may I comment on the present state of the British dog-breeder? It strikes me that there are far too few breeds of breeder for comfort's sake. We all know the Northamptonshire Nutter, with his friendly tweed coating, the Cotswold Colonel, and the ever popular Gloucester Gorgon. But whatever happened to breeders like the Northern t'Dog Fancier, or the TV Sheep Trial Commentator, or the Stately Home-Owner, who could breed dogs indistinguishable from hearth rugs?

What we are getting instead is fancy breeds like the Klub Kennel Klique, the Quarantine Importer and the Shampooing Set and Blow Specialist. Frankly, I shudder at some of the examples I see around me. I am not even sure that old fighting breeds like the Cotswold Colonel are still capable of the tasks for which they were bred, and it grieves me to see them combing dogs when they should be out battling with Afghan tribesmen.

Yours,

"Adorning the Upper Cruft", The Independent

Terence Brady

The more I see of dog shows, the less I like people. I'm not talking Cruft's here. I'm talking local. And rural. And small. They can be quite unnerving experiences as I discovered. I was invited to adjudicate in "The-Dog-You'd-Most-Like-To-Take-Home-With-You" class recently at one of our friendly neighbourhood canine expos, and since the risk content appeared low if not indeed non-existent, I accepted. Shows just how wrong you can be. I got savaged.

And not by a dog either. Nor by an owner. By several owners. All the proud proprietors of Dogs-You'd-Most-Like-To-Take-Home-

With-You. And they weren't kidding. Two middle-aged ladies of indeterminate sex, who are usually to be found arranging the flowers in the Church, gave me a public and extremely abusive dressing down for passing over their most unappealing pug. A hitherto quite amenable ex-military gentleman now blatantly turns his back on me in the snug of The Mason's Codpiece the moment I have bought him his gin and tonic for ignoring his rickety and foul-breathed whippet.

Worst of all, I receive regular anonymous hate mail from the little old lady down the road in Thistle Cottage who looks like Mrs Tiggywinkle. I know the letters are from her because she signs them Yours anonymously, Miss Ada Woolridge, Thistle Cottage. Apparently she will never forgive me till her dying day for failing to call into the final line-up her aging and toothless dachshund, who rumour unkindly has it is in fact not a dog at all but a stoat.

But as anyone who has ever adjudicated knows only too well, the business of amateur arbitration more often than not veers inevitably towards the subjective. So the fact that I gave the Blue Ribbon in the class to the lookalike of my own first and beloved of canine companions, a sort of sheepdog thing, all hair, George Robey eyebrows, size ten and a half paws, and straight off the Walt Disney drawing board, should come as no great surprise to anyone. Particularly to anyone who had known Bobby.

Bobby was a Catalan Sheepdog, and came into my existence when I was a boy. Such was the power of his personality that he has coloured my judgment of canines ever since. Indeed, my childish affection for him ran so deep that, eschewing the inevitable derision of my sporting childhood chums, I was even prepared to take up knitting for his sake.

You see, in those days even the most modest of family saloons often had what is now classed as a Desirable Executive Extra, namely leather upholstery. And owing to my new four-footed friend's propensity for turning cartwheels every time we were out driving and he saw another dog, let alone a cat or, heaven forbid, worst of all, a horse, my father had forbidden him further transportation *en voiture*.

In order to bypass this prohibition, instead of fishing or footballing I spent long days knitting a double set of drawstring blue woollen bootees, mostly in plain, but with the odd purl thrown in now and then for good measure. It was worth the ridicule of the locker room to see Rover restored to the back of the Rover.

He had other faults, unfortunately, his main vice being the organization of canine orgies. In other words, he was a pimp, and although he attempted to use trainspotting as a cover for his unsalutary activity, it didn't fool anybody. When he hared off after a O-6-o side tank J72 Goods, we all knew the pursuit was spurious, and the real game lay much further afield. Sure enough, a day or so later he'd be handed over to the local fuzz, having been recaptured in some distant farmyard, exhausted but happy and accompanied by the cream of the neighbourhood riffraff. The dog would then be bailed out, taken home and put in the slam to do a few hours' solitary. This, interestingly enough, was how we came to discover that, apart from being a pimp, he was also a pianist.

He'd kept this particular light well hidden under his bushel, and only chose to reveal it upon release from a longer than usual spell in solitary, brought about by a longer than usual spell AWOL. When his cell door finally swung open, and having bounded out and turned his usual half dozen overjoyed somersaults, he suddenly made for the joanna, leapt up on the stool and began to extemporize. It wasn't exactly Mozart. But then Mozart wasn't exactly a sheepdog. Seeing the sensation it caused, it soon became a regular habit. Subsequently, you had only to open the piano lid, and he'd be up there at the keyboard busking away. He had one hell of a repertoire, too. That dog never played the same tune twice.

None of us knew from whence his extensive musical knowledge sprang. He may well have got it from some of the books he so avidly devoured, because after a session at the keyboard there was nothing he enjoyed more, leaving aside farmyard saturnalia, than a good book. He'd wander into the study, take down some leather-bound volume, and eat it. This resulted in further spells in the cooler, and a lifelong ban from the family reading room. But this was no usual canine. This wasn't a dog to be denied. Thereafter he simply drew any books he required from the mobile library.

He was a very positive sort of person, and like all positive people, encouraged positive reactions. You either loved him, or were completely dotty about him. He was the sort of friend you never make once you're grown up, because once you're grown up you stop making that sort of friend.

Sometimes, after a perfect day out fishing together, or a summer's evening jointly spent chasing rabbits back to their warrens. I used to wish he could talk so that we could chew over the day's events together. But whenever I mentioned this to him, he used to give me a look of such extraordinary pity that even I, boy that I was, realized that the reason that dogs don't speak is because it's totally unnecessary for them to do so.

He's long gone now, of course, up there somewhere in the blue yonder chasing an intergalactic express no doubt, or trying to work out the proper fingering for Bach's Prelude in C sharp major. But once bitten . . .

So now, as I write, at my feet lies my latest Bobby lookalike, an Almost Bearded Collie named PG, after Wodehouse. He too is something special. He doesn't chase trains. PG chases other dogs. When we lived in London, taking him for a walk was about as much fun as a winter break in Cambodia. It finally got so bad I had to exercise him at times when I knew sane dog owners – and by that I mean dog owners who own sane dogs – were fast in their houses, namely in the middle of Force Ten hailstorms, or around 0400 hours.

I was forced to adopt this ambulatory routine after he severely jeopardized my career. In the early days, before he savaged his first chihuahua, I used to walkie him during normal walkie hours in Richmond Park. One fine spring morning, when my head was full of other things and PG was chasing squirrels and trying to work out why God hadn't given him the ability to climb trees, I chanced upon a friend and neighbour who also happened to be a rather important television factotum for whom I was writing a projected television comedy series. We stood and chatted about this and that for a while, and too late I suddenly realized he was also walkieing his dog. And it was the sort of dog which, next to Chows, is top of PG's hit list, viz. a Poodle.

Neither of us saw the actual moment of impact because my dog came for his out of the sun, like a Spitfire dropping on a Fokker, which I think was one of the things my TV producer friend called my dog as we tried vainly to separate them.

But PG had the poodle by the ear and was swinging him round his head like a rag doll. It wasn't until the TV producer started attacking me that the dog let go of the poodle and began attacking the TV producer. And he wouldn't let go of him until the Park

Police arrived with an Alsatian, which PG promptly seized by the throat. And which he wouldn't let go until the policeman attacked me. We'd probably all still be there now if someone hadn't thrown a bucket of water over us.

All told, what with vet's bills, and tailor's bills, and lawyer's fees, and a contribution to the Policeman's Ball, and the fact that I haven't worked for the perforated poodle's owner since, it ended up as a rather expensive walkie. Which is why today, whenever I go walking and PG attacks anything, I give my name as Tom Stoppard.

"Bobby's Main Vice was Orgies", *Living,*

* * *

William Shakespeare

SLENDER. How does your fallow greyhound, sir? I heard say he was outrun on Cotsall.

PAGE. It could not be judged, sir.

SLENDER. You'll not confess, you'll not confess.

SHALLOW. That he will not: 'tis your fault, 'tis your fault. 'Tis a good dog.

PAGE. A cur, sir

SHALLOW. Sir, he's a good dog, and a fair dog; can there be more said?

from *The Merry Wives of Windsor,* 1602

Sir Walter Scott

'Twas when fleet Snowball's head was grey,
A luckless lev'ret met him on his way;
Who knows not Snowball? He whose race renowned
Is still victorious on each coursing ground:
Swaffham, Newmarket and the Roman Camp
Have seen them victors o'er each meaner stamp.

"Snowball"

Anonymous

In a field near the Welsh Harp, at Hendon, a course has, in fact, already been laid off for hunting an "artificial hare". For distance of 400 yards in a straight line a rail has been laid down in the grass. It is traversed through its whole length by a groove, in which runs an apparatus like a skate on wheels. On this sort of shuttle is mounted the "artificial hare". It is made to travel along the ground at any required pace, and so naturally to resemble the living animal that it is eagerly pursued by Greyhounds. On Saturday afternoon, at half past three o'clock, a trial was made of the new mechanical arrangement. A considerable number of persons were present.

The whole scene was that presented by a race-course. The rail, over which the sham hare runs, is hid in the grass, and the windlass by which the apparatus is moved does not catch the eye of the spectator. When the hour came all that was seen was the "artificial hare" bounding out, quite naturally, like the real animal from its bag, followed at once by the hounds like so many kittens after a cork. It was amusing to watch the eager Greyhounds in their headlong race, striving in vain with all their might to overtake the phantom hare, which a touch of the windlass could send spinning like a shadow out of their reach. This new sport is undoubtedly an exciting and interesting one.

"Coursing by Proxy", *The Times*, 11 September 1876

Ellangowan (pseud.)

"Country-side coursing matches" have always been popular in Scotland, and in far-away places neighbours for miles around go to look on, harvest being over and care banished for a time. On such occasions laird and tenant meet on terms of perfect equality, the best man being the man who for the time has the best dog; and, when a greyhound of one locality is matched against a greyhound of another locality, the interest rises to what may be called a white heat. The sport, however, has this great disadvantage, namely that men can do no more than look on, while the dogs do the work. There are those who call coursing a cruel sport, but there are people who are never satisfied. "Hares apparently were created to be coursed," said Dr Gregory, "and, when killed, to be made into soup."

from *Out-Door Sports in Scotland*, 1890

Jack London

One man stated that his dog could start a sled with five hundred pounds and walk off with it; another bragged six hundred for his dog; and a third, seven hundred.

"Pooh! pooh!" said Thornton; "Buck can start a thousand pounds."

"And break it out! and walk off with it for a hundred yards?" demanded Matthewson, a Bonanza King, he of the seven hundred vaunt.

"And break it out, and walk off with it for hundred yards," John Thornton said coolly.

"Well," Matthewson said, slowly and deliberately, so that all could hear, "I've got a thousand dollars that says he can't. And there it is." So saying, he slammed a sack of gold dust of the size of a bologna sausage down upon the bar.

Nobody spoke. Thornton's bluff, if bluff it was, had been called. He could feel a flush of warm blood creeping up his face. His tongue had tricked him. He did not know whether Buck would start a thousand pounds. Half a ton! The enormousness of it appalled him. He had great faith in Buck's strength and had often thought him capable of starting such a load; but never, as now, had he faced the possibility of it, the eyes of a dozen men fixed upon him, silent and waiting. Further, he had no thousand dollars; nor had Hans or Pete.

"I've got a sled standing outside now, with twenty fifty-pound sacks of flour on it," Matthewson went on with brutal directness; "so don't let that hinder you."

Thornton did not reply. He did not know what to say. He glanced from face to face in the absent way of a man who has lost the power of thought and is seeking somewhere to find the thing that will start it going again. The face of Jim O'Brien, a Mastodon King and an old-time comrade, caught his eyes. It was as a cue to him, seeming to rouse him to do what he would never have dreamed of doing.

"Can you lend me a thousand?" he asked, almost in a whisper.

"Sure," answered O'Brien, thumping down a plethoric sack by the side of Matthewson's. "Though it's little faith I'm having, John, that the beast can do the trick."

The Eldorado emptied its occupants into the street to see the test. The tables deserted, and the dealers and gamekeepers came forth to see the outcome of the wager and to lay odds. Several hundred men, furred and mittened, banked around the sled within easy distance. Matthewson's sled, loaded with a thousand pounds of flour, had been standing for a couple of hours, and in the intense cold (it was sixty below zero) the runners had frozen fast to the hard packed snow. Men offered odds of two to one that Buck could not budge the sled. A quibble arose concerning the phrase "break out." O'Brien contended it was Thornton's privilege to knock the runners loose, leaving Buck to "break it out" from a dead standstill. Matthewson insisted that the phrase included breaking the runners from the frozen grip of the snow. A majority of the men who had witnessed the making of the bet decided in his favour, whereat the odds went up to three to one against Buck.

There were no takers. Not a man believed him capable of the feat. Thornton had been hurried into the wager, heavy with doubt; and now that he looked at the sled itself, the concrete fact, with the regular team of dogs curled up in the snow before it, the more impossible the task appeared. Matthewson waxed jubilant.

"Three to one," he proclaimed. "I'll lay you another thousand at that figure, Thornton. What d'ye say?"

Thornton's doubt was strong in his face, but his fighting spirit was aroused – the fighting spirit that soars above odds, fails to recognize the impossible and is deaf to all save the clamor for battle. He called Hans and Pete to him. Their sacks were slim, and with his own, the three partners could rake together only two hundred dollars. In the ebb of their fortunes, this sum was their total capital; yet they laid it unhesitatingly against Matthewson's six hundred.

The team of ten dogs was unhitched, and Buck, with his own harness, was put into the sled. He had caught the contagion of the excitement, and he felt that in some way he must do a great thing for John Thornton. Murmurs of admiration at his splendid appearance went up. He was in perfect condition, without an ounce of super-fluous flesh, and the one hundred and fifty pounds that he weighed were so many pounds of grit and virility. His furry coat shone with the sheen of silk. Down the neck and across the shoulders, his mane, in repose as it was, half bristled and seemed to lift with every movement, as though excess of vigour made each particular hair alive and active. The great breast and heavy forelegs were no more than in proportion with the rest of the body, where the muscles showed in tight rolls underneath the skin. Men felt these muscles and proclaimed them hard as iron, the odds went down to two to one.

"Gad, sir! Gad, sir!" stuttered a member of the latest dynasty, a king of the Skookum Benches. "I offer you eight hundred for him, sir, before the test, sir; eight hundred just as he stands."

Thornton shook his head and stepped to Buck's side.

"You must stand off from him," Matthewson protested. "Free play and plenty of room."

The crowd fell silent; only could be heard the voices of the gamblers vainly offering two to one. Everybody acknowledged Buck a magnificent animal, but twenty fifty-pound sacks of flour bulked too large in their eyes for them to loosen their pouch strings.

Thornton knelt down at Buck's side. He took his head in his two hands and rested cheek to cheek. He did not playfully shake him, as was his wont, or murmur soft love curses; but he whispered in his ear. "As you love me, Buck. As you love me," was what he whispered. Buck whined with suppressed eagerness.

The crowd was watching curiously. The affair was growing mysterious. It seemed like a conjuration. As Thornton got to his feet, Buck seized his mittened hand between his jaws, pressing in with his teeth and releasing slowly, half-reluctantly. It was the answer, in terms, not of speech, but of love. Thornton stepped well back.

"Now, Buck," he said.

Buck tightened the traces, then slacked them for a matter of several inches. It was the way he had learned.

"Gee!" Thornton's voice rang out, sharp in the tense silence.

Buck swung to the right, ending the movement in a plunge that took up the slack and with a sudden jerk arrested his one hundred and fifty pounds. The load quivered, and from under the runners arose a crisp crackling.

"Haw!" Thornton commanded.

Buck duplicated the maneuver, this time to the left. The crackling turned into a snapping, the sled pivoting and the runners slipping and grating several inches to the side. The sled was broken out. Men were holding their breaths, intensely unconscious of the fact.

"Now, MUSH!"

Thornton's command cracked out like a pistol shot. Buck threw himself forward, tightening the traces with a jarring lunge. His whole body was gathered compactly together in the tremendous effort, the muscles writhing and knotting like live things under the silky fur. His great chest was low to the ground, his head forward and down, while his feet were flying like mad, the claws scarring the hard-packed snow in parallel grooves. The sled swayed and trembled, half-started forward. One of his feet slipped, and a man groaned aloud. Then the sled lurched ahead in what appeared a rapid succession of jerks, though it never really came to a dead stop again . . . half an inch . . . an inch . . . two inches . . . The jerks perceptibly diminished; as the sled gained momentum, he caught them up, till it was moving steadily along.

Men gasped and began to breathe again, unaware for a moment they had ceased to breathe. Thornton was running behind, encouraging Buck with short, cheery words. The distance had been measured off, and as he neared the pile of firewood which marked the end of the hundred yards, a cheer began to grow and grow, which burst into a roar as he passed the firewood and halted at command. Every man was tearing himself loose, even Matthewson. Hats and mittens were flying in the air. Men were shaking hands, it did not matter with whom, and bubbling over in a general incoherent babel.

But Thornton fell on his knees beside Buck. Head was against head, and he was shaking him back and forth. Those who hurried up heard him cursing Buck, and he cursed him long and fervently, and softly and lovingly.

"Gad, sir! Gad, sir!" spluttered the Skookum Bench king. "I'll give you a thousand for him, sir, a thousand, sir — twelve hundred, sir."

Thornton rose to his feet. His eyes were wet. The tears were streaming frankly down his cheeks, "Sir," he said to the Skookum Bench King, "no, sir. You can go to hell, sir. It's the best I can do for you, sir."

Buck seized Thornton's hand in his teeth. Thornton shook him back and forth. As though animated by a common impulse, the onlookers drew back to a respectful distance; nor were they again indiscreet enough to interrupt.

from *The Call of the Wild*, 1903

Cecil Day-Lewis

A shepherd stands at one end of the arena.
Five sheep are unpenned at the other. His dog runs out
In a curve to behind them, fetches them straight to the shepherd,
Then drives the flock round a triangular course
Through a couple of gates and back to his master; two
Must be sorted there from the flock, then all five penned.
Gathering, driving away, shedding and penning
Are plain words for the miraculous game.

An abstract game. What can the sheepdog make of such
Simplified terrain? – no hills, dales, bogs, walls, tracks,
Only a quarter-mile plain of grass, dumb crowds
Like crowds on hoardings around it, and behind them
Traffic or mounds of lovers and children playing.
Well, the dog is no landscape-fancier; his whole concern
Is with his master's whistle, and of course
With the flock – sheep are sheep anywhere to him.

The sheep are the chanciest element. Why, for instance,
Go through this gate when there's on either side of it
No wall or hedge but huge and viable space?
Why not eat the grass instead of being pushed around it?
Like blobs of quicksilver on a tilting board
The flock erratically runs, dithers, breaks up,
Is reassembled; their ruling idea is the dog;
And behind the dog, though they know it not yet, is a shepherd.

The shepherd knows that time is of the essence
But haste calamitous. Between dog and sheep

There is always an ideal distance, a perfect angle;
But these are constantly varying, so the man
Should anticipate each move through his dog, his medium.
The shepherd is the brain behind the dog's brain,
But his control of dog, like dog's of sheep,
Is never absolute – that's the beauty of it.

For beautiful it is. The guided missiles,
The black-and-white angels follow each quirk and a jink of
The evasive sheep, play grandmother's steps behind them,
Freeze to the ground, or leap to head off a straggler
Almost before it knows that it wants to stray,
As if radar-controlled. But they are not machines –
You can feel them feeling mastery, doubt, chagrin:
Machines don't frolic when their job is done.

What's needfully done in the solitude of sheep-runs –
Those tough, real tasks – becomes this stylized game,
A demonstration of intuitive wit
Kept natural by the saving grace of error.
To lift, to fetch, to drive, to shear, to pen
Are acts I recognize, with all they mean
Of shepherding the unruly, for a kind of
Controlled woolgathering is my work too.

"Sheepdog trials in Hyde Park", *c.*1960

CHAPTER 13

A Dog's Worth

Puppy farming, however that ignominious term might be defined, is a label designed to blacken breeders. Those whom the label fits deserve to have their names blackened, but it should not be forgotten that their unhappy trade thrives only because of the readiness of the gullible puppy-buying public to pay high prices for badly bred, indifferently reared and often sickly puppies.

Not that commercial dog breeding is anything new. Round about AD 10 Gratius Falicus, about whom little is known, other than that he was a contemporary of Ovid, wrote his *Cynegeticon*, later translated into English by Christopher Wade in 1654.

Gratius showed that international trade in dogs, even nearly 2,000 years ago, was no new thing and there is no doubt but that this trade has helped to develop and modify many breeds, though the nature and extent of the influence may sometimes be exaggerated (See p. 24).

Marcus Terentius Varro

Be careful not to buy dogs from hunters or from butchers, for the dogs of butchers are too idle to follow the flock, while hunting dogs, if they see a hare or stag, will chase after it instead of after the sheep. Thus the best is one that has been bought from shepherds and has been trained to follow sheep or has had no training at all.

from *De Re Rustica, c.* 10 BC

Gratius Faliscus

But can you waft, across the British tide,
And land undangered on the farther side,
O what great gains will certainly rebound,
From a free traffic in the British hound.
Mind not the badness of their forms or face;
That the sole blemish of the generous race,
When the bold game turns back upon the spear,
And all the furies wait upon the war.
First in the fight the whelps of Britain shine,
And snatch Epirus, all the palm from thine.

from Cynegeticon, AD 8

William Harrison

There is no countrie that maie (as I take it) compare with ours, in number, excellencie, and diversitie of dogs. And therefore if Ploycrates of Samia were now alive, he would not send to Epyro for such mercandize: but to his further cost provide them out of Britaine, as an adornament to his countrie, and peece of Husbandrie for his common wealth, which he furnished of set purpose with Molossian and Laconian dogs, as he did the same also with sheepe out of Attica and Miletum, gotes from Scyro and Narus, swine out of Sicilia, and artificiers out of other places. Howbeit the learned doctor Caius in his Latine treatise upon Gesner "De canibus Analicis", bringeth them all into three sorts: that is the gentle kind serving the game: the homelie kind apt for many sundrie uses: and the cuirrish kind meet for many toies. For my part I can say no more of them than he hath done alreadie.

from Description of England, 1577

Earl of Nottingham

You spake unto me for a water spaniel for to send to the French King. I could have sent you sundry ones, but not such a one as I thought fit for you to send till now. But I think I send you one by this bearer, which for beauty and goodness will hardly be believed. His name is Hercules. Your man must have a care of him and tie him in a chain for his only suit is that he wyll sher, because he hath been ever used to go loose.

Letter to Sir Robert Cecil, June 1598

Prestwich Eaton

A good Mastive dogge, a case of bottles replenished with the best lickour, and pray proceur mee two good bulldoggs, and let them be sent by ye first shipp.

Letter to George Wellingham, 1631

Dorothy Osborne

When your father goes into Ireland, lay your commands upon some of his servants to get you an Irish greyhound. I have one that was the General's; but 'tis a bitch, and those are always much less than the dogs. I got it in the time of my favour there, and it was all they had. Henry Cromwell undertook to write to his brother Fleetwood for another for me; but I have lost my hopes there. Whomsoever it is that you employ, he will need no other instructions but to get the biggest he can meet with; 'tis all the beauty of those dogs, or of any kind, I think. A masty is handsomer to me than the most exact little dog that ever lady played withal.

Letter to Sir William Temple, c. 1660

Alexander Pope

A young Bounce is ready for you at my lord Oxford's. The sooner you send for the dog the better; but care must be taken: he can but just lap, and I know your humanity extends to all the creatures that have life.

Letter to Ralph Allen, *c.* 1730

Charles Dickens

"If you'd like to have him, he's at the door. I brought him on purpose for you. He ain't a lady's dog, you know," said Mr Toots, "but you won't mind that, will you?"

In fact, Diogenes was at that moment, as they presently ascertained from looking down into the street, staring through the window of a hackney cabriolet, into which, for conveyance to that spot, he had been ensnared, on a false pretence of rats among the straw. Sooth to say, he was as unlike a lady's dog as a dog might be; and in his gruff anxiety to get out presented an appearance sufficiently unpromising, as he gave short yelps out of one side of his mouth, and overbalancing himself by the intensity of every one of these efforts, tumbled down into the straw, and then sprang panting up again, putting out his tongue, as if he had come express to a dispensary to be examined for his health.

But though Diogenes was as ridiculous a dog as one would meet with on a summer's day; a blundering, ill-favoured, clumsy, bullet-headed dog, continually acting on a wrong idea that there was an enemy in the neighbourhood, whom it was meritorious to bark at: and though he was far from good-tempered, and certainly was not clever, and had hair all over his eyes, and a comic nose, and an inconsistent tail, and a gruff voice; he was dearer to Florence, in virtue of that parting remembrance of him, and that request that he might be taken care of, than the most valuable and beautiful of his kind. So dear, indeed, was this same ugly Diogenes, and so welcome to her, that she took the jewelled hand of Mr Toots and kissed it in gratitude. And when Diogenes, released, came tearing up the stairs and bouncing into the room (such a business as there was first to get him out of the cabriolet!) dived under all the furniture, and wound a long iron chain, that dangled from his neck, round legs of chairs and tables, and then tugged at it until his eyes became unnaturally visible, in consequence of their nearly starting out of his head; and when he growled at Mr Toots, who affected familiarity; and went pell-mell at Towlinson, morally convinced that was the enemy whom he had barked at round the corner all his life and never seen yet; Florence was as pleased with him as if he had been a miracle of discretion.

from *Dombey and Son*, 1846–1848

Henry Mayhew

JACK BLACK

"When I found I was master of the birds, then I turned to my rat business again. I had a little rat dog – a black tan terrier of the name of Billy – which was the greatest stock dog in London of that day. He is the father of the greatest portion of small black tan dogs in London now, which Mr Isaac, the bird-fancier in Princess street, purchased on of the strain for six or seven pounds; which Jimmy Massey afterwards purchased another of the strain for a monkey, a bottle of wine, and three pounds. That was the rummest bargain I ever made.

"I've ris and trained monkey by shoals. Some of mine is about now in shows exhibiting; one in particular – Jimmy.

"One of the strain of this little black tan dog would draw a badger twelve or fourteen lbs. to his six lbs., which was done for a wager, 'cos it was thought the badger had his teeth drawn, but he hadn't, as was proved by his biting Mr P— from Birmingham, for he took a piece clean out of his trousers, which was pretty good proof, and astonished them all in the room.

"I've been offered a sovereign a-pound for some of my little terriers, but it wouldn't pay me at that price, for they weren't heavier than two or three pounds. I once sold one of the dogs, of this same strain, for fourteen pounds, to the Austrian Ambassador. Mrs H the baker's lady, wished to get my strain of terriers, and she gave me five

pounds for the use of him; in fact, my terrier dog was known to all
the London fancy. As rat-killing dogs, there's no equal to that strain
of black tan terriers."

★

The dog-sellers are a sporting trading, idling class. Their sport is now
the rat-hunt, or the ferret-match or the dog-fight: as it was the
predecessors of their stamp, the cock-fight; the bull, bear, and
badger bait; the shrove-tide cock-shy, or the duck hunt. Their
trading spirit is akin to that of the higher-class sporting fraternity, the
trading members of the turf. They love to sell and to bargain, always
with a quiet exultation at the time – a matter of loud tavern boasts
afterwards, perhaps, as respects the street-folk – how they "do" a
customer, or "do" one another. "It's not cheating," as the remark
and the apology of a very famous jockey of the old times, touching
such measures: "it's not cheating, it's outwitting." Perhaps this
expresses the code of honesty of such traders: not to cheat, but to
outwit, to over-reach. Mixed with such traders, however, are found
a few quiet, plodding, fair-dealing men, whom it is difficult to
classify, otherwise than that they are "in the line, just because they
likes it." The idling of these street-sellers is a part of their business.
To walk by the hour up and down a street, and with no manual
labour except to clean their dogs' kennels, and to carry them in their
arms, is but an idleness, although, as some of these men will tell you,
"they work hard at it."

from London Labour and London Poor, 1851

Samuel Butler

The righteous man will enslave his horse and his dog,
Making them serve him for their bare keep and for nothing further,
Shooting them, selling them for vivisection when they can no
    longer profit him,
Backbiting them and beating them if they fail to please him;
For his horse and his dog can bring no action for damages,
Wherefore, then, should he not enslave them, shoot them, sell them
    for vivisection?

from The Righteous Man, 1879

Revd Jack Russell

I will send off the two terrier puppies by train to Charleton tomorrow morning and "hope they will arrive fresh." Take your choice of them, and send on the other to Pat Carnegy with my best wishes to the missus and himself. We hadn't much sport last week at Ivybridge, but the meeting and the dinner were both a great success. I was staying at Delamore, where you were often toasted. Please put a few potatoes into the hamper and send it back – not that I want the hamper, but I do the potatoes.

. . .

Believe me my dear Jack,
Yours affectionately.

Letter to Colonel Jack Thomson, Tuesday, 8 April 1879

Thorstein Veblen

The commercial value of canine monstrosities such as the prevailing styles of pet dogs both for men's and women's use, rests on their high cost of production, and their value to their owners lies chiefly in their utility as items of conspicuous consumption.

from *The Theory of the Leisure Class*, 1899

Anonymous

When the dog men have boarded the steamer, they scatter in all directions – one steering aft to the officers' quarters, another making a bee-line for the cook's galley, and a third one, with surprising alacrity, in spite of his game leg, climbing down into the forecastle – all in search of the dainty Japs. Many of the ship's officers are acquainted with the doggy visitors, and a bargain is quickly struck with them for their living possessions. The case is quite different amidships, where the steward and the cook – two fairly well civilized Chinamen, apparently from the north country – are partners in a trio of Japanese Spaniels, which, judging from their protestations, are the pick of the dogs of the Flowery Kindgom, and represent the sum total of their combined life's savings.

Armed with this knowledge, the visitors, who are able to converse in the "lingo" of the Chinese coast, called Pidgin English, will politely inquire for the price set upon "him doggie," and when the figure is mentioned he is not quite certain of the purpose which brought him aboard, but his general impressions will be that he has been invited to purchase the entire steamship line, with the docking-privileges and water-rights thrown in. He promptly declines to make a counter offer, with a polite "you speak." When mentioning a figure – by the way, about one-half of what the dog man is prepared to pay for the dogs – this is generally followed by polite shrugs and bows, and a request to "speak again." The haggling is now on in earnest, the merits of the "man dogs" and the "woman dogs" thoroughly demonstrated, and the visitor finally emerges from the galley the owner of the three "priceless beauties." He has paid his earnest money on his purchases, and has been requested to bring the balance in gold. It seems that all Chinamen prefer gold, as they can exchange American gold to greater advantage at home, than bills.

from *Dogs In America,* 1909

Mrs Lesmoir-Gordon

There are few occupations in which the advance of the times is more clearly shown than in that of dog-dealing, which has now risen to the height of one of the fine arts. It used in bygone days to be considered a business somewhat lacking in artistic refinement, generally redolent, linked indissolubly with short black pipes, neck-mufflers, and hoarseness, and a with a local habitation some-where in Seven Dials. Rat matches were an allied feature of dog dealing in those distant days, and the value of the dog depended not at all on its pedigree, of which it had little, or its beauty, of which it had less, but upon its record of rats, and trade was brisk or the reverse according to whether the dog killed his 100 rats in 5½ minutes or failed to beat another dog at the gentle sport owing to his time handicap.

Hard bitten champions of pit encounters – fighting dogs as to whose ownership there were "no questions asked" – these were what were required of the dog merchant of old days; and if the London dealers of about 60 years ago had been permitted a vision of 1910 dog dealing and its conditions they would have disbelieved their eyes. No clay pipes, no pot boys, no fusty straw, no crowded pens, no cellars full of darkness and dogs. Instead, Regent Street, a picture-adorned shop, and business in two minutes on the telephone: incredible!

And the shock to them might have proved fatal to learn that a lady could start a dog bureau, could turn dog dealer with perfect calm, and could not only organise such an innovation without loss of dignity, but actually enjoy the opportunity of employing her energies in a shop of her own, in which the "stock" was of such congenial kind as dogs. "C'est le progrès?"

The Entente Cordiale Bureau is one of the latest advances of woman's enterprise, and Mrs Lesmoir-Gordon, who lived in America until her marriage, and has travelled widely, has the satisfaction of starting a new profession for ladies, one in which not even America, that pioneer of new enterprises, has as yet come to the front. And modernity is the keynote of the whole establishment at 289 Regent Street.

*

There are many entertaining incidents that arise in connection with dog shops, apart from the people who always come in and ask with an air of profound wisdom for quite non-existent breeds. On one occasion a man came in and bought every dog in the place, and ordered twenty more. All were to be sent that night to his hotel; but, as enquiries at the said hotel showed there was "no sich person", he was presumably a canomaniac.

Then there was a lady who brought in two fox cubs with the request that they might be placed in the window, which was done, but the cubs jumped over the partitions and cleared the whole shop out!

And, finally, there was the young lady who brought in her dog to have roller skates fitted for him. She said the dog could dance and she had no doubt he would learn to skate, especially as she and all the rest of the family were mad on rinking.

from "Methods of a Modern Dog Dealer", *The Kennel*, 1910

Judith Anne Lytton, Baroness Wentworth

There is no reason why dog dealers should not be honest, and my experience of the poorer dealers is, that they are far more so than those that are well to do. The worst kind of dog dealer is the "lady" dealer, who pretends to be what she is not. Kennels that buy up all the cheap stuff that is to be had, and whose premises are always full of new dogs, are inevitably always contaminated by mange and distemper. Anyone who has tried the experiment of constantly buying new dogs even with the most careful isolation will know what I say is true. These people will never have their show dogs in good coat and always have some excuse ready. The bitches have always just whelped, and the dogs are always just changing their coats.

Therefore beware of buying from big kennels unless you have been all over them yourself, and verified that the dogs are in first-class condition. If this is so you may be sure that the owner is a bona fide breeder and not a dealer only, and my advice is to buy from a bona fide breeder or from a small dealer, never from a big dealer, unless his dogs stand the test above mentioned.

from *Toy Dogs and their Ancestors*, 1911

James Watson

My connection with the Chihuahua began in the spring of 1888, when I made my first judging trip to the Coast. I had stopped of at El Paso so as to cross the river and say I had been in Mexico. As I was awaiting the arrival of the train for the West, I saw a Mexican standing with a very small dog in his hand. I knew enough Spanish to ask him "How much?" He replied $5, and as I was pulling out the money another man rushed up and advised me that he could speak English, so I amusedly said, "Ask him if he will take $4." After a most animated conversation I was advised that he would take $3. That purchase rankled on my conscience for many years, and not until I had confided in a doggy Father of the church and he said I was justified in paying the $3, did the matter settle in my mind.

from "The Chihuahua Dog", *Country Life in America*, March 1914

Sir Hugh Walpole

Having no children, Isabelle thought that it would be pleasant to have a dog. Many of her lady friends had them. There were, in fact, far more hospitals for dogs in Beverly and Hollywood than for human beings. And everybody said that the dog hospitals were so perfectly run that it was worth having a dog just for that reason alone. Isabelle wanted a dog, but there were problems to be settled. She understood that unless you had it as a puppy, it never became really fond of you. On the other hand, puppies had to be trained, and one's beautiful rugs and carpets suffered in the process. Then, what kind of dog should she have? There were the darling Cockers, the adorable Scotch Terriers, the amusing Dachshunds and the great big splendid Setters and Airedales. Some very lonely women had Pekingese, and then there were French Bulldogs. She couldn't make up her mind and used to ask William which sort he preferred. And William, while he was trying to guess what she wanted him to say, would look at her with that slow, puzzling stare, which Isabelle always interpreted as a tribute of gratified recognition of her brilliance and beauty.

from *Having No Hearts, c.* 1935

Elizabeth, Countess von Arnim

I recommend those persons of either sex, but chiefly, it would seem of mine, whose courage is inclined to fail them if they are long alone, who are frightened in the evenings if there is nobody to speak to, who don't like putting out their own lights and climbing silently to a solitary bedroom, who are full of affection and have nothing to fasten it on to, who long to be loved, and, for whatever reason, aren't – I would recommend all such to go, say, to Harrods, and buy a dog. There, in eager rows, they will find a choice of friends, only waiting to be given a chance of cheering and protecting. Asking nothing in return, either, and, whatever happens, never going to complain, never going to be cross, never going to judge, and against whom no sin committed will be too great for immediate and joyful forgiveness.

from *All the Dogs of my Life,* 1936

Thomas Thompson

Sam Ingham, and Gladys his wife, first saw the pup in a kind of box-cum-cage outside a household pets shop, and it looked so much like a pretty snowball that Gladys said, "Eee!" and Sam said, "What's to do?"

"Look at that lovely pup," said Gladys.

"It's more like a mop-rag," said Sam.

"Buy it, Sam," said Gladys. "Ah've allus longed for a pet."

"Well," said Sam, "tha's getten me."

"Ah – but," said Gladys. "Ah mean a proper un."

"If yo're thinkin o' buyin that pup," said the shopkeeper, who had just come to see what it was all about, "yo're good judges – that's all Ah con say at present."

"Has it a pedigree?" asked Sam cautiously.

"Well – look at it," said the shopkeeper. "Hasn't it breed written all ower it?"

"There isn't mich on it," said Sam.

"What there is is good," said the shopkeeper. "Th' chap as sowd it me said its gron' feythor wor Simon o' Sheffield."

"If Simon wor owt like my gron'feythor he're nowt to be proud on," said Sam.

"Ah never knew my gron'feythor," said Gladys.

"Tha happen missed nowt," said Sam. "Ah reckon nowt o' ancestry. Deeper tha digs an' more they stink."

"Pups is different," said the shopkeeper. "Breed will tell."

"What breed is it?" asked Sam.

"Happen it's too early to tell," said Gladys. "An' Ah dunnot care what bred it is if it'll tent th' door."

Just then the pup wakened up and tried to sit on its hind legs, but couldn't just manage it.

"Aw . . . look at it," said Gladys. "Aw . . . buy it, Sam."

"How mich dosta want for it?" asked Sam.

"Seven an' six," said the dealer.

"Lemme look at its pedigree," said Sam.

"It had one," said the dealer, "but it etten it."

"It etten it?" asked Sam incredulously.

"Aye," said the dealer, "it etten it."

"There wor some carelessness somewhere," said Sam, "or else it couldn't ha' etten it."

"It pedigree wor on the table, an' our little Charley poked it through th' bars," said the dealer, "an' th' pup etten it. Its pedigree's theer all reet."

"But what mun Ah do if anybody wants to see its pedigree?" asked Sam.

"Tell 'em it etten it," said Gladys.

"They'll not believe me," said Sam, "Ah connot reckon to oppen th' pup to show its pedigree."

"Ah'll tell thee what Ah'll do," said the dealer, "Ah'll let thee have it for five shillin', pedigree or no pedigree. That's nobbut mongrel price."

"Ah'll gi' thee five bob," said Sam. "But Ah'd sooner its pedigree wor outside."

"It'll not be a big dog, mesthor?" asked Gladys.

"Them soart never gets big," said the dealer. "Wilta have it i' thi' big pocket?"

"Naw," said Sam. "Ah've getten a brown loaf in mi big pocket."

"Ah'll carry it in mi shoppin basket," said Gladys.

When they got the pup home they lined a small basket with the remains of a cotton blanket. The pup rolled into the bottom and promptly fell asleep.

"Aw . . . just look at it," said Gladys. "Isn't it bonny?"

"Ah wish it hadn't etten its pedigree," said Sam.

"Give o'er mitherin about its pedigree," said Gladys impatiently. "As long as it geet here, what's it matter?"

"Tha connot show it bout pedigree," said Sam.

"It's a bonny little thing," said Gladys.

A month after it was still a bonny little thing, but not as little as it was. Two months later its size was disturbing, and at the end of seven months the pup could rest its chin on the table.

"Ah thowt it wor a Pekinese when Ah bowt it," said Sam. "Ah wor mistakken."

"It isn't a Pekinese," said Gladys.

"Tha sees what it is to get a pedigree wi' 'em," said Sam. "If Ah'd ha' sen its pedigree when Ah bowt it Ah shouldn't ha' bowt it."

"What breed would tha say it wor?" asked Gladys.

"Tha'rt axin' me summat," said Sam. "There doesn't seem to be mich in th' breed line as is left out. Its ears is Alsatian, its back legs is Airedale. Ah should say its nose is Irish. Its back is . . . tha could give a lecther on th' damn pup. Tha could show it in ony class."

"Ah wanted one Ah could dad on mi knee," said Gladys.

"Ah'll tak' it back an' see what he says about it," said Sam in sudden indignation. "Ah think he's chetted us. He towd us it wouldn't grow big."

So Sam allowed the giant pup to tug him round to the dealer's. That worthy was smoking a pipe at the door.

"Heigh, thee!" said Sam. "This is that pup as tha sowd us."

"It's thrivin'," said the dealer.

"Thrivin' 'ell," said Sam crisply. "It shifts more for its dinner nor me an' th' wife put together."

"That shows it's healthy," said the dealer.

"Ah'd like to sell it thee back," said Sam.

"Ah couldn't do that," said the dealer. "Ah only buy pups. Ah haven't room for grown dogs."

"Tha could keep it in th' Drill Hall," said Sam. "Tha said it wouldn't grow big."

"Tha connot allus tell when they're little," said the dealer. "It's surprisin' how they turn out, some on 'em. It's like puttin' a seed in th' ground an' it comes up a margowd."

"Aye," said Sam. "An' this un's come up a ruddy sunflower."

"Tha connot have it every road," said the dealer. "Ah bet that dog's a rare ratter."

"That's wheer tha'rt wrong," said Sam. "It runs out o' th' road o' a mouse. It's neither a pet nor a hunter. It wags it tail at tramps an' hawkers. An' if it goes in a puddle it doesn't shake until it gets whoam."

"Tha connot guarantee 'em, tha knows," said the dealer. "It had a pedigree when it come here."

"Ah'd ha' gaen summat to ha' seen it," said Sam. "That theer dog has a bit in it o' all th' twelve lost tribes o' Israel. A pedigree o' that dog'd look like a photygraph o' th' front-line trenches."

"They breed back a bit some times," admitted the dealer.

"Well, look at it," said Sam. "It's grown while Ah've been stonnin' here."

"Ah'll tell thee what Ah'm prepared to do," said the dealer. "If Ah con find thee a customer Ah will. Ah connot say fairer nor that."

"Tha con tell him it'd make a good chain-horse," said Sam. "If we could train it to bat th' carpets wi' its tail it'd be worth summat to us."

"When tha buys a litter o' pups tha con never swear how they'll turn out," said the dealer contemplatively. "If somebody let that pup's grondmother out when they shouldn't ha' done it might come out even unto th' third an' fourth generation."

"Ah think its mother had a neet out too," said Sam.

"Ah once bowt a pup for a red setter an' it turned out a Dalmatian," said the dealer.

"One of them curran'-puddin' dogs?" asked Sam.

"It's as thrue as Ah'm stonnin' here," asserted the dealer.

"Ah wouldn't ha' cared, but we kessumed it Tiny," said Sam. "It'll answer to nowt else."

"Is it obaydeyant?" asked the dealer.

"Aye," said Sam. "We con make it do owt it wants."

"What dun yo' feed it on?" asked the dealer. "Yo're happen feedin' it wrong."

"It'll eat owt," said Sam. "It's etten th' basket it should sleep in, an' th' blanket too. It's etten th' hond broosh at side o' th' fireplace, and it'd getten hawf o' th' clooas-line down when th' missus poo'ed it back. It refuses nowt."

"Ah dunnot like 'em to tickle about their meat," said the dealer.

"Ah dunnot like 'em tickle misel'," said Sam. "But there's a mite o' difference between bein' tickle and shiftin' hawf o' th' doormat."

"Ah'll bet tha could train that dog to a gun," said the dealer.

"Tha could train it to a cannon," said Sam. "Tha'll ha' to have it back."

"Ah couldn't do that," said the dealer.

"If tha doesn't Ah'll set it on thee," said Sam. "It worried two cats last neet. See 'im off, Tiny."

Tiny bared a couple of tusks and imitated the rumble of a train.

"Ah'm prepared to allow thee discount," said the dealer. "Ah'll knock thee a shillin' off . . . or tha con have a pup chucked in."

"One as 'as etten its pedigree?" asked Sam sarcastically. "Ah'm havin' no more pups fro' thee. Ah'll swap thee this dog back again for a globe o' gowdfeesh. Them'll none jump on mi bed th' fust thing in a mornin'."

"Ah couldn't do that," said the dealer.

"Seck 'im, Tiny," said Sam.

Tiny "secked 'im" until the leash threatened to break.

"Tie 'im up theer," said the dealer, "an pick thi' gowdfeesh."

"Ah'll ha' that lot," said Sam. "What dun yo' feed 'em wi'?"

"Ants' eggs," said the dealer.

"Uncle to thee," said Sam. "Ah'll set it at thee again if tha starts thi' anky-panky wi' me."

"These is 'em," said the dealer. "Fourpence a packet."

"Ah thowt tha wor pooin' mi leg," said Sam. "Anyhow, Ah'm fain they dunnot eat pedigrees, or else there might be another Jonah do at our house."

So Sam made his way home with his bowl of goldfish, with the despairing howls of Tiny growing fainter and fainter in his ears.

"What's tha done wi' Tiny?" asked Gladys.

"Ah've swapped 'im for these gowdfeesh," said Sam.

"What good are they?" asked Gladys. "Con we eat 'em?"

"They look nice in th' window," said Sam.

"Ah'd sooner 'ave a aspidistra," said Gladys.

"It's allus wrong so what Ah do," said Sam. "Ah getten shut o' Tiny ony road."

"Ah's miss him," said Gladys. "'E met me wi' a smile every time Ah come in."

"'E met me like a troop o' cavalry," said Sam. "Ah con manage very weel bout 'im meetin' me."

"Ah weesh tha hadn't left 'im," said Gladys. "Ah'd just getten used to 'im."

"Wheer could we ha' kept 'im if he'd grown ony more?" asked Sam. "It wor like keepin' a camel."

"Th' house'll not be th' same," said Gladys.

"Ah'm gooin' a 'avin a gill," said Sam in disgust.

He donned his billycock and opened the door. The next moment he was on his back in the lobby and Tiny was over him to lick the outstretched hands of Gladys.

"He's come back, Sam," said Gladys. "An' we'n getten the gowdfeesh an' o'."

Sam raised himself from the floor, picked up his billycock, and rattled the ribs of the yelping Tiny as the dog dashed through the door of the front room.

"Ah'll murder it," said Sam.

"Tha'll do nowt o' th' soart," said Gladys. "It didn't mean owt by it."

When they both went into the front room Tiny was sitting there on the hearthrug with a seraphic smile on its face, and its tail wagging genially.

"It looks as though butter wouldn't melt in its mouth," said Gladys.

"Wheer's th' gowdfeesh?" asked Sam. "It's etten th' gowdfeesh . . . an' it's supped th' watter."

"Eee! Tha nowty dog," said Glayds.

"Tha nowty dog," mimicked Sam. "If it eat mi arm up to mi elbow tha'd pat its head an' say 'tha nowty dog'."

"It must ha' been hungry," said Gladys.

"It wor," said Sam. "It allus is. Tha could feed that dog all day an' it'd be lookin' at thee wi' its een comin' out o' its head, an' its tongue lollin' about like a big red bowster. Tha has to stoke that dog, not feed it."

"It doesn't eat that mich, Sam," said Gladys.

"It etten mi gowdfeesh," said Sam, "an' it etten its pedigree."

"Ah wonder what made it eat its pedigree?" asked Gladys.

"Ah expect it'd read it," said Sam. "It meant keepin' it dark."

from The Pedigree Pup. c. 1948

Bob Merrill

How much is that doggie in the window?
The one with the waggly tail.
How much is that doggie in the window?
I do hope that dog is for sale.

How much is that doggie in the window?
Song, 1953

Kathleen Szasz

The fact that Americans spend five to six billion dollars a year on their pets and the British well over £100 million, that there are 8 million dogs and cats in West Germany and 16½ million in France, can be, and often is, ascribed to affluence and one of its side-effects, leisure. It may be due to modern methods of advertising that the pet trade and industry record an annual increase of 15 per cent in their turnover and that the circulation of pet magazines and the number of pet books published attain astronomical figures. However, before trade, industry, advertising and publishing discovered this new and highly profitable market and threw themselves wholeheartedly into exploiting it and creating new needs, the basic need, man's growing dependence on pet animals as an emotional crutch, was already there.

This basic need springs from the same frustrations that drive man to the psychoanalyst's couch, to indiscriminate sex, to alcohol, drugs and crime. From an alienation from himself and from society he can no longer control or even understand, from the mental agony of loneliness, from deracination and from the anonymity of urban living, from his feeling of inadequacy in a world that demands a moral flexibility and intellectual alertness of which few are capable. And, last but not least, from the breakdown of human communication.

from *Petishism: Pet Cults of the Western World*, 1968

Frank Jackson

FOR SALE: ILL HEALTH OBLIGES ME TO PART WITH LOVELY, WELL-BRED 14 MONTH OLD BITCH. COULD GO TO THE TOP. GOOD HOME MORE IMPORTANT THAN PRICE ALSO DUE TO CANCELLED EXPORT ORDER QUALITY PUPPY AVAILABLE.
Apply: Miss D. Crummock
Rose Cottage, Penny Way.

Dear Madam,

I have been looking for a good show and breeding bitch at a price within my means for some time now. I would be obliged if you could supply me with further information about the bitch recently advertised. If details are satisfactory and the price is right I would be free to inspect her at the end of the month.

Yours faithfully,
Capt. J. A. H. McGregor
Sebastopol, East Cheam Lane.

Dear Captain McGregor,

Thank you for your kind enquiry. There are so many enquiries for dear Rosy; my wretched health just will not permit me to show her and that would be such a loss to the breed, she is so lovely. I am enclosing a copy of her pedigree and one of my snapshots of her which sadly does not do her justice. The puppy in the photograph is hers and very promising but I fear I will have to part with her too. My health really won't allow me to show her. I am asking 250 gns for the bitch but could possibly let her puppy go even more cheaply especially to someone like yourself who could do justice to her, it would be such a joy to see her in the ring and well worth the sacrifice. I wonder if you know my dear friend Colonel Bagwash who is one of Rosy's greatest admirers.

Yours sincerely,
D. Crummock (Miss)
Rose Cottage, Penny Way.

Dear Madam,

I fear the price you ask is well beyond my means, however, I spoke to Colonel Bagwash in the club on Friday and he strongly advises that I direct my attention towards the pup which is, I believe, by his dog. Would you kindly let me know precisely what price you are asking for the pup?

Yours faithfully,
Capt. J. A. H. McGregor
Sebastopol, East Cheam Lane.

Dear Mrs Fox-Willoughby.

Thank you for your charming latter. I've had so many enquiries for my darling Rosy and all from such lovely homes, Colonel Bagwash has a friend who absolutely insists on having her but seems to want her for nothing and I do think it is a mistake to give dogs away. One can't be too careful, I would only ask you for £250 for her and shall be losing money I can ill afford but it would be such a comfort to know she was with you. I am enclosing a pedigree and a photograph of her father who is a champion and who she much resembles. My studio portraits are with Colonel Bagwash's friend.

Yours very truly,
Davinia Crummock
Rose Cottage,
Penny Way.

Dear Miss Crummock.

I received your letter when I returned from a few days in Capri to find the whole place in an uproar, one can't rely on staff these days I'm afraid. Rosy sounds delightful and I'm sure would be very happy with me but I'm afraid that since my husband is no longer with me I couldn't possibly pay more than £100 and would need to have a vet's opinion of her. Could you tell me why she has not been shown? I do hope she is on the Active Register (though I know how terribly difficult that is these days, the trouble I have had). It would be possible for me to come to see Rosy on Sunday or subject to conditions being acceptable, you could put her on the 11. 10 train on Friday.

Sincerely yours,
Hernia Fox-Willoughby
The Manor,
Fosse Lane.

Dear Hernia,

I was so pleased to speak to you last night. I have been so worried about Rosy and it is such a relief to know that she is to have such a wonderful home. The Americans are anxious to have her but Rosy's happiness must come before my financial problems. She is so very spirited I have been afraid my poor back would not stand the strain if I showed her. The vet thought Rosy was a little thin but I think the poor dear is pining because of my unhappiness at the thought of parting but as you know life is full of partings and I must be strong. If I receive your cheque for £150 on Friday I will put Rosy on the 11.10 train, I just know you will love one another.

Truly,
Davinia
Rose Cottage,
Penny Way.

Dear Davinia.

You are being so very brave about Rosy. I have been working at her pedigree and am very excited. My cheque for £150.50 is enclosed, please do not present it before the weekend, I assume your price includes transport and vets fees.

Sincerely,
Hernia
The Manor,
Fosse Lane.

Dear Captain McGregor,

I am so pleased to know you are such a friend of the dear Colonel's. I do hate dealing with strangers and a mutual friend makes me feel that we too are friends. It is so wonderful to have such people looking after our interests at the Kennel Club. So very many people have been trying to buy Rosy both at home and abroad it has all been such a terrible strain. She is now going to a lovely home and at such a generous price. It would have been hateful to have let her go abroad. Her puppy is not the Colonel's dog. I had to let them all go because they were so boisterous and rather coarse, so unlike my dear Rosy. The puppy, Daisy, is by my dear friend Lady Smedley's young dog which she was anxious to mate to Rosy, and Rosy so loves her puppies. I would like £200 for the puppy, it would be most unfair to

Lady Smedley to let it go for less. I wonder, Captain. if you could use your influence at the Kennel Club to get some Registrations done for me quickly, it is so difficult when one is alone.

Yours very sincerely,
Davinia Crummock
Rose Cottage,
Penny Way.

My Dear Hernia,

Rosy has gone but her empty bed is here to reproach me. I received your cheque and have asked the vet to send his account direct to you. I had to go shopping on Friday morning so that I would not see her go. I forgot to tell you that Colonel McGregor, a friend of dear Lady Smedley's offered me a great price for Rosy and I had to refuse another from America so felt that she was destined to come to you.

Truly,
Davinia
Rose Cottage,
Penny Way.

Dear Miss Crummock.

I did not realize you were a friend of Lady Smedley's. I had the honour of serving with her late husband, but have not met Lady Smedley. I wonder if you could arrange an introduction so that I could see the pup's sire. The pup sounds ideal for my purpose. However I could not pay more than £100 and that only because she is so highly recommended. If this is acceptable to you I propose to inspect her on Friday when I shall be in the area prior to visiting Major Harrington who is, I believe, a near neighbour of Lady Smedley. If you let me have your registration applications I will get them processed when I am next in the Club.

Yours sincerely,
J. A. Horace McGregor
Sebastopol,
East Cheam Lane.

Dear Miss Crummock,

I met the bitch at the station and was surprised how very different she is from her father, she is so small and thin. At home I put her in a kennel with a lovely, sweet bitch, one of my own breeding and so very valuable. When I returned to my horror I found that your animal had savagely attacked my Dinkums and the vet now fears for her life. I telephoned Sebastian Bagwash who says that if the bitch is the same one Mr Green gave to you she has always had a reputation for savagery and could not be shown for that reason. He told me his dog is still reluctant to mate bitches after yours had attacked him. When I showed the bitch to my vet he was appalled at her condition and when he examined her found a fearful Caesarean scar under all the matted hair. Until your last letter you had not said she had been bred from and now I find she has had two litters in six months both needing a Caesarean. I had hoped to let her have a family just for the joy of the experience but I cannot do that now and my husband's solicitors are being difficult about my accounts. You have used me most harshly and I must insist that you take the bitch back and return my cheque.

Yours sincerely,
J. H. Fox-Willoughby,
Manor Kennels,
Fosse Lane.

Dear Mrs Fox-Willoughby,

It was such a shock to receive your letter and as you know my heart is not strong. I do not see how you can hold me responsible if your bitch does not get on with darling Rosy. I told you she was spirited but that is just youthful playfulness and shows that she is in good condition, in spite of your innuendos to the contrary. You have no right to ring Mr Bagwash, he obviously does not remember Rosy at all. I paid a high price for her from my friend Julian Green and only let you have her as a favour. It would have been much better for me to sell her to an influential member of the Kennel Club who is absolutely in love with her.

> Yours sincerely,
> Davinia Crummock
> Rose Cottage,
> Doggie Hols,
> Penny Way.

Dear Miss Crummock,

As you well know the bitch is completely unmanageable. I have to get the girls, who are terrified of her, to put her in a kennel well away from other dogs and visitors. My husband is very angry and insists you take her back and reimburse the full price. Otherwise I must contact my solicitors.

> Yours sincerely,
> J. H. Fox-Willoughby
> Manor Kennels,
> Fosse Lane.

Dear Captain,

I'm afraid I have a long standing appointment, which I dare not break, with my doctor on Friday and I could not trust my staff to entertain you properly. I'm sure you know what staff is like these days – I would so love to meet you on your return from Major Harrington's. Although your offer is much less than others I have had I would so like Daisy to go to a friend and so will accept it. I am bitterly disappointed with the home I found with such care for Rosy, Daisy's dear mother, and I will have to send my head girl to get her back no matter what the cost. I could not stand the thought that she is not loved and the Doctor insists I must avoid all worry. Life is so hard for one so alone. Perhaps you or one of your friends would like Rosy, a good understanding home would be much more important than price.

> Yours sincerely,
> Davinia Crummock (Miss)
> Rose Cottage,
> Penny Way.

Dear Mrs Willougby,

From your letter it is obvious that darling Rosy has been most dreadfully misused. I ran a temperature of 104° last night worrying about her, but as I have no one else I must stand up for myself. Goodness knows what harm was done when your dog savaged poor Rosy. I am prepared to take her back and will return £40 to you, for she cannot now be the same lovely creature and will need constant nursing and goodness knows what expense. My head girl can collect her on Thursday. This is without prejudice.

Yours truly,
D. Crummock
Rose Cottage,
Penny Way.

Madam.

I have not previously acknowledged your letter as I wanted to consult my uncle the judge. He advises me that you haven't a leg to stand on. Your animal's savagery was well known though you chose to conceal it, nor did you tell me that the poor thing had already had two litters. It is obvious she has been ill-used as you say but not by me. I insist you take her back and reimburse the full price.

Yours faithfully,
J. H. Fox-Willoughby
Manor Kennels,
Fosse Lane.

Dear Madam,

I write to inform you I am no longer interested in purchasing a dog from you because during the weekend I was able to discover the truth of your situation. You are fortunate, madam, I did not fall for your subterfuge or I would have had no alternative but to lay the entire matter before the disciplinary committee.

Yours faithfully,
Captain J. A. H. McGregor
Sebastopol,
East Cheam Lane.

Mrs Willoughby,

If you had said you wanted a stuffed toy I would not have
bothered in the first place. Rosy is just spirited as the breed should be
and can be handled by anyone who knows anything about dogs. Of
course I will take her back. I wouldn't want her to stay with you but
you can hardly expect me to return the full price after what you have
done to her. I refer you to the terms in my earlier letter. Please do
not ring again. The Doctor insists I must have quiet.

Faithfully,
D. Crummock
Rose Cottage,
Penny Way.

Madam,

Against the advice of my uncle the judge but to avoid having
this awful animal in my kennels one moment longer I am prepared
under protest and without prejudice to accept £50 providing you
collect the dog on Tuesday at the very latest, after which she will
be kept at your expense. I enclose a schedule of my normal
boarding charges.

Yours faithfully,
J. H. Fox-Willoughby
Manor Kennels,
Fosse Lane.

Dear Mrs Fox-Willoughby,

Miss Crummock has told me to collect Bogus Rosewater on
Tuesday evening. Could you please tell me the best way from you to
Smethwick where the bitch is to go as a guard in a breakers' yard.

Yours sincerely,
Jane Slaver
c/o Rose Cottage Doggie Coiffures,
Penny Way.

Madam,

Your girl has written to me about collecting the bitch. She must arrive before 4.30 when reception closes on Tuesdays. I insist she brings cash and a note absolving me from all and any further expense. Did I tell you my uncle is judging in Surrey next week?

Yours faithfully,
J. H. Fox-Willoughby
Manor Kennels,
Fosse Lane.

Dear Captain,

Your letter came as such a shock to me especially since you know my Doctor insists I should be protected from all stress. I had thought that we had become friends but now I find you prefer to believe gossip. A lady on her own is always at a disadvantage among men. Fortunately not everyone believes gossip and Rosy has now gone to a lovely home as companion for an industrial magnate in the Midlands, who I know will appreciate her. I think I will try to keep Daisy and hope my health improves sufficiently to allow me to show her. Certainly after this experience I am no longer prepared to give her away to anyone who pleads poverty and claims mutual friendships. Thank you for getting my registrations done. They came through so quickly. I have written to the Wing Commander to tell him how kind you have been.

Yours sincerely,
Davinia Crummock
Rose Cottage,
Penny Way.

Dear Mrs Fox-Willoughby,

I felt sure we would come to an amicable agreement. These silly misunderstandings are so very upsetting. Rosy has now gone to a lovely home with a very wealthy family and I know will be very happy. My silly head girl forgot to collect Rosy's collar, muzzle

437

and lead. Please send them to me so that I will have something to remember her by. I realize now how much you wanted Rosy's bloodlines and could offer you her daughter by Lady Smedley's dog. She is developing into such a beautiful animal and my health won't allow me to do her justice and it would be such a comfort to know that she was with such a knowledgeable person as yourself. Brigadier McGregor a friend of Lady Smedley's wanted her but he is such a rude man I couldn't let her go no matter how much he offered. Daisy has a wonderful temperament, just like Rosy before she was attacked by that awful dog of Colonel Bagwash's.

Yours sincerely,
Davinia Crummock
Rose Cottage,
Doggie Hols,
Penny Way.

Dear Mrs Crummock,

Your girl delivered the bitch to Gibsons yard while I was picking up some stuff, she seems a right goer and your girl said you had a pup out of her, my brother in law was looking for one of the same sort for his pub yard. I could offer £30 (cash) for the pup if your girl could deliver.

Cheers,
Bill Carter
10 Station Crescent,
Smethentry.

Dear Mr Carter,

It's so good to know that darling Rosy is appreciated. I had hoped to keep Daisy who is so like her mother and very dear to me but my health will not allow me. I know she would be very happy in a hotel and getting such a good home is so important – I could let you have her for £30 plus the first and second pick of her first two litters. She is the last of a very valuable line which I must somehow keep. A member of the Kennel Club wants her but

I would prefer her to be in a family like yours where she would be loved.

Yours sincerely,
Miss O. Crummock
Rose Cottage,
Penny Way

"Caveat Emptor", *Our Dogs Christmas Annual,* 1978

* * *

Lost, or Stolen?

Prince Rupert

On Wednesday, the Ninth instant were lost a brace of Greyhounds of his Highness Prince Ruperts, the one a large white young Dog, with a thick black head, with a chain and small coller: The other a cole black Dog, with a small coller. If any person hath taken them up they are desired either to send or bring them to his Highness lodgings in the Stone Gallery at Whitehall, where they shall be well rewarded for them.

London Gazette, 16 October 1667

Lost in Dean's-yard, Westminster, on the 26th of October last, a young white Spaniell about six months old, with a black head, red eye-browes, and a black spot upon his back. Lost also about the same time near Camberwell, a Yorkshire Buckhound, having black spots upon his back, red ears, and a wall-eye, and PR upon his near shoulder; both belonging to his Highness Prince Rupert. If any one can bring them or tydings of them to Prince Ruperts lodgings in the Stone Gallery at Whitehall he shall be well rewarded for his pains.

London Gazette, November 1667

439

Jonathan Swift

Pray steal me not; I'm Mrs Dingley's,
Whose heart in this four-footed thing lies.

Inscription on the collar of "Tiger",
Mrs Dingley's lap-dog

Henry Mayhew

OF THE FORMER STREET-SELLERS, "FINDERS,"
STEALERS, AND RESTORERS OF DOGS

The "finders" and "stealers" of dogs were the more especial subjects of a parliamentary inquiry [1844], from which I derive the official information on the matter. . . .

In their Report the Committee observe, concerning the value of pet dogs: — "From the evidence of various witnesses it appears, that in one case a spaniel was sold for 105£., and in another, under a sheriff's execution, for 95£. at the hammer; and 50£. or 60£. are not unfrequently given for fancy dogs of first-rate breed and beauty." The hundred guineas' dog above alluded to was a "black and tan King Charles's spaniel" – indeed, Mr Dowlino, the editor of Bell's Life in London, said, in his evidence before the Committee, "I have known as much as 150£ given for a dog." He said afterwards: "There are certain marks about the eyes and otherwise, which are considered 'properties;' and it depends entirely upon the property which a dog possesses as to its value."

I cannot better show the extent and lucrativeness of this trade, than by citing a list which one of the witnesses before Parliament, Mr W. Bishop, a gunmaker, delivered in to the Committee, of 4 cases in which money had recently been extorted from the owners of dogs by dog-stealers and their confederates. There is no explanation of the space of time included under the vague term "recently"; but the return shows that 151 ladies and gentlemen had been the victims of the dog-stealers or dog-finders, for in this business the words were, and still are to a degree, synonyms, and of these 62 had been so victimized in 1843 and in the six months of

1844, from January to July. The total amount shown by Mr Bishop to have been paid for the restoration of stolen dogs was 977£. 4s. 6d., or an average of 6£ 10s. per individual practised upon.

These dog appropriators, as they found that they could levy contributions not only on royalty, foreign ambassadors, peers, courtiers, and ladies of rank, but on public bodies, and on the notaries of the state, the law, the army and the church, became bolder and more expert in their avocations – a boldness which was encouraged by the existing law. Prior to the parliamentary inquiry, – stealing was not an indictable offence. The only mode of punishment for dog-stealing was by summary conviction, the penalty being fine or imprisonment; but Mr Commissioner Mayne did not know of any instance of a dog-stealer being sent to prison in default of payment. Although the law recognised no property in a dog, the animal was taxed; and it was complained at the time that an unhappy lady might have to pay tax for the full term upon her dog, perhaps a year and a half after he had been stolen from her. One old offender, who stole the Duke of Beaufort's dog, was transported, not for stealing the dog, but his collar.

The difficulty of proving the positive theft of a dog was extreme. In most cases, where the man was not seen actually to seize a dog which could be identified, he escaped when carried before a magistrate. "The dog-stealers," said Inspector Shackell, "generally go two together; they have a piece of liver; they say it is merely bullock's liver, which will entice or tame the wildest or savagest dog which there can be in any yard; they give it to him, and take him from his chain. At other times," continues Mr Shackell, "they will go in the street with a little dog, rubbed over with some sort of stuff, and will entice valuable dogs away. . . . If there is a dog lost or stolen, it is generally known within five or six hours where that dog is, and they know almost exactly what they can get for it, so that it is a regular system of plunder." Mr G. White, "dealer in live stock, dogs, and other animals," and at one time a "dealer in lions, and tigers, and all sorts of things," said of the dog-stealers: "In turning the corners of streets there are two or three of them together; one will snatch up a dog and put it into his apron, and the others will stop the lady and say, "What is the matter?" and direct the party who has lost the dog in a contrary direction to that taken."

In this business were engaged from 50 to 60 men, half of them actual stealers of the animals. The others were the receivers, and the go-betweens or "restorers." The thief kept the dog perhaps for a day or two at some public-house, and he then took it to a dog-dealer with whom he was connected in the way of business. These dealers carried on a trade in "honest dogs," as one of the witnesses styled them (meaning dogs honestly acquired), but some of them dealt principally with the dog-stealers. Their depots could not be entered by the police, being private premises, without a search warrant – and direct evidence was necessary to obtain a search warrant – and of course a stranger in quest of a stolen dog would not be admitted. Some of the dog-dealers would not purchase or receive dogs known to have been stolen, but others bought and speculated in them. If an advertisement appeared offering a reward for the dog, a negotiation was entered into. If no reward was offered, the owner of the dog, who was always either known or made out, was waited upon by the restorer, who undertook "to restore the dog if terms could be come to." A dog belonging to Colonel Fox was once kept six weeks before the thieves would consent to the Colonel's terms. One of the most successful restorers was a shoemaker, and mixed little with the actual stealers; the dog-dealers, however, acted as restorers frequently enough. If the person robbed paid a good round sum for the restoration of a dog, and paid it speedily, the animal was almost certain to be stolen a second time, and a higher sum was then demanded. Sometimes the thieves threatened that if they were any longer trifled with they would inflict torture on the dog, or cut its throat. One lady, Miss Brown of Bolton-street, was so worried by these threats, and by having twice to redeem her dog, "that she has left England," said Mr Bishop, "and I really do believe for the sake of keeping the dog." It does not appear, as far as the evidence shows, that these threats of torture or death were ever carried into execution; some of the witnesses had merely heard of such things.

from *London Labour and London Poor*, 1851

Mrs Isabella Mary Beeton

The Skye is the oddest member of the family. It would be worth enquiring how it is that this dog is so constantly losing himself. That this is the case, anyone taking ordinary notice of window-bills and placards must have discovered. It can't be that the dog's extraordinary value tempts the dog thief, for many dogs allowed as much freedom as the Skye are of much more value, and are but seldom "lost or stolen". Is it that the poor creature's vision is so obstructed by his hirsute furniture that he can but dimly make out where he is going? Is it that he is a stupid, blundering dog, who really doesn't care which way he goes, or what becomes of him? Or is he a dog of so much intelligence and of such an enquiring turn of mind that he is impelled to investigate each and every odd matter that may turn up in the course of a morning's walk?

from *Home Book of Pets*, 1862

Virginia Woolf

"This morning Arabel and I, and he with us," Miss Barrett wrote, "went in a cab to Vere Street where we had a little business, and he followed us as usual into a shop and out of it again, and was at my heels when I stepped up into the carriage. Having turned, I said 'Flush', and Sarabel looked round for Flush – there was no Flush! He had been caught up in that moment, from under the wheels, do you understand?" Mr Browning understood perfectly well. Miss Barrett had forgotten the chain; therefore Flush was stolen. Such, in the year 1846, was the law of Wimpole Street and its neighbourhood.

Nothing, it is true, could exceed the apparent solidity and security of Wimpole Street itself. As far as an invalid could walk or a bathchair could trundle nothing met the eye but an agreeable prospect of four-storeyed houses, plate-glass windows and mahogany doors. Even a carriage and pair, in the course of an afternoon's airing, need not, if the coachman were discreet, leave the limits of decorum and respectability. But if you were not an invalid, if you did not possess a carriage and pair, if you were – and many people were – active and able-bodied and fond of walking, then you might see sights and hear language and smell smells, not a stone's throw from Wimpole Street, that threw doubts upon the solidity even of Wimpole Street itself. So Mr Thomas Beames found when about this time he took it into his head to go walking about London. He was surprised; indeed he was shocked. Splendid buildings raised themselves in Westminster, yet just behind them were ruined sheds in which human beings lived herded together above herds of cows — "two in each seven feet of space." He felt that he ought to tell people what he had seen.

But in the summer of 1846 that hint had not yet been given; and the only safe course for those who lived in Wimpole Street and its neighbourhood was to keep strictly within the respectable area and to lead your dog on a chain. If one forgot, as Miss Barrett forgot, one paid the penalty, as Miss Barrett was now to pay it. The terms upon which Wimpole Street lived cheek by jowl with St Giles were well known. St Giles stole what St Giles could: Wimpole Street paid what Wimpole Street must. Thus Arabel at once "began to comfort me by showing how certain it was that I should recover him for ten pounds at most." Ten pounds, it was reckoned, was about the price that Mr Taylor would ask for a cocker spaniel. Mr Taylor was the head of the gang. As soon as a lady in Wimpole Street lost her dog she went to Mr Taylor; he named his price, and it was paid; or if not, a brown paper parcel was delivered in Wimpole Street a few days later containing the head and paws of the dog. Such, at least, had been the experience of a lady in the neighbourhood who had tried to make terms with Mr Taylor. But Miss Barrett of course intended to pay. Therefore when she got home she told her brother Henry, and Henry went to see Mr Taylor that afternoon. He found him "smoking a cigar in a room with pictures" — Mr Taylor was said to make an income of two or three thousand a year out of the dogs of Wimpole Street — and Mr Taylor promised that he would confer with his "Society" and that the dog would be returned next day. Vexatious as it was, and especially annoying at the moment when Miss Barrett needed all her money, such were the inevitable consequences of forgetting in 1846 to keep one's dog on a chain.

But for Flush things were very different. Flush, Miss Barrett reflected, "doesn't know that we can recover him"; Flush had never mastered the principles of human society. "All this night he will howl and lament, I know perfectly," Miss Barrett wrote to Mr Browning on the afternoon of Tuesday, the 1st September. But while Miss Barrett wrote to Mr Browning, Flush was going through the most terrible experience of his life. He was bewildered in the extreme. One moment he was in Vere Street, among ribbons and laces; the next he was tumbled head over heels into a bag; jolted rapidly across streets, and at length was tumbled out – here. He found himself in complete darkness. He found himself in chilliness and dampness. As his giddiness left him he made out a few shapes in a low dark room – broken chairs, a tumbled mattress. Then he was seized and tied tightly by the leg to some obstacle. Something sprawled on the floor – whether beast or human being, he could not tell. Great boots and draggled skirts kept stumbling in and out. Flies buzzed on scraps of old meat that were decaying on the floor. Children crawled out from dark corners and pinched his ears. He cowered down on the few inches of damp brick against the wall. Now he could see that the floor was crowded with animals of different kinds. Dogs tore and worried a festering bone that they had got between them. Their ribs stood out from their coats – they were half famished, dirty, diseased, uncombed, unbrushed; yet all of them, Flush could see, were dogs of the highest breeding, chained dogs, footmen's dogs, like himself.

He lay, not daring even to whimper, hour after hour. Thirst was his worst suffering; but one sip of the thick greenish water that stood in a pail near him disgusted him; he would rather die than drink another. Yet a majestic greyhound was drinking greedily. Whenever the door was kicked open he looked up. Miss Barrett – was it Miss Barrett? Had she come at last? But it was only a hairy ruffian, who kicked them all aside and stumbled to a broken chair upon which he flung himself. Then gradually the darkness thickened. He could scarcely make out what shapes those were on the floor, on the mattress, on the broken chairs. A stump of candle was stuck on the ledge over the fireplace. A flare burnt in the gutter outside. By its flickering, coarse light Flush could see terrible faces passing outside, leering at the window. Then in they came, until the small crowded room became so crowded that he had to shrink back and lie even closer against the wall. These horrible monsters – some were ragged, others were flaring with paint and feathers – squatted on the floor; hunched themselves over the table. They began to drink; they cursed and struck each other. Out tumbled from the bags that were dropped on the floor, more dogs – lapdogs, setters, pointers, with their collars still on them; and a giant cockatoo that flustered and fluttered its way from corner to corner, shrieking 'Pretty Poll! Pretty Poll!' with an accent that would have terrified its mistress, a widow in Maida Vale. Then the women's bags were opened, and out were tossed on to the table bracelets and rings and brooches such as Flush had seen Miss Barrett wear and Miss Henrietta. The demons pawed and clawed them, cursed and quarrelled over them. The dogs barked. The children shrieked, and the splendid cockatoo – such a bird as Flush had often seen pendant in a Wimpole Street window – shrieked 'Pretty Poll! Pretty Poll!' faster and faster until a slipper was thrown at it and it flapped its great yellow-stained dove-grey wings in frenzy. Then the candle toppled over and fell. The room was dark. It grew steadily hotter and hotter; the smell, the heat were unbearable. Flush's nose burnt; his coat twitched. And Miss Barrett did not come.

Miss Barrett lay on her sofa in Wimpole Street. She was vexed; she was worried, but she was not seriously alarmed. Of course Flush would suffer; he would whine and bark all night; but it was only a question of a few hours. Mr Taylor would name his sum; she would pay it; Flush would be returned.

from *Flush*, 1933

Jaroslav Hašek

The lieutenant began to take a great interest in this doggy love, and so Schweik was able to continue without hindrance:

"Dogs can't dye their own hair, like ladies do, so that's always a job for the one who wants to sell him. When a dog's so old that he's all grey, and you want to sell him as a one-year pup, you buy some silver nitrate, pound it up and then paint the dog black so that he looks like new. And to give him more strength you feed him arsenic like they do horses, and you clean his teeth with emery paper like they use to clean rusty knives with. And before you show him to a customer, you make him swallow brandy, so that he gets a bit tipsy and then he's merry and bright and barks as jolly as can be, and chums up with everyone, like people do when they're boozed. But this is the most important part of the business, sir. You must talk to the customers, keep on talking to 'em, till they're sort of flabbergasted. If a man wants to buy a house dog and all you've got is a greyhound, you've got to have the gift of the gab, as they say, to talk the man over, so that he takes the greyhound instead of a house dog.

Or supposing someone wants a savage bulldog to keep burglars away, you've got to bamboozle him so that instead of a bulldog he takes one of these here midget lapdogs away in his pocket. When I used to deal in animals, there was a lady came one day and said that her parrot had flown away into the front garden and that some boys who were playing at Indians in front of her house had caught this parrot and torn all the feathers out of its tail and decorated themselves with them like policemen. Well, this parrot felt so ashamed at losing his tail that he fell ill and a vet had finished him off with some powders. So she wanted to buy a new parrot, a well-behaved one, not one of those vulgar birds that can do nothing but swear. Well, what was I to do, not having any parrot, and not knowing where to lay hands on one? But I had a bad-tempered bulldogs, quite blind he was too. And I give you my word, sir, I had to talk to that lady from four in the afternoon till seven in the evening, before she bought the blind bulldog instead of the parrot. That was a more ticklish job than any of their diplomatic stuff, and when she was going away, I said to her: "Those little boys had better not try to pull his tail off." And that's the last words I spoke to that lady, because she had to move away from Prague on account of that bulldog, because he bit everyone in the house. You wouldn't believe, sir, how hard it is to get hold of a really first-rate animal."

from *The Good Soldier Schweik*, 1920–3

Anonymous

Chicago, whose misfortune it is to have not more crime than other American cities, but more versatile criminals, has again achieved unenviable notoriety. Gangsters there are now kidnapping not men but dogs. The latest victim of their activity is Kid Boots Ace, a prize-winning Boston Terrier. He was stolen on Monday, February 29, from his owner, Mr Louis Rudginsky, of Boston (Mass.), who was notified by telephone that the dog was being held for a ransom of $500 (£100). He informed the police, and nothing has been heard from the kidnappers since.

The Times, March 1934

CHAPTER 14

The Proper Remedy

The methods used to try to cure dogs of their various ills may always have been well intentioned but all too often resulted in suffering which was as bad or worse than the supposed affliction. It is a continued source of puzzlement as to how some of these remedies came into being and how some, which could not have had the slightest beneficial effect, retained the confidence of dog owners for hundreds of years.

In AD 65 Junius Lucius Moderatus Columella included in his *De Re Rustica*, possibly for the first time, a recommendation that biting off the end joint of a dog's tail forty days after its birth renders the dog immune from madness.

This may have been the original reason for docking dogs' tails, since justified by a number of very different but sometimes equally unlikely reasons.

The petfood industry is not new. The Domesday book (1085) recorded "*ter mille panes canibus*" – three thousand cakes of dog bread – being produced in Chintenham (Cheltenham?), Gloucestershire. This reference taken with those in *Master of the Game* show that the manufacture of food intended for dogs was already established in the eleventh century. The industry now directly employs over 5,000 people in Britain alone and makes a significant contribution to the country's economy. The benefits which accrue from dog ownership are not only felt by their owners but by the entire community.

Dowager Empress T'zu Hsi

Let the Lion Dog be small, let it wear
the swelling cape of dignity around its neck, let it
display the billowing standard of pomp over its back.
Let its face be black, let its forefront be shaggy,
let its forehead be straight and low, like unto
the brow of an Imperial harmony boxer.
For its colour let it be that of a lion, a
golden sable, to be carried in the sleeve of a yellow
robe, or the colour of a red bear, or striped like
a dragon, so that there may be dogs appropriate to
every costume in the Imperial wardrobe.
Whose fitness to appear at public ceremonies and
functions shall be judged by their colour, and by
their aristocratic contrast with the Imperial robes.

Let it venerate its ancestors and deposit
offerings in the Canine Cemetery of the Forbidden
City on each new moon.

Let it be taught to refrain from gadding about,
let it comfort itself with the dignity of a Duchess.
Let it learn to instantly bite the foreign devils!

Let it wash its face like a cat with its paws,
let it be dainty in its food, that it shall be known
for a Royal and Imperial dog by its fastidiousness.

Let its eyes be large and luminous
let its ears be set like the sails of a war junk,
let its nose be like that of the Monkey God of the Hindu.

Let its forelegs be bent so that it shall not desire
to wander far or leave the Imperial precincts.

Let its body be shaped like that of a hunting
lion spying for its prey.

Let its feet be tufted with plentiful hair that
its footfalls may be noiseless, and for its standard
of pomp, let it rival the whisk of the Tibetan yak,
which is flourished to protect the Imperial
litter from the attack of flying insects.

Let it be lively that it may afford
entertainment by its gambols,
let it be wary that it may not involve itself in
danger, let it be sociable in its habits, that it
may live in amity with the other beasts fishes or
birds that find protection in the Imperial Palace.

Shark's fins and curlews' livers and the breasts of
quails, on these may it be fed, and for drink give it
the tea that is brewed from the Spring buds of the
bush that groweth in the province of Han Kon, or the
milk of antelopes that pasture in the Imperial parks,
or broth made from the nests of sea swallows.

Thus shall it preserve its integrity and self-respect,
and in the day of sickness let it be anointed with the
clarified fat of the leg of a sacred leopard and give
it to drink a throstle's egg shell – full of the juice
of the custard apple in which has been dissolved
three pinches of shredded rhinoceros horn – and apply to it
    piebald leaches –

So shall it remain, but if it die, remember that
thou, too, art mortal. . . .

from *Pearls of Wisdom*, translated by Annie Coath Dixey, 1931

William Harrison

Besides these also we have sholts or curs dailie brought out of
Iseland, and much made of among us, bicause of their sawcinesse and
quarrelling. Moreover they bite verie sore, and love candles

exceedlinglie, as do men and women of their countrie: but I may saie no more of them, bicause they are not bred with us. Yet this will I make report of by the waie, for pastime's sake, that when a great man of those parts came late into one of our ships which went thither for fish, to see the forme and fashion of the same, his wife apparelled in fine sables, abiding on the decke whilest hir husband was under the hatches with the mariners, espied a pound or two of candles hanging at the mast, and being loth to stand there idle alone, she fell to and eat them up everie one, supposing hir selfe to have beene at a jollie banket, and shewing verie pleasant gesture when hir husband came up againe unto hir.

from *Description of England*, 1577

James Hart

Man is of far different structure in his guts from ravenous creatures as dogs, wolves, etc., who, minding only their belly, have their guts descending almost straight down from their ventricle or stomach to the fundament: whereas in this noble microcosm man, there are in these intestinal parts many anfranctuous circumvolutions, windings and turnings, whereby, longer retention of his food being procured, he might so much the better attend upon sublime speculations, and profitable employment in Church and Commonwealth.

from *Diet of the Diseased*, 1633

Revd James Woodforde

In the afternoon my dog Pompey came home shot terribly, so bad that I had her hanged directly out of her Misery. My greyhound Minx who was with her did not come and we suppose she has met with the same fate. It is supposed that Mr Townshend's gamekeeper who goes by the name of black Jack, shot Pompey.

from *The Diary of a Country Parson*, 21 September 1777

Colonel George Hanger

When a dog looks unkindly in his coat, though he has been physicked, give him three doses of powdered glass, as much as will lie heaped up on a shilling to each dose. This will make his coat very fine, and he will look well in his skin; besides it is a very great cleanser. The powdered glass must not be made of the green glass bottles, but from broken decanters and wine-glasses, powdered and ground in an iron mortar, then sifted through a fine muslin sieve.

I have ever, throughout life, fed my own dogs, after they come home from the day's sport. If I had twenty servants, one should prepare the food for them; but I would not so much as allow him to be present when they are fed. The advantages you acquire are very great, by doing this yourself; first, you make each dog attached to you, and only to you; for which reason he will hunt the better for you, and infallibly be more obedient. If your servant feeds him, the dog is always looking after him, and cares not one curse for you. What a pretty situation you are in, with an ignorant groom, who knows not, in the smallest degree, how to hunt or treat a dog in the field:- by heavens! you had as well stay at home, either for the pleasure or the sport you will have!

from *To all Sportsmen, and particularly to Farmers and Gamekeepers,*
1814

George Gordon, Lord Byron

He saw the lean dogs beneath the wall
Hold o'er the dead their carnival,
Gorging and growling o'er carcass and limb;
They were to busy to bark at him!
From a Tartar's skull they had stripp'd the flesh,
As ye peel the fig when its fruit is fresh;
And their white tusks crunch'd o'er the whiter skull,
As it slipp'd through their jaws, when the edge grew dull,
As they lazily mumbled the bones of the dead,
When they scarce could rise from the spot where they fed;

So well had they broken a lingering fast
With those who had fallen for that night's repast.

from The Siege of Corinth, 1816 `

Anonymous

We find that Mr Smith, who has introduced his biscuits on our
Magazine cover, has met that encouragement and patronage which
we trust will ever follow the endeavours of all who study to promote
the pleasures and conveniences of the Sporting World. We have
seen a letter from our valuable correspondent, NIMROD, who
states: — "I approve of them very much, and shall not fail to
recommend them to my sporting friends;" — also, from E. Cripps
Esq. whose black bitch, Emerald, won the Ashdown Cup, stating, "I
must say it is the best food for Greyhounds I have tried."

The Sporting Magazine, 1826

Somerville and Ross (pseud.)

The first object that met my eyes was the original sinner, Venus,
mounted on a long and highly adorned luncheon table, crunching
and gulping cold chicken as fast as she could get it down; on the
floor half a dozen of her brethren tore at a round of beef amid the
debris of crockery and glass that had been involved in its overthrow.
A cataract of cream was pouring down the table-cloth, and making a
lake on the carpet for the benefit of some others; and President, the
patriarch of the pack, was apparently seated on the wedding cake,
while he demolished a cold salmon. I had left my whip in the stable,
but even had this paralysing sight left me the force to use it, its
services would not have been needed. The leaders of the revel
leaped from the table, mowing down colonies of wine glasses in the
act, and fled through the open window, followed by the rest of the
party, with a precipitancy that showed their full consciousness of sin
— the last scramblers over the sill yelping in agonized foretaste of the
thong that they believed was overtaking them.

from "The Pug-nosed Fox",
Further Experiences of an Irish R. M., 1908

It has been said by an excellent authority that children and dogs spoil conversation. I can confidently say that had Madame de Sévigné and Dr Johnson joined me and my family on our wonted Sunday afternoon walk to the kennels, they would have known what it was to be ignored. This reflection bears but remotely on the matter in hand, but is, I think, worthy of record. I pass on to a certain still and steamy afternoon in late September, when my wife and I headed forth in the accustomed way, accompanied by, or (to be accurate), in pursuit of, my two sons, my two dogs, and a couple of hound puppies, to view that spectacle of not unmixed attractiveness, the feeding of hounds.

Flurry Knox and Michael were superintending the operation when we arrived, coldly observing the gobbling line at the trough, like reporters at a public dinner. It was while the last horrid remnants of the repast were being wolfed that my wife hesitatingly addressed Mr Knox's First Whip and Kennel Huntsman.

"Michael," she said, lowering her voice, "you know the children's old donkey that I spoke to you about last week – I'm afraid you had better –"

"Sure he's boiled, ma'am," said Michael with swift and awful brevity; "that's him in the throch now!"

Philippa hastily withdrew from the vicinity of the trough, murmuring something incoherent about cannibals or parricides, I am not sure which, and her eldest son burst into tears that were only assuaged by the tactful intervention of the kennel boy with the jawbone of a horse, used for propping open the window of the boiler-house.

"Never mind, Mrs Yeates," said Flurry consolingly, "the new hounds that I'm getting won't be bothered with donkeys as long as there's a sheep left in the country, if the half I hear of them is true!" He turned to me. "Major, I didn't tell you I have three couple of O'Reilly's old Irish hounds bought. They're the old white breed, y'know, and they say they're terrors to hunt."

"They'd steal a thing out of your eye," said Michael, evidently reverting to an interrupted discussion between himself and his master. "There's a woman of the O'Reillys married back in the country here, and she says they killed two cows last season,"

"If they kill any cows with me I'll stop the price of them out of your wages, Michael, my lad!" said Flurry to his henchman's back. "Look here, Major, come on with me to-morrow to bring them home!"

from "The Whiteboys", *Further Experiences of an Irish R. M.*, 1908

Andrew Lang

The dog's worst peril awaits him at the moment of his highest fortune, when he has become the pet and protégé of women. . . . Under their enervating patronage he may gradually lose some of his most cherished qualities, until he whines with the poet, "What is it, in this world of ours, that makes it fatal to be loved?" For fatal it would be if the dog were gradually evolved into a thing of tricks, a suppliant for sugar at afternoon tea, a pert assailant only of the people who never mean to rob the house, or a being deaf to the cry of "rats", but fiercely active in the pursuit of a worsted ball – a fine-coated dandy with his initials embroidered on his back. His affection, his fidelity, his reasoning power are very good things, but it is not all a blessing for him that they are finding their way into literature. For literature never can take a thing simply for what it is worth. The plain dealing dog must be distinctly bored by the ever-growing obligation to live up to the anecdotes of him in the philosophic journals. These anecdotes are not told for his sake; they are told to save the self-respect of people who want an idol, and who are distorting him into a figure of pure convention for their domestic altars. He is now expected to discriminate between relations and mere friends of the house, to wag his tail at "God save the Queen"; to count up to five in chips of firewood, and to seven in mutton bones; to howl for all deaths in the family above the degree of second cousin; to post letters, and refuse them when they have been insufficiently stamped; and last and most intolerable, to show a tender solicitude when the tabby is out of sorts. He will do these things when they are required of him, for he is the most good-natured and obliging fellow in the world, but it ought never to be

456

forgotten that he hates to do them, and that all he really cares for is his daily dinner, his run, his rat, and his occasional caress.

from *Daily News*, 1919

Walter Hutchinson

Metropolitan Drinking Fountain and Cattle Trough Association exists with the avowed object of supplying and installing fountains or water troughs for the use of animals in localities where it is deemed such would be of great humanitarian service. It has agreed to provide the water drinking facilities for the new Royal Veterinary College which is under construction at Camden Town, London. Some five hundred drinking troughs for dogs and cats have been supplied to this college during the year 1933–34, in addition to twenty troughs for the North London Dogs' Home, and a great number over various parts of the country. Seventeen hundred and twenty six dog troughs were supplied in the Metropolitan area during the same twelve months, and four hundred and eighty-eight in the provinces and abroad.

Hutchinson's Dog Encyclopaedia, 1934–5

John Steinbeck

They called him The Pirate because of his beard. Every day people saw him wheeling his barrow of pitchwood about the streets until he sold the load. And always in a cluster at his heels walked his five dogs.

Enrique was rather houndish in appearance, although his tail was bushy. Pajariti was brown and curly, and these were the only two things you could see about him. Rudolph was a dog of whom passers-by said "He is an American dog," Fluff was a Pug and Señor Alec Thompson seemed to be a kind of Airedale. They walked in a squad behind the Pirate, very respectful toward him, and very solicitous for his happiness. When he sat down to rest from wheeling his barrow, they all tried to sit on his lap and have their ears scratched. . . .

457

The Pirate lived in a deserted chicken house in the yard of a deserted house on Tortilla Flat. He would have thought it presumptuous to live in the house itself. The dogs lived around and on top of him, and the Pirate liked this, for his dogs kept him warm on the coldest nights. If his feet were cold, he had only to put them against the warm belly of Señor Alec Thompson. The chicken house was so low that the Pirate had to crawl in on his hands and knees.

Early every morning, well before daylight, the Pirate crawled out of his chicken house, and the dogs followed him, roughing their coats and sneezing in the cold air. Then the party went down to Monterey and worked along an alley. Four or five restaurants had their back doors on the alley. The Pirate entered each one, into a restaurant kitchen, warm and smelling of food.

Grumbling cooks put packages of scraps in his hands at each place. They didn't know why they did it.

When the Pirate had visited each back door and had his arms full of parcels, he walked back up the hill to Munroe Street and entered a vacant lot, and the dogs excitedly swarmed about him. Then he opened the parcels and fed the dogs. For himself he took bread or a piece of meat out of each package, but he did not pick the best for himself. The dogs sat down about him, licking their lips nervously, and shifting their feet while they waited for food. They never fought over it, and that was a surprising thing. The Pirate's dogs never fought each other, but they fought everything else that wandered the streets of Monterey on four legs. It was a fine thing to see the pack of five, hunting fox-terriers and Pomeranians like rabbits.

from *Tortilla Flat*, 1935

Victor Chapple

Serve me to the dogs when I die, says Lord Eric!

Pet-loving peer Lord Avebury is adding an eccentric request to his will – he wants to be dished up as dinner for the dogs.

The 12-stone former MP Eric Lubbock – who could fill 168 11b tins of doggydins – is determined to be a pedigree chum to the strays at Battersea Dogs Home.

And he says he will offer them money to accept him. Lord Eric's family are horrified. And the offer was turned down flat last night.

But chunky Lord Eric, 59, now a Buddhist, said: "It's a terrible waste to cremate bodies. I don't want to waste heat and energy being cremated. Anyway, it's a nice gesture to give the doggies a good meal."

Lord Eric's decision has deeply upset his second wife Lindsay.

But alarmed daughter Victoria said last night: "He is threatening to disinherit us unless we see his wishes are fulfilled."

Vet Bill Wadham-Taylor, manager of the home, said last night: "The dogs aren't fussy. But we just could not do it — it is not ethical."

"Pedigree Chump", *The Sun*, 22 January 1987

* * *

Pliny the Elder

The sure and soveraigne remedie for them that are bitten with a mad dog, was revealed by way of Oracle: to wit, the root of a wild rose, called the sweet Brier or Eglantine.

And there bee some againe, who burne the haires of the same mad dogges taile, and conveigh their ashes handsomely in some tent of lint into the wound.

from *Historia Naturalis*, c. AD 70,
translated by Dr Philemon Halland

Edward, 2nd Duke of York

OF THE SIKNESSE OF HOUNDES AND OF HER CORRUPCIONS
The houndes haven many dyvers sekenesse and ye grettest siknesse is ye rage. Wher of ther ben ix maners of the which I will you telle a partis. The first is cleped [called] furyous woodnesse madness; the houndes yat ben woode of yat woodnesse cien and howlynm wit. Avoid and nouygt in ye wise yat thei wer wonned whan thei were in helthe, whan thei may escape thei goon overalle byteng both

men and women and alle yat thei biforn funde. And thei han a
wonder pilous biteng, for yif thei biten eny thing, with grett payne
it shal eskape thereof yif he drawe bloode, yat it ne shal wax
woode what thing ever it be. A tokennyng for to knowe hym and
ye bygynnyng, is thes, yat thei eten not so wel as thei were
wonned, and thei beten ye other houndes, making hem cher with
ye taile and first sembleth upon hem and likketh hem, and than he
bloweth a gret blast with his nose and than he loketh fersliche; and
by holdeth his owyn sides and maketh tokenyngis men shuld take
him from ye other in to the iiij day for yan may men se her
siknesse al openly or ellis that he is nat wode, hor somtyne many
men ben gyles, in yat wise yat any hounde is woode of eny of ye
ix woodnesse os knowe by thise signes in ye bigynneng; as I have
saide, he dooth, sauf yat thei ne biten neither man ne beestis but
oonly houndes: as pilous is ye biteng of ye first, and evermore thei
goon up and down with out eny abiding; and this woodnesse is
cleped rennyng woodnesse. and thise ij woodnesse biforesaid taken
ye other houndes that thei bene youge thei byte hem nougt. That
other woodnesse is cleped ragerhunt, for thei ne byten not ne thei
rennen not, eke thei wil not ete for her mouthe is somdele gapyng
and yif thei were enbosed in her throte, and also thei day with the
terme bifore said, with out deyeng of any harme. And some men
seyn that it cometh to hem of a worme yat thei have under ye
tunge, and ye shuld fynde but fewe houndes yat thei ne han a
worme under ye tunge, and many men seyn yat yif yat worm were
take from hem thei shuld never wax woode. but therof make I
noon affirmacion, natheless it is goode to take it from hem and
men shulde take it away in this maner.

Take the hounde when he is passed half a yeere and hoolde fast his
fowre feet, and put a staf over wherte is mouthe that he shuld not
bite, and after take the tounge and ye shall fynde the worme undir
the toungue. Than shul ye slitte the tounge undirnethe and put a
nedel with threde bytwix the worme and the tongue and knyt it and
draw the worme out with the threde or ellis with a small pynne of
tre.

from *Mayster of the Game*, 1406–13

George Turbervile

A CHARME OF WORDES, TO PRESERVE DOGS FROM MADNESSE
A Gentleman of Brittaine taught the Author (for the Translatour wil learne no suche devices) to make two little rolles wherein were written but two lynes, and those he put in an eggshell, and so put them downe a dogges throate, which was bitten withe a madde dogge. And the wryting contaayned but this, Y Ran Qui Ran, cafram cafratrem caratrosque. This he sayde would preserve a dogge from being madde: believe it he that list, for I do not.

from *The Noble Arte of Venerie,* 1575

Richard Surflet

Shut up a dog close in some place, for three daies in such sort as that he may gnaw nothing but bones, then gather his dung and drie it: the powder of this dung is good against all bloudie fluxes, if it be taken twice a day with milke, and so continued for the space of three daies, remembering moreover before you mixe the saide milke, to quench divers small pebbel stones made red hot in the fire in it.

from *Translation of Maison Rustique by a Practitioner in Physicke,* 1600

Robert Burton

Hydrophobia is a kind of madness well known in every village, which comes by the biting of a mad dog, saith Aurelianus; touching, or smelling alone sometime, as Slenkius proves, and is incident to many other creatures as well as man.

from *The Anatomy of Melancholy,* 1621

Thomas de Gray

Take the hearb which groweth in dry and barren hils, called "the starre of the earth;" you must give it three dayes together: the first time you must gather three of these hearbs with all the whole roots, and wash them clean, then pound them well, loosing no part of them; which done, give it your horse in milke, beer, ale or white wine, but be careful the horse take all the hearbs and roots; but if you will, you may make up these hearbs and roots in fresh or sweet butter, which will do as well; the second day give your horse five of these hearbs and roots, like as you gave him them the day before; and the third day give him seaven. Doe this punctually as I have here prescribed you, and be well assured your horse will be perfectly cured, for albeit I myselfe have never tryed this medicine, yet I dow know the party of whom I had this cure hath cured much cattel of all sorts therewith, for it cureth all sorts of living creatures which shall be bitten by a mad dog; I myselfe can say this much of this receit, that I knew it cure a whole kennell of hounds of a Gentlemans, one Beagle excepted, which they did not suspect to be bitten, which indeed was bitten, so he fell mad and dyed, but all the residue escaped and did very well. Another time a Gentlemans sonne of my acquaintance was unfortunately bitten by a mad dog, who was cured by the party who taught me this receipt; and this young Gentleman (for he was then a boy of ten years old) was so far spent with the rancour of the disease, before the man tooke him in hand, as that his head began to addle, and he to talke very idly, yet he cured him, so he lived and did well and is at this houre living, he being now come to man's state, and a very handsome and proper man, whose parents whilst they lived I very well knew, and with whom I was very intimately acquainted.

from *The Compleat Horseman and Expert Farrier*, 1639

William Somervile

> Of lesser ills the Muse declines to sing,
> Nor stoops so low; of these each groom can tell
> The proper remedy. But O! what care!

What prudence can prevent madness, the worst
Of maladies? Terrific pest! that blasts
The huntsman's hopes, and desolation spreads
Thro' all th' unpeopled kennel unrestrain'd.
More fatal than th' envenom'd viper's bite;
Or that Apulian spider's pois'nous sting,
Heal'd by the pleasing antidote of sounds.
When Sirius reigns, and the sun's parching beams
Bake the dry gaping surface, visit thou
Each ev'n and morn, with quick observant eye,
Thy panting pack. If, in dark sullen mood
The glouting hound refuse his wonted meal,
Retiring to some close, obscure retreat,
Gloomy, disconsolate; with speed remove
The poor infectious wretch, and in strong chains
Bind him suspected. Thus that dire disease,
Which art can't cure, wise caution may prevent.
  But this neglected, soon expect a change,
A dismal change, confusion, frenzy, death.
Or in some dark recess, the senseless brute
Sits sadly pining: deep melancholy,
And black despair, upon his clouded brow
Hang low'ring; from his half-op'ning jaws
The clammy venom, and infectious froth,
Distilling fall; and from his lungs inflam'd
Malignant vapours taint the ambient air,
Breathing perdition: his dim eyes are glaz'd,
He droops his pensive head, his trembling limbs
No more support his weight; abject he lies,
Dumb, spiritless, benumb'd, till death at last
Gracious attends, and kindly brings relief.
  Or if outrageous grown, behold, alas!
A yet more dreadfull scene; his glaring eyes
Reden with fury, like some angry boar
Churning he foams, and on his back erect
His pointed bristles rise; his tail incurv'd
He drops, and with harsh broken howlings rends
The poison-tainted air, with rough hoarse voice
Incessant bays, and snuffs th' infectious breeze;

This way and that he stares aghast, and starts
At his own shade; jealous, as if he deem'd
The world his foes. If haply tow'rd the stream
He cast his roving eye, cold horror chills
His soul; averse he flies, trembling, appall'd
Now frantic to the kennel's utmost verge
Raving he runs, and deals destruction round.
The pack fly diverse; for whate'er he meets
Vengeful he bites and ev'ry bite is death.

from *The Chace*, 1735

Oliver Goldsmith

Good people all, of every sort,
   Give ear unto my song;
And if you find it wondrous short,
   It cannot hold you long.

In Islington there lived a man,
   Of whom the world might say,
That still a godly race he ran,
   Whene'er he went to pray.

A kind and gentle heart he had,
   To comfort friends and foes;
The naked every day he clad,
   When he put on his clothes.

And in that town a dog was found,
   As many dogs there be,
Both mongrel, puppy, whelp, and hound,
   And curs of low degree.

This dog and man at first were friends;
   But when a pique began,
The dog, to gain some private ends,
   Went mad and bit the man.

Around from all the neighbouring streets
   The wondering neighbours ran,
And swore the dog had lost its wits,
   To bite so good a man.

The wound it seem'd both sore and sad
   To every Christian eye;
And while they swore the dog was mad,
   They swore the man would die.

But soon a wonder came to light,
   They show'd the rogues they lied:
The man recover'd of the bite,
   The dog it was that died.

"Elegy on the Death of a Mad Dog", *c.*1760

Rudolph Erich Raspe

A mad dog, which soon came running against me in a narrow street
at St Petersburg. Run who can, I thought; and to do this the better, I
threw off my fur cloak, and was safe within doors in an instant. I sent
my servant for the cloak, and he put it in the wardrobe with my
other clothes. The day after I was amazed and frightened by Jack's
bawling, "For God's sake, sir, your fur coat is mad!" I hastened up to
him, and found almost all my clothes tossed about and torn to pieces.
The fellow was perfectly right in his apprehensions about the fur
cloak's madness. I saw him myself just then falling upon a fine full-
dress suit, which he shook and tossed in an unmerciful manner.

from *The Travels and Surprising Adventures of Baron Munchausen*, 1785

Public notice

MAD DOGS

Whereas there have lately been many MAD DOGS in this town and
neighbourhood: We hereby give Notice, that we have appointed

465

proper Persons to pursue and destroy all such as are suspected of being Mad; and do request, that all Persons will confine their Dogs, in Order to prevent, as much as possible, the spreading of this dreadful Evil.

JAMES ENTWISTLE, Boroughreeve.
EDWARD HOBSON, Constable
SAMUEL SMITH, Constable.

Manchester, 2nd. May, 1794.
Borough proclamation, 1794

Sarat Chandra Das

The poison of a white rabid dog with red, flushed nose affects at all times; that of a red or brown dog is more dangerous when one is bitten at midday, midnight, or sunrise; that of a parti-coloured dog, between 8 a.m. to 1 p.m.; of spotted ones at 9 p.m. or at twilight; of iron-grey ones at night and dawn; and that of a yellow rabid dog is sure to be fatal when one is bitten at dusk or 9 a.m. The baneful effects of this dangerous malady break out seven days after the bite of a white dog, one month after that of a black dog, 16 days after that of a parti-coloured, 26 days after that of an ash-grey, from one month to 7½ months in the case of a red, 3 to 7 months in that of a blackish-yellow, one year and a half-month in that of a spotted, and a year and 8 months after the bite of a bluish-black or tiger-coloured rabid dog. It is difficult to cure the disease when caused by a bite of the last kind of dogs at 7 p.m. or dusk, or by that of a black dog at dawn; but if a blue dog bites at midday, a red one at midnight, a spotted one at dawn, or a white one early in the morning, the patient can easily be cured.

from *Narrative of a Journey to Lhasa*, 1885

William Youatt

A child was bitten by a rabid dog at York, and became hydrophobous. All possibility of relief having vanished, the parents, desirous of putting an end to the agony of their child, or fearful of its doing mischief, smothered it between two pillows. They were tried for murder, and found guilty. They were afterwards pardoned; but the intention of the prosecutor was that of deterring others from a similar practice, in a like unfortunate situation.

from Rev. William B. Daniels, *Rural Sports,* 1807–13

Anonymous

John Evans, Vicar of Bronant, was attacked by a dog which when dissected, was found to be mad which at the time of the attack had not been realised. If at the time it had been realised the poor vicar would have had his arm amputated to prevent the spread of the poison, but it was now too late for that measure. "The Rev. gentleman is perfectly tranquil in mind and awaits the onset of madness and his death with a serenity becoming his cloth."

Carmarthen Journal, 23 March 1811

Robert Southey

To about six grains of calomel add thirty of powdered jalap and ten of scammony; make them into a pill with honey, or any other convenient vehicle, and give it to the dog immediately. In all probability an abundant evacuation will succeed, from which alone the cure sometimes results. This medicine, however, should not be solely relied on, but should be followed up by pills of about the size of a very large marrow-fat pea, given half-hourly. These pills are to be made of pure camphor, dissolved sufficiently to be worked into a mass, by means of a few drops of spirit wine, which should be added drop by drop, as it is very easy to render the camphor too liquid. A short time will decide the case: if the medicine take proper effect, the jaws will be freed from that slimy, ropy excretion occasioned by the disease, and in its stead, a free discharge of saliva will appear, rather inclined to froth like soapsuds. I can only assure the reader, that I have more than once saved the life of dogs by these means, although

467

they were so far gone as to snap at me whilst administering the medicine.

from Commonplace Book, c.1819

Charles Lamb

Excuse my anxiety – but how is Dash? – (I should have asked if Mrs Patmore kept her rules, and was improving – but Dash came uppermost. The order of our thoughts should be the order of our writing). Goes he muzzled or *aperto ore?* are his intellects sound, or does he wander a little in *his* conversation? you cannot be too careful to watch the first symptoms of incoherence. The first illogical snarl he makes, to St Luke's with him! All the dogs here are going mad, if you believe the overseers; but I protest they seem to be very rational and collected. But nothing is so deceitful as mad people to those who are not used to them. Try him with hot water. If he won't lick it up, it is a sign he does not like it. Does his tail wag horizontally or perpendicularly? That has decided the fate of many dogs in Enfield. Is his general deportment cheerful? I mean when he is pleased – for otherwise there is no judging. You can't be too careful. Has he bit any of the children yet? If he has, have them shot, and keep *him* for a curiosity, to see if it was the hydrophobia.

Letter to P. G. Patmore, c.1822

Somerville and Ross

As I spoke something darted past Mrs Knox, something that looked like a bundle of rags in a cyclone, but was, as a matter of fact, my faithful water-spaniel, Maria. She came on in zigzag bounds, in short maniac rushes. Twice she flung herself by the roadside and rolled, driving her snout into the ground like the coulter of a plough. Her eyes were starting from her head, her tail was tucked between her legs. She bit, and tore frantically with her claws at the solid ice of a puddle.

"She's mad! She's gone mad!" exclaimed Philippa, snatching up as a weapon something that looked like a frying pan, but was, I believe, the step of the phaeton.

Maria was by this time near enough for me to discern a canary-coloured substance masking her muzzle.

"Yes, she's quite mad," I replied, possessed by a spirit of divination. "She's been eating the rabbit curry."

from "The Man that came to Buy Apples", *Further Experiences of an Irish R.M.*, 1908

John and Jean Lang

A certain root, too, was of sovereign efficacy in the prevention of rabies in human beings who had been bitten by a mad dog. In Gerard's "Herbal", a medical work published in 1596 – "Gathered by John Gerarde of London, Master in Chirurgerie" – it is laid down that "the root of the Briar-bush is a singular remedy found out by oracle against the biting of a mad dog." Then, as now, rabies was regarded with a sickening dread, but in that remote day there had arisen no Pasteur, and dread too frequently degenerated into panic, and, panic, as it ever does, revealed itself in brutality.

In olden days the remedies generally administered to patients suffering from the bite of a dog were many and curious, and probably by the average patient they were regarded in reality rather as something in the nature of a charm than as medicines. Doubtless they gave confidence to the person who had been bitten, and, so far, were good. But in very many cases they got the credit of being infallible remedies solely because in most instances the dog which had given the bite was no more afflicted with rabies than was the person whom it bit; probably it was some poor, hunted, frightened beast which had lost its master, against which some panic-stricken individual had raised the senseless cry of "mad dog."

One remedy prescribed by a famous physician who lived so late as mid-eighteenth century, was "ash-coloured ground liver-wort a half-ounce, black pepper a quarter-ounce," to be to taken, fasting, in four doses, the patient having been bled prior to beginning the cure. Thereafter for a month, each morning he must plunge into a cold spring or river, in which he must be dipped all over, but must stay no longer than half a minute. Finally, to complete the cure, he must for a fortnight longer enter the river or spring three times a week. It is all eminently simple, and tends at least to show that our ancestors after all were not ignorant of the virtues of cold water. Amongst other remedies, also, was a medicine composed of cinnabar and musk, an East Indian specific, and one of powdered Virginian snake-root, gum asafoetida, and gum camphire, mixed and taken as a bolus. So far, at least, if the various treatements did little good, they did no great harm. Brutality began where a person had been bitten by a dog that really was mad, and when undoubted symptoms of hydrophobia had shown themselves. Then it was no uncommon practice to deliberately bleed the unhappy patient to death, or, worse still, to smother him between mattresses or feather beds.

from *Stories of the Border Marches*, 1916

Virginia Woolf

Fleas leapt to life in every corner of the Florentine houses; they skipped and hopped out of every cranny of the old stone; out of every fold of old tapestry; out of every cloak, hat and blanket. They nested in Flush's fur. They bit their way into the thickest of his coat. He scratched and tore. His health suffered; he became morose, thin and feverish. The Brownings, trying various means – powders and scouring – finally had to clip him all over into "the likeness of a lion."

from *Flush*

Don Marquis

i heard a
couple of fleas
talking the other
day says one come
to lunch with
me i can lead you
to a pedigreed
dog says the
other one i do not care

what a dog s
pedigree may be
safety first
is my motto what
i want to know
is whether he
has got a
muzzle on
millionaires and
bums taste
about alike to me.

from *"certain maxims of archy"*,
archy and mihitabel, 1927

Gervase Markham

Now for the cutting or shaving him from the Navill downward, or backward, it is two wayes to be allowed of that is, for summer hunting or for the water; because these water dogges naturally are ever most laden with haires on the hindr parts, nature as it were labouring to defend that part most, which is continually to be employed in the most extremity, and because the hinder parts are ever deeper in the water than the fore parts, therefore nature hath given them the greatest armour of haires to defeet the wette and coldnesse; yet this defence in the Sommer time by the violence of the heate of the Sunne, and the greatness of the Dogges labour is very noysome and troublesome, and not onely maketh him sooner to faint and give over his sport, but also makes him by his overheating, more subject to take the Maungie.

And so likewise in a matter of water, it is a very heavy burthen to the Dogge and makes him swimme lesse nimbly and slower, besides the former offences before receited; But for the cutting and shaving of a Dogge all quite over, even from the Foote to the Nostrill that i utterly dislike, for it not only takes from him the general benefits which Nature hath lent him, but also brings such tendernesse and chilnesse over all his body, that the water in the end will grow yrksome unto him; for howsoever men may argue that keeping any creature cold will make it the better indure colde, yet we finde by true experience both in these and divers other such things, that when Nature is thus continually kept at her uttermost ability of indurance, when any little drope more is added to that extremity, presently she faints and grows distempered, whereas keepe Nature in her full strength and she will very hardly be conquered, and hence it shall come that you shall see an ordinary land Spaniell being lustily and well kept, will tyre 20 of these overshaven Curres in the cold water.

from *Hunger's Prevention; or the whole Arte of Fowling by Water and Land,* 1655

Anonymous

Wanted a Nurse. – The Signora Marchesa Siffanti di San Bartolomeo is in want of a young healthy wet nurse; and in order to avoid any future loss of milk she must be unmarried. Her services will be required for a small litter of five English spaniels thorough-bred, the maternal parent having died, whilst giving them birth; nurse to reside in the house, wages 100 francs per month; chocolate in the morning; breakfast with the Marchesa; dine with the servants; and sleep with the dogs.

Thacker's Courser's Annual, 1850, reproduced from an Italian journal

Jack London

Oh, you charity-mongers! Go to the poor and learn, for the poor alone are charitable. They neither give nor withhold from their excess. They have no excess. They give, and they withhhold never, from what they need themselves, and very often from what they cruelly need themselves. A bone to the dog is not charity. Charity is the bone shared with the dog when you are just as hungry as the dog.

from "Confession", *The Road,* c.1913

★　★　★

Nicholas Cox

It is necessary for several reasons to cut off the tip of a Spaniel's stern when it is a whelp. First, by doing so worms are prevented from breeding there; in the next place, if it be not cut he will be the less forward in pressing hastily into the covert after his game; besides this benefit, the dog appears more beautiful.

Gentleman's Recreation, 1674

Jean de la Fontaine

"What have I done, to be thus mocked,
By my own lord and master docked?
Oh, the unspeakable disgrace!
To other Dogs how dare I show my face?
Ye Kings, nay rather tyrants of my race,
If such a trick were played on you . . .!"
Thus the young mastiff Towzer rent the skies
When with small heed for his shrill anguish'd cried
They seized his ears and shore them through.
He thought it was a loss: but as he grew
Found advantage. He was born to fight,
And many a time would come home at night,
When he had got the worst of matters,
With those appendages in tatters;
By the ear we know the quarrelling hound.

The less there is of one for foes to bite,
The better; and 'tis common sense,
Having one vulnerable ground,
To concentrate thereon our whole defence.
Thus Master Towzer, with his gorget round
His throat, and not a trace of ear
For Wolves to grab him by, had nought to fear.

"The dog whose ears were cropt", *c.*1680

473

William Youatt

Then the tail of the dog does not suit the fancy of the owner. It must be shortened in some of these animals, and taken off altogether in others. If the sharp, strong scissors, with a ligature, were used, the operation, although still indefensible, would not be a very cruel one, for the tails may be removed almost in a moment, and the wound soon heals; but for the beastly gnawing off of the part – and the drawing out of the tendons and nerves – these are the acts of a cannibal; and he who orders or perpetrates a barbarity so nearly approaching to cannibalism deserves to be scouted from all society.

from *The Dog*, 1845

Stonehenge (pseud.)

If terriers are to be cropped, the beginning or end of the fourth month is the best time to choose; and, before sending out to walk, hounds are branded with the initials of the master or of the hunt, a hot iron shaped like the letter itself being used. This practice is, however, now abandoned in some kennels, notably the Fitzwilliam. Both cropping and rounding require practice to perform them well, a large pair of scissors being used, and care being necessary to hold the two layers of skin in the ear in their natural position, to prevent the one rolling on the other, and thus leaving one larger than the other. Foxhounds have so much work in covert that rounding is imperatively called for to prevent the ears being torn, and it always has been adopted as a universal practice, different huntsmen varying in the quantity removed. Some people after cutting one ear lay the piece removed on the other; but this is a clumsy expedient, and, if the eye is not good enough to direct the hand without this measurement, the operation will seldom be effected to the satisfaction of the owner of the dog. It is usual to round foxhound puppies after they come in from their walks; but it would be better to perform the operation before they return, as it only makes them more sulky and unhappy than they otherwise would be, and it is a poor introduction to their new masters.

from *The Dog in Health and Disease*, 1859

Idstone (pseud)

Let me recommend exhibitors to abstain from mutilating God's work, with the foolish notion that they can improve it by trimming ears and tails, and impress upon those who break or train the dog, that they are never so likely to bring out his good qualities as when they are gaining his confidence by kindness, and stimulating him to fresh exertions of his wonderful brain by encouragement and rewards. Punishment is always perilous.

> from *The Dog: with Simple Directions for his Treatment and notices of the best dogs of the day and their breeders or exhibitors*, 1872

Francis Knollys

Marlborough House, Pall Mall, S. W.,

Sir,

I am desired by the Prince of Wales to acknowledge the receipt of your communication, and to inform you in reply that he has kept dogs for many years, and frequently sends them to exhibitions, but that he has never allowed any dog belonging to him to be "mutilated".

His Royal Highness has always been opposed to this practice, which, he considers, causes unnecessary suffering, and it would give him great pleasure to hear that owners of dogs had agreed to abandon such an objectionable fashion.

I am, sir, your obedient servant,

Francis Knollys.

> Letter to Edgar Farman, Esq., January 1895

Thomas Thompson

"Ah'm soft-hearted meself," said Sam. "Ah once had a litter o' Airedales an' Ah hadn't th' heart to dock their tails either. What does tha think Ah did?"

"Drowned 'em o'," said Owd Snack.

"Don't be callous," said Enoch.

"Ah seed they were fond o' chasin' their tails," said Sam. "So Ah rubbed their tails wi' beef drippin', an' when they'd chewed their tails to th' reet length Ah rubbed 'em wi' bitter aloes an' that did th' trick."

from *Cat and Dog Life,* 1952

CHAPTER 15

A Too Short Life

Dogs' lifespan means that their owners usually have to cope with several bereavements during their own life. The loss of a much loved canine companion cannot be lightly dismissed as a mere inconvenience that can easily be overcome by acquiring a replacement.

After Patrick landed in Ireland in 432 to begin his saintly mission, he set about building a number of churches, among them the church that is now at Davidstown in Ossory. Work had begun and Patrick was resting from his labours when he was offered a dish of broth by a pagan woman. He took the offering with gratitude but was horrified, when his healthy appetite had been satisfied, to find a dog's paw at the bottom of the dish. He fell to his knees and prayed for the poor creature's restoration to life, whereupon, it is said, a huge yellow hound leapt from the dish and ran away towards Waterford.

Having accomplished the miracle for which he had prayed, Patrick then decided that the hound would kill everything in its path and so called on his workmen to pursue and slay the beast. This was quickly achieved and the hound, having briefly been restored to life, was killed for a second time. The unfortunate dog was ceremonially buried under a white thorn bush, *sgeithin-na-chon*, The Little Thornbush of the Hound. The imprint of the Saint's knees at the place at which he had prayed for the hound's brief restoration to life became known as *Glun Phadruig*, Patrick's Knee.

An ambivalent attitude towards dogs is nothing new.

Plutarch

A good man will take care of his horses and dogs, not only while they are young, but when old and past service. . . . Many have shown particular marks of regard in burying the dogs which they had cherished and been fond of; and, among the rest, Xanthippus, of old, whose dog swam by the side of his galley to Salamis, when the Athenians were forced to abandon their city, was afterwards buried by his master upon a promontory, which to this day is called the *Dog's Grave*. We certainly ought not to treat living creatures like shoes or household goods, which, when worn out with use, we throw away, and were it only to learn benevolence to humankind, we should be merciful to other creatures.

from *Symposiaca, c.* AD 100

John Rastell

He lyved lyke a lyon and dyed lyke a dogge.

Of Gentylness and Nobylyte, 1529

Robert Herrick

Now thou art dead, no eye shall ever see,
For shape or service, Spaniell like to thee.
This shall my love doe, give thy sad death one
Teare, that deserves of me a million.

"Upon his Spaniell Tracie", *Hesperides,* 1648

Dr John Arbuthnot

TO THE MEMORY OF
SIGNOR FIDO,
AN ITALIAN OF GOOD EXTRACTION:
WHO CAME INTO ENGLAND,

NOT TO BITE US, LIKE MOST OF HIS COUNTRYMEN,
BUT TO GAIN AN HONEST LIVELIHOOD:
HE HUNTED NOT AFTER FAME,
YET ACQUIRED IT:
REGARDLESS OF THE PRAISE OF HIS FRIENDS,
THOUGH HE LIVED AMONG THE GREAT,
HE NEITHER LEARNED NOR FLATTERED ANY VICE:
HE WAS NO BIGOT,
THOUGH HE DOUBTED NONE OF THE THIRTY-NINE ARTICLES:
AND IF TO FOLLOW NATURE,
AND TO RESPECT THE LAWS OF SOCIETY,
BY PHILOSOPHY,
HE WAS A PERFECT FRIEND,
AN AGREEABLE COMPANION,
A LOVING HUSBAND,
DISTINGUISHED BY A NUMEROUS OFFSPRING,
ALL OF WHICH HE LIVED TO SEE TAKE GOOD COURSES:
IN HIS OLD AGE HE RETIRED
TO THE HOUSE OF A CLERGYMAN IN THE COUNTRY,
WHERE HE FINISHED HIS EARTHLY RACE,
AND DIED AN HONOUR AND EXAMPLE TO THE WHOLE SPECIES,
READER,
THIS STONE IS GUILTLESS OF FLATTERY,
FOR HE TO WHOM IT IS INSCRIBED
WAS NOT A MAN,
BUT A
GREYHOUND

Epitaph, *c.*1700

Alexander Pope

Not louder Shrieks to pitying heav'n are cast,
When husbands, or lap-dogs breathe their last.
Beauties in vain their pretty eyes may roll;
Charms strike the sight, but merit wins the soul.

from *The Rape of the Lock,* 1712

John Gay

No – To some Tree this Carcase I'll suspend. –
But worrying Curs find such untimely end!

from *The Shepherd's Week. Friday*, 1714

Alexander Pope

Lo, the poor Indian! whose untutor'd mind
Sees God in clouds, or hears him in the wind;
His soul proud Science never taught to stray
Far as the Solar Walk, or Milky Way;
Yet simple Nature to his hope has giv'n,
Behind the cloud-topp'd hill, an humbler heav'n;
Some safer world in depth of woods embrac'd,
Some happier island in the wat'ry-waste,
Wher'er slaves once more their native shore behold,
No fiends torment, no Christians thirst for gold,
To be, contents his natural desire, –
He asks no angel's wing, no seraph's fire;
But thinks, admitted to that equal sky,
His faithful dog shall bear him company.

from *Essay on Man*, 1733

Lord John Hervey, 1st Earl of Bristol

Dyed dear Kickaninny, a perfect pattern to all her sex for constancy,
fidelity and friendship, which she shewed towards me in a most
exemplary manner from her birth to her death.

Epitaph, 1741

Anonymous

The Dog will bark,
I dare not to stir;
Take a Halter
And Hang up the Cur,
No, no, Why, Why,
I would not for a Guinea
My dog should die.

from *The Famous Tommy
Thumb's Little Story-Book, c.*1760

Thomas Erskine, 1st Baron

Approach, vain man! and bid thy pride be mute;
Start not! – this monument records a brute.
In sculptured shrine may sleep some human hog –
This stone is sacred to a faithful dog.
Though reason lend her boasted ray to thee,
From faults which make it useless he was free:
He broke no oath, betrayed no trusting friend,
Nor ever fawned for an unworthy end;
His life was shortened by no slothful ease,
Vice-begot care, or folly-bred disease.
Forsook by him he valued more than life,
His generous nature sank beneath the strife;
Left by his master on a foreign shore,
New masters offered – but he would no more –
The ocean oft with seeming sorrow eyed,
And pierced by man's ingratitude he died.

Epitaph on a Dog left by a brother officer
on the island of Minorca, 1772

Horace Walpole

Sweetest roses of the year
Strew around my Rose's bier.
Calmly may the dust repose
Of my pretty faithful Rose!
And if yon cloud-topped hill behind,
This frame dissolved, this breath resigned,
Some happier isle, some humbler heaven
Be to my trembling wished given,
Admitted to the equal sky
May sweet Rose bear me company!

Epitaph to Rosette, 1773

John Wilkes

At Thieves I bark'd, at lovers wagg'd my tail,
And thus O pleas'd both Lord and Lady Frail.

*Epitaph on Lady Vane's Lap Dog Veny;
At the time of the publication of her Memoirs,
under the name of Lady Frail, eighteenth century*

Anonymous

Let this perpetuate the memory,
Of an Animal, when living, deservedly esteemed
For his uncommon Sagacity, and Honesty.
Th' of American Original,
He was no Rebel;
But faithful, constant, and unvariable in his Attachments.
His Anger sometimes got the better of that Discretion,
With which he was endowed by Nature:
But it was then only, when he found
Unjustifiable Opposition

To his delegated, legal Authority.
Possessed of every amiable Quality,
His Resentment for any Affront or rough Treatment,
Soon subsided,
And he became at once
Placable, loving, and sincere.
Such was "Pierro Grande":
Whose Misfortune it was to die of Poison.
Seduced by a false "Brother" of an opposite "currish Spirit";
After a Day's Confinement to avoid the Danger
He took, alas! the fatal Dose
That put a Period to his Existence,
To the general Regret of all who knew him,
March 6th, 1780.

His Skin being tanned for the Purpose,
Made the Covers of two Books.

Inscription to a favourite dog, 1780

William Cowper

Though once a puppy, and though Fop by name,
Here moulders one, whose bones some honour claim;
No sycophant, although of spaniel race!
And though no hound, a martyr to the chase!
Ye squirrels, rabbits, leverets, rejoice!
Your haunts no longer echo to his voice.

This record of his fate exulting view,
He died worn out with vain pursuit of you.
   "Yes!" the indignant shade of Fop replies,
"And worn with vain pursuit, man also dies."

Epitaph on Fop, c.1780

Revd William B. Daniel

In October 1811, as Mr W., a gentleman in the neighbourhood of Lewes, Sussex, was shooting Partridges with a double-barrelled gun, and attended by a brace of excellent "Pointers", his Dogs stood, the Covey rose, and he discharged both barrels, bringing down his Bird to the right and left; finding his Dogs still "stationary" in the first high stuff, from which the Birds had risen, he re-loaded, but found that by the first Fire, he had not only shot the "Partridges" quite dead, but his two "Pointers" also! This "sporting" casualty was occasioned by the Dogs standing on a small Eminence, and the Birds going off nearly close to the "lower" ground, immediately in a "Line" with them.

from *Rural Sports*, 1807–13

George Gordon, Lord Byron

Near this spot
Are deposited the remains of one
Who possessed Beauty without vanity,
Strength without insolence,
Courage without Ferocity,
And all the Virtues of Man without his Vices.
This Praise, which would be unmeaning Flattery
If inscribed over human ashes,
Is but a just tribute to the memory of
Boatswain, a Dog,
Who was born at Newfoundland, May 1803
And died at Newstead Abbey, 18 Nov, 1808.

Epitaph to Boatswain, 1808

When some proud son of man returns to earth,
Unknown to glory, but upheld by birth,

The sculptor's art exhausts the pomp of woe,
And storied urns record who rest below:
When all is done, upon the tomb is seen,
Not what he was, but what he should have been:
But the poor dog, in life the firmest friend,
The first to welcome, foremost to defend,
Whose honest heart is still his master's own,
Who labours, fights, lives, breathes for him alone.
Unhonour'd falls, unnoticed all his worth,
Denied in heaven the soul he held on earth,
While man, vain insect! hopes to be forgiven,
And claims himself a sole exclusive heaven.
Oh man! thou feeble tenant of an hour,
Debased by slavery or corrupt by power,
Who knows thee well must quit thee with disgust,
Degraded mass of animated dust!
Thy love is lust, thy friendship all a cheat,
Thy smiles hypocrisy, thy words deceit!
By nature vile, ennobled but by name,
Each kindred brute might bid thee blush for shame.
Ye! who perchance behold this simple urn,
Pass on – it honours none you wish to mourn:
To mark a friend's remains these stones arise;
I never knew but one, – and here he lies.

> Inscription of the tomb of a favourite
> Newfoundland dog buried at Newstead Abbey, 1808

Alas, poor Prim
I'm sorry for him;
I'd rather by half,
It has been Sir Ralph.

> On the death of
> his wife's toy
> spaniel, c.1815

Sir Walter Scott

We must not omit one other remarkable figure in the group – a gigantic dog, which bore the signs of being at the extremity of canine life, being perhaps fifteen or sixteen years old. But though exhibiting the ruin only of his former appearance, his eyes dim, his joints stiff, his head slouched down, and his gallant carriage and graceful motions exchanged for a stiff, rheumatic, hobbling gait, the noble hound had lost none of his instinctive fondness for his master. To lie by Sir Henry's feet in the summer or by the fire in winter, to raise his head to look at him, to lick his withered hand or his shrivelled cheek from time to time, seemed now all that Bevis lived for. His faithful dog did not survive him many days.

Woodstock, 1826

William Wordsworth

On his morning rounds the Master
Goes to learn how all things fare;
Searches pasture after pasture,
Sheep and cattle eyes with care;
And, for silence or for talk,
He hath comrades in his walk;
Four dogs, each pair of different breed,
Distinguished two for scent, and two for speed.

See a hare before him started!
– Off they fly in earnest chase;
Every dog is eager-hearted,
All the four are in the race;
All the four are in the race:
And the hare whom they pursue,
Knows from instinct what to do;
Her hope is near: no turn she makes;
But, like an arrow, to the river takes.

Deep the river was, and crusted
Thinly by a night's frost;
But the nimble Hare hath trusted
To the ice, and safely crost;
She hath crost, and without heed
All are following at full sped,
When, lo! the ice, so thinly spread,
Breaks – and the greyhound, DART, is overhead!

Better fate have PRINCE and SWALLOW –
See them cleaving to the sport!
MUSIC has no heart to follow,
Little MUSIC, she stops short.
Hers is now another part:
A loving creature she, and brave!
And fondly strives her struggling friend to save.

From the brink her paws she stretches,
Very hands as you would say!
And afflicting moans she fetches,
As he breaks the ice away.
For herself she hath no fears, –
Him alone she sees and hears, –
Makes efforts with complainings; nor gives o'er
Until her fellow sinks to re-appear no more.

Incident

Sydney Smith

Here lies poor Nick, an honest creature,
Of faithful, gentle, courteous nature;
A parlour pet unspoiled by favour,
A pattern of a good dog behaviour.
Without a wish, without a dream,
Beyond his home and friends at Cheam,
Contentedly through life he trotted
Along the path that fate allotted;

Till Time, his aged body wearing,
Bereaved him of his sight and hearing,
Then laid him down without a pain
To sleep, and never wake again.

"An Honest Creature", *c.*1835

Revd Richard Barham

It was a litter, a litter of five,
Four are drown'd, and one left alive,
He was thought worthy alone to survive;
And the Bagman resolved upon bringing him up,
To eat of his bread and drink of his cup,

"The Bagman's Dog",
The Ingoldsby Legends, 1840–1847

Oh! where shall I bury my poor dog Tray,
Now his fleeting breath has passed away? –
Seventeen years, I can venture to say,
Have I seen him gambol, and frolic, and play,
Evermore happy, and frisky, and gay,
As though every one of his months was May,
And the whole of his life one long holiday –
Now he's a lifeless lump of clay,
Oh! where shall I bury my faithful Tray?
. . .
   Affliction sore
   Long time he bore,
Physicians were in vain! –
   Grown blind, alas! he'd
   Some Prussic Acid,
And that put him out of his pain!

"The Cynotaph", *The Ingoldsby Legends*

Thomas Babington Macaulay

I went to Oatlands and walked with Margaret and Alice to a most singular monument of human folly. The Duchess of York had made a cemetery for her dogs. There is a gateway like that under which coffins are laid in the churchyard of this part of the country; there is a sort of chapel; and there are the gravestones of sixty-four of her Royal Highness's curs. On some of these mausoleums were inscriptions in verse. I was disgusted by this exceeding folly. Humanity to the inferior animals I feel and practice, I hope, as much as any man; but seriously to make friends of dogs is not my taste. I can understand, however, that even a sensible man may have a fondness for a dog. But sixty-four dogs! Why it is hardly conceivable that there should be warm affection in any heart for sixty-four human beings.

from *Life and Letters*, c.1850

Alexis Soyer

We must beg pardon of the reader for informing him that the dog presented a very relishing dish to many nations advanced in culinary science. To them, one of these animals, young, plump, and delicately prepared, appeared excellent food.

The Greeks, that people so charming by their seductive folly, their love of the arts, their poetic civilization, and the intelligent spirit of research presiding over their dishes – the Greeks (we grieve to say it) ate dogs, and even dared to think them good: the grave Hippocrates himself – the most wise, the least gluttonous, and therefore the most impartial of their physicians – was convinced that this quadruped furnished a wholesome and, at the same time, a light food.

As to the Romans, they also liked it, and no doubt prepared it in the same manner as the hare, which they thought it resembled in taste.

However, it is but right to add, that this dish, which we will not even hear mentioned, was never favourably received by the fashionable portion of Roman society, and that the legislators of ancient gastrophagy even repulsed it with disdain.

There is every reason to believe that the people regaled themselves with a roast or boiled dog, especially once a year, at that period when they celebrated the deliverance of the Capitol from the siege of the Gauls.

from *The Pantropheon*, 1853

Thomas Carlyle

Fife had done his mistress, and still more him, a great deal of good. But, alas, in Cook's grounds here, within a month or two, a butcher's cart (in her very sight) ran over him, neck and lungs: all winter he wheezed and suffered; Feb. 1st, 1860, he died (prussic acid, and the doctor obliged at last!) I could not have believed my grief then and since would have been the twentieth part of what it was — nay, that the want of him would have been to me other than a riddance. Our last midnight walk together (for he insisted on trying to come), Jan. 31st, is still painful to my thought. "Little dim, white speck, of Life, of Love, Fidelity, and Feeling, girdled by the Darkness as of Night Eternal!" Her tears were passionate and bitter, but repressed themselves as was fit, I think, the first day. Top of the garden, by her direction, Nero was put underground. A small stone tablet with the date she also got, which, broken by careless servants, is still there — a little protected now.

Letter, 1860

George Borrow

Beth Gelert is situated in a valley surrounded by huge hills, the most remarkable of which are Moel Hebog and Cerrig Llan; the former fences it on the south, and the latter, which is quite black and nearly perpendicular, on the east. A small stream rushes through the valley, and sallies forth by a pass at its south-eastern end. The valley is said by some to derive its name of Beddgelert, which signifies the grave of

Gelert, from being the burial-place of Gelert, a British saint of the sixth century, to whom Llangeler in Carmarthenshire is believed to have been consecrated, but the popular and most universally received tradition is that it has its name from being the resting place of a faithful dog called Cetert or Gelert, killed by his master, the warlike and celebrated Llewelyn ab Jorweth, from an unlucky misapprehension.

Llewelyn during his contests with the English had encamped with a few followers in the valley, and one day departed with his men on an expedition, leaving his infant son in a cradle in his tent, under the care of his hound Gelert, after giving the child its fill of goat's milk. Whilst he was absent a wolf from the neighbouring mountains, in quest of prey, found its way into the tent, and was about to devour the child, when the watchful dog interfered, and after a desperate conflict, in which the tent was torn down, succeeded in destroying the monster. Llewelyn returning at the evening found the tent on the ground, and the dog, covered in blood, sitting beside it. Imagining that the blood with which Gelert was besmeared was that of his own son devoured by the animal to whose care he had confided him, Llewelyn in a paroxysm of natural indignation forthwith transfixed the faithful creature with his spear.

Scarcely, however, had he done so when his ears were startled by the cry of a child from beneath the fallen tent, and hastily removing the canvas he found the child in its cradle, quite uninjured, and the enormous wolf, frightfully torn and mangled, lying near. His breast was now filled with conflicting emotions, joy for the preservation of his son, and grief for the fate of his dog, to whom he forthwith hastened. The poor animal was not quite dead, but presently expired, in the act of licking his master's hand. Llewelyn mourned over him as over a brother, buried him with funeral honours in the valley, and erected a tomb over him as over a hero. From that time the valley was called Beth Gelert.

from *Wild Wales*, 1862

Charles Stuart Calverley

And then I bought a dog — a queen!
　　Ah Tiny, dear departing pug!
She lives, but she is past sixteen
　　And scarce can crawl across the rug.
I loved her, beautiful and kind;
　　Delighted in her pert Bow-wow:
But now she snaps if you don't mind:
　　'Twere lunacy to love her now.

I used to think, should e'er mishap
　　Betide my crumple-visaged Ti,
In shape of prowling thief, or trap,
　　Or coarse bull-terrier — I should die.
But ah! disasters have their use;
　　And life might e'en be too sunshiny:
Nor would I make myself a goose,
　　If some big dog should swallow Tiny.

from "Disasters",
Verses and Translations, 1862

Matthew Arnold

. . . We lay thee close within our reach,
Here where the grass is smooth and warm,
Between the holly and the beech,
Where oft we watch'd thy couchant form.

Asleep, yet lending half and ear
To travellers on the Portsmouth Road —
There build we thee, Oh guardian dear,
Mark'd with a stone, thy last abode!

Then some, who through this garden pass,
When we too, like thyself, are clay,

Shall see they grave upon the grass,
And stop before the stone, and say:

People who lived here long ago
Did by this stone, it seems intend
To name for future times to know
The dachs-hound, Geist, their little friend.

from "Geist's Grave", *c.*1867

Norah M. Holland

High up in the courts of Heaven today
    A little dog-angel waits,
With the other dogs he will not play,
    But he sits alone at the Gates:
"For I know my master will come," says he
"And when he comes, he will call for me."

He sees the spirits that pass him by
    As they hasten towards the throne,
And he watches them with a wistful eye
    As he sits at the gate alone;
"But I know if I just wait patiently
"That someday my Master will come," says he.

And his Master far down on the earth below,
    As he sits in his easy chair
Forgets sometimes, and he whistles low
    For the dog that is not there;
And the little dog-angel cocks his ears
And dreams that his Master's call he hears.

And I know when at length his Master waits
    Outside in the dark and cold
For the hand of Death to open the gates
    That lead to the Courts of Gold,
The little dog-angel's eager bark
Will comfort his soul while he's still in the dark.

"The Little Dog Angel", *c.*1870

Jerome K. Jerome

"What's that?"

"What's what?" asked Harris and I.

"Why that!" said George, looking Westward.

Harris and I followed his gaze, and saw, coming down towards us on the sluggish current, a dog. It was one of the quietest and peacefullest dogs I have ever seen. I never met a dog who seemed more contented – more easy in its mind. It was floating dreamily on its back, with its four legs stuck up straight into the air. It was what I should call a full-bodied dog, with a well-developed chest. On he came, serene, dignified, and calm, until he was abreast of our boat, and there, among the rushes, he eased up, and settled down cosily for the evening.

George said he didn't want any tea, and emptied his cup into the water. Harris did not feel thirsty, either, and followed suit. I had drunk half mine, but wished I had not.

from *Three Men in a Boat*, 1889

Harding Cox

It was during our sojourn in Twickenham that I suffered a loss which caused me dire distress. I have been, from my earliest days, more of a "cynophilist," than a "hippophilist." Though forming attachments to various units of the equine race, I generally regarded them as a means to an end; whereas my own particular canine pals claimed a place even nearer to my heart than some of the indispensable females of the human race, who from time to time, claimed my temporary allegiance. Of all my familiars none has been dearer than a certain fox-terrier registered as Coxswain, but known to me and my friends as Cockie. It was from this little chap that I derived my own sobriquet. A fair friend had declared that I and my canine attendant were strangely alike, not only in appearance, but also as regards temperament, and that, therefore, it behoved all and sundry to address us by the same name. As my terrier was a particularly handsome specimen of his breed I raised no objection on the grounds of personal appearance; but when it came to a question of character, I was inclined to demur, for my tyke was a rascal of the deepest dye, and possessed of a cayenne pepper temper which brooked no interference by any one except his master. He was absolutely fearless of God, man, devil, or the creatures of the wild, including the harmless, necessary cat, against which he waged eternal warfare. Here was a striking example of hereditary temperament for his sire, Mr Skinner's "General," was a holy terror and when visited by the opposite sex, for the purposes of eugenic propagation, it was always a toss-up whether he would proceed to amorous gymnastics, or would elect to tear the windpipe out of his would-be inamorata. Cockie's dam was the darling of Ted's heart – Stella, by name, sprung directly from the primitive Nottingham strain, being by Old Sam, ex Cottingham Nettle.

My favourite had the run of the premises and was the terror of all interlopers. I had taught him to be a dog of all works. He was as keen as mustard on fur and feather, and did duty for spaniel, pointer or retriever; though as regards the last-named industry, I always had to race to the kill; for Cockie was decidedly of iron jaw, and would reduce a partridge to a mélange of blood and plumage in an incredibly short space of time.

The sad day arrived when, returning from a cutting-out expedition to the Metropolis, there was no little pal to greet me with his usual demonstrations of joy. Cockie had disappeared, utterly and irretrievably. Rewards of £5, £10, and finally £25, elicited no response. I put a detective on the track of possible dog-stealers. He followed what he deemed to be a slender clue into the purlieus of the East, where he was so heavily drugged that he died within a week. Thus tragedy trod on the track of tragedy.

Cockie has passed; but his name survived; for as "Cockie" I have ever since been known to my intimates and to the sporting public in general.

from *Chasing and Racing*, 1921

Rudyard Kipling

There is sorrow enough in the natural way
From men and women to fill our day;
But when we are certain of sorrow in store,
Why do we always arrange for more?
Brothers and sisters, I bid you beware

Buy a pup, and your money will buy
Love unflinching that cannot lie.
Perfect passion and worship fed
By a lick in the ribs or a pat on the head.
Nevertheless it is hardly fair
To risk your heart for a dog to tear.
When the fourteen years which nature permits
Are closing in asthma, or tumour or fits,
And the vet's unspoken prescriptions runs
To lethal chamber or loaded guns,
Then you will find – it's your own affair –
But . . . you've given your heart for a dog to tear.

When the body that lived at your single will,
When the whimper of welcome is stilled (how still!)
When the spirit that answered your every mood
Is gone – wherever it goes – for good
You will discover how much you care,
And will give your heart to a dog to tear.

We've sorrow enough in the natural way,
When it comes to burying Christian clay,
Our loves are not given, but only lent
At compound interest of cent per cent.
Though it is not always the case! I believe,
That the longer we've kept 'em the more do we grieve;
For when debts are payable, right or wrong,
A short time loan is as bad as a long –
So why in heaven (before we are there!)
Should we give our hearts for a dog to tear?

"The Power of the Dog", 1925

Hilaire Belloc

Here lies a Dog: may every Dog that dies
Lie in security – as this Dog lies.

> Epitaph on the Favourite
> Dog of a Politician, 1925.

William Henry Davies

When I was once a wandering man,
    And walked at midnight, all alone –
A friendly dog, that offered love,
    Was threatened with a stone.

"Go, go", I said, "and find a man
    Who has a home to call his own;
Who, with a luckier hand than mine,
    Can find his dog a bone."

But times are changed, and this pet dog
    Knows nothing of a life that's gone –
Of how a dog that offered love
    Was threatened with a stone.

> "Dogs", c. 1930

Anonymous

The horse and mule live thirty years
And nothing know of wines and beers.
The goat and sheep at twenty die
And never taste of Scotch or Rye.
The cow drinks water by the ton
And at eighteen is mostly done.
The dog at fifteen cashes in

Without the aid of rum and gin.
The cat in milk and water soaks
And then at twelve short years it croaks.
The modest, sober, bone-dry hen
Lays eggs for nogs, then dies at ten.
All animals are strictly dry:
They sinless live and swiftly die;
But sinful, ginful, rum-soaked men
Survive for three score years and ten.
And some of them, a very few,
Stay pickled till they're ninety-two.

"Poor Beasts"

Frances, Countess of Warwick

Nearly everyone knows the Dogs' Cemetery in Kensington Gardens. The little, secluded sanctuary, which contains the graves of over four hundred dogs, is known practically all over the world. It was founded many years ago by the Duchess of Cambridge. She was riding in her victoria in the Park one day and ran over her own dog, which was running beside the carriage. She asked that the body should be buried in the little garden of the keeper's lodge, and thus was started the graveyard that has since become so famous.

The cemetery is long since full – in fact it is now thirty years since a new grave was dug. All the dogs whose resting-places the tombstones mark are therefore the dogs of a past generation, and, as anyone who cares to visit the place will see, the epitaphs engraved on the small headstones reflect the attitude towards dogs of that generation. The predominant tone is sentiment. "Darling Dolly, my beam, my consolation, my joy," runs one inscription, and it fairly represents the way many people regarded their pets half a century ago; in those days a person either loved dogs with an effusive, sentimental love, or held a callous disregard for them. Of course there were exceptions (as the epitaph to a dog called Cora "Here lies a pal asleep" reveals), but in general it was either the one extreme or the other; fulsome love, or callous indifference.

Preface to *The Understanding of a Dog*, 1935

Evelyn Waugh

"Mr W. H., all happiness," said Dennis involuntarily.

"Pardon me?"

"I am the Happier Hunting Ground," said Dennis.

"Yes, come along in."

Dennis opened the back of the wagon and took out an aluminium container. "Will this be large enough?"

"Plenty."

They entered the house. A lady, also dressed for the evening in a long, low gown and a diamond tiara, sat in the hall with a glass in her hand.

"This has been a terrible experience for Mrs Heinkel."

"I don't want to see him. I don't want to speak of it," said the lady.

"The Happier Hunting Ground assumes all responsibility," said Dennis.

"This way, said Mr Heinkel. "In the pantry."

The Sealyham lay on the draining-board beside the sink. Dennis lifted it into the container.

Together he and Mr Heinkel carried their load to the wagon.

"Shall we discuss arrangements now, or would you prefer to call in the morning?"

"I'm a pretty busy man mornings," said Mr Heinkel. "Come into the study."

There was a tray on the desk. They helped themselves to whisky.

"I have our brochure here setting out our service. Were you thinking of internment or incineration?"

"Pardon me?"

"Buried or burned?"

"Burned, I guess."

"I have some photographs here of various styles of urn."

"The best will be good enough."

"Would you require a niche in our columbarium or do you prefer to keep the remains at home?"

"What you said first."

"And the religious rites? We have a pastor who is always pleased to assist."

"Well, Mr—?"

"Barlow."

"Mr Barlow, we're neither of us what you might call very church-going people, but I think on an occasion like this Mrs Heinkel would want all the comfort you can offer."

"Our Grade A service includes several unique features. At the moment of committal, a white dove, symbolizing the deceased's soul, is liberated over the crematorium."

"Yes," said Mr Heinkel, "I reckon Mrs Heinkel would appreciate the dove."

"And every anniversary a card of remembrance is mailed without further charge. It reads: *Your little Arthur is thinking of you in heaven today and wagging his tail.*"

"That's a very beautiful thought, Mr Barlow."

"Then if you will just sign the order. . . ."

Mrs Heinkel bowed gravely to him as he passed through the hall. Mr Heinkel accompanied him to the door of his car. "It has been a great pleasure to make your acquaintance, Mr Barlow. You have certainly relieved me of a great responsibility."

"That is what the Happier Hunting Ground aims to do," said Dennis, and drove away.

At the administrative building, he carried the dog to the refrigerator. It was a capacious chamber, already occupied by two or three other small cadavers. Next to a Siamese cat stood a tin of fruit juice and a plate of sandwiches. Dennis took his supper into the reception room, and, as he ate it, resumed his interrupted reading.

from *The Loved One*, 1948

Somerville and Ross

It is not too much to say that no one would be more shocked and surprised at being relegated to, as it were, the Heel of the Hunt, than those to whom these later thoughts refer. It is indeed almost with awe that one reflects on the greatness of soul, the self-respect, the self-consciousness (a quality that is attributed erroneously, I believe — to man only) of a very small terrier.

Especially are these present in the terrier that is accredited to a pack of Foxhounds. When it is considered what it can accomplish with that tiny rough body, those indomitable little legs, that absurdly small head, packed with constructive intelligence yet with a brain-pan no bigger than an apple, it is impossible to deny that its high opinion of itself is justified.

There was once a little white rough dog who was – or thought he was – in charge of a small pack of Fox-hounds in the South of Ireland. He was born of a noted strain of his sort in very distinguished surroundings, no less than the Kildare Hunt Establishment, and perhaps it was as well that, like Joseph, he was sold into captivity when he was too young to realize how very far he had come down in the world, geographically and otherwise. But, like Joseph, he soon rose to eminence. He was little more than a year old when his career as a Hunt terrier began, and the way in which he recognized and adapted himself to the conditions of his job came little short of genius. He soon realized the need of conserving his strength, and submitted to being parted from the Pack and carried by any available means to the Meet. Once there, however, he would break from control and, asserting himself as a foxhound among foxhounds, would become merged with the Pack.

But he had a technique of his own. Realizing that to struggle through the intricate jungles of those southern haunts of the Fox would exhaust him unduly before the more serious business began, he would, as soon as the Hounds were thrown into covert, post himself outside it on a convenient hillock, and there would sit, rigid, ears pricked, waiting for the first questioning note. When it came he would spring to attention. One could see that every fibre of his little body was hearkening for the next, and when certainty followed, Tatters – such was his unassuming name – like an arrow from the bow, would join his comrades, and in any interval of the melodious hound-music his small shrieks would fill the silence.

In the wild country which had become his there are seldom runs that do not find their earthly close in a drain or gully or similar place of refuge. Many were the occasions when the Hounds, having marked to Ground, would be found vainly endeavouring to thrust the greater, themselves, into that which could only contain the less, the Fox. The Huntsman, dragging by the stern a futile enthusiast out of the mouth of the hole, might then be seen looking over his shoulder, and asking, with pardonable violence, where that terrier had got to. "And then", as Lord Macaulay has said – certain quotations are so applicable that they must be corrupted to my purpose — "Then," I repeat, "the cry is 'Tatters!' and lo, the ranks divide, and —" but the quotation ceases to apply, for it is less like the stately stride of the Great Lord of Luna than a bullet leaving a gun when Tatters comes through the Field. He bores his way like an eel or an auger into the clamouring Pack, and if there is — as there generally is — a back-door to the drain, it is seldom long before the Fox has decided to leave by it, and, since the Hounds have been removed to a reasonable distance, the waiting and watching Field can view his retreat, relentlessly pursued by a little creature that is now dark brown and half its normal size, because drains are usually wet and muddy.

The Fox melts away — it is impossible to express the imperceptible way in which a fox can disappear. Even though he is — as an excited follower avers — the size of a chestnut horse, he is in a single instant incredibly lost to sight. The Hounds are laid on. Tatters is overtaken. Not so the Fox. In that hilly country of rocks and gullies and of what, locally, are spoken of as "His Dungeons", he, having been given his chance, far more often than not takes it.

Little Tatters soon became the idol of the Huntsman's heart. Every indulgence was his — rats, served up in a lordly trap, to gratify his zest for blood; the choicest morsels from the Hounds' kitchen; a barrel packed with straw and placed, in winter, as near the boiler-stove as possible. Even though those Kennels were not those of the Killing Kildares, Tatters was a happy little dog. A bride was found for him, white, like himself, with fascinating fair hair (her ears only, and one spot on her back) and with the similar tastes for rats and petty robbery that are so all-important in ensuring a happy married life. The little couple were established at the Huntsman's cottage, in due season a daughter blessed their union, and for a time all went well.

Unfortunately, however, Tatters began after a time to regard the comfortable cottage kitchen as his Capua, and craved for the original and sterner barrel at the Kennels. He had early developed a passion for the Doghounds. He preferred their society even to that of his wife and daughter, and he lost no opportunity of slipping into their kennel and spending his days among them.

One morning, early in Tatters' third season, the Huntsman, with the Hounds, met the Master at the Kennel-gates as usual. They were going hunting. The Huntsman, a North-country little man, who had come from the Bramham Moor Hounds, saluted the Master, lifting his cap with solemnity, but said no word of greeting. Something was wrong. The Master said, not without anxiety:

"Hounds all right?"

"I can't 'ardly bear to look at 'em!" was the remarkable response.

"Good heavens! What's wrong?"

"They've killed little Tattoo!"

This was Tatters' pet name. Tears ran down the little Huntsman's red face.

"'E got in among 'em last night, through the bars some way; I suppose they was startled like and didn't know it was 'im –"

That was a sad day's hunting. And as if to emphasize the fact of the recent tragedy, the only fox, found after a long day of trailing over the hills, got to ground immediately, and there was no little Tatters to fetch him out.

The widowed Mrs Tatters had never showed any fancy for the Chase. Her only game was rats, and even these, without the late Tatters to back her up at critical moments, soon ceased to interest her. She developed embonpoint and kept the house.

Maria and Some Other Dogs, 1949

Robert Garioch

My dug? If he wes killed, ye'll unnerstaun,
I'd murn as sair as gin they'd killed my brither.
Thon dug, ken this, there isnae sic anither,
Ye'll niver find his marra in the laun.

Ye suid jist see him eating breid, and gaun,
the dear wee thing, to seek things fir me, whither
to fesh my hat, or sneeshin-mull, whitiver,
and he duis things like we wad dae by haun.

When I win hame he wringles like an eel,
syne in the morn, ye suid see him stalk
to greet me, and he taks ma bairns to schuil.

He'll gae the messages, save me a walk
doun til the baker's and the pub . . . I feel
that the wan thing he vannae dae is talk.

"The Dug", *c.*1950

Ogden Nash

My little dog ten years ago
Was arrogant and spry,
Her backbone was a bended bow
For arrows in her eye.
Her step was proud, her bark was loud,
Her nose was in the sky,
But she was ten years younger then,
And so, by God, was I.

Small birds on stilts along the beach
Rose up with piping cry,
And as they flashed beyond her reach
I thought to see her fly.
If natural laws refused her wings,
That law she would defy,
For she could do unheard-of things,
And so, at times, could I.

Ten years ago she split the air
To seize what she could spy;
Tonight she bumps against a chair,
Betrayed by milky eye.
She seems to pant, Time up, time up!
My little dog must die,
And lie in dust with Hector's pup;
So, presently, must I.

"For a good dog", *The Private Dining
Room and other Verses*, 1953

Anonymous

IN COMMEMORATION OF TIP,
the sheepdog which stayed by the body of her dead master,
Mr Joseph Tagg,
on the Howden Moors for fifteen weeks
from 12th December 1953 to 27th March 1954.
Erected by public subscription.

Epitaph, 1954

A Northumbrian Gentleman (pseud.)

Once many years ago an old retriever bitch of his went wrong in her
waterworks through age. She had become completely unreliable
about the house and she should have been put down, but for a long
time he funked sending her to the vet. He finally decided that the
kindest thing he could do was to put her down himself.

He took her out with his gun as if he was about to shoot a rabbit.
They had had many a hunt together the man and the dog in the past.
The retriever would put the rabbits out of the gorse bushes for the
man to shoot.

The old man thought he would kill the bitch quickly whilst she
was hunting. He tried three times to raise his gun to her but found
that he could not bring himself to press the trigger. He felt a moral
coward. Finally he gave it up and came home with the bitch. He had
to ring up his daughter two days later to ask her to come and take the
old retriever to the vet to have her destroyed.

He felt parting with his animals keenly. The older he grew the
more painful were the farewells. Even now he dreaded having to
part with the cob he was riding, whenever he allowed himself to
think of it.

"That's the trouble with all animals," he thought. "They're so
much shorter lived than us humans, which means so many partings
in one's lifetime."

The Old Man Hunts, 1959

Dewey Gram

Californians have discovered a new way to cope with their grief when their pet dies: they freeze-dry the loved one and mount it in their living room.

Tasha, who died two years ago, still keeps Karen Nastasuk company. The freeze-dried Pekinese, his pink tongue sticking out as it always did, looks as if he is having a nap in her home in the San Francisco Bay area.

Nastasuk says: "I grew up with Tasha. He's been through two marriages with me. I guess I just couldn't let him go."

Freeze-drying is simpler and less gory than traditional taxidermy, which involves skinning the animal, removing biodegradables (eyes, footpads) then curing, stretching and forming the hide over a sculpted mannequin.

Freeze-drying leaves an animal substantially whole. It is shampooed, gutted, dipped in insect repellent, shot with preservatives, then posed with stiff internal wires, given artificial eyes and popped in a commercial freezer for a few days.

Lastly the pet goes into a $50,000 freeze-drying apparatus: a specimen chamber connected to a condensing chamber connected to a vaccuum-pump chamber. At 0 degrees F. moisture from the pet's frozen body sublimates, changing from ice to gas, and is drawn into the condensing chamber and removed.

The procedure is expensive ($400 for a small dog or cat, $1,000 for a German shepherd, $1,500 for a pit bull), and slow. It takes up to nine months. But Rod Skelton, the leading freeze-dryer in the West, says business is doubling every year.

Museums have been freeze-drying for 25 years but the use of the process for pets has angered traditional taxidermists, who see a crude technology replacing their art.

Michael O'Donnell, a taxidermist in Burbank, California, says: "You wouldn't stick old Grandma in the corner just because it makes you feel better. You should also have a little respect for your pet."

Nastasuk, who grooms Tasha every day with hair-spray and a blow-dryer, believes critics miss the point. "When Tasha died I couldn't work, I couldn't sleep. When I finally found a place that would preserve him, I could finally get on with my life."

"A perfect pet comes frozen to the core", *The Sunday Times*, 6 October 1985

Milan Kundera

Dogs do not have many advantages over people, but one of them is extremely important: euthanasia is not forbidden by law in their case; animals have the right to a merciful death. Karenin walked on three legs and spent more and more of his time lying in a corner. And whimpering. Both husband and wife agreed that they had no business letting him suffer needlessly. But agree as they might in principle, they still had to face the anguish of determining the time when his suffering was in fact needless, the point at which life was no longer worth living.

If only Tomas hadn't been a doctor! Then they would have been able to hide behind a third party. They would have been able to go back to the vet and ask him to put the dog to sleep with an injection.

Assuming the role of Death is a terrifying thing. Tomas insisted that he would not give the injection himself; he would have the vet come and do it. But then he realized that he could grant Karenin a privilege forbidden to humans: Death would come for him in the guise of his loved ones.

Karenin had whimpered all night. After feeling his leg in the morning, Tomas said to Tereza, "There's no point in waiting."

In a few minutes they would both have to go to work. Tereza went in to see Karenin. Until then, he had lain in his corner completely apathetic (not even acknowledging Tomas when he felt his leg), but when he heard the door open and saw Tereza come in, he raised his head and looked at her.

She could not stand his stare; it almost frightened her. He did not look that way at Tomas, only at her. But never with such intensity. It was not a desperate look, or even sad. No, it was a look of awful, unbearable trust. The look was an eager question. All his life Karenin had waited for answers from Tereza, and he was letting her know (with more urgency than usual, however) that he was still ready to learn the truth from her. (Everything that came from Tereza was the truth. Even when she gave commands like "Sit!" or "Lie down!" he took them as truths to identify with, to give his life meaning.)

His look of awful trust did not last long; he soon laid his head back down on his paws. Tereza knew that no one ever again would look at her like that.

They had never fed him sweets, but recently she had bought him a few chocolate bars. She took them out of the foil, broke them into pieces, and made a circle of them around him. Then she brought over a bowl of water to make sure that he had everything he needed for the several hours he would spend at home alone. The look he had given her just then seemed to have tired him out. Even surrounded by chocolate, he did not raise his head.

She lay down on the floor next to him and hugged him. With a slow and labored turn of the head, he sniffed her and gave her a lick or two. She closed her eyes while the licking went on, as if she wanted to remember it forever. She held out the other cheek to be licked.

Then she had to go and take care of her heifers. She did not return until just before lunch. Tomas had not come home yet. Karenin was still lying on the floor surrounded by the chocolate, and did not even lift his head when he heard her come in. His bad leg was swollen now, and the tumor had burst in another place. She noticed some light red (not blood-like) drops forming beneath his fur.

Again she lay down next to him on the floor. She stretched one arm across his body and closed her eyes. Then she heard someone banging on the door. "Doctor! Doctor! The pig is here! The pig and his master!" She lacked the strength to talk to anyone, and did not move, did not open her eyes. "Doctor! Doctor! The pigs have come!" Then silence.

Tomas did not get back for another half hour. He went straight to the kitchen and prepared the injection without a word. When he entered the room, Tereza was on her feet and Karenin was picking himself up. As soon as he saw Tomas, he gave him a weak wag of the tail.

"Look," said Tereza, "he's still smiling."

She said it beseechingly, trying to win a short reprieve, but did not push for it.

Slowly she spread a sheet out over the couch. It was a white sheet with a pattern of tiny violets. She had everything carefully laid out and thought out, having imagined Karenin's death many days in advance. (Oh, how horrible that we actually dream ahead to the death of those we love!)

He no longer had the strength to jump up on the couch. They picked him up in their arms together. Tereza laid him on his side, and Tomas examined one of his good legs. He was looking for a more or less prominent vein. Then he cut away the fur with a pair of scissors.

Tereza knelt by the couch and held Karenin's head close to her own.

Tomas asked her to squeeze the leg because he was having trouble sticking the needle in. She did as she was told, but did not move her face from his head. She kept talking gently to Karenin, and he thought only of her. He was not afraid. He licked her face two more times. And Tereza kept whispering, "Don't be scared, don't be scared, you won't feel any pain there, you'll dream of squirrels and rabbits, you'll have cows there, and Mefisto will be there, don't be scared . . ."

Tomas jabbed the needle into the vein and pushed the plunger. Karenin's leg jerked; his breath quickened for a few seconds, then stopped. Tereza remained on the floor by the couch and buried her face in his head.

Then they both had to go back to work and leave the dog laid out on the couch, on the white sheet with tiny violets.

They came back towards evening. Tomas went into the garden. He found the lines of the rectangle that Tereza had drawn with her heel between the two apple trees. Then he started digging. He kept precisely to her specifications. He wanted everything to be just as Tereza wished.

She stayed in the house with Karenin. She was afraid of burying him alive. She put her ear to his mouth and thought she heard a weak breathing sound. She stepped back and seemed to see his breast moving slightly.

(No, the breath she heard was her own, and because it set her own body ever so slightly in motion, she had the impression the dog was moving.)

She found a mirror in her bag and held it to his mouth. The mirror was so smudged she thought she saw drops on it, drops caused by his breath.

"Tomas! He's alive!" she cried, when Tomas came in from the garden in his muddy boots.

Tomas bent over him and shook his head.

They each took an end of the sheet he was lying on, Tereza the lower end, Tomas the upper. Then they lifted him up and carried him out to the garden.

The sheet felt wet to Tereza's hands. He puddled his way into our lives and now he's puddling his way out, she thought, and she was glad to feel the moisture on her hands, his final greeting.

They carried him to the apple trees and set him down. She leaned over the pit and arranged the sheet so that it covered him entirely. It was unbearable to think of the earth they would soon be throwing over him, raining down on his *naked body*.

Then she went into the house and came back with his collar, his leash, and a handful of the chocolate that had lain untouched on the floor since morning. She threw it all in after him.

Next to the pit was a pile of freshly dug earth. Tomas picked up the shovel.

Just then Tereza recalled her dream: Karenin giving birth to two rolls and a bee. Suddenly the words sounded like an epitaph. She pictured a monument standing there, between the apple trees, with the inscription *Here lies Karenin. He gave birth to two rolls and a bee.*

It was twilight in the garden, the time between day and evening. There was a pale moon in the sky, a forgotten lamp in the room of the dead.

Their boots were caked with dirt by the time they took the shovel and spade back to the recess where their tools stood all in a row: rakes, watering cans, hoes.

from *The Unbearable Lightness of Being*, 1984 trans. Michael Heim

T. H. White

Brownie, I am free of you,
Who ruled my heart for 14 years!
O Freedom, all begun anew,
O iceblock heart, O tears!

My gentleness, my trustfulness,
My looker-up, my life,
My coward who leaned on my care
In vain, my child and wife.

My mother with the golden pelt,
Myself with melting eye,
My Brownie, rooted in the core,
My hoping lover – lie.

"Brownie, I am free of you,"
A Joy Proposed

Acknowledgements

Every effort has been made to trace copyright holders; in a few instances this has not proved to be possible. I am grateful that permission has so readily and generously been given to quote from:

Lt Col. G. H. Badcock, *The Understanding of a Dog* (Herbert Jenkins 1935); Les Barker, 'Mrs Ackroyd's retreat from Crufts' (*Our Dogs*); Robert Bernen, 'The Yellow Dog', *Tales from the Blue Stacks*; Terence Brady, 'Bobby's Main Vice was Orgies' (*Living*); Victor Chapple, 'Pedigree Chump' (*The Sun*); Jim Corbett, *Man-eaters of Kumaon* (Oxford University Press); William Henry Davies, 'The Dog', 'D is for Dog', 'Dogs' (Jonathan Cape, London); Cecil Day-Lewis, *Sheepdog Trials in Hyde Park* (Jonathan Cape, London); Gerald Malcolm Durrell, *My Family and Other Animals* (Curtis Brown); Robert Garioch, *The Dug* (Macdonald); Roy Hattersley, 'Me and My Dogs' (*The Listener*); Montague H. Horn, 'On the Working-Terrier Class' (*Our Dogs*); Frank Jackson, 'The Company in Session', 'Dirty Dog', and 'Caveat Emptor' (*Our Dogs*); James Joyce, *Ulysses* (Faber and Faber); Miles Kington, 'Adorning the Upper Cruft' (*The Independent*); Rudyard Kipling, *The Cat that walked by himself, Old Man Kangaroo, A Sea Dog, The Power of the Dog* (Macmillan); Donald Robert Perry Marquis, *certain maxims of archy, the merry flea* (Macmillan); John Masefield, *Reynard the Fox* (Heinemann); Harold Monro, *Dog* (Duckworth & Co); Dr Desmond Morris, *Dogwatching* (Jonathan Cape); Michael Murray, 'A Pipsqueak with the Heart of a Lion' (Northern Border Club); Ogden Nash, 'For a good dog', 'Two dogs have I' (Dent); D. Nunn, 'The Show that Cruft Built'

(*Our Dogs*); Proteus; *A Lady of Seniority*; E. Arnot Robertson, review of *Thurber's Dogs* (*The Spectator*); Damon Runyon, 'The Blood-hounds of Broadway', *More than Somewhat* (Constable); Siegfried Sassoon, *Man and Dog* (Faber); Edith Somerville and Martin Ross, 'Trinket's Colt', 'The Man that Came to Buy Apples', 'The Pug-nosed Fox', 'The Whiteboys', *Further Experiences of an Irish R.M.* (Longmans, Green and Co.); John Steinbeck, *Travels with Charley*, *Tortilla Flat* (William Heinemann 1935); Frederick Watson, *Hunting Pie*, *In the Pink* (Witherby); Evelyn Waugh, *The Loved One*, 1947 (Peters Fraser and Dunlop); Terence Hanbury White, *Once and Future King*, 'Brownie, I am free of you', *The Goshawk*, *England Have My Bones* (Martin Secker & Warburg); Virginia Woolf, *Flush* (Faber and Faber).

Index of Authors

Acosta, Father Joseph de [16c] 232
Addison, Joseph [1672–1719] 318–20, 345
Aelianus, Claudius [c.220] 49–50, 317
Aldrovandi, Ulisse [1522–1605] 200–1, 317
Alken, Henry Thomas [1785–1851] 180–1
Anonymous 80, 91–2, 99–100, 108, 111–12, 114, 123–5, 136, 181–
   2, 188–9, 257, 272–4, 285, 328–30, 345–9, 357, 366, 368–9, 371–
   2, 403–4, 417–18, 447, 454, 467, 472, 481, 482–3, 497–8, 505
Arbuthnot, Dr John [1667–1735] 478–9
Arnim, Elizabeth, Countess von [1866–1941] 421
Arnold, Matthew [1822–88] 300, 492–3
Arrian (Flavius Arrianus) [95–180] 341
Aubrey, John [1626–97] 135

Badcock, Lt. Col. G. H. [20c] 388–9
Bacon, Francis [16c] 233
Barham, Revd Richard [1788–1845] 323, 488
Barker, Les [20c] 396–7
Barkley, H. C. [20c] 313–14
Barnes, Dame Julyans [14c] 19–20, 127–8
Beckford, Peter [1740–1811] 28, 158
Beeton, Mrs Isabella Mary [1836–65] 442–3
Bell, Isaac [1878–?] 355–6
Bell, Professor Thomas [1792–1800] 16–17
Belloc, Hilaire [1870–1953] 497
Benét, Stephen Vincent [1898–1943] 76

Bennett, Alan [b.1934] 270
Bernen, Robert (20c) 334–7
Bewick, Thomas [1753–1828] 8–9, 138, 284
Bierce, Ambrose Gwinett [1842–c.1914] 209
Billings, Josh (pseud. Henry Wheeler Shaw) [1818–85] 95
Blunden, Edmund [1896–1974] 241
Boece, Hector [c.1465–1536] 82–3
Borrow, George [1803–81] 183–4, 325–6, 490–1
Bradford, John [16c] 173
Brady, Terence [20c] 399–403
Brontë, Anne [1820–49] 182
Brontë, Emily Jane [1818–48] 205–6
Browning, Elizabeth Barrett [1806–61] 65–7
Browning, Robert [1812–89] 94–5
Burns, Robert [1759–96] 240–1
Burton, Robert [1577–1640] 461
Butler, Samuel [1612–80] 8, 237, 416
Byron, George Gordon, 6th Baron of Rochdale [1788–1824]
    453–4, 484–5

Calverley, Charles Stuart [1831–84] 39, 492
Camerarius, Joachim [1500–74] 53–4
Campbell, Roy [1901–57] 266
Campbell, Thomas [1777–1844] 244–5
Canute the Great (Sveinsson Knut) [c.970–1035] 108
Carlyle, Jane Baillie Welsh [1801–66] 207
Carlyle, Thomas [1795–1881] 64–5, 490
Carroll, Lewis (pseud. Charles Ludwidge Dodgson) [1832–98]
    327–8
Caxton, William [c.1422–91] 200
Cecil, William, Lord Burghley [1520–98] 54
Cervantes Saavedra, Miguel de [1547–1616] 133
Chalmers, Patrick [1872–1942] 149, 261
Chapple, Victor [20c] 458–9
Chaucer, Geoffrey [c.1345–1400] 200
Chesterton, Gilbert Keith [1874–1936] 352
Chestre, Thomas [14c] 50–1
Cicero, Marcus Tullius [106–43BC] 49
Clapham, Richard [1878–?] 155–8

Clare, John [1793–1864] 91
Cobbett, William [1763–1835] 161
Colvin, Sir Sidney [1845–1927] 70–1
Corbett, Jim [20c] 167–70
Cotgrave, Randle [d.c.1634] 21
Cowper, William [1731–1800] 56, 89–91, 241, 483
Cox, Harding [20c] 257–9, 309–11, 494–5
Cox, Nicholas [17c] 473
Crabbe, George [1754–1832] 59, 61
Crowley, Robert [16c] 172–3

Daniel, Revd William Barker [1753–1833] 243, 321–2, 484
Darbyshire, E. [19c] 77–8
Dare, Shirley [19c] 367
Darwin, Charles [1809–82] 9–10, 354–5
Das, Sarat Chandra [19c] 466
Davies, E. W. L. [c.1840–?] 367–8
Davies, Sir John [c.1565–1618] 5, 175–6
Davies, William Henry [1871–1940] 71, 77, 497
Day, J Wentworth [20c] 30–1
DeLong, Lt. Com. George Washington 11
Dickens, Charles [1812–70] 13, 63–4, 69–70, 93–4, 370–1, 414–15
Dillon, Francis (Ed) [20c] 374–5
Diogenes the Cynic [c.410–320BC] 9
Doyle, Sir Arthur Conan [1859–1930] 287–8
Drayton, Michael [1563–1631] 54, 282
Druid, The (pseud. Henry Hall Dixon) [1822–70] 139–40, 324–5
Durrell, Gerald Malcolm [1925–95] 267

Eardley-Wilmot, Sir J. [1811–92] 142–3
Eaton, Prestwich [17c] 413
Edward, 2nd Duke of York [c.1373–1415] 2–3, 19, 125–7, 459–60
Edward the Confessor [c.1003–66] 122
Eliot, George (pseud. Mary Ann Evans) [1819–80] 284
Ellangowan (pseud.) [19c] 404
Elliott, Ebenezer [19c] 245
Erskine, Thomas, 1st Baron [1750–1823] 481
Eustis, Dorothy [20c] 100–1
Evelyn, John [1620–1706] 176

Fawcett, William [20c] 153–4
Fitz-Barnard, Captain Lawrence [20c] 191–4, 356–7
Fitzpatrick, Sir Percy [19c] 289–99
Fitzroy, Robert [1805–65] 322–3
Fleming, Abraham [16c] 51–2, 83–6, 128–31, 151–2, 173–4, 201–2, 206, 280–2
Fortesque, John W [20c] 165–6
Frankau, Gilbert [1884–1953] 214–17
Froissart, Jean [c.1333–c.1404] 230–1
Fuller, Revd Thomas [1608–61] 176–7

Galsworthy, John [1867–1933] 78–9, 212
Garioch, Robert (Robert Garioch Sutherland) [1909–1981] 269–70, 503–4
Garst, Shannon [20c] 101–3, 312–13
Gaskell, Mrs Elizabeth Cleghorn [1810–65] 68–9
Gay, John [1685–1732] 22–3, 88–9, 158–9, 480
Gaza, Theodorus [1398–1478] 2, 50
Goldsmith, Oliver [1728–74] 3–4, 31, 464–5
Googe, Barnabe [1540–94] 23–4
Gram, Dewey [20c] 506–7
Gratius Faliscus [c.1st century] 24–5, 412
Graves, John Woodcock [1786–1886] 144–5
Gray, Thomas [1716–71] 204
Gray, Thomas de [17c] 462
Greene, (Henry) Graham [1904–91] 222–5
Grenfell, Julian Henry Francis [1888–1915] 20–1
Guilpin, Edward [16c] 175

Haakonsson, Magnus VI, the Law-Reformer [1238–80] 110
Hallam, Henry [1777–1859] 62–3
Halliwell-Philips, James Orchard [1820–89] 204–5
Hamilton, William [1704–54] 16
Hanger, Colonel George [1760–1824] 453
Hardy, Thomas [1840–1928] 299–300
Harington, Sir John [1561–1612] 132, 174–5, 233–5
Harrison, William [1534–93] 412, 451–2
Hart, James [17c] 452
Hašek, Jaraslov [1883–1923] 300–1, 446–7

Hattersley, Roy Sidney George [b.1932] 218–22
Hawker, Lt Col. Peter [1786–1830] 113, 116–17
Hazlitt, William [1788–1830] 204
Heinemann, Arthur Blake [1871–1930] 194–7, 379–81
Henry, O. (pseud. William Sydney Porter) [1862–1910] 252–6
Herrick, Robert [1591–1674] 478
Hervey, Lord John, 1st Earl of Bristol [1696–1743] 480
Hodgkins, Thomas [19c] 58
Hogg, James [1770–1835] 62
Holland, Norah M. [19c] 493
Homer [8th century BC] 48
Hopkins, Matthew [d.1647] 318
Horace [65–8BC] 121
Horn, Montague H. [20c] 390
Houghton, John [17c] 178–9
Hudson, William Henry [1841–1922] 11–13, 211, 301–8
Hutchinson, Walter [20c] 457
Hutchinson, Woods [20c] 44–5
Huxley, Thomas [19c] 115

Idstone (pseud. Thomas Pearce) [19c] 286–7, 475
Irving, Washington [1783–1859] 61–2

Jackson, Frank [b.1933] 274–7, 391–6, 428–39
Jefferies, Richard [1848–87] 147, 208
Jerome, Jerome Klapka [1859–1927] 31–3, 208–9, 248–9, 288, 494
Jesse, George R. [19c] 109–10
Joyce, James [1882–1941] 15
Juvenal [c.55–c.140] 230

Kington, Miles [20c] 397–9
Kipling, Rudyard [1865–1936] 45–6, 312, 496
Knollys, Francis [19c] 475
Krehl, George R. [19c] 96–9
Kundera, Milan [20c] 507–10

Labouchère, Henry du Pré [1831–1912] 207
La Fontaine, Jean de [1621–95] 112, 134, 473
Lamb, Charles [1775–1834] 468

Lang, Andrew [1844–1912] 330–1, 456–7

Lang, John and Jean [20c] 469–70

Lee, Rawdon Briggs [1845–1908] 373

Lehmann, Rudolph Chambers [1856–1929] 250–2

Lennox, Lord William Pitt [19c] 133–4

Lesmoir-Gordon, Mrs [20c] 418–19

Lewis, Percy Wyndham [1882–1957] 312

Lewis, Cecil Day- [1904–72] 409–15

London, Jack [1876–1916] 71–3, 210–11, 256–7, 405–8, 472

Lucas, Sir Jocelyn M. [20c] 189–91

Lucas, Edward Verrall [1868–1938] 260

Luther, Martin [1483–1546] 128

Lytton, Judith Anne, Baroness Wentworth [20c] 14, 375–7, 420

Macaulay, Thomas Babington [1800–59] 246, 489

Mackie, Sir Peter Jeffrey [19c] 378–9

Macpherson, James [1736–96] 136–7

Maeterlinck, Count Maurice [1862–1949] 79

Malory, Sir Thomas [d.1471] 231

Mansfield, Katherine [1888–1923] 213

Manwood, John [16c] 108–9

Markham, Gervase [1568–1637] 21–2, 25–8, 343–4, 471–2

Markland, George [18c] 153

Marples, Theophilus [1848–1931] 115–16

Marquis, Donald Robert Perry [1878–1937] 384, 470–1

Marston, John [?1575–1634] 202–3

Martial [c.40–c.104] 229

Masefield, John Edward [1878–1967] 146, 165

Mayhew, Henry [1812–87] 92–3, 184–7, 415–16, 440–2

McLachan, David [19c] 369–70

McLeod, Irene [20c] 350

Merrill, Bob [20c] 427

Mitford, Mary Russell [1787–1855] 323–4

Monro, Harold [1879–1932] 259–60

Moore, Thomas [1779–1852] 244

Moorman (pseud. William Carnegie) [19c] 148–9

More, Sir Thomas, St [1478–1535] 128

Morris, Dr Desmond [b.1928] 103

Murray, Michael [20c] 339–40

Nash, Ogden Frederick [1902–71] 217–18, 504
Nashe, Thomas [1567–1601] 87
Newcastle, William Cavendish, Duke of [17c] 177
Nightingale, Florence [1820–1910] 93
Nimrod (pseud. Charles Apperley) [1779–1843] 160, 355
Nixon, Richard Milhous [1913–95] 266
Northumbrian Gentleman (pseud.) [20c] 505
Nottingham, Earl of [16c] 413
Nunn, D. [20c] 386–7

Ogilvie, Will H. [1869–1962] 17–18, 154–5, 166, 213, 349
Ollivant, Alfred [19c] 74–6, 288–9
Orwell, George (pseud. Eric Blair) [1903–50] 262
Osborne, Dorothy [1629–95] 413
Ovid, (Publius Ovidius Naso) [43BC–17AD] 122

P., J. M. [20c] 73–4
Pennycuik, Dr Alexander [18c] 283
Pepys, Samuel [1633–1703] 87–8, 236–7
Petronius (1st century) 228–9
Plato [c.428–c.348BC] 5–7
Pliny the Elder, (Gaius Plinius Secundus) [AD 23–79] 459
Plutarch [AD 46–120] 49, 230, 478
Polo, Marco [1254–1324] 122–3
Poole, Revd Robert [18c] 111
Pope, Alexander [1688–1744] 135, 239, 284, 414, 479, 480
Pound, Ezra Loomis [1885–1972] 8
Pratt, Samuel [?] 60–1
Prior, Matthew [1664–1721] 55
Proteus (pseud.) [20c] 337–8
Public notice [1794] 465–6

Queneau, Raymond [1903–76] 332–4

Raleigh, Sir Walter Alexander [19c] 248
Ramsay, Allan [1713–84] 238–9
Raspe, Rudolph Erich [1737–94] 465
Rastell, John [1475–1536] 478
Ray, John [1627–1705] 316–17

Reach, Angus Bethune [19c] 140–1
Ring-Ouzel (pseud.) [?] 158
Ritson, Lady Kitty [20c] 384–5
Robertson, E. Arnot [20c] 214
Rogers, Samuel [1763–1855] 320
Ross, Martin (pseud. Violet Martin) [1862–1915]
Rostand, Edmond [1868–1918] 289
Rousseau, Jean-Jacques [1712–78] 7
Runyon, Damon [1884–1946] 263–6
Rupert, Prince [1619–82] 439
Ruskin, John [1819–1900] 247–8
Russell, Revd John (Jack) [1795–1884] 417

Salter, Dr John Henry [1841–1932] 162–4, 187–8, 373–4, 377–8
Sand, George (pseud. Amandine Aurore Lucie Dupin, Baronne
   Dudevant) [1804–1876] 327
Sartre, Jean-Paul [1905–80] 261
Sassoon, Siegfried [1886–1967] 79
Scott, Robert Falcon [1868–1912] 350
Scott, Sir Walter [1771–1832] 10, 138–9, 403, 486
Scrutator (pseud. K. W. Horlock) [b.c.1800] 141–2
Shakespeare, William [1564–1616] 232–3, 342–3, 403
Shelley, Percy Bysshe [1792–1822] 322
Sheridan, Richard Brinsley [1751–1816] 179
Sinclair, Sir John [1754–1835] 113
Sloan, A. and Farquar, A. [20c] 42–4
Smart, Christopher [1722–71] 239–40
Smith, Sydney [1771–1845] 487–8
Smollett, Tobias [1721–71] 240
Somervile, William [1675–1742] 28–9, 89, 462–4
Somerville, Edith Anna Oenone [1858–1949] 29–30, 145, 210,
   381–2, 454–6, 468–9, 500–3
Sorel, Agnes [c.1422–50] 231
Southey, Robert [1774–1843] 179–80, 243, 467–8
Soyer, Alexis [1809–58] 489–90
Sparrow, John Hanbury Angus [b.1906] 270
Spencer, Sir Stanley [1891–1959] 270
Spenser, Edmund [1552–99] 86–7, 175
St John, Charles [?] 161–2, 325

Steele, Sir Richard [1672–1729] 238
Steinbeck, John Ernest [1902–68] 269, 457–8
Stevenson, Robert Louis Balfour [1850–94] 328
Stonehenge, (pseud. John Henry Walsh) [d.1888] 474
Stowe, Harriet Elizabeth Beecher [1811–96] 35–9
Strindberg, August [1849–1912] 249
Sturgeon, A. G. [20c] 382
Surflet, Richard [16c] 461
Surtees, Robert Smith [1779–1834] 142, 143–4, 162, 164–5
Swift, Dr Jonathan [1667–1745] 203–4, 440
Szasz, Kathleen [20c] 427–8

Taplin, William [17c] 35, 137–8, 320–1
Taylor, John [?1578–1653] 23, 133
Tennyson, Alfred, Lord [1809–92] 243
Thompson, Thomas [1880–1951] 150–1, 422–7, 475–6
Thurber, James [1895–1961] 389–90
Tickell, Thomas [1686–1740] 135–6
Tickner, John [20c] 271–2, 391
Todd, D. P. [20c] 387–8
Topsell, William [d.1638] 202
Toynbee, Arnold [1889–1975] 267
Turbervile, George [c.1540–c.1610] 131–2, 461
Twain, Mark (pseud. Samuel Langhorne Clemens) [1835–1910]
  252, 331
T'zu Hsi, Dowager Empress (d.1860) 450–1

Varro, Marcus Terentius [116–27BC] 18, 411
Veblen, Thorstein [1857–1929] 417
Vest, George Graham [19c] 246–7
Vigne, Gace de la [14c] 4, 127, 341–2
"Vincent" [?] 59, 159–60

Walpole, Horace [1717–97] 112–13, 482
Walpole, Sir Hugh Seymour [1884–1941] 311–12, 421
Walsh, I. [17c] 283
Walton, Izaak [1593–1683] 344–5
Warwick, Frances, Countess of [20c] 498
Watson, Frederick [1885–1935] 350–2, 382–4

Watson, James [20c] 420
Watson, John [19c] 147–8
Watts, Isaac [1674–1748] 10
Wentworth, Baroness, *see* Lytton
Waugh, Evelyn Arthur St John [1903–66] 499–500
White, Revd Gilbert [1720–93] 33–4
White, Terence Hanbury [1906–64] 167, 267–9, 510–11
Wilkes, John [1727–97] 482
William of Wykeham, Bishop of Winchester [1324–1404] 111
Winner, Septimus [19c] 246
Wodehouse, Sir Pelham Grenville [1881–1975] 262–3
Wood, Revd J. G. [19c] 207
Woodforde, Revd James [1740–1803] 452
Woolf, Virginia [1882–1941] 14, 443–6, 470
Wordsworth, William [1770–1850] 56–8, 242, 486–7
Wotherspoon, Ralph [?] 214

Xenophon [*c.*435–354BC] 120–1

Yates, Dornford [1885–1960] 212
Youatt, William [19c] 46–8, 228, 466–7, 474

Index of Subjects

affection, disinterested 48
Agaseus 129–30
aged dogs 79, 337–8, 486, 487–8, 492, 504, 505
ailments 286, 449–76
Airedale 368
Alaskan dogs 312–13
Alice in Wonderland 327–8
Allan, types of 21
Alsatian 384
American foxhounds 29–30
animal cult 262
Aquaticus sevinquisitor 152
Argus 235

badger-baiting 182, 188
badger bites 195
badger-digging 132, 158, 189–91, 195, 196–7
Baian 122
Balaban 301
Baldy 313
Ball 282
Bandogge 24, 173, 281
Barnaby 97, 98
Barnet 283
Basset 1
Battersea Dogs' Home 114, 115, 458–9
Bawty 238–9
baying 350
Beagle 24, 25–6, 137–8, 343

bear baiting 172–3, 174, 177
bear baiting pits 172
Bear Garden 176, 177
beating dogs 68–9, 100
Beau 241
Beauty 222–5
Bedlington Terrier 368, 380
Bellman 144
bereavement *see* death
Beth Gelert 490–1
Biblical references to dogs 228
Bill Sikes' dog 63–4
Billy 360
bites
    badger 195
    dog 114, 116, 462, 464–5
    fox 195
    rat 187
    remedies 459
Blenheim Spaniel 247–8, 303
blind, companions to the 60–1, 93–4, 100–1
blood-dogs 36
Bloodhound 83–5, 96–9, 136, 264–6, 322
    cross-breeding 354
    in former lives 320
    scenting powers of 84
blush, a dog's inability to 252
Boar-hound 31
Boatswain (Byron's dog) 244, 484
Bob 329–30

Bobby 400–1
The Bold 212
Boney 181
Border Terrier 391
Borzoi 1
boundaries, laws of 14
brachet (hound) 123, 231
Bran 136, 137
branding 474
breeding 139–40, 284, 353–7
    commercial breeding 276, 411
    costs 393
    hybrids 281–2, 285
    pedigrees 313–14
    see also cross-breeding;
        interbreeding
Bridget 191–2
Brownie 510–11
bubonic plague 107
Buck 71–3, 404–8
bull baiting 172, 174–5, 176, 177–80
bull baiting pits 172
Bulldog 1, 31, 32, 36, 68–9, 240
    as food for humans 207
    bred for fighting 31, 36, 356–7
    cross-breeding 286, 354, 356
    in former lives 321
Bull-terrier 357, 369
Bungey 235
Burgho 97, 98
burials 478
butchers' dogs 175, 359, 411
buying dogs 420, 422–7
Byron, Lord 244

Caesar 230
Cairn terrier 220
calming influence of dogs 81, 103
Canute's Forest Laws (1016) 105
carcases, utilisation of 115–16
Carolina foxes 120
Catalan Sheepdog 400
Cathenarius 173, 174
cat-killing 188
cats 238
Celtic dogs 341
cemeteries for dogs 489, 498

Cerberus 288
character and habits 1, 2–80
charity, dogs and 472
Charles II 243
Charley 269
charm to preserve dogs from madness
    461
Chesapeake Bay Retriever 30, 31
chicken killing 310
Chihuahua 1, 81, 420
children, dogs as substitutes for 206,
    230
Chinese dogs 25, 34, 42–3
Chinuchi 122
Chowder 240
church, attendance at 37, 111, 328–9
Church attitude towards animal
    suffering 171
Cleveland Agricultural Society 362
clipping dogs 471–2
Clumber Spaniel 309
coat, condition of 453
Cockie 494–5
cold, affected by the 38–9, 161–2
college dogs 106, 207
collies 31, 32
communication 167, 212, 325,
    332–4, 337–8
companions, dogs as 421
competitions 359–410
computer-age dog 397–8
conspicuous consumption, dogs as
    items of 417
control of dogs 105–17
    laming dogs 105, 108–10
    legislation 105
    licensing system 107–8
    muzzling 115, 116, 302, 308
    wholesale slaughter 107
conversation spoilers 246
Coonhound 247
Corgi 353
Court, keeping dogs at 111–12
Cribb 324
cropped ears 473, 474, 475
cross-breeding 286–7, 354, 355
    hybrids 281–2, 285

Cruft's 363, 385–6, 387, 396–7
"Crufts" (hypothetical breed) 397–8
Cuban dog 64
cunning 306, 307
currour 280
curs 279–80
curtail-dog 279–80

Dachshund 249, 300, 359, 493
Dan 330–1
dancing dogs 92–3, 281, 282
Dandie Dinmont 18, 197, 368, 380
Dangerous Dogs Act 1991 105
Dart 487
Dash 248, 309–11, 468
Daunser 281
death
  cemeteries 489, 498
  epitaphs 55, 246–7, 478–9, 480,
    481, 482–3, 484–5, 497, 505
  freeze-drying the dog 506–7
  putting a dog down 505, 507–10
  right to a merciful death 507
  undertakers and funeral services
    499–50
death, faithfulness unto 42, 48,
  49–51, 54, 57–8
Deerhound 363
deer hunting 119–20, 133
dhole 16
Dido 321–2
Dinah (Roy Hattersley's dog)
  218–19, 221–2
dingoes 16, 348
Dino 332–4
Diogenes 414–15
disagreeable habits 12–13, 225
distemper 382, 420
docking 449, 473, 474, 475–6
dog dealers 300–1, 416, 418–19,
  428–9
  "lady" dealers 420
dog fighting 171, 176, 180–4, 187–8
dog-haters 103, 214–15, 270
dogmen 274–7
Dog Order (Northern Ireland) 107–8
dog population 199, 262

dog races 313
  sled-dog races 313, 364, 365
dog-rose 243
Dogs' Cemetery, Kensington Gardens
  498
dog-sellers see dog dealers
dog's eye view 252–6, 260
dog shows 359–410
  American shows 384–5
  commercial side 388–9
  dishonesty 394–5
  effect on the sporting dog 31, 357,
    377–8
  establishment of in Britain 360–1
  exhibitor behaviour 370, 381–2,
    399–400
  first recorded 359
  judges 369–70, 372, 375–6, 388–9,
    394–5
  judges, bribing 371
  puppy shows 382–3
  in Russia 373–4
Dogue de Bordeaux 1
dog-violet 243
domestic disputes over dogs 236–7
drinking troughs 457
drover's dog 69–70
drowned and drowning dogs
  299–300, 487, 494
drowning, saving children from 94–5
dyeing dogs 301, 394, 446

ears 34
  cropped 473, 474, 475
earth dogs 271
earth-stoppers 145
eating dogs 34, 207, 489–90
eczema 311
Egyptian veneration of dogs 228
Elizabeth I 119–20, 171
Elizabeth II 353
endearments 243, 253
epileptic seizures in humans,
  detecting 82, 315
epitaphs 55, 246–7, 478–9, 480, 481,
  482–3, 484–5, 497
expectations of dogs 456–7

expenditure on dogs 427–8
extinction of dogs 270

"fairy dog" 325–6
familiars, dogs as 318
fanciers 275, 367
faults of the dog 328
Favorite 92
feeding 453
   burying food 12, 13
   dislikes of certain foods 4
   human flesh 458–9
female maltreatment, absence of
   256–7
ferrets 186
fewterers 123
fidelity 41, 46, 48, 49–58, 60–3,
   246–7
fighting dogs 191–4
   breeding 356–7
   natural instinct 10, 11, 303
Fillan 137
finders 152
Finette 92
Fizzy 14
fleas 383, 470–1
flogging 113
Flush (Elizabeth Barrett Browning's
   dog) 65–7, 444–6, 470
food for humans, dogs as 34, 207,
   489–90
food, thieving 454
Fop 483
fowling 152–3, 168–9
fox dog see Pomeranian
foxes
   bites 195
   reaction to music 348
foxhounds 287, 500–3
   American 29–30
   breeding 353, 355–6
   cropped ears 474
foxhunting
   on foot 140–1
   with terriers 195
Fox Terrier 32–3, 215, 303, 369
   as sheepdog 375

freeze-drying the dog 506–7
French dogs 202
Fullerton 364
furyous woodnesse madness 459–60

Gas 181
Gasehound 135
Geist 492–3
Gelert 490–1
Gilpin 244
Golden Retriever 30
gold, finding 316
Gordon Setter 30
graves 492–3
Gray 155–8
Greyhound 24, 50–1, 106, 108, 122,
   135, 208, 230–1, 286, 323–4,
   344–5, 413
   characteristics 19–20
   cross-breeding 354
   in former lives 321
   hare coursing 363–4, 404
   interbreeding 354–5
Griffon 303
guard dogs 3–4, 23, 37, 52, 80, 173,
   327
guide dogs for the blind 100–1
Gustavus Adolphus 208–9

Half-and-Half 286
hambling 109
Hamlet (Sir Hugh Walpole's dog)
   311–12
hanging a dog 104, 452, 480
hare coursing 122, 128, 363–4, 403–4
   artificial hares 403
harness-dogs 286
Harry Hanks 176
Haydon 153
health hazards 391
hearing 315
Heathcliff's dogs 205–6
Hector 37
herding instinct 36
Hockley 172
hospitals for dogs 421
hounds 36, 41–2

characteristics 2–3, 19, 26–8, 36,
    120–1
colours 26, 121
feeding 127–8
in former lives 321
music of the 341–6, 349–52
puppies 139–40
puppy shows 382–3
pursuit by 120–1
rearing 267–8
rennyng hounde 19, 125–7
smell, sense of 36, 344
types of 26
house cur 280
housetraining 236–7
Howell's Code 280
hoxing 109
human chastity, discerning 318–19
humanitarian attitudes towards dogs
    171
human remains, eating 458–9
humans, attacking 110
    see also bites
human souls, dogs as recipients of
    320–1
hunting
    moral concerns 128
    "proper exercise for knights and
        princes" 133
hunting dogs 4, 18
hybrid animals 281–2, 285
hydrophobia 116, 287, 461, 466–7,
    470

ice, accidents on the 162–4
idle dogs 209
Index 151
Indies 232
intelligence, cross-breeding and 286
interbreeding 286, 354–5
Irish Grey-hound 133
Irish Setter 71
Irish Terrier 366, 369–70
Irish Wolfhound 1, 176
Issa 229
Italian Greyhound 1, 303

Jack 189, 324–5
jackals 348
Jacko 360–1
James I 227–8, 236
James II 243
Jess 289, 290
Jowler (James I's dog) 227–8

Kaiser 300
Keeper (Emily Bronte's dog) 68–9
Kennel Club 364
Kerry Beagle 29
Kiar 136
kidnapping 447
King Charles Spaniel 243, 303
King Koffee 162
kitaeog 280
kitchen service 88–9, 281
Komondor 1

Labrador 353
Lacoena 281
ladies and hunting 137–8
Lakeland Terrier 387–8
a lamb in dogs' company 211
laming dogs 105, 108–10
language of dogs 81
lap-dogs
    death of 479
    in former lives 321
legislation
    anti-cruelty 114
leopards, encounters with 91–2, 169,
    340
Leporarius 130
Levararios Hariers 129
Levinarius 130
licensing system 107–8
lifespan 477
Lion Dog 450–1
lion, encounter with a 176
litter size 357
"little dog-angel" 493
"little red dogs" 304–8
London
    dead dogs in 112–13
    slaughter of dogs in 115

(London *cont.*)
stray dogs 301–12
longevity, dog ownership and 103
lost dogs 439
Lu-a 136
Lurcher 147, 149, 150, 153
in former lives 321
Lyciscus 281
Lyme Hall mastiffs 42

mad dogs 4, 460–70
Malines sheep dog 99
Maltese dogs 200–1, 303
man and dog
distinction between 328
man's dependence on dogs 428
relationship 36, 43–8, 78–9, 103
mange 420
manhunts 41–2, 96–9
Man's Best Friend 271
Maria 210, 468–9
Marylebone Fields 172
Mary Queen of Scots' dog 54
Master MacGrath 364
Mastiff 23, 31, 36, 42, 80, 81, 91–2,
105, 106, 122–3, 176, 413
bull and bear baiting 172, 175, 178
character 36, 80
in former lives 321
hybrids 285
maudlin sentiment 249
Max 300
Mayflower 323–4
medical experiments 87–8
Melitaeusor Fotor 201
Mick 219
Mingan 122
Mithe 230–1
monastery dogs 81
mongrels 286–7, 288, 299–300, 312
Monkey 182
Montmorency 33
Mountain dogs 359
murder, avengers of 49
music, influence of 346–9
Mutilatus 109
muzzling 115, 116, 302, 308

National Show of Sporting Dogs 362
Neart 136
neglect of dogs 38–9
Nero (Thomas Carlyle's dog) 64–5,
490
neutering 105–6
Newfoundland dog 31, 38, 95,
210–11, 241
cross-breeding 286
Nick 487–8
Nig 71, 72
Nobby 212
nunneries, dogs in 111

obsession with dogs 272–4
Old Drum 247
origins of breeds 24–5
otter hunting 195, 196
ownership
camaraderie among owners 227
commercial side 388–9
dog population 199
owners and dogs, resemblance
between 80
women owners 456
Ozor 92

pack behaviour 8–9, 11, 36, 44–5
pariah dogs 301, 304, 305
Paris Gardens 172, 176
paupers as dog owner 113
pedigrees 313–14
false 300–1
pedlar's dog 315–16
Peel, John 144–5
Pekinese 43, 213, 223–5, 257, 262–3,
506
Pelléas 79
performing dogs 92–3, 281, 282
petfood industry 449, 454
pet keeping, folly of 262
pets, dogs as 199–225
PG 401–2
physical appearance 1
Pilgrim 141–2
Pincha 167–70
Pipsqueak 339–40

poaching dogs 147–9
pointers 9, 158–60, 161, 329–30
    in former lives 320
police dogs 99–100
pollution by dogs 270
Pomeranian 35, 303
Pomero (W.S. Landor's dog) 70–1
Pompey 162
Ponto 164–5
Poodle 31, 32, 207, 249, 347, 359,
    402
popularity of dogs as companions 199
prehistory and legend, dogs in 17–18,
    42–6
premonition 315, 323
Prim 485
Prince 487
Prince Rupert (retriever) 162–4
products from dogs 115–16
professed shots 161
psychic experiences 329–31
Pug 237, 303, 359
    in former lives 321
pugnacious temperament 303
Punch 210–11
punishment 68–9, 100, 113
puppies
    puppy farming 276, 411
    selecting 317
Pyrenees Shepherd 359

quarantine 223
quick-wittedness 325

rabies 116, 469–70
railway workers' dogs 147
Randy 256–8
Ranter 144
The Rat 289–99
rat-catching 150–1
rat-killing 184, 186, 188, 360–1, 418
    by a man 187
reason 316
Reddie 305–6
regimental dogs 348
rescues by dogs 37, 94–5
retrievers 31, 162–3

Richard II 230–1
Robin 231
roller skates, dogs on 419
Rosette 482
Royal 144
Royal Pit 172
Ruby 144
Rufus 250–2
Russian dog shows 373–4
Russian wolfhound 359
Ryno 137

Sacarson 176
Saddleworth weavers 140–1
sagacity 141
Sagax 128
St Bernard 1, 31, 37, 43, 359, 363,
    367
St Hubert hound 96, 139
St Patrick 276, 477
St Roch 276
Saltator 281
Sanguinarius see Bloodhound
savage dogs, curtailing 110
scavengers 44, 301–2
Scotch Terrier 36–7
Scottish Forest Laws (1130) 106
Scylax 229
Sealyham 189–90, 197, 212
Segusians 341
selling dogs 446–7
    see also dog dealers
services to man 41, 81–2
setters 9, 151, 160, 161, 166–7, 321–2
    cross-breeding 286
    in former lives 320
    sheep dogs 4, 80
    characteristics 23–4
    fox terriers as 375
sheep dog trials 364, 408–9
    international trials 374–5
sheep worrying 257–9, 327
shepherd dogs 18, 37, 85–87
    cross-breeding 354
    in former lives 321
    reaction to music 348
shepherd's/herdsman's cur 280

ships, dogs on board 417–18
shooting dogs 452
    in error 484
Siberians 367
Sicilian dogs 317, 318–20
    enemy of adulterers 317
    the sick and the handicapped: dogs
        as helpmates to 81–2, 93, 200
sight 315
size 1
Skeet 71, 72
Skip 189
Skye Terrier 36, 368, 442–3
slaughter as a means of control 107
sled-dog races 313, 364, 365
sled dogs 34, 100, 101–3, 313, 404–8
sleeping with dogs 267, 268
sleuthhound 41–2, 82–3
small dogs 201, 217–18, 271
smell, sense of 14, 315, 318–19, 344
smoking, a dog's attitude to 260
smugglers' dogs 348
snakes, encounters with 339–40
Society of Experienced Hunters 359
"soul of brutes" 316–17
South American dogs 34
spaniels 22–3, 30, 36, 89–90, 202,
        203–4, 243, 250–2, 266, 366
    character 36
    cross-breeding 286
    in former lives 320–1
    tampering with the breed 378
    toy 360
Spitz 38, 359
sportsmen 133–4
stealers and restorers of dogs 275,
        440–6, 495
stray dogs 114, 116–17, 301–2
superstition 36
surgical mutilation 105–6
Swaffham Club 363
Swallow 487

Taborine 92
Tailless Tyke 75–6, 288–9
talents 12
"talking dogs" 332–4

Tatters 501–3
tavern, bath-house and privy
    control of dogs in 110
taxing dog owners 107, 441
temple dogs 318–20
Terrars 129
terriers 36, 136, 138, 194–7, 204,
        271–2, 337–8, 356, 386–8,
        389–90, 415–16, 494–5
    badger-digging 158, 195, 196–7
    characteristics 271–2, 380
    cross-breeding 286, 380, 390
    dog shows 369, 378–80
    feeding 196
    in former lives 320
    foxhunting 195
    old dogs 337–8
    otter hunting 195, 196
    ratting 196, 415–16
    rough terrier 138
    smooth terrier 138
    starting to hunt with 131–2, 158
    toy 303, 368
    types 36, 131
    working terriers 194–7, 378–80
territorial behaviour 81
time, sense of 216
Tiny 422–7, 492
Tip 505
Toby 311, 334–7
Tracie 478
trail hunts 140
training 46
Tray 94–5, 244–5, 488
tricks 281
Tumblers 130–1, 132, 136
turnspits 88–9, 281, 321
Tuttle Fields 172
Tympanista 281

"unclean beast", dog as the 36, 228
undertakers and funeral services
        499–500
unselfishness 247
Urcanus 281, 282

Vertagus 130

Villaticus 173
vivisection 87–8
Vixen 284

waking their owners 269
walks 259–60, 267
"warset" 106
war, use of dogs in 101–3
watch cur 280
watch-dogs *see* guard dogs
Water dogge 21–2
Waterloo Cup 363
Water Spaniel 152, 413
Welsh curs 280
West Highland Terrier 197
Westminster Kennel Club 362–3
Westminster Pit 172, 181, 182
wet nurses 472
whelping 236–7

Whippet 23
Whitechapel murders 96–9
Wideawake 143, 144
wild dogs 16–17
Wimpole Street 443–4
winter shooting 161–2
Wiseacre 144
witchcraft 318, 323
wolf-like characteristics 16–17, 36,
   81, 354
wolves 24, 452
   reaction to music 347–8
women owners 456
Wonder Tiny 360
woodman's dog 56
working certificates 390
writing about dogs 214

Xoloizcuintle 1